RUSSIA: THE POST-WAR YEARS

RUSSIA
THE POST-WAR YEARS

ALEXANDER WERTH

Epilogue by
HARRISON E. SALISBURY

TAPLINGER PUBLISHING COMPANY
NEW YORK

First published in the United States in 1971 by
TAPLINGER PUBLISHING CO., INC.
New York, New York

ISBN 0-8008-6930-3
Library of Congress Catalog Card Number 75-143223

PRINTED IN GREAT BRITAIN

Contents

To Aline

Introduction

The interest shown in *Russia at War* has encouraged me to write this sequel, which deals with the immediate post-war period. My original plan was to cover in one book the whole period between the end of the Second World War and Stalin's death in 1953. But after some reflection I decided to confine myself in this volume to the Soviet Union between 1945 and about the middle of 1948. It was a time rich in events of world importance, and it was during these years that the foundations were laid for the world in which we now live. Stalin's obvious desire to turn the post-war world into one based on a Big Three peace came to nothing. Germany, far from being placed under three-power (or, including France, four-power) control with a central government, for which the Russians put up an extremely tough diplomatic battle in 1945-7, inevitably drifted towards a division into two separate states. The rest of Europe split into two water-tight spheres of influence—more tightly sealed off from each other than they might have been if the Cold War had not assumed the vicious character it did in 1945-8. It has now become a truism to say—as some of the most eminent American historians have been saying—that, but for the death of Roosevelt on 12th April 1945, there would have been no Cold War of the kind that developed so rapidly, especially after Harry Truman, in possession of the A-bomb, declared himself a crusader against "world communism".

Several things characterized these immediate post-war years, as will be seen from the narrative that follows. First, a rapid deterioration in the relations between the Soviet Union and her wartime allies in the West, particularly the United States and Britain, where the Foreign Secretary in the 1945-elected Labour government was every bit as "anti-Russian" as Harry Truman. The Russians, not having the A-bomb, were very largely on the defensive, and, at least to the spring of 1947, Stalin himself continued to make conciliatory gestures towards the West. Nevertheless, with the Cold War growing more intense, he was increasingly obsessed with security, and although he had made up his mind as early as 1943 (if not before) to turn a basically anti-Russian Poland into an obedient satellite, he decided in 1947–8 to "Stalinize" the rest of Eastern Europe too, the last of the East European countries to come under strict Russian control being Czechoslovakia in 1948. But then, a few months later, Yugoslavia rebelled against her status of "Soviet satellite". Stalin had the good sense not to send tanks to Belgrade (as Brezhnev was to send tanks to Prague twenty years later), but instead enormously increased the pressure on the rest of Eastern Europe, declaring at the same time that Titoism was the most dangerous heresy. And so, from the Stalinist point of view, it was, as we know from later attempts to loosen Moscow's stranglehold—in Poland, Hungary, Czechoslovakia and—in a different way—in seemingly meek and obedient Rumania.

This build-up of Stalin's East European empire is one of the main subjects of this book. Another is the Russian "economic miracle" of the extraordinary post-war reconstruction. Still another is the rejection of that post-war "liberalization" inside Russia, the prospects of which seemed so promising, especially to the Russian intellectuals, during the war, at the height of the Anglo-American Soviet alliance. "Ideological coexistence", which undoubtedly existed (within limits) during the war, was now declared completely unthinkable. A frantic Russian nationalism, combined with a great deal of anti-Western xenophobia (and, before long, anti-semitism), began more and more to dominate the Soviet home scene. In science, the dictatorship of Lysenko was established in 1947–8; and a thorough purge in philosophy, literature, the theatre, the cinema, the plastic arts and even music was undertaken, on Stalin's instructions, by Andrei Zhdanov, one of the greatest Party thugs in Stalin's entourage. By the end of 1947—and the real breaking-point had come with the breakdown of the Foreign Ministers' Conference in Moscow in March/April 1947 which foreshadowed the division of Germany into two parts—these cultural purges were accompanied by a wave of more or less artificially worked-up xenophobia, a "vigilance campaign" and a spy-mania. Many people who, during and after the war, had been associated in one way or another with foreigners began to be arrested. It was the beginning of that Little Terror which was to mark the years between 1948 and Stalin's death five years later.

This book on the immediate post-war years in Russia was, in many respects, a more difficult book to write than *Russia at War*. For the years between the end of the Second World War and Stalin's death in 1953, and particularly the 1945–8 period, is the most unexplored period in the whole history of the Soviet Union. The Russians still consider it as a kind of taboo subject, of which the less said the better. I do not know of a single serious Russian study covering this period. When, in desperation, I wrote some months ago to Professor V. M. Trukhanovsky, one of the foremost Russian authorities on recent and contemporary history, and asked his advice, all he found to recommend to me was the shorthand account of the Nineteenth Congress of the CPSU, held in October 1952, a few months before Stalin's death—a document which includes the long General Report by G. M. Malenkov, who was then considered the most likely successor of an ailing and rapidly ageing Stalin. The latter delivered only a very short speech at the very end of the Congress. Whereas, especially since the "de-Stalinization" Twentieth Congress of 1956, hundreds and even thousands of books, as well as countless articles, have been written in Russia on the war years—and some, as readers of *Russia at War* know, are of the greatest historical value—nothing, almost literally nothing, has been written in Russia on the period between the end of the Second World War and Stalin's death nearly eight years later. There is, of course, the Russian daily, weekly and monthly press of the period to fall back on, but all this is marred by the "personality cult". Apart from some economic studies on the post-war development of the Soviet Union (parts of which are devoted to the immediate post-war years, with their "economic miracle") there is no history of this period of any kind in Russian.

The position in the West concerning these eight years of Russian history is only a little better. But one must distinguish between Western, and particularly American, books written during

1945 and 1953 and more recent works. The vast majority of
books on Russia written during the last years of Stalin are "Cold
War" books, in which angry anti-Russian and anti-Soviet
propaganda holds an infinitely larger place than any search for
historical facts. Thus, the "historical" value of a classic of the
Cold War literature of the time, Victor Kravchenko's *I Chose
Freedom*, though for several years a tremendously potent weapon
of propaganda against Russia, with its clear implication that
dropping an atom bomb on Moscow was the only possible
solution to "the Russian problem", is precisely nil. Dozens of
other books of the same kind were published in the West between
1945 and 1953, and practically all of them are worthless to the
present-day historian as sources of solid information, though
they are, of course, significant as manifestations of the war
hysteria that existed among many (fortunately not all) people in
the West in the immediate post-war years.

A very different story can be told of more recent studies of the
period. Hundreds of books, many of them of great value, have
been written in the West, and particularly in the United States, on
the Cold War years—including the especially violent years of,
say, 1946 to 1953. I cannot list them all, but should like to mention
with special appreciation such first-class studies as Professor
D. F. Fleming's monumental two-volume work, *The Cold War
and Its Origins, 1917–1960*, published in 1960; André Fontaine's
two-volume *History of the Cold War*, the first volume of which was
published in Paris in 1965, and which is now also available in
England and the United States; W. A. Williams's *The Tragedy of
American Diplomacy*, published in 1962; and George Kennan's
Memoirs, which, significantly, stress the "wrong" American
approach to Russia (including Kennan's own) in 1947, and the
"more correct" approach ten years later.

But all these books, strictly speaking, deal with diplomatic
history, and not with the history of Russia of 1945–53, except
insofar as the Soviet government manifested itself at Foreign
Ministers' conferences, in various diplomatic changes, and, of
course, at the United Nations. The UN, though of very little
practical value to them (since they were nearly always in a
minority there), was nevertheless a highly effective platform
for stating their views to world opinion, and on occasion even
for influencing it. It is also widely known what the Soviet

press was saying during those years, but its articles on world affairs were little more than paraphrases of what Mr. Molotov and Mr. Vyshinsky had already said at such-and-such a Foreign Ministers' conference, or during a UN debate. The only real contributions to an understanding of Russian policy came from certain *Pravda* or *Izvestia* editorials, and, more important still, from the fairly frequent statements Stalin made from 1946 onwards, when the Cold War was getting into its stride, to either Soviet or foreign (mostly British and American) correspondents and visitors. What provoked him into making his first post-war statement since his speech on the capitulation of Japan in September 1945 was Winston Churchill's Fulton speech of March 1946 delivered, moreover, in the presence, and with the blessing, of President Harry Truman.

The argument which is central to my narrative—namely, that things both in Russia and the world in general would have been very different if Roosevelt had not died in April 1945 and had continued at the White House for several years longer—is, of course, not original. Innumerable studies demonstrating precisely this point have been published in America by eminent scholars, some of whom I have already mentioned. But at the time it was considered by many an outrageous thing to say, and in 1947 voices like that of Walter Lippmann were little more than voices crying in the wilderness. Today, I think, everybody in the United States with any sound historical judgement agrees that the Cold War was unnecessary. But Harry Truman, who knew infinitely less about European, including Russian, history than Roosevelt, was, once he had his atom bomb, fired by an anti-communist crusading spirit which did not in fact come to an end until the Russians, too, had not only A-bombs but also H-bombs. Truman got it into his head that Stalin's Russia was dangerous—perhaps even more dangerous than Hitler's Germany, and even if he personally could not make up his mind to "drop the Bomb on Moscow" (for one thing, Britain and France and the rest of Western Europe were very far from cherishing the prospect, which might have ended in utter disaster to themselves), there were a good many people in America and a few even in England (including Winston Churchill) who regarded such a preventive war against Russia with considerable relish and as the only salvation for the free world.

The Russians knew about all this. One of the great features of those post-war years was the behaviour of Stalin and, consequently, of the whole Soviet establishment. Uppermost in Stalin's mind was the fact that Russia was economically weak and desperately war-weary (she had lost 20 million people in the war, though this figure was not officially admitted until 1959) and her economy was largely in ruins. During those years Stalin handled the former Allies with extreme caution. At least until April 1947, when the Foreign Ministers' conference broke down in Moscow, he missed no opportunity to repeat that the Soviet Union wanted to live in peace with America, with Britain, with everybody. Almost with desperation, he continued to cling to the wartime concept of a Big Three peace, and it was galling for him to find, very soon after the defeat of Germany, if not before, that nothing was less suited to a man like Harry Truman. Also, the Western press, both in the United States and in Western Europe, was becoming increasingly anti-Russian. The great pretext—and sometimes even the real reason—for this anti-Soviet crusade was the "enslavement" by the Russians of Eastern Europe. Roosevelt had at least tacitly agreed that there was something to be said for the Russian "security" arguments for controlling the countries of the former Western *cordon sanitaire*, where governments "friendly" to Russia had now replaced the pre-war governments of those countries, which, with the exception of Czechoslovakia, had been uniformly "unfriendly" to the Soviet Union. But all this is well known, and there seems very little disagreement on these questions now.

If Russian historians have been discouraged to write about Stalin's last years, there were also very few opportunities for non-Russians to observe Russia from inside. During the war, life for the foreign correspondent (as readers of *Russia at War* know) was rather easier than it became after the war, and above all after April 1947, when a kind of curtain began to come down on foreign observers. One could travel about extensively and meet hundreds of Russians in every walk of life—soldiers, workers, officials, officers, generals and even marshals of the Soviet Union, to say nothing of the intellectuals—writers and artists among them—who, as a rule, were extremely friendly and cordial to most representatives of the "allied" press. True, Stalin and other top members of the Party and government hierarchy were not particularly accessible to Western journalists, but they had other things to do than give interviews to the foreign press.

The Russian attitude to foreigners began slowly to change after the capitulation of Germany, and especially after Hiroshima. But by the middle of 1947 the Russians became distrustful of practically everybody foreign—even of loyal Poles and Czechs, who, for all they knew, might be British or American spies.

Fortunately, I myself managed to stay in their confidence for longer than most others (apart from those who simply "chose freedom" on the Russian side—and even then the Russians were never quite certain about these people's real motives in doing so), and I did not notice any appreciable difference in the attitude towards me of "ordinary Russians", or even of officials. Together with a Polish friend, Ziemowit Fedecki, I was even granted permission to go on an unconducted tour to Rostov, the Caucasus and Transcaucasia in August 1946.

So a large part of this book is devoted to something about which little is known outside Russia—the "economic miracle" of restoring Russian industry within three years of the war, and with no outside help (except the reparations and the loot collected in East Germany and the various countries of Eastern Europe, by means of "joint-stock companies" with Rumanians, Hungarians, Yugoslavs, etc., and certain other equally dubious devices). But the bulk of the gigantic reconstruction effort came, of course, from the Russian people themselves, just as had come the Russian people's war effort. Lend-Lease to the USSR, representing only some 3 per cent of America's war expenditure during the Second World War, amounted to no more than 11 billion dollars.

Still less known outside Russia (and even inside Russia) are the conditions in which this enormous work of restoration and reconstruction had to be done. One of the most important pieces of evidence, which I quote in an early chapter of this book, concerns the truly merciless exploitation of the peasantry by the state. This exploitation had gone on throughout the war, but it also continued for at least two years after the war, and the peasants in the Archangel village described here were even hungrier in 1947 than they had been in 1944. It took a man of a typically Russian statebuilder's ruthlessness like Stalin to enforce this reconstruction. The great tradition of Ivan the Terrible and Peter the Great (whose new capital, St. Petersburg, had been built "on the bones of thousands of peasant serfs") was being maintained.

At least until the latter half of 1947, Stalin had been on the defensive. In the spring of that year, he had still spoken to Senator Harold Stassen of "peaceful coexistence" and is even believed to have mentioned the possibility of a great American reconstruction loan. But the Truman Doctrine, quickly followed by the breakdown of the Foreign Ministers' Moscow Conference on Germany and Austria in April 1947 (which meant the end of Stalin's dream of a four-power control of a united Germany), and the Marshall Plan soon after, all meant that the world had been split in two. Stalin (who did not give a hang for Lenin's world revolution, but was interested only in the Soviet Union's security, which implied control of Eastern Europe and, if possible, of bits of Iran and a part-control of the Turkish Straits, so that atom-bomb-carrying American aircraft carriers could not enter the Black Sea) now felt forced to change his line.

I do not believe that Stalin was mad—except perhaps during the last few weeks of his life. For if there was much madness in what Stalin did, before, during and since the war, there was a certain method in it.

One of the very nastiest aspects of the last years of Stalin were the Zhdanov purges in literature, philosophy, history, painting, and finally music. In this book I have dealt with all these, but above all with music. Was this *Zhdanovshchina*, this terrorization of writers and musicians by Andrei Zhdanov, one of the worst thugs in Stalin's entourage, really necessary?

Even here one cannot but fail to detect a certain method in Stalin's madness. In 1946, when the country was about to face the worst famine winter within human memory (except perhaps for the fearful winter of 1941–2 at the beginning of the war); when Churchill had, shortly before, made his "Iron Curtain" speech at Fulton, Missouri; and when, altogether, the immediate prospects for either peace or prosperity were more than dubious, it may well have occurred to Stalin that this was not a time for escapist poetry and "cheap wisecracks" about Soviet humanity. The country was expected to put every ounce of energy, every drop of sweat into reconstruction. Hence the decision to fight "escapism" at any price: even at the price of making the Soviet Union odious in the eyes of the world.

I think this largely explains the seemingly ridiculous and odious Akhmatova/Zoshchenko affair of September 1946. One important point deserves to be noted: Akhmatova and Zoshchenko were expelled from the Writers' Union, but that was all. They were made to suffer great humiliations and serious material hardships, but they were not sent to a camp or prison, as Siniavsky and Daniel were under the Brezhnev regime, besides many others—not to mention the perhaps even more monstrous persecution of a major Russian writer, Alexander Solzhenitsyn.

Many of us think of Stalin as an unequalled ogre. Yes, there were the purges and all the other acts of brutality in the 1930s. But is there not something significant in the fact that during the Zhdanov purges of 1946–8 (abominable though they were) nobody—except the unfortunate "Dodik", whom I later mention —was arrested among the writers and other artists, still less deported or shot. If in the early 1950s a large number of Yiddish-writing authors were shot, this was not a literary but a political "anti-Zionist" matter. But neither under Stalin since 1941, nor under Khrushchev, was any writer or artist actually arrested, still less shot. The deportation of writers did not start till 1966, with the Siniavsky/Daniel trial, after a twenty-eight-year interval since the end of the great Stalin purges.

The Zhdanov purge among the composers and musicians is even more grotesque and absurd, at first sight, than that of the writers. It is, in fact, hard to say why exactly Stalin, after not bothering for years about music, should suddenly have unleashed Zhdanov against Prokofiev, Shostakovich, Khachaturian, and others who had done so much to make Soviet music popular with the Western world. Was it just his personal dislike of "complicated" music like Shostakovich's? Was he angry about these "geniuses" living in a little world of their own, with its rivalries and its mutual-admiration societies? Or was he angry that an *élite* had emerged among the musical public, who did not give a hang, at heart, for five-year plans, for the hardships of ordinary Soviet humanity? The great composers had been the spoilt children of the regime. So they had to be given a hard knock, and no one was better at this job than that ubiquitous brute, Andrei Alexandrovich Zhdanov. Whether he knew anything about music or not did not matter at all. In addition, Prokofiev and Shostakovich did not *quite* belong to the Soviet Union; one was too sophisticated, too "European", infinitely cleverer than the ordinary run of Soviet composers, and a craftsman none could even approach; the other was too introspective, too concerned with himself and his own depths and chasms, even though sometimes he did feel passionately about the sufferings of his own country—during the war, and since. But the real essence of the music purge was probably the super-nationalism of a Stalin obsessed, as he was in February 1948, with the possibility of a war in which, even a year before, he had not believed. And the composers were, except the popular-song hacks, mostly Western in their education; Prokofiev certainly, but also Shostakovich, with his cult of Beethoven and Mahler. In short, they were being accused of being "un-Russian", just as people on the other side of the Atlantic were being accused of being "un-American". The last years of Stalin—especially 1948 to 1953—were marked by a peculiar kind of Russian McCarthyism.

The Zhdanov Decree on music, coinciding almost day-for-day with the communist *coup* in Prague, to be followed by a further intensification of the Cold War, and the ever-growing threat of an atomic attack on Russia. Improbable, yes; impossible, no. And Russian people in February 1948 were acutely conscious of the danger. Ten-year-old youngsters—I saw it myself—would viciously tear down from the walls coloured posters of Uncle Sam, with A-bombs sticking out of every one of his pockets. And in those days, the composers were looking for further and further refinements. In 1967, I was talking in Leningrad to an elderly woman intellectual. She was extremely liberal in her views, and yet, when I came to talk of the Zhdanov purge in music, she said: "I really think that in 1948, and with everything threatening to fall on top of us, it was necessary. And what I mean is that today all this persecution of writers is totally unnecessary."

My relations with the Soviet authorities had deteriorated since the end of the Foreign Ministers' conference in April 1947. I was furious at the ever-diminishing facilities for travel and for meeting "ordinary" Russians, and not just officials, And the censorship had become so utterly fiendish that I had to resort to all kinds of subterfuges to by-pass it, and this did not escape the Press Department's notice. They also knew I regarded Prokofiev as a great composer and that I was strongly opposed to all this nonsense about his music. In short, after April 1947 it had become more and more difficult to learn anything definite about Russia from "ordinary" Russian people; instead, I took as active a part as I could in the defence of Prokofiev; and this did not make me popular. But worse still, beginning, roughly, with January/February 1948, Stalin unleashed his Little Terror. First "Dodik" was arrested; then more and more Russians one had known began to "disappear"; and one soon learned that they had been arrested for "associating with foreigners". One day, in February, I met a weedy little man, whose name, I think, was Beliayev, not far from the Lubianka Square. He stopped me, but said: "Just one second: I've got to say something to you." And he whispered in my ear: "This is going to be 1937 the [year of the Great Purge] all over again." And then, in a frightened whisper he added: "And now go, and let's pretend we don't know each other." A few weeks later, I heard that poor Beliayev, who had had during the war a minor translating job at the American Embassy, had been arrested and deported. In 1959 I heard he was "very ill in hospital in Karaganda". And then, it seems, he died soon after for he was never heard of again,

Besides, I was beginning to hear all sorts of rumblings about Yugoslavia, and, having one good acquaintance at the Yugoslav Embassy in Moscow, I one day went to see him. But a Soviet policeman turned me away. I felt something very serious was happening. Was Stalin's East European empire being threatened by a new heresy? Or had he been asking for trouble by treating the Yugoslavs as a subject race?

I left Moscow by the night train for Leningrad on 27th May 1948, and barely a month later I was on my way to Belgrade. Stalin had outlawed Tito.

It is on this Yugoslav episode that I end this book. The next few years were marked by the final splitting of Germany into two states, and by the appearance on the Russian political scene of two formidable new characters who were both to affect to this day the course of history—the Russian A-bomb (soon to be followed by an H-bomb) and Mao Tse-Tung.

ONE

Retrospect: The Soviet-German War

The capitulation of Germany did not come as a surprise to the Soviet people. But that was in May 1945. There had been moments, in 1941 and 1942, when the thought crossed many Russians' minds that the battle against the formidably efficient German army and air force was a hopeless one, and that, with the Allies "doing nothing to help",* the war would sooner or later be lost. The gloom and pessimism were deepest during the first months of the German *blitzkreig*, when vast territories were overrun in a short time by the Wehrmacht—the whole of the Baltic provinces, the whole of Belorussia, and most of the Ukraine. By the autumn the Germans were rapidly approaching Moscow, which they very nearly captured on 16th October, and had by then been fighting on the outskirts of Leningrad—now completely encircled, except for the precarious little lifeline across Lake Ladoga—since the end of August, two months after the invasion. All the great industrial areas of the Ukraine, including the Donbas, Kharkov and Krivoi Rog—and, before long, Rostov, the "gate to the Caucasus"—were lost. The press and radio propaganda was making less and less impression, and although not a word was said of the loss of millions of Russian soldiers captured by the Germans in the gigantic encirclements in the summer and autumn of 1941, ordinary Russians knew, or at least strongly suspected, that the country was in danger of suffering the most disastrous defeat in its whole history. Stalin's blood-sweat-and-tears speech of 3rd July was a remarkable

---

* In fact, up to Pearl Harbor, the only major official ally was Britain.

action programme for the Soviet people; but, as the agonizing weeks of July, August, and September crawled on, even faith in Stalin was being shaken as never before.

Stalin himself was fully aware of the catastrophic situation. Although he knew that sooner or later a showdown between Russia and Germany would be inevitable, he still believed that by "avoiding the slightest provocation" he could postpone a German invasion at least until 1942—by which time the Red Army would be in a much stronger position to meet it. When the Germans struck out on 22nd June, he spoke in his 3rd July broadcast of Hitler's "perfidious attack"; and in private the effect on him of the invasion was such that he would say that "all Lenin's work has now gone to hell". Sergo Mikoyan, the son of Anastas Mikoyan, one of Stalin's closest associates, later told me that during the first days of the war Stalin had lost his head completely and stayed alone at his *dacha* at Kuntsevo, near Moscow, abandoning himself to his black, perhaps even suicidal, thoughts. The first announcement of the invasion had not been made by him, but by Molotov on 22nd June, several hours after the war had begun, and according to Sergo it was Molotov and Mikoyan who wrote Stalin's broadcast of 3rd July; they almost had to drag him physically to the microphone. Although the speech was of the greatest morale-building value, most people realized how nervous Stalin sounded, and noticed how, every few minutes, he had to sip water from a glass that clattered against his teeth.

For three months, until the Battle of Moscow, something happened which had never happened in Russia since the late 1920s: pictures of Stalin disappeared from the Soviet press almost completely. It was not "Stalin's war", but a plain war of national survival. Stalin, indeed, knew it. Whether he, or Mikoyan, or Molotov had, in reality, written the script of the 3rd July broadcast, its predominant theme was the battle for national survival, for *Russia's* survival; any mention of Lenin or the Soviet system was merely incidental.

True, when Harry Hopkins first visited Stalin at the end of July, Stalin had regained some of his former self-confidence. At the time, the German advance was meeting with ever-growing Russian resistance and had appreciably slowed down, and at Smolensk, on the direct road to Moscow, their advance had been temporarily stopped.* Stalin even assured Hopkins that the Germans were most unlikely to advance more than another sixty miles and that, in any case, not only Moscow and Leningrad but also Kiev would never be abandoned. Kiev, however, was to fall within a few weeks and it was at least partly in order to keep his "promise" to Hopkins that Stalin engaged in its defence several hundred thousand troops, who were then killed or captured, together with the Ukrainian capital (600,000 according to the Germans; some 200,000 according to the official post-war Russian history of the war). At the time, of course, not a word was said about this or any other of the major *débâcles* of the summer and autumn of 1941. People had no means of knowing much: all wireless sets (except those of highly privileged and official persons) had to be handed in to the police a few days after the invasion; only official news was available from the press and the local radio network; but even this news could not conceal the loss of enormous territories, great cities and huge industrial areas. In his letters to Churchill in August, Stalin openly spoke of the "mortal danger" threatening Russia. This, of course, went together with an appeal, both threatening and plaintive, for an immediate opening of the Second Front, even though Britain, with the United States still not a belligerent, was in no position, militarily, to do anything of the slightest importance.

Nevertheless, the fact that Russia had "allies"—or rather, one major ally, Britain—and that America was going to "help" was of some psychological importance to the Russians; they did not feel entirely alone, and soon after the invasion the thought had become deeply ingrained that the war *would* be won, no matter how terrible and how long it was. Much was, of course, made of minor military successes, such as the slowing-down of the *blitzkreig* at Smolensk (which, curiously, created for several weeks almost a feeling of euphoria, at least in Moscow), and of the small Russian counter-offensive at Yelnya, south of Smolensk in September 1941, when a few hundred square miles were re-captured from the Germans—the first to be recaptured anywhere in Europe since the beginning of the Second World War. At that time, in bombed and half-devastated Vyazma, the future

* It was the tough Russian resistance at Smolensk which ultimately determined Hitler, much to some of his generals' disgust, to divert his main forces on the Central Front to the Ukraine.

Marshal V. D. Sokolovsky made to the foreign press the significant remark that, fearful though the war was, the Russians were "gradually grinding down" the German war machine, and that in any case Moscow would not be lost.

Yet Moscow was very nearly lost a month later, after the Germans had launched their "final" offensive against the Soviet capital on 30th September. "Oh damn you, Nineteen-Forty-One!" the Russian soldier-poet Simeon Gudzenko wrote soon after the war,[*] and truly catastrophic sentiments were also expressed in 1941 by many other poets, such as Simeon Kirsanov. But it was, in one way, a war different from any other—not only a "patriotic" war in the deepest sense, but a war in which literally the only choice was between death and victory; and the Russians *were*, by the millions, ready to die. As distinct from France in 1940, where it was merely "the Germans' turn to win", the conquest of Russia by the Germans was *inconceivable*, since it could only result in death for everybody, or, at best, the worst kind of slavery. If, at the very beginning of the war, some soldiers simply surrendered to save their skins, it soon became perfectly clear that such a surrender was no different from death—though perhaps a slower death.[†]

The situation was most catastrophic of all in October 1941, with Leningrad encircled, with the Germans on the point of breaking into Moscow and with practically the whole of the Ukraine and the Crimea in their hands. What was the mood in the country in these appalling conditions? Pessimism there certainly was; but not defeatism and utter hopelessness, as there had been in France in June 1940. Everybody knew, of course, that something had gone seriously wrong. For years before the war the Russians had been told that if ever there *was* a war, it would be fought "on enemy territory", and it was clear that some hideous mis-calculations had been made "at the top"—that is, by Stalin himself. Never had "the great genius's" stock fallen so low.

---

[*] His poem—like many similar ones—was not published until long after Stalin's death.

[†] These attitudes do not, of course, apply to the entire Soviet population, but they are practically universal among the Russians, Belorussians, and the great majority of Ukrainians. On the other hand, the majority of Lithuanians, Latvians and Estonians obviously preferred the Germans to the Russians, and later in the war so did the Crimean Tartars and other Moslem nationalities, notably in the Caucasus.

Even during the great purges of the 1930s, it was "explained" to everybody why this was necessary; but what had happened now seemed wholly incomprehensible, and the usual argument that Hitler had stabbed Russia in the back and that this had come to her as a complete surprise could scarcely carry much weight with anyone. But there could be no question of "replacing" Stalin, still less of suing for peace with Nazi Germany.

Much has been written of the panic in Moscow in the middle of October, and of the disorderly flight to the East of more than half the population. The simple explanation for this exodus is simply that most Muscovites did not wish, on any account, to stay under German occupation, which to them seemed almost inevitable. The official warnings that Moscow was "in mortal danger" made this flight perfectly justifiable, though, with the benefit of hindsight, they were later charged with cowardice and gutlessness. What if Moscow had fallen? I talked to numerous Muscovites soon after, as well as later in the war. They admitted that "a few" did believe that the fall of Moscow would mean the end of the war, but the vast majority merely thought that the war would go on, though in even more difficult conditions. The moral effect of the fall of Moscow would be terrible, but after all there was still "a lot of space" in Russia and, more important still, all the war industries had been, or were being, evacuated to the Urals, Siberia and Central Asia. Also, before very long, the Allies "would get a move on".

Despite the statements in the press, which were even supported by a Moscow Party leader like A. S. Shcherbakov, that Moscow was in danger, it was somehow later assumed that Stalin in particular had never even contemplated the possibility of the fall of Moscow. Much was also made of the fact that even in the most critical days in October he had remained in Moscow, as had the General Staff, the Chief Command and anyone who really mattered to the defence of the city. As we know, the announcement on 17th October on Moscow radio that Stalin was in Moscow had an immensely heartening effect on what was left there of the population. It meant to them that there never had been, and never would be, any question of surrendering the capital. But this, as I discovered much later, was not entirely true. It is correct that Stalin (as the radio announced) was in Moscow on 17th October; but, in the course of a conversation in 1967 with the poet Alexei

Surkov (an old friend whom I had first met on the Smolensk front in the grim September of 1941, a few weeks before the Battle of Moscow) he said:

"Yes, Stalin had plenty of guts, but even he did not assume that Moscow could never, never fall. I may tell you that if, on 17th October, he was indeed in Moscow, he had *returned* there that day. During the two previous days—the 15th and 16th, when all seemed lost—he had gone to Kineshma, on the Volga, some 200 miles north-east of Moscow to set up the Supreme Command headquarters there—in case of need." And Surkov added: "Of course, the loss of Moscow in 1941 would have been infinitely more serious than it was in 1812, but the war would still have gone on, in terrible conditions no doubt, and perhaps for years; but even then we would have worn the Germans out. It might have been mainly a partisan war, but to the enemy a partisan war can be even more terrible than an ordinary one. See how the Chinese communists went on fighting for years and years; and remember also what terrible trouble Tito's partisans were to the Germans and Italians in Yugoslavia! And our partisan war— if it had come to that—would have been on an infinitely larger scale, and the Germans' nerves would have finally cracked. And, what's more, we might in the end have lost *fewer* people than we did by 1945, since the British and Americans would have had to do much more actual fighting."

The first real turning-point in Russian morale after the invasion was, of course, the Battle of Moscow. It demonstrated to the Russians for the first time that the Germans could be defeated, not just in some minor local operation, but in an immense battle that had lasted for several months.

Between the middle of October and the first week of December, Moscow was saved. Then came the great Russian counter-offensive, which in a few weeks drove the Germans a good distance to the west—anything from 60 to 250 miles.

The effect on Russian morale was amazing. The people now regained full faith in their ability not only to hold out indefinitely, but to win the war—and even to win it soon. In his famous Red Square speech on 7th November, with the Germans only a few miles outside Moscow, Stalin had spoken of winning the war within "a *godik*", "a little year", and had also boosted the great power of the Allies—even though it was still a month before

Pearl Harbor. More strongly even than in July, he had appealed above all to the national sentiment, the national pride of the Russian people—stressing, indeed, the word *Russian* and scarcely mentioning the other nationalities of the Soviet Union.

True, the counter-offensive of December/January proved disappointing, owing mainly to a desperate shortage of equipment and had practically petered out by February. But the national pride aroused in every Russian heart by the Moscow victory was immense, and this helped them to bear the appalling hardships they suffered during that winter—the worst of all the wartime winters. Nearly half the population of encircled Leningrad died of starvation. Nearly everywhere in Russia food-conditions were terrible, not least among the industrial workers in the Urals, where in incredible winter conditions and with practically nowhere to live they were setting up thousands of war factories moved from the invaded and threatened areas of European Russia. The East was rich in food, but with practically all the food-growing areas in European Russia overrun by the Germans the whole country now had to depend for food on the East; and the rule in Russia—which was to be observed till the very end of the war— was *"Vse dlya fronta, vse dlya pobedy"*—"everything for the Front, everything for Victory". Civilian rationing, introduced in the major cities on 18th July, was of the utmost severity, except that there were certain "top" rations which were shockingly generous. Officials, scientists, and, I am ashamed to say, foreign diplomats and even journalists hardly ever lacked anything; and writers, no matter how worthless and useless to the war-effort, all belonged to some more-or-less highly privileged category. Even in Leningrad in the winter of 1941-2, when thousands were dying of hunger every day, Zhdanov and the other Party bosses at the Smolny were having plentiful and even luxurious meals every day.

But it is true enough to say that the army (except at Leningrad) was getting enough to eat even at the worst of times. Perhaps the most fearful food-shortages, surprisingly, were not in the towns, but in the villages. Few in Moscow knew about it at the time, and even if they knew they never mentioned it. Anyway, this was wartime, and everybody had to suffer. The peasants—now almost solely women and very old men or youngsters—for it was they who ran the whole of Soviet agriculture, the men being in the

army—gladly gave all they could, both out of patriotism and
out of the love for their own men in the army. But even this was
not enough: the local Party officials extracted from them, by every
kind of pressure, every ounce of food they could short of letting
them die of starvation. Later I shall quote a remarkable example of
this which shows that not only during the war but even long
after it was over the same methods of intimidation and extortion
were used, no longer in the name of Victory, but in the name
of Reconstruction.

Despite these fearful living conditions in the winter of 1941-2,
morale still remained high, thanks above all to the effect of the
Moscow victory. But Russia's troubles were far from over. The
conviction that victory would be won in a *godik* after November
1941 was still alive in the spring of 1942. Then much was made
of the Anglo/Soviet Alliance signed at that time, and of the
Anglo/American "promise" of a Second Front "in 1942".
"Victory in 1942" became, for a few short weeks, the Soviet
government's official slogan. But soon the slogan was called off,
and the thousands of posters bearing these words were taken down.

In a sense, 1942 was an even more terrible year than 1941.
Then at least all the country's misfortunes could be attributed, as
they were by Stalin, to the "suddenness" and "perfidiousness"
of the German invasion. Now there was no longer this excuse.
Instead of "Victory in 1942", the Russians were to suffer between
May and the autumn of 1942 defeats almost on the 1941
scale. The German *blitzkrieg* was resumed in the south, and by
the middle of August the Wehrmacht had reached the Lower
Volga at Stalingrad, capturing in the process all the fertile
country east of Rostov, and the northern foothills of the Caucasus.
This meant the loss of the Kuban, another enormously rich
agricultural area of European Russia. Some oil centres (such as
Maikop) were captured by the Germans, others (such as Grozny
and Baku) were heavily bombed, and in the main Russia now had
to depend for her oil supplies on the "new Bakus" east of the Volga.
Stalin was later to say that by far the most critical month of the war
had not been October 1941, but October 1942. This is undoubtedly
true; if during that summer and autumn the Germans had
captured Voronezh, which would have enabled them to cut
Moscow's supply lines from the East, and if Stalingrad had
fallen in October, as it very nearly did, the Russians' chances of

continuing the war would have been infinitely more slender even than they would have been if Moscow had fallen during the previous winter. Stalingrad was the key to the rest of the country still in Russian hands—the whole of European Russia east of Moscow, the Urals and Siberia—while the capture of the whole Caucasus would have brought Turkey into the war on Germany's side, and the whole Middle East would have been overrun by the Germans, too.

The atmosphere in Moscow in the summer and autumn of 1942 was infinitely gloomier than it had been even during the agonizing first months of the invasion. With the Germans rapidly overrunning the northern Caucasus and aiming at Stalingrad, the feeling both in the army and among civilians was that there was "nowhere else to retreat to". The only thought that saved people from utter despair was that the disasters of 1941 had ended in the great Moscow victory, and something similar might yet happen. As early as June (long before the actual battle), people spoke of "Stalingrad", which became like a symbol of life or death. It was not in 1941 but in 1942 that very large numbers of Russians, both in the towns and at least for a time in the army, came nearest of all to defeatism, as is openly admitted in the bitter and angry first part of General Chuikov's book on Stalingrad.*

In that autumn, scapegoats were needed; hence the furious press campaign against the Allies, and even against the Red Army itself, in which numerous officers were charged with incompetence and countless soldiers with cowardice. During his visit to Moscow in August 1942, Churchill gave the Russians only a fifty-fifty chance of surviving; his military advisers took an even gloomier view.

Stalingrad proved the turning point of the Soviet/German war in every sense. It showed that at last Russia was able to provide the army with all the necessary equipment, which had been sorely lacking (especially as regards aircraft) during the previous summer's campaign. The change in Russian morale was overwhelming. For the first time the Russian people were totally convinced that they would win the war. Stalin, of whom little had been heard during the black summer and autumn of 1942,

* *The Beginning of the Road*, 1963; also fully summarized in the author's *Russia at War*, 1964.

took full credit for the Stalingrad victory, and phrases like "Stalin's military genius" appeared for the first time in the Soviet press, which was scarcely to the liking of the generals, the true artisans of Stalingrad. Some credit, however, was given to them, and the names of Zhukov, Rokossovsky, Yeremenko, Chuikov, Vassilevsky and many others became immensely popular in the country. As a Russian woman told me at the time: "For the first time in my life, I think we are a very great people, perhaps the greatest people in the world."

The fearful wartime hardships of the workers and the rest of the civilian population, which continued even after Stalingrad, had become easy to bear. The peasantry continued to be mercilessly exploited in the name of "everything for the Front, everything for Victory", but they now bore their semi-starvation even better than before. Their sceptical patriotism had now given way to a proud and exalted patriotism—it was also *their* war, in the sense that the highest proportion of soldiers in the army had come from the villages.

Except for a moment of disappointment in March, when Kharkov—which had been liberated a month earlier—was lost again, and some nervousness on the eve of the battle of Kursk in July 1943, the Russian people lived till the end of the war in a state of exalted and exuberant optimism. The only question that worried them was how long it would last; and if victory came neither in 1943 nor 1944, the fault was entirely, in the Russian view, that of the Allies. But life was not easy. Although the soldiers were now better fed than ever before (and after Stalingrad, though not before, their diet was greatly improved, thanks to Lend-Lease shipments), very little Lend-Lease food, except in schools, hospitals and some crucially important industries, reached the civilian population. There were still hundreds of thousands, if not millions, of personal tragedies every year, for even in retreat the German soldiers were as tough as ever, and Russian casualties continued to be high—though not nearly as high as in 1941–2. Their equipment was now equal or superior to that of the Germans, and the earlier nightmare of those vast encirclements, as a result of which millions of Russians perished especially in 1941, was a thing of the past. Now it was the Russians, not the Germans, who were capturing hundreds of thousands of prisoners.

Food-rationing in the cities was now at least regular, and ration-cards were usually honoured, which was far from being true in 1941-2. But except for industrial workers and other privileged number one ration-card holders, Russia continued to be a hungry, or at any rate a badly undernourished country. In the villages, where there were no ration-cards, the peasants had to be content with what little was not taken from them by the state and Party officials. The top bureaucracy, however, suffered no food-shortage at all; perhaps one of my most obscene memories was that of the vast reception given by Molotov on 7th November 1943, at which, in the midst of hungry Moscow, several enormous buffets were laden with mountains of caviare, smoked salmon, suckling pigs and countless other delicacies. No doubt on an all-Russian scale it was just "a drop in the bucket"; but by 1944 the same "drop in the bucket" principle was being applied to the new so-called "commercial restaurants", where anybody with a lot of money could eat and drink himself silly. Especially to Britons, with their austere rationing system, it was truly shocking, though, as some Russians explained to me, only "truly deserving people" could afford to go to these places—mostly industrial executives, officers on leave, well-paid writers, actors and scientists —and in Moscow, in particular, it was important to give the city a certain "glamorous" look, and make people feel that life was "returning to normal". The "commercial shops", run on the same principle, were psychologically, it was claimed, a godsend even to the poor, for, even if only once a month, they could at least buy, outside the ration, some tiny little luxury (say, a couple of cream-cakes) that took their fancy.

Perhaps these "commercial restaurants" were not really as wicked and absurd as they looked. Though limited only to a very tiny privileged minority, they did give the happy illusion towards the end of the war of being a small, though very small, beginning of a return to normal. It was expected that once the war was over prices in both commercial shops and restaurants would rapidly become low enough for "almost everybody". Also, it was confidently hoped that before very long rationing would disappear altogether. These forecasts were, indeed, fully justified, and rationing would probably have been abolished very soon after the war, but for the disastrous drought of 1946. As a result, rationing was not abolished until the end of 1947, and it went together, as we shall see, with one of the most ruthless and drastic monetary reforms in human history.

The combination of the abolition of rationing and the introduction of the monetary reform was, of course, both logical and inevitable, since the post-war rouble was almost worthless, except as payment for rationed goods. For unrationed goods (as in the commercial shops and restaurants) altogether exorbitant prices had to be paid. The same was of course also true of the "free" *kolkhoz* markets for agricultural produce, and the black market. Black-marketing began, indeed, to flourish towards the end of the war. Among the most active black-marketeers were soldiers who could well afford to sell to the civilians all kinds of little extras they could spare. A very common black-market commodity were army tins of American spam. On the whole, the government turned a blind eye to black-marketing; after all, it was making life a little easier for countless hungry civilians.*

Towards the end of the war, life was getting better and easier not only materially, but also psychologically. The war had, of course, brought into the lives of millions of families fearful personal tragedies. There were families who had lost *all* their sons and other men. But life seemed freer than it had ever been under Stalin before. During the war, there was relatively very little police persecution, people were not only immensely patriotic and proudly nationalist, but they also spoke—and even wrote— with infinitely greater freedom than they had done previously— above all during the hideous years of the Stalin police terror in the 1930s. True, at the end of the war, there was the great tragedy of the hundreds of thousands who were now being punished for having fallen into German captivity, or (worse still) for having allowed themselves to be forced into the Vlasov Army, or who had, however innocuously, "collaborated" with the Germans in the occupied areas. But only a very small minority was affected by this new purge, and apart from the repatriated war prisoners, none of these people aroused much sympathy on the part of the population. But I shall deal with this and with what remained of the labour camp system by 1945 in a later chapter. At the end of the war, none of this seemed a major problem; victory was what

---

*I regret to say that among the worst black-market profiteers were the foreign diplomats in Moscow.

mattered, and every citizen, whether soldier or civilian, was proudly conscious of having done his bit.

Proudest of all, of course, were the soldiers, practically all of whom wore military decorations, some as many as a dozen or more. Many of these decorations were awarded automatically, especially the Moscow, Leningrad, Odessa, Stalingrad, Bucarest, Belgrade, Budapest and Berlin medals and the like—places in whose defence, capture or liberation they had taken part. Such medals were also lavishly awarded to civilians, and there were corresponding medals in the industries, so practically everybody felt a hero. The highest award was the title of Hero of the Soviet Union, but even of these (some of them "double" and even "treble" Heroes) there were several thousands, as there were also thousands of "Heroes of Socialist Labour". War decorations were the most fantastically successful application, as it were, of the "Stakhanovite" principle—any soldier would have been ashamed to come home after the war without at least one or two decorations—in addition to the "automatically" awarded ones. Decorations were given only very sparingly in 1941-2; after Stalingrad, nearly everybody was decorated. It was not until some months after the war that the government became conscious of the dangers of this kind of "inflation", and warned even the greater war heroes that their wartime achievements were a thing of the past and were no excuse now for relaxation.

But on V.E. Day (which, significantly, was one day later than in the West) the whole country was in an exuberantly self-congratulatory mood:

> May 9th was an unforgettable day in Moscow. The spontaneous joy of the two or three million people who thronged the Red Square that evening, and the Moscow River embankments, and Gorki Street, all the way up to the Belorussian Station, two miles distant, was of a quality and a depth I had never yet seen in Moscow before. They danced and sang in the streets; every soldier and officer was hugged and kissed; outside the US Embassy the cheering crowds shouted "Hurray for Roosevelt!" (even though he had died a month before);* they were so happy that they did not even have

---

* The British Embassy, being on the other side of the Moscow River, some distance from the main scene of the mass-rejoicing, was given only a few minor friendly demonstrations; besides this, the feelings towards Britain and Churchill were very different from those towards the United States and Roosevelt. The

to get drunk, and, under the tolerant gaze of the militia, young men even urinated against the walls of the Moskva Hotel, flooding the wide pavement. Nothing like *this* had happened in Moscow before. For once, Moscow had thrown all reserve and restraint to the winds. The fireworks display that evening was the most spectacular I have ever seen. (*Russia at War*, p. 969.)

No doubt almost everybody, no matter how poor, would have liked to celebrate victory in a "commercial restaurant", regardless of cost. But there were, of course, so few that only very important Soviet personages were admitted, as well as officers of the very highest ranks and, of course, foreigners—diplomats, no matter how insignificant, and journalists. I did not go, and preferred to mix with the crowds, frantic with joy as never before.

President was regarded as a real friend; Churchill never was. Of Harry Truman, the new President, the Russians still knew practically nothing.

TWO

The Difficult Summer of 1945

It is often assumed that the adoration of Stalin was never so great in Russia as at the end of the war, but this is not entirely true. As regards popularity and hero-worship, Stalin had for the first time in the course of his leadership, which dated back to the mid-twenties, some very serious rivals, namely, the greatest of the Russian generals—men like Zhukov, Konev and Rokossovsky; above all Zhukov. Stalin was extremely conscious of this, and, realizing the immense popularity of the army, he did his utmost after V.E. Day (as, indeed, he had already done during the war, or rather since Stalingrad) to identify himself completely with the army. He had been Commander-in-Chief, and by no means a negligible one. It must, however, be said that some of the main Russian reverses in the war could be attributed to Stalin's personal decisions—such as the disastrous Kharkov operation in May 1942 when, after the victory of Moscow (very much a "generals' victory"), he was determined to "reassert" his own exclusive authority as Commander-in-Chief. But this disaster, in which the Russians lost several hundred thousand men, taught him in the end a salutary lesson. He had, after that, to be content to be the "chairman" of a collective army command, and though the final decisions in any major battle were his own, they were taken after long consultations with the top generals. Stalingrad was a "collective" victory, and so was Kursk and virtually every other major victory between then and the end of the war.

Only once, as far as we know, did Stalin overrule the generals. It was in February 1945, when Zhukov and other generals in the field were all set for a rapid offensive against Berlin, which in their opinion they could easily have captured within a few days. But Stalin firmly vetoed the operation—which would almost certainly have ended the war three months earlier than it did end—because he declared it rash and dangerous. In reality, his reasons for this veto were unquestionably diplomatic—he thought that such an early victory by the Russians, and one "uncoordinated" with the Western allies, who were then still dragging their feet on the other side of the Rhine, might cause the greatest alarm in the West and so seriously complicate future relations with them. For, at that time, Stalin attached the greatest importance to a harmonious three-power peace and victory, from which he expected the greatest benefits. And one can, indeed, easily imagine the panic which the Russian capture of Berlin in February would have caused in a man like Churchill. Highly significantly, Stalin's peremptory order was phoned to Zhukov from the Yalta conference.

It was, of course, a hard decision for Stalin to take, and the generals were furious, as we know from Marshal Chuikov's account of this episode. In the end, it cost the Russians hundreds of thousands of lives. Between February and April, the Germans had time to build powerful fortifications between the Oder and Berlin, and the final Russian victory was incomparably more costly to them than it would have been three months earlier.*

Very soon after that Stalingrad victory, Stalin assumed the title of Marshal of the Soviet Union. After V.E. Day he went one better, and became "Generalissimo" (no one in Russia had borne this title since Suvorov, the famous Russian general of the Napoleonic wars!). During the war and for a short time after, he wanted to be seen by the Russian people as a soldier above all else, as head of the government second, and as head of the Party as a bad third. But, always suspicious, he distrusted the generals and particularly such (in his view) "Bonapartist" types as Zhukov, a man who, with good reason, regarded himself as the greatest of all the great generals to have emerged in the course of the Second World War. It did not take long for Zhukov, after a short spell as head of the Soviet Military Administration in Germany, to be

---

* See Chuikov, *The End of the Third Reich*, 1966, pp. 56–8, and Erich Kuby, *The Russians and Berlin*, 1968, pp. 24–5. Both writers, however, describe Stalin's decision as "inexplicable", and do not mention what I am certain was the real reason.

removed to the obscure post of regional commander of the Odessa district. It was not till after Stalin's death that Zhukov re-emerged in Moscow as Minister of Defence; but even then he did not last long; in Khrushchev's view, too, he was not sufficiently "Party-conscious", and although the head of the government and Party "used" him in his shabby political operation against the "anti-Party" group (Malenkov, Molotov, Kaganovich), he soon after got rid of him on the grounds that he had built up a "personality cult" of his own, especially inside the army!

For a time after V.E. Day Stalin basked in the glory of the army—but for only a very short time. This period was, in fact, over long before Russia declared war on Japan, which she did on 8th August, less than a month before Japan's official capitulation was signed on board the *Missouri*.

In May and June there were, of course, many spectacular celebrations in the army's honour. The most famous was that of 24th June when, after the gigantic Victory Parade, in the course of which hundreds of captured German banners were thrown down in the Red Square at Stalin's and the other leaders' feet, the greatest Moscow banquet ever was given at the Kremlin to thousands of marshals, generals and other distinguished officers.

This banquet was the final apotheosis of the victorious army, but it was, significantly, also an apotheosis of a different kind. The speech Stalin made at that banquet was not only the most *nationalist* but also the most *Russian-nationalist* he ever made. He described the Russian people as "the most remarkable of all the nations in the Soviet Union" and as "the leading nation, remarkable for its clear mind, its patience and its firm character". The Soviet government, he added (an almost unique admission coming from Stalin), had made many mistakes, but the Russian people had not told the government to go, had never thought of making peace with Germany, had shown confidence in the Soviet government and had decided to fight till final victory, whatever the cost.

The implications of this speech were clear enough: the Russians were not only quantitatively the greatest of the Soviet nations, but also qualitatively. They were the ones who had shown the greatest faith and devotion to the Soviet system, while of the smaller nationalities the Crimean Tartars and a number of small Moslem nationalities in the Caucasus in particular had been plainly

treasonable and pro-German, and others were more than doubtful
from the Soviet and Russian point of view (for instance the Baltic
Republics, reannexed, after their twenty years' independence, in
1940). The speech was particularly unfair to the Ukrainians;
a great many, it is true, had collaborated with the Germans, but
millions had fought and died in the Red Army, and their war
record was no worse than that of the Russians.

This priority given to the Russians was not without significance.
All the other nationalities, and perhaps even most Ukrainians,
whose country was overrun by the Germans in 1941–2 were, in
the main, convinced at the time that the Germans had practically
won the war. The Russians alone (obviously with a few exceptions) simply did not, at any moment, even admit the possibility
that all might be lost, no matter how desperate things looked.

This Russian (though not exclusively Russian) nationalism, from
being merely desperate in 1941–2, developed after Stalingrad into
an immensely proud nationalism, the like of which had never been
seen in Russia before. The mood continued for a few weeks after
V.E. Day. The two reasons why it suddenly disappeared were
(a) the tremendous "back-to-normal" campaign, which aimed
at an immediate restoration of the Party's absolute supremacy
over the army, and the soldiers' supreme patriotic duty to forget
about his war victories and his decorations, no matter how high,
and to get back to "ordinary" work; and (b) the Hiroshima bomb
in August, which cast an understandable gloom on Russia; some
pessimists went so far as to say—and many more to think—that
their four years' fighting and the millions of lives lost had all
been for nothing.

But paradoxically, Stalin's supreme exaltation of Russian
patriotism—which before long became simply Soviet patriotism
—related not only to the wartime past, but also to the future; and
never in all Russian history was the "innate" Russian (or Soviet)
superiority over *all* nations of the world, and above all over Western Europe and the United States, exalted with such seemingly
insane extravagance as between 1947 and 1950. This propaganda
had, as we shall see, a clear purpose, too. At the height of the Cold
War, with the Soviet people genuinely nervous about the atom
bomb, which until July 1949 was the sole monopoly of the United
States, it was essential to reassure the people that in the past,
even in the distant Tsarist part, Russia had produced scientists

far superior to any the West had ever produced, and that there was therefore very little need to worry. In fact, as early as November 1947, Molotov announced that there were no atom-bomb secrets the Russians did not know—which meant, except to the extreme sceptics, that Russia had already "practically" made her bomb. This, as it happens, proved perfectly true: eighteen months later the first Russian atom bomb was exploded—many years before American scientists had expected it.

Among Soviet civilians living conditions had been extremely hard in 1943–5, though not quite as desperately hard as during the two *années terribles* of 1941 and 1942. After V.E. Day, despite the people's exuberantly happy mood, these living conditions were no better than during the last two years of the war. In fact, they were slightly worse—and for a curious reason: almost immediately after V.E. Day (and without even waiting for the end of the war with Japan, which Russia had undertaken to join three months after the defeat of Germany), Harry Truman stopped Lend-Lease shipments to Russia. An important proportion of this Lend-Lease material consisted of food, and this, during the latter stages of the war, accounted for about one-half of what the (roughly) 10 million Russian soldiers ate; also a few odds and ends of this Lend-Lease food went to the civilian population, particularly to children. This meant, in effect, that the equivalent of say, 5, 6 or 7 million Russians were living solely on what America was supplying. The figure may seem negligible, but it mattered in the war-devastated Russia of 1945, which had, practically overnight, to provide extra food to several millions out of her own extremely meagre resources.

During the war, as we have seen, the rural population, which had to provide "for Army and Victory" every ounce of food except a bare subsistence minimum, was living in the main even more poorly than the town-dwellers, who at least had the advantage, because of rationing, of knowing (except in frequent cases of breakdowns) what to expect. This was not the case in the villages, where there were no ration-cards. Many desperate stories were heard, both during and after the war, about fearful conditions in such-and-such a village, but this information was fragmentary. Not till many years after the war and after Stalin's death could the real truth be told. Thus, in 1968, *Novy Mir* (Nos. 1, 2, and 3) published a remarkable novel by Fedor Abramov,

Two Summers and Three Winters, set in a village in the Russian
far north, on the Pinega river, some 200 miles north-east of
Archangel. No other book, as far I know, has ever covered so
concisely *all* the tragic "problems" that beset the Russian peasantry
both during the war and in the immediate post-war period—
from 1945 to 1948. First, the extermination of practically the
entire adult male peasant population. During the war, the vast
majority of the Red Army had, indeed, consisted of peasants, not
of town-dwellers, since most of these were required to keep the
war industries, the railways and the administration going. It is
true that in the cities a very large number of people conscripted
into the army were replaced by women; but agriculture depended
exclusively on female labour, plus very old men, adolescents and
even small children. Whatever hatreds may have been accumulated among the peasantry during the twelve years before the
war against Stalin for his ruthless collectivization of agriculture,
they no longer mattered once the war had begun. Besides being
naturally patriotic (and in Abramov's novel the scene is an exclusively *Russian* village), all the women had their husbands and
their sons over 18 in the army, and they were working, as it were,
not only for the country, but also for their own husbands and
boys. Life in the godforsaken village in the Arctic had been bleak
enough before the war, but at least since 1935 or so food at any
rate had not been a problem. Once the war had started, every
single scrap of food, apart from an absolute minimum necessary
to survive at all, had to be surrendered in the name of "the Front
and Victory". The peasant women worked as they had never
worked before and the enforcement of the various economic
"plans" was carried out by the local Party officials with the utmost
ruthlessness. The simplest pleasures were denied to the villagers
once the war had begun; as one of Abramov's characters says:
"The *aurora borealis* is now our only free cinema."★

Abramov's characters are also symbolic of the times. First, the
hard-working Pryaslin family who, after the father is killed in
the war in 1942, owe their survival to the 15-year-old son Mikhail,
a boy without education but with an inexhaustible physical
energy which he displays both in the *kolkhoz* fields and in the
timber camp some miles outside the village. Despite fearful

★ There was no local cinema in a village like Pekashino before the war, but,
like all villages, it enjoyed frequent visits from ambulating cinemas.

physical fatigue, Mikhail is always exuberantly cheerful and never complains. Then there are Lizka, his young sister, his mother Anna, and three small boys of about 7 to 10. All these, even the children, have to work incredibly long hours to help the family to survive "till after the war". The small boys contribute by catching fish in the river. There is no mention in the novel of anybody literally dying of hunger, but to earn even a bare minimum as many hours as humanly possible have to be devoted to cripplingly hard work, especially in the timber camp. Russia being in desperate need of timber during the war, much higher wages are paid than for any ordinary agricultural work, but even then, to maintain even a bare minimum of prosperity—very relative prosperity, of course—the daily "plan" must be "overfulfilled" to a very large extent.

The "village economics" are perhaps best of all illustrated by the story of 16-year-old Lizka. She is being continually pestered by Yegorsha, a swaggering, cynical, promiscuous 19-year-old lad. After his failure to seduce Lizka, he is, however, wholly successful in marrying her, despite the girl's obvious dislike for him. If Lizka agrees to marry him, it is in order to save the whole family from utter destitution: Lizka simply has not the heart to reject the young rogue, since, by hook and by crook, he had succeeded in getting a cow for her family. The death of their own cow Zvezdonya a few months before had reduced the whole Pryaslin family to near-starvation.

Another unforgettable character is Anfisa Petrovna, a war-widow, a woman beloved by all the villagers. She is dismissed from the chairmanship of the *kolkhoz* precisely because of her *babya zhalost*, her infinite "female pity" for her fellow-villagers. Anfisa Petrovna's opposite is Podresov, the secretary of the *raikom*, the CP's local committee. He is not a bad man at heart, but not to be ruthless in his demands that the timber and other "plans" be fulfilled or, better still, overfulfilled is more than his own life is worth. Also, regardless of everything, the priorities of the "plan" must be absolutely respected. Thus, when the villagers on one occasion tell the Party secretary that they must on no account miss the time for their spring sowing, they receive the typical answer that the state is not interested in the wretched rye and barley grown in the far north, but is desperately in need of timber, which must therefore receive top priority. That is undoubtedly the chief reason why, throughout the war and for at least three years later, the people of Pekashino never saw a piece of bread, while in 1944 they were literally reduced to eating moss.

The story begins around V.E. Day, and its historically most significant theme is that peace did not bring any improvement for a very long time. The exploitation by the state remained every bit as ruthless, with just this difference, that all these sufferings and hardships were now continuing, not for "the Front and Victory", but for "Reconstruction". A striking episode relating to the post-war years is the merciless bullying of the villagers by the local Party boss and the tax-collector into "voluntarily" subscribing to the 1946 Reconstruction Loan. The wretched people, though desperately short of money, have to subscribe to the loan to the extent of two or three months' earnings. Harsher still was the "meat tax". Those who had a cow or a calf or one or two sheep could pay the "tax"; but half the peasants had no live-stock of any kind, and had to buy the meat at exorbitant prices from their more "prosperous" neighbours.

Representative of the whole of Russia is Abramov's account of war losses in his village. Of all the men mobilized into the army, only three (out of about 100) return at all, one a war-cripple, one in perfect health and with scarcely a scratch, and one after long captivity in Germany. The wife of the one lucky man organizes a party to celebrate his return, but the party is boycotted by practically all the village women, since they have all lost their own husbands and could not bear to take part in the celebration. As for the man who returns from German captivity, he is met with the greatest hostility—as a "traitor" who has saved his life by surrendering, though nobody bothers to ask in what conditions he had fallen into German hands; he was "lucky", most probably, through his own "fault". Only when the man dies of cancer a few weeks later do the women begin to feel some pity for him— and to wonder. . . .

Here, in miniature, is the whole tragedy of the Russian peasantry during the war, and for three years after. No doubt, conditions in this Arctic village were even worse than in more clement parts of Russia, but the system of taxation was the same everywhere. I did occasionally come into contact with peasants soon after the war, among them Marusya, a pathetic "old" peasant woman who was a servant at the Metropole Hotel. She would sit there at night, nibbling at a crust of black bread. She seemed desperately undernourished and was pathetically grateful for any little gift, like a tin of meat and vegetables from our NAAFI store. But when I said to her that she would probably be much better off in her village near Kazan, she replied that, miserable and hungry though she was in Moscow, life "at home" was much more terrible now, and people were fleeing from the villages into the cities. Marusya looked old—at least 50; in reality she was not perhaps even 30, and those last years had been filled with endless grief. Her only baby, born in Moscow in the fearful winter of 1941, had died of cold, and her husband and both her brothers had been killed in the war.

Was there ever cannibalism in Russia? Undoubtedly there were several cases of it in the winter of 1941–2 in besieged Leningrad, when, especially in December/February, about 10,000 people a day were dying of starvation. In other parts there were, as far as I know, no cases of "conscious" cannibalism; but, as a *Pravda* correspondent, who had lived as a child during the war at Kuibyshev, told me a few years ago, human flesh (posing as minced pork) was sold in the local market and was eagerly bought up for making *kotlety* (meat rissoles) by the starving population.

Yes, both the war years and the immediate post-war years were periods of acute undernourishment for a large part of the population—for the peasantry and for those in the cities holding "dependants'", "employees'" and children's ration-cards, which provided about a pound of bread, but very little else. The industrial and other "heavy" workers were, however, reasonably well fed, except in the winter of 1941–2, when the distribution system had become altogether chaotic; I report in an earlier book an armaments worker's remark in 1942: "Enough work to kill you, *no zhrat' ni huya* (but not a f—ing thing to eat)."* In short, British wartime austerity was a Savoy banquet in comparison with Russian wartime rationing.

This situation continued till the end of 1947, when rationing was abolished, following the good harvest that year, which was in happy contrast with the disastrous drought of 1946.

The dire poverty of the villages for at least two years after the war had an immediate effect in producing a significant population shift. The soldiers returning from the war found life in the villages

* *The Year of Stalingrad*, 1946.

so lamentable that many of them fled to the cities, where, thanks to rationing, living conditions were more bearable. Although every change of employment was subject to government approval, this drift was condoned at first and then simply encouraged by the government. Men were needed for rebuilding the country's shattered economy, and during the first five years of peace the urban population increased by 12 millions and was, despite the appalling war losses, higher by 8 millions than in 1940. As during the war, so after the war, agriculture continued to be run predominantly by women—57 per cent—the rest of the rural population consisting mostly of old men, adolescents and children. But the same was almost true in the cities. The urban economy after the war employed 51 per cent of women; in building, nearly one-third of the workers were women; in other, more congenial, branches of the economy, such as textiles, they formed two-thirds or even four-fifths of the labour force.*

The reason for this anomaly is not far to seek. As the 1959 census showed, in the age groups that had borne arms there were at the end of the war only 31 million men left,† as against 52 million women. This vast gap is still very far from closed.

In the midst of the general exaltation and euphoria of the summer of 1945—except for the continuing food-shortage and a growing friction with the Western Allies—of which more later—there were two new tragedies affecting hundreds of thousands of people—tragedies about which the Soviet press, naturally, said next to nothing, but about which there was much whispering at the time in Moscow and elsewhere. Apart from the war casualties—which were then officially put at 7 million by Stalin, though, as was revealed in 1959, they amounted (civilians included) to at least 20 million—and the permanent war cripples (men with amputated arms and legs and other permanent injuries, of whom there were at least several hundreds of thousands in the country), there were also the "suspected collaborators" and the Russian soldiers taken prisoner by the Germans. As in all other countries, there were of course in Russia (or rather in the non-Russian parts of the Soviet Union) many genuine collabo-

* Isaac Deutscher, *Stalin*, 1961 edn., p. 560.

† These figures show the value of those Cold War books of 1948 which "demonstrated" that 10 or 15 million men were in forced labour camps, that is a third or a half of the whole adult male population.

rators who would, indeed, have been punished as they were in all occupied countries; but in Russia it was often sufficient merely to be "suspected" of collaboration to be sent to a labour camp.

More iniquitous still was the system whereby (with many exceptions, it is true) Russian soldiers who had been captured by the Germans were sentenced to more or less long periods in a camp for having "betrayed" their country. This was all the more horrible since, of the 5 million Russians captured by the Germans in the course of the war (almost exclusively in 1941 and 1942), only 1 million, that is one-fifth, survived the almost systematic extermination of Russian war prisoners through murder or plain starvation. It was not until after Stalingrad that Hitler decided that the few survivors and any new prisoners (there were very few) might, after all, be of some economic, and even military, value.*

It is untrue that all the repatriated war prisoners were sent to camps. Many returned in very poor health, many others could prove that they had been captured after being severely wounded, and officers, as a rule, were not punished. Nevertheless a stigma attached to those who had been taken prisoner; it was difficult, if not impossible, for the Soviet authorities to be entirely convinced that a prisoner had not surrendered "voluntarily". On the top of the black-list were of course those Russians who had joined Hitler's Russian "quisling" army, under the command of the notorious General Vlasov, who had himself been taken prisoner in the spring of 1942 and almost immediately decided that his brilliant career in the Red Army (he had been one of Stalin's greatest favourites) could be continued only in the German army —perhaps an understandable reflex by a fanatically ambitious man who in 1942 thought, perhaps not unreasonably, that the Germans were sure to win the war.† What the Russian authorities chose to overlook was that the great majority of Russians in the Vlasov army had simply been blackmailed into it—"either you join or you die of starvation". But this, for the Russians, was no valid excuse; such a man's duty was to die, however horribly, rather than serve the enemy.

No figures of the number of the repatriated war prisoners sent to camps are available, but it is reasonable to suppose that it was about half the total—that is, about 500,000.

* For full details, see the author's *Russia at War*, pp. 703–9.
† Ilya Ehrenburg, *Memoirs, Vol. IV, The War*, London 1964, pp. 47–52.

As regards collaborators sent to camps during and after the war, no reliable figures are available either. During the war, a number of "disloyal" nationalities—Volga Germans, Crimean Tartars, Kalmuks and several Caucasian Moslem nationalities—had been deported *en masse* to Siberia, including all the women, children and even communists and Komsomols. The operation was in the nature of a resettlement, and if some were sent to actual forced labour camps, they were in a small minority.

Regarding the other nationalities who were not deported *en masse*, those which had the highest number of genuine and suspected collaborators were undoubtedly the Baltic Republics, which had been reannexed by the Soviet Union barely a year before the German invasion, and the Western Ukraine (acquired as a result of the "partition" of Poland between the Soviet Union and Germany in 1939). The Baltic Republics, which had become independent "bourgeois republics" in 1918–19, naturally would have greatly preferred the Germans to the Russians, had they been able to make a choice in 1939–40. The only pro-Russians in these countries were their numerically almost negligible working class. The Latvian workers had, indeed, a powerful revolutionary tradition, and Latvians—having escaped from their "bourgeois" homeland—were extremely prominent in Russia in the early years of the Revolution—as soldiers, commissars (including many with "cabinet rank"), economic experts and, above all perhaps, as Cheka officials and executioners. But the vast majority in the three Baltic States were bourgeois *kulak* and, therefore, pro-German and often pro-Nazi and savagely anti-Semitic. Probably least hostile to Russia of the three Baltic Republics was Estonia, though, oddly enough, in the 1946 "election results"—for what they are worth—there were slightly more abstention and "No" votes in Estonia than in either Latvia or Lithuania.

Since the great majority of the population (apart from the Jews) could be said to have "collaborated" in some measure with the Germans after having been re-incorporated by Russia for only a year, no particular loyalty to the latter could in fact have been expected, and the Baltic deportees, though numerous, did not apparently run into more than 10,000 or 20,000—fewer than had been deported during the first Russian takeover in 1940. Moreover, the most violently anti-Soviet people had fled in very large numbers to Germany when, in the summer and autumn of 1944, the Russians were about to overrun or had already overrun the Baltic States.

Proportionately to their numbers, very many more people were deported from the Western Ukraine than from the Baltic States. Cities like Lwow were hotbeds of the most extreme Ukrainian nationalism, fascism and anti-semitism; and the Western Ukraine was by far the most pro-Nazi part of the Soviet Union to have been occupied by the Germans. For at least two years after the war a savage guerrilla war was waged by Ukrainian nationalists, with Nazi officers, against the Russians. In 1947 I had a long talk with a young Russian I knew who had been drafted into the NKVD troops who fought the Ukrainian guerrillas, as well as the *Armija Krajowa* Polish guerrillas on either side of the Polish/Ukrainian border. It was a very fierce business, and both sides had to be completely ruthless:

"I was too young to be called up before the end of the war, and it was all quite new, and pretty horrible to me. We had to go on punitive expeditions, we lost a lot of people ourselves, and the most unpleasant thing of all, for me, was to stand some of these Poles and Ukrainians against the wall and shoot them. I know that if we didn't shoot them, they would shoot us; but, all the same, it was beastly. I had never shot anybody in my life, and had even hated killing a chicken."

Some years later I met the same boy. He had taken to drink, and his heavy drinking, he said, had started during that guerrilla war.

Although there were many points in common between Eastern and Western Ukraine, which had formed part of Poland between the two wars (until 1918 it had been about half-Russian, half-Austro-Hungarian), above all their anti-semitism, Eastern Ukraine had been Russian for centuries and for over twenty-five years Soviet, and was still very different from the Western Ukraine. Soviet indoctrination of a whole generation had after all considerably weakened the traditional Ukrainian anti-semitism. Moreover, to the vast majority of Eastern Ukrainians, Russia *was* their homeland, and their Soviet, or Russian, patriotism was as great as that of the Russians themselves. True, for a short time after the invasion of 1941, the Germans behaved like "liberators" of the Ukraine, and were far less brutal there than in Russia proper. But this did not last long. By the beginning of 1942 Eastern Ukraine became the chief German reservoir for slave labour in the East. At least 2 or 3 million people—men and women—were deported to Germany. Alfred Rosenberg's "theory" that the Ukrainians were real Aryans, while the Russians were "*Untermenschen*", and that the former should, therefore, be given preferential treatment was dismissed by other top Nazis and Hitler himself as unrealistic; to Erich Koch, the Nazi Reichskommissar of the Ukraine, the Ukrainians had, indeed, been *Untermenschen* from the start.*

Compared with those in the Western Ukraine, only part of which had ever been Russian, the wartime collaborators in the Eastern Ukraine had in proportion been incomparably fewer, and the Eastern Ukraine got off very lightly. Sleeping with German soldiers was not regarded as "collaboration", though the police no doubt put a black mark against the sinner's name. I remember how even in Moscow at the height of the war, the famous Ukrainian film director, Alexander Dovzhenko, begged for leniency towards minor forms of "collaboration". Thus he argued that many Russian and Ukranian women may well have slept with Germans simply as a means of obtaining more food for their own children.

Apart from the whole nationalities who were re-settled in the East during the war, I should say that at most a million people were actually sent to labour camps after the war: some 10,000 or 20,000 from the Baltic States; about as many—perhaps more— from the Western Ukraine; perhaps 50,000 from the rest of the territories occupied by the Germans. The number of Russian war prisoners sent to camps is unlikely to have exceeded half a million.†

How many people were actually in camps by the end of the war? According to my estimates and the figures commonly mentioned in Russia, there were around 3 million people in forced labour camps at the beginning of the war. I am not con-

* For the various Nazi "theories" of what the Ukrainians were, and of how they should be treated, see the author's *Russia at War*, pp. 599–618.

† In A. Solzhenitsyn's *Ivan Denisovich*, describing life in a labour camp soon after the war, many of the characters are, significantly, either Balts or West Ukrainians. The naval captain who was sent to a camp for having received a souvenir from a British admiral belongs, almost certainly, to a later period— 1948 or 1949.

cerned here with the number of victims of the Stalin purges in the 1930s. Some Soviet, or rather anti-Soviet, "experts" have put forward the harrowing figure of 20 million deaths as a result of these purges—this figure being particularly attractive as showing that the Soviet Union lost exactly as many people during them as during the war. That many people died in the 1930s is of course certain, but by far the largest number died as a result not of the Stalin purges proper but of the collectivization of agriculture during the earlier part of the decade. In the liquidation of the *kulaks* many were killed, since they desperately and often violently resisted collectivization, but a far greater number were deported, together with their families, to timber camps. This deportation in itself would not have brought about many deaths had it not been for the deliberate slaughter by the peasants (and not only the *kulaks*) of an immense proportion of the country's livestock. Together with the chaotic state of agriculture during the few years that followed the collectivization drive (aggravated moreover by some severe droughts), this produced perhaps the worst famine Russia had ever known. It reached its peak in 1931-2 and as a result several million people died of hunger or acute undernourishment, and not just in the timber camps to which the *kulaks* had been deported, but in the country generally. The consequences of the mass-slaughter of livestock were to be felt for many years after, and by the time the war broke out in 1941 meat and dairy produce were still lamentably short. A campaign was launched around 1934 in favour of enormously multiplying the number of rabbits in the country, to make up for the meat shortage, even though rabbit meat is not usually eaten by Russians. (The rabbit became known as the "Stalin cow".)

Even long after the war, in 1959, there were many fewer cattle in the Soviet Union than there had been in 1916, before the Revolution, and today their number scarcely exceeds the 1916 figure. This is, of course, in fantastic contrast with industrial production, which, since the Revolution, has increased about seventy times. During the intervening period Russia had developed from a near-undeveloped country into the second-largest industrial power in the world.

Compared with the loss of life caused directly and indirectly by collectivization the deaths caused by the great Stalin purges of the late 'thirties were almost negligible, which does not of course mean that in human terms they were not one of the most odious episodes in the whole of human history. But apart from those executed (for example those sentenced to death in the famous open purge trials of 1936–8, and in the trial of Marshal Tukhachevsky and other army leaders) and those shot in greater "privacy", the deaths directly caused by the purge resulted from the overzealousness of certain "examining magistrates" whose tortures of those unwilling to "confess" merely led to the prisoner's death.

But, as we know from numerous accounts written in recent years by those who had been tortured, or were about to be tortured, the vast majority of prisoners soon realized that the only real salvation lay in "confessing" *anything*, since failure to "confess" could lead only to the greatest physical suffering by torture and could in no case shorten the sentence, but only aggravate it. As for the prisoners serving their sentence in the camps few, probably none, were actually tortured, since the "confessions" had already been extracted from them in the prisons. Extra-severe punishment (such as imprisonment for a fortnight or more in the kind of icy cell that Solzhenitsyn describes) could result in death, either immediately or soon after. Thus, those who, in the late 1930s, actually died in the camps of various causes were very few, probably a matter of not more than 10,000.[*] According to the great anti-Soviet mythology especially after the war, the Soviet labour camps were almost exactly the same as Hitler's extermination camps: in the Soviet camps people "died like flies". In reality they were like the camp described by Solzhenitsyn in *Ivan Denisovich*. This, in recent years (when one could, at last, at least privately talk to those who had been in camps), was confirmed to me by a very large number of Russians. Naturally, some camps were worse than others, according to the personality of the camp commandant, but everything suggests that the Solzhenitsyn camp was "average". In addition, most, though not all of the people I interviewed confirmed that until the war prisoners could—and did—receive letters and food-parcels from home. There were exceptions to this, however, in some extra-

---

[*] Probably a large number of these deaths occurred not in the camps themselves, but in transit to the camps. For a particularly gruesome account of such a journey, see Evgenia Ginzburg's *Into the Whirlwind*—another book that was published abroad (in England in 1968), but not in the Soviet Union.

severe camps, where no such favours were allowed—for instance the camp referred to in Lydia Chukovskaya's *Deserted House*, one of the most poignant "purge novels" I know.*

Between 1938 and 1941 a considerable number of prisoners were released—particularly among the officers who had been deported at the height of the "military" purge in 1938. By the end of that year, with the international situation becoming increasingly menacing, Stalin realized that the officers deported were now desperately needed, though even then he released only a relatively small proportion. A probably slightly greater number were released in 1941 after the German invasion. (Only to this extent is Isaac Deutscher's phrase, in his book *Stalin*, about the "replenishment" of the camps after the war correct.)

The vast majority of camp prisoners were not released during the war, not even if they begged to be given a chance to "die for their country". So we get a paradoxical situation in which the "criminals" lived an almost perfectly safe life, while millions of loyal Soviet citizens died in the war. In *Russia: Hopes and Fears* I relate the story of a Leningrad teacher who in 1937 was sent to a labour camp, and who remarked with grim humour: "Thank God for Stalin and Yezhov!" It was they who literally saved his life by sending him to a camp, for even if he had not been killed in the war he would almost certainly have died of starvation in Leningrad. The chances of surviving both the war and the Leningrad blockade were, he said, precisely nil.

Relatively very few people were sent to camps *during* the war, but there were cases, and I knew of one or two at the time. At the very beginning of the war, when I first arrived in Russia, I met a somewhat shifty and shady Italian called Colombo (whether that was really his name I do not know). As far as I remember, he acted as secretary to one of the foreign correspondents, but he also liked to visit all other correspondents and fill them up with good anti-Soviet propaganda. Though as ugly as sin (his teeth, he said, had been knocked out while being tortured by the

* Published in London in 1967. Although there was every chance of its being published in Russia soon after *Ivan Denisovich*, the outcry amongst the Stalinist *ultras* against washing dirty linen in public, and so unnecessarily discrediting Stalin, was such that its publication was in the end prohibited. It was, of course, read by thousands of Russians in typescript, under the *Samizdat* ("self-publisher") system, and like many other books, was smuggled out and published abroad.

Chinese, who had also disfigured his face with numerous scars, all of which was probably true), he had succeeded before I met him in marrying a very beautiful Russian woman of 25 or so, and a member of the "former classes"—in this case of an aristocratic Moscow family. She spoke French, English (and I believe German) perfectly. When I met her in the summer of 1941, with her mother (still very much a *grande dame* of the old regime), I soon discovered that both she, and even more so her mother, did not like Stalin. The reason for this was not far to seek: several members of the family, including two of Madame Colombo's brothers, had been deported in 1937.

When I returned to Russia in May 1942 Colombo was still there, but soon I learned from his wife (who was also by now a correspondent's secretary) that her husband had been suddenly arrested. She thought he had done a very foolish thing: while Moscow was being part-evacuated just before the Battle of Moscow, he had taken his more treasured possessions to the Japanese Embassy, where he had many friends, and had even attempted to stay in Moscow, though all foreigners, with rare exceptions, had been compulsorily evacuated. The grim sequel did not come till the autumn of 1943, when Catherine (Madame Colombo) was arrested. I visited her mother, but she received no news from Catherine until about two months later, when she wrote as follows: The journey to Siberia, at the height of winter, had been appalling. Most of the prisoners on the train were women; several died of cold and Catherine herself arrived at Novosibirsk, after an endless journey, with both her feet severely frost-bitten. The prisoners were herded into a large barracks, with an infirmary of sorts. She had not been sent to a camp, but had merely been "deported" as the wife of a man who had apparently been guilty of some serious crime. However, as luck would have it, the wife of one of her arrested brothers lived, also as a deportee, in a town about 100 miles away; she was employed as a local teacher, and was living in relative comfort. Catherine was permitted to join her, and before long was also given a reasonably good job. Not long after Catherine's deportation, I learned from her mother that she had received an official communication informing her that Colombo had been shot as a *vrag naroda* ("enemy of the people") and, more precisely, as a Japanese spy. I cannot say that I was unduly surprised. His friendship with the Japanese had struck me as more than suspect. As for the old lady, she had obviously received the news with undisguised pleasure. She had regarded the marriage of her charming and beautiful daughter *de très bonne famille* to a particularly shady foreigner as a *mésalliance* of the worst sort. I last heard of Catherine about 1958. She had only recently been allowed to return to Moscow, and was now happily married. The old lady had, of course, died long before, with all her children except one deported; and this only "lucky" one had been killed in the war.

The hundreds of women who had shared Catherine's terrible journey to Siberia were, almost without exception, wives of other "enemies of the people", who had either proved to be spies or had done something particularly disgraceful at the Front—and had almost invariably been shot, there and then.

After Catherine's arrest, I moved heaven and earth to get her released. In desperation, I even wrote to Stalin personally. There was absolutely no response from anybody. Finally I called on the head of the Foreign Ministry Press Department; but my mere mention of the case made him turn green with fear and the only response I got was a frightened mutter: "I should very, very strongly advise you to leave such cases strictly alone." And this from a man—the late A. A. Petrov—who, a few months later, was to be appointed Soviet Ambassador in China. When I raised the question with a close Russian friend and asked why on earth a wife had to share the punishment of her husband, he explained: "Well, you see, there are very close sexual relations between man and wife, and it is inconceivable that they should keep secrets from each other. To take your case, he simply *must* have told her something about his spying for the Japanese. . . ."

Probably not many more than, say, 10,000 people like Catherine were deported during the war for "guilt by association", and it is probable that very few people (apart from ordinary criminals) were actually sent to labour camps. Any soldier who had committed a serious offence was either shot or made to join some *shtrafnoi batalyon*—one of those "penalty battalions" in the Red Army which were given near-suicidal missions.

So, throughout the war, the forced-labour population remained practically stationary—the figure usually quoted to me by Russians being about $2\frac{1}{2}$ millions, only a very small proportion (less than one-tenth) of them women. This figure marked a drop from

3 million in 1938, about half a million having been released from camps for various reasons between 1938 and 1941. Once the war had begun, life became even harder in the labour camps than before. Food parcels which had previously helped to improve the prisoners' diet and relieve the fearful and nauseating monotony of the meals, with their everlasting *balanda* broth, were stopped almost as soon as the war had begun. Nor were letters allowed to be sent to camps any more. In *Russia: Hopes and Fears* I record the story of a man who had spent all the war years in a camp in northern Russia. He told me that food became extremely short after the war had broken out; there was very little food available in the country, and the forced-labour camps were at the very bottom of the list of priorities. The year 1942, he said, was the most terrible of all. Towards the autumn of that year, people in the camps began literally to die of starvation. In his particular camp some ten or twenty people out of 2,000 died of hunger every week, while he, like most others, was so swollen with hunger that he could hardly move, still less do any physical work. There was a slight improvement in 1943, when occasional packets of American calcium and vitamin pills, as well as some precious tins of American spam, would reach the camp infirmary. He reckoned that, as a result of this famine or acute undernourishment in the camps, particularly in 1942, perhaps 100,000 prisoners died out of a total camp population of, say, $2\frac{1}{2}$ million.

During the months following the war, the camps were "replenished", as we have seen, by about 1 million new prisoners (or perhaps a little fewer). As a result, by the end of 1945 there were over 3 million "forced labourers" in the Soviet Union, not counting, of course, the many hundreds of thousands of German and Japanese war prisoners who were extensively used for restoration work for a good number of years after the war. Thus, in the summer of 1946, I saw thousands of German war prisoners in the Caucasus being engaged in road-building.

To look a little further ahead, "forced labour" in the Soviet Union was to be used, especially after 1947, as the most potent weapon of anti-Soviet propaganda. The most fraudulent figures, bearing no relation whatsoever to the real facts, were produced by "Russian experts", the biggest fraud of all being the seemingly academic and scholarly work by two old Mensheviks, David Dallin and Boris Nicolaevsky. Anyone who dared challenge their assertion in their *Forced Labour in Russia* that the camp population was around 10 or 12 million people was treated *ipso facto* as a communist or Soviet agent, though even the most elementary study of the problem would have shown up the utter absurdity of the Dallin/Nicolaevsky figures.*

Except to the repatriated war prisoners and to thousands of real or "suspected" collaborators, arrests and deportations did not become a daily obsession (as they had been in the late 1930s) with a large number of Russians until the beginning of 1948. It was during that year, as we shall see, that another era of "Stalin purges" began, not to end till Stalin's death in 1953. It never assumed the proportions of the Yezhovshchina of 1937–8, but nevertheless affected thousands of people, among them even such "improbable" victims as Mr. Ivan Maisky, former Soviet Ambassador in London, and his First Secretary there, Mr. K. Zinchenko, who had, shortly before his arrest, been a high Soviet official at the UN. Probably the biggest purge of all during that period was in Leningrad, a city against whose independent, *frondeur* and "anti-Moscow" spirit Stalin had always been acutely prejudiced. In the course of the "Leningrad Affair" of 1949 practically the whole of the Leningrad Party Organization was wiped out, along with Nikolai Voznesensky, a member of the Politburo, head of the Gosplan, and one of Stalin's own closest and ablest associates during the war. Other well-known victims of the "second" Stalin purge were many prominent Jews, suspected of "Zionist" sympathies, particularly dozens of the most famous Yiddish-writing authors, and many hundreds, if not thousands, of Russians who had, during and soon after the war, maintained close and friendly relations with foreigners, particularly with Britons and Americans.

So in the first two or two and a half years after the war, Russia was in the main still free of that fear which had made it such a nightmarish country only ten years before. Living conditions were hard for nearly everybody and the industrial workers had to work almost as hard as during the war. A vast, nation-wide reconstruction drive characterized this period. Many vast areas, especially in the southern and western parts of European Russia, were in ruins. Thousands of villages had to be rebuilt, and hundreds of major towns and cities, such as Stalingrad, Sebastopol,

* See the author's *Russia: Hopes and Fears*, p. 97.

Rostov, Smolensk, Kiev, Kursk, Orel, Pskov, Minsk and nearly all the other Belorussian cities, had to be raised from the ruins, as well as great industrial areas like practically the whole of the Donbas in the Ukraine, with its coal-mines and its great engineering works.

Most villages were more or less rebuilt within a few months after the war (or had already been since their liberation). The reconstruction of the destroyed or half-destroyed towns and cities took, of course, much longer—usually between three and five years. During that period very little building was done on an almost wholly undamaged city like Moscow,* despite a great population influx in the immediate post-war years.

---

* The only time Moscow was damaged was during a few ineffective air-raids in 1941.

THREE

The Cold War

When one examines carefully the origins of the Cold War, one almost inevitably comes to the conclusion that it began not at some relatively recent date, but simply in 1917, the year the Soviet regime was established in what had been the Tsar's Russian Empire. At least two major recent histories of the Cold War start the story in 1917: Professor D. F. Fleming's *The Cold War and Its Origins, 1917–1960* and André Fontaine's *History of the Cold War*, the first volume of which bears as a subtitle: *From the October Revolution to the Korean War*. The establishment in Russia of a socialist or communist regime was, *ipso facto*, an unprecedented challenge to the entire capitalist system by which the rest of the whole globe was then ruled. Worse still, it made no secret of its ambition to overthrow this capitalist system; the Russian Revolution was, to Lenin and the other Soviet rulers, merely the small beginning of an "inevitable" world revolution, and nothing, as we know, disappointed Lenin more than the failure of the German working class in 1918–19 to bring about a revolution, similar to the Russian one, in highly industrialized Germany, where in Lenin's view conditions for such a revolution were infinitely more favourable than in a backward, politically uneducated and "underdeveloped" country like Russia. Germany, at that time, had an enormous and class-conscious working class; though the Russian working class was also politically highly educated, it was, numerically, extremely small. Yet—except for some isolated attempts which were doomed to failure—the homeland of Marx and Engels refused, almost unanimously, to follow in Lenin's footsteps, even in the near-famine conditions in Germany in

37

1918–19 and in the midst of all the frustration caused to the German people by their military defeat in November 1918 at the hands of the Western Allies.

This enormous initial failure to "export" the Revolution to Germany did not, however, discourage Lenin. In 1919 the Third International, or Communist International (Comintern), was set up in Moscow, its purpose being defined as

> an international revolutionary proletarian organization representing the unification of the communist parties of the different countries. It proclaimed as its historical aims the winning-over of the majority of the working class and all other toilers to the cause of communism; the struggle for the dictatorship of the proletariat, the liquidation of the capitalist system and its replacement by the socialist system. The Comintern was the historical successor of the First International, and inherited the best traditions of the Second International, though it firmly rejected the latter's opportunism. The Comintern adopted the Marxist-Leninist ideology in its struggle against social-democratism, and against the opportunism of the leaders of the Second International and of the separate social-democratic parties, as well as against anarcho-syndicalism and other tendencies hostile to Marxism. (*Malaya Sov. Entsiklopedia*, vol. 4, p. 1090, 1959.)

The constituent Congress of the Comintern was held in March 1919, and here thirty-five communists parties were represented, though not all were yet called that officially. The principal countries represented at that Congress were the various Soviet republics of the former Russian Empire, Germany, Austria, Poland, Hungary, Finland, France, the USA, China and Korea. It was between 1918 and 1921 that most of the principal communist parties of the world were officially created: Austria, Germany and Finland, 1918; Hungary, Bulgaria and the USA, 1919; Great Britain, Indonesia (then Dutch East Indies), Spain and France, 1920; China, Rumania, Czechoslovakia and Italy, 1921. Later other communist parties were formed, for instance Japan (1922), Korea and Poland (1925), India (1933), Albania (1941). At the Sixth Congress of the Comintern in 1928, no fewer than fifty-five countries were represented, and at the Seventh Congress in 1935, sixty-five countries. But by now, and indeed long before, the true aim of the Comintern was no longer world revolution, but the defence of humanity (and, in the very first place, of the

Soviet Union) against the growing threat of military aggression from the "fascist and imperialist" forces of the world. In fact, the Comintern had gradually become nothing more than part of the Soviet Establishment and a weapon in the hands of the Soviet government. It had, indeed, become that increasingly ever since Stalin had proclaimed his policy of "Socialism in One Country". The Comintern's almost sole purpose was to give orders to the various communist parties abroad—orders which were determined exclusively by what was most important to the Soviet Union and often quite regardless of the interests of the foreign communist parties to which these orders were given.*

Although anyone familiar with the Soviet scene knew that there was nothing internationalist about the Cominform, at least in the original Leninist sense, that the organization had little more than a theoretical interest in the world revolution (despite the usual Leninist/Trotskyist verbiage it continued to use) and that the Comintern was merely a tool in the hands of an increasingly chauvinist and nationalist Russian nation-state, all the anti-Soviet forces of the outside world continued to treat the Comintern as a fearful menace and deliberately continued to identify it, in their anti-Soviet propaganda, with the famous "hand of Moscow". The Comintern continued, indeed, to be the biggest stick to beat Moscow with. But even apart from that, the capitalist governments and the capitalist press continued to regard Russia as a great menace to the established order, since she was the only socialist country in the world and was so setting a dangerous and tempting example to the working class and other left-wing opposition elements in the capitalist countries themselves. The capitalists also remembered only too well how, in the early years of the Russian Revolution, they had to make very substantial financial concessions to their own working class in order to convince them that, to improve their lot and their standard of living, they did not need to start any violent revolutions after the

* The most famous example of this total disregard were the orders given by the Cominform in 1939 to the French communists to sabotage as far as possible the "imperialist war", since Stalin thought it in Russia's interests to do nothing that might antagonize Hitler. These orders created for the French CP its most tragic dilemma, which I discuss at great length elsewhere—notably in *France 1940–1955* (1956). It was literally a case for the French communists of sacrificing themselves for Russia against their own national instincts and better judgement.

Russian model. Hence the paradoxical effect of the Russian Revolution: as a result of the capitalists' concessions, the Western working classes became not *more* but *less* revolutionary than they had been.

Not that the danger of their "imitating" the Russian communists could be written off, even after Stalin's "Socialism in One Country"; the great slump between 1929 and the mid-thirties made large parts of the Western working classes turn for salvation to Russia—a country which did not suffer from slumps or from unemployment. It is scarcely surprising that at the height of the slump, in 1931–2, there should have been, for instance, 6 million Germans to vote for the German Communist Party—the communists alone seeming capable to their voters of putting an end to the German people's miseries and hardships. It took a Hitler to show the Germans that there *was* an alternative to a communist dictatorship. Hence no doubt the great interest and even sympathy shown to Hitler by a large part of the ruling class, even in some of the most "democratic" countries of Western Europe, as well as in the United States.

To the capitalist, the Soviet Union also constituted an enormous danger in another field. If, in the 1920s, they had "appeased" their own working class by creating better living conditions for them, they had done practically nothing for the hundreds of millions of people in the colonies under their rule. And to these multitudes of Indians, Africans and Latin-Americans, Russia was already the answer, or would, at any rate, and within a foreseeable future, provide such an answer, to the hideous problems of their own unspeakable poverty and backwardness. The Tsars also had had their "colonial" peoples, notably in Central Asia, and under the Soviet regime and particularly under Stalin's "nationalities policy" the Uzbeks, Tadjiks, Bashkirs, Kazahks and the rest became equal partners of the Russians and Ukrainians. Better still, the Soviet regime took special pride in improving the lot of these backward people, and of making them feel genuinely grateful to the Russians; and it is, of course, perfectly true that if, under the Tsarist regime, as much wealth as possible was pumped *out* of the Russian "colonies" of Central Asia, the Soviets pumped wealth and money *into* them. If there was, at times, resistance, even violent resistance, against the Soviets in Central Asia, it was not for economic reasons, but almost exclusively for religious reasons, the Soviets' atheism being wholly unacceptable to certain traditional Moslem communities.

But the British ruling classes naturally knew what effect these far-reaching reforms and the "equal national status" in Central Asia would have, sooner or later, in countries like India, not to mention Indo-China, whose people (or whose intellectuals, at any rate) were much quicker than the traditional, fatalist and deeply religious Indians in grasping the lessons of the Russian Revolution and of Stalin's nationalities policy in relation to their own country. Besides China, one of the strongest and most dynamic communist parties to develop in the colonial world in the 1920s was the Indo-Chinese CP, already then under the leadership of Ho Chi Minh.* The only answer the French colonialists had to this "menace" was prisons, concentration camps, tortures and executions.†

How deeply prejudiced most of the leaders of the capitalist world were against the Soviet Union—even when a *rapprochement* or alliance with her could alone have kept Nazi Germany in check—we know from the example of Neville Chamberlain, for instance, who deliberately ignored any possible Russian help to Czechoslovakia on the eve and at the time of Munich,‡ and who, in 1939, agreed with only the utmost reluctance to enter into diplomatic talks with Russia, let alone those military talks which he deliberately sabotaged in the summer of 1939,

* Ho Chi Minh had attended the historic Congress of Tours in December 1920 which resulted in a split of the French Socialist Party; the larger of the two factions assumed the name of Communist Party.

† See notably Andrée Viollis, *Indochine S.O.S.* (Paris, 1931). Since Hitler we have read countless books on mass-murders and mass-atrocities; in 1931 Andrée Viollis's remarkable book still had very few to equal it for sheer horror. When, a year or two later, I became acquainted with that brilliant French journalist, she could scarcely speak of Indo-China without tears in her eyes, and without saying how profoundly ashamed she was of her country—the country of the French Revolution and the Rights of Man. It was indeed as a result of what she had seen in Indo-China that she joined the French Communist Party, although nothing was more anti-communist than the newspaper, *Le Petit Parisien*, which employed her as one of its top reporters. If I am not mistaken, *Le Petit Parisien*, after publishing her series of articles on Indo-China, dismissed her, despite the enormous sensation these articles had caused among the unsuspecting French public.

‡ The Soviet Union had undertaken to come to the help of Czechoslovakia, provided her Western ally, France, did not violate her military obligations to Czechoslovakia were the latter to be attacked by Germany.

when Russian military action against Germany could alone have saved Poland from quick defeat by Germany.

To men like Chamberlain (though this was never stated publicly) the "free hand in the East" for Germany was already clearly implied in the Munich "settlement", soon to be followed by the officially inspired British and French press, which launched their famous campaign in favour of a German annexation of Soviet Ukraine. The French government took precisely the same line, notably during Ribbentrop's visit to Paris in December 1938, when Foreign Minister Georges Bonnet not only implicitly approved a German expansion to the East, but even favoured the adoption by France of something very like Hitler's policy as regards the Jews. As Ribbentrop wrote after his visit to Paris:

> During my second talk with Bonnet on 7th December we examined the Jewish problem. Although I told him that I could not discuss this matter with him officially, he replied that he would like to tell me privately that France was greatly interested, too, in solving the Jewish problem. I said to Bonnet I was surprised that France should consider it a problem. He then explained that, on the one hand, he did not wish to admit any more Jewish refugees from Germany, and asked that the German Government take appropriate measures for stopping them from coming to France; on the other hand, it was important for France to get rid of 10,000 Jews, and to send them anywhere. In fact, the French Government had been thinking of Madagascar. (*Les archives secretes de la Wilhelmstrasse IV*, Paris, 1953, quoted by Roger Errera, *Les libertés à l'abandon*, Paris, 1968, pp. 155–6.)

This shows to what extent even "great Republicans" like Georges Bonnet, in pining for a political and even military *rapprochement* with Nazi Germany, were prepared to ingratiate themselves with Hitler by adopting some of the most odious aspects of the Nazi regime—all the more so as France, with her vast colonial empire, had plenty of places to which she could deport her Jews—10,000 to begin with.*

---

* Although everybody knew at the time that Bonnet had made it quite clear to Ribbentrop that France was in favour of giving Germany a "free hand in the East", no one knew that he had discussed France's "Jewish problem" with Hitler's Foreign Minister. What everybody, however, knew was that the two Jewish ministers in the Daladier government (Zay and Mandel, both subsequently murdered by Vichy killers) had been excluded from the French

That the "free hand in the East" was also highly popular as a way of avoiding a war between Germany and Britain, if not with Chamberlain himself (though what his secret thoughts were on the subject can scarcely be doubted), at least with numerous members of his entourage, notably Sir Horace Wilson, is made obvious enough—if anyone still had any doubts on the subject— by the *Dircksen Papers*, later discovered in Germany and published by the Russians in 1948. These papers from the archives of Herbert Dircksen, the German Ambassador in London shortly before the war, clearly show that not only some of Chamberlain's closest associates, but also at least two press lords, Rothermere and Kemsley, were "free-hand-in-the-East" men, Rothermere quite openly, Kemsley a little more discreetly. The editor of Rothermere's *Daily Mail* was in the habit of informing the German Ambassador on the paper's foreign policy.*

After Munich, the Russians were profoundly disgusted with the world powers' betrayal of Czechoslovakia, their total departure from Litvinov's "indivisible peace", and their obvious gang-up with Hitler during the months that followed Munich, complete with the Western press campaigns in favour of a German conquest of the Ukraine. While regarding Nazi Germany as potentially far more aggressive than Britain and France, Stalin, in his famous speech of 10th March 1939, took in effect a "plague on both your houses" line and almost congratulated the Germans on not having followed their friends' "advice" in the West to conquer the Ukraine. But when, five days later, the Germans marched into Prague, he was willing, and indeed anxious, to consider a *rapprochement* and even an alliance with the Western powers. He knew that at least some leading public figures in the West— ex-President Millerand in France and Winston Churchill in England, though both fanatical former interventionists in the Russian Civil War—saw a Western alliance with the Soviet Union as the only salvation. But it soon became clear that the actual governments of both France and Britain were hesitant and reluctant to start any *serious* talks with the Russians. In the case of

government receptions given in Ribbentrop's honour, in case this top Nazi took offence!

* *Dokumenty i materialy kanuna 2-oi Mirovoi Voiny. Tom II Arkhiv Dircksena 1938–39.* Published by the Foreign Ministry of the USSR, Moscow, 1948.

Britain, this was all the more disconcerting since Chamberlain had just given his "guarantee" to Poland; and how Poland was to be saved without Russian help was totally incomprehensible.

When "negotiations" between France, Britain and the Soviet Union began soon after the German invasion of Czechoslovakia, it became clear at once that what Chamberlain aimed at was simply to get the Soviet Union to give unilateral "guarantees" to Poland, Rumania and other border states. The first serious proposal for a military alliance between Britain, France and the Soviet Union was made on 14th April by Foreign Commissar Maxim Litvinov; and its virtual rejection by the British government resulted, a fortnight later, in the dismissal of Litvinov and his replacement by V. M. Molotov. I need not here repeat the now all-too-familiar story of the diplomatic exchanges during that fateful summer between Russia and the Western powers, Germany and the Western powers, Germany and Russia.* It all ended, as we know, in the conclusion of the Soviet/German Pact of 23rd August. Far from enthusiastic about an alliance with France and Britain, and more and more convinced, as time went on, that the French and especially British governments loathed the very idea of a genuine military alliance with Russia, Stalin saw no alternative to this Soviet/German Non-Aggression Pact, if Russia was not to be invaded by the Germans that year, after their now imminent conquest of Poland. It was, in effect, Stalin's answer to Munich; if Munich implied for Germany a "free hand in the East", the Molotov/Ribbentrop pact meant a "free hand in the West" for Hitler.

This pact aroused the highest "moral indignation" in the West; it was a "stab in the back", a Russian betrayal of "collective security" etc. etc.—all these indignant people conveniently forgetting that Munich was *their* stab in the back to Russia and just as blatant a betrayal of "collective security" as Munich had been. Moreover, at Munich France had cynically betrayed Czechoslovakia, a country with which she had a firm military alliance. By signing their pact with Nazi Germany, the Russians did not at the time "betray" or throw to the wolves any country. If, soon after, they took part with Germany in the "partition" of Poland, it was only because Poland had been defeated anyway, and the Russians had to choose between either abandoning the

* See for details for example Part I of the author's *Russia at War.*

whole of Poland to the Nazis (which would have brought them to a frontier almost within marching distance of Moscow) or taking over Eastern Poland themselves. This, moreover, had the advantage of having only a very small Polish population, the bulk of the people being Belorussians and Ukrainians. Nevertheless, the "moral indignation" over Stalin's participation in the "partition of Poland" was even greater in the West than over the Soviet/Nazi Pact itself.

But the greatest boon to all the anti-Soviet maniacs and secret Nazi sympathizers in the West came at the end of November, when the Russians attacked Finland. It was perfectly clear even at the time why they had done this. Their share in the "partition" of Poland had pushed the Soviet Union's frontier with German-occupied Poland several hundred miles to the West; and now the most vulnerable spot on Russia's Western frontier was precisely on her border with Finland, which ran only some thirty miles north-west of Leningrad. Even if the Russians could be 100 per cent certain that the Finns would never attack them, they still had no guarantee that Finland might not be occupied by the Germans, who could then either capture Leningrad or, failing that, more or less destroy it by intensive artillery bombardment from Finnish territory. For the Russians knew all along that a German attack on them was almost inevitable, and only a question of time; and the Soviet/Nazi Pact had given them at least a breathing-spell for strengthening Russia's frontier defences and increasing the power of their armed forces.

Practically the whole of public opinion in the West was shocked by the Russian attack on Finland, but those who were savagely anti-communist and more or less secretly pro-Nazi saw in the Russian invasion an undreamed-of opportunity for turning the Anglo/French war against Nazi Germany into one against the Soviet Union. This was also, in fact, the point of view of the French and British governments, or at least of several of their members. It was, indeed, extraordinary how they hastened to get the League of Nations to expel the Russian "aggressor", even though neither Japan had been expelled for having invaded Manchuria, nor Mussolini's Italy for her blatant aggression against Ethiopia. Except for some naval incidents, the war against Germany had as good as vanished from the greater part of the British and French press, whose front pages and banner headlines were virtually monopolized by the "Russian aggression against Finland". Not content with expressing their verbal sympathy, both the French and British governments* started very soon to give substantial military help to "gallant little Finland", with promises of ever-increasing help, complete with volunteers; significantly, as a result of a hysterical press campaign, there were many more such volunteers to fight the Russians in Finland than the Germans on the Franco/German frontier. If this Western help did not assume huge proportions, it was because the Scandinavian countries refused most of the transit facilities Daladier and Chamberlain were demanding from them and because a peace was signed between the Soviet Union and Finland in March 1940, almost the moment the Russians had achieved all that they needed—a shifting of the frontier from thirty to 100 miles north-west of Leningrad. This peace treaty also provided for the establishment of a Russian naval base at Hangö at the entry into the Gulf of Finland—another vital security measure to the Russians in the event of a war with Germany.

Hitler's attitude to the Soviet/Finnish War was one of "neutrality", and he was not going to allow it to upset his plans for striking at the West. A month after the end of the Finnish war, he attacked Denmark and Norway, and after another month launched his *blitzkrieg* against the Low Countries and France, thus profiting from the "free hand in the West" that the Soviet/German pact had implied.

How did Russia react to the German invasion in the West? Among the intellectuals, there was much sympathy for France and England, both of which, to such Russians, were far less detestable than Nazi Germany. Many, however, thought with some glee of France and England now getting what they had wanted Russia to get. To the politically minded there was great satisfaction at the thought that the capitalist powers were now "devouring each other", and that in the end both sides would be terribly weakened (it was precisely what Harry Truman said a year later, when Germany attacked the Soviet Union—the more people killed on both sides, the better for America). But what did come as a shock to the Russians was the complete military rout of France within less than two months; for the German losses

* The USA was particularly friendly to Finland, since she was the only country to have fully paid her First World War debts to her.

in the war in the West proved negligible, and had not weakened Germany in the least. Worse still, her victory had enormously increased her economic resources. A Nazi attack on Russia was now only a question of time; and immediately after the fall of France the Russians hastened to push forward their frontiers in two more places—by "incorporating" the Baltic States in the Soviet Union and by annexing Bessarabia and North Bukovina from Rumania.

During all those first years of the Second World War, the Comintern lay dormant. If its chief spokesman, George Dimitrov, preached defeatism to the French communists, he was only carrying out the Kremlin's instructions. Similarly, the abortive Russian puppet government for Finland was not an invention of the Comintern, but of the Kremlin—even though its head, Otto Kuusinen, had been very active on the Comintern for years. It is just possible that the idea of this Finnish puppet government was originally his; if so, he was responsible for one of the Kremlin's biggest diplomatic fiascos.

Between the fall of France and the German attack on Russia, the Cold War assumed a peculiar character; if during the Finnish war there was between Russia and the Western powers a Cold War which threatened at any moment to become a shooting war, after the fall of France there was a carefully camouflaged but still very genuine Cold War between Russia and Germany, and, at the same time, a slight, though very slight, *rapprochement* between Moscow and London, which, among other things, sent Sir Stafford Cripps as its Ambassador to Moscow. His cautious overtures to the Russians met, officially, with no response. Nevertheless, the Kremlin must have noted with some satisfaction that speaking terms between the Russians and the British were being slowly restored. With Hitler now ruling the greater part of Europe, Moscow's relations with the British were beginning to assume some importance in the eyes of the Soviet government. But, for fear of offending Hitler, even this faint *rapprochement* was kept extremely secret—so secret that even Cripps was scarcely allowed to be aware of it!

On 22nd June 1941 the Germans attacked Russia, and on that very night Churchill declared Britain's full support for the Soviet Union, though stressing at the same time that he had always been an enemy of communism, and always would be. A few weeks

5

later a *de facto* alliance was concluded between Britain and the Soviet Union, and less than a year later a formal military alliance was signed by the two countries. Though less officially, the United States also joined in what came to be known as the Big-Three Alliance. Did that, however, mean that as Britain, the USA and the Soviet Union were fighting the same enemy, the Cold War between them had completely ended? Certainly not. Although very little was said at the time, there were mental reservations on both sides. The two great Western allies represented a capitalist society traditionally hostile to communism, and vice versa. While welcoming the existence of a military ally (Britain), the Russian people could not but deeply distrust Churchill, who was remembered as one of the chief interventionists who had tried desperately to strangle the Soviet regime in its cradle. Nothing could be entirely forgotten—the Zinoviev Letter forgery of 1924, the Arcos Raid, the break-off of diplomatic relations with Russia in 1927. And although Churchill had nothing to do with Munich, and had even condemned it, he belonged to the same "class" as the Chamberlains and Halifaxes who had taken part in the Munich settlement. On 22nd June, the Russians indeed heaved a loud sigh of relief in finding Britain and Churchill by their side; since Hess's landing in Britain on 11th May, they had suspected the worst—an Anglo/German gang-up against the Soviet Union. When I landed at Archangel on 3rd July, the one question almost every Russian asked was whether I was "quite sure" that no deal had been made between the British and Hess.

It was, of course, well known that there were still plenty of Munichites, not only in the Conservative Party but even inside the British government—people with a chronic loathing for all that the Soviet Union stood for. One of the first disagreeable episodes after the German invasion of Russia arose from a speech by Colonel Moore-Brabazon, the Minister of Aircraft Production in the Churchill government, who declared that he hoped the Russian and German armies would exterminate each other, and that, while this was taking place, Britain would develop her air force and other armed forces and become the dominating power in Europe. It was at the TUC meeting in London on 2nd September 1941 that Jack Tanner, President of the Amalgamated Engineering Union, asserted that these were indeed the words Moore-Brabazon had used; such a point of view, he said, would result in the nullification of the whole war effort, since it meant that Britain should *not* help Russia with armaments. All that Moore-Brabazon found to reply in a statement published on his behalf was that Tanner was "evidently referring to a passage in a recent extempore speech which was open to misinterpretation", but he made sure not to issue a verbatim report of the remarks in question.★

Such sentiments were, of course, expressed on both sides of the Atlantic, as we know, for instance, from the speech which Senator Harry Truman, the future President, made the day after the German invasion of Russia, in which he said he would like to see the mutual extermination of Russians and Germans; and that the USA should always support the weaker side, so that the carnage was complete and went on for as long as necessary. But although, in the long run, it mattered more what Harry Truman thought of the Russians than what Moore-Brabazon said, he was in 1941 at least not a member of an allied government pledged to supporting the Soviet Union in her war effort!

People like Moore-Brabazon were, in a sense, "optimistic". His speech implied that the war in Russia might be a very long one, and one in which Germany would suffer grave losses and be considerably weakened. The prevalent opinion among British military "experts", including those of the War Office, was that the defeat of the Soviet Union was a matter of weeks or, at most, of a few months. When G. Bernard Shaw, in a letter to *The Times*, said in effect that he thanked God for Hitler's attack on Russia, for with Stalin "on our side" we could be certain of victory, most people thought that GBS was standing on his head, as usual. Genuine authorities on Russia, like the late Sir Bernard Pares, who declared that, for Russia, this would be a genuine people's war, just as 1812 had been, and that her defeat was by no means a foregone conclusion, but indeed highly improbable, were few and far between. In Moscow, Sir Stafford Cripps, the British Ambassador, and General Mason Macfarlane, head of the British Military Mission, took a gloomy though by no means a hopeless view of the Russians' chances of "holding out". At the American Embassy in Moscow, opinions were sharply divided, the great majority being highly pessimistic, and only a minority,

★ For fuller details, see W. P. and Z. K. Coates, *A History of Anglo-Soviet Relations*, vol. I, London, 1944, pp. 684–6.

headed by General Philip Faymonville, rating the Russians' chances highly. Ambassador Laurence Steinhardt held a middle-of-the-road position. The most important diplomatic event during that grim summer, with the German *blitzkrieg* at its height, was the arrival in Moscow of Harry Hopkins, who, after several talks with Stalin and Molotov, took back to the President a sober and, in the main, favourable assessment of the Russians' chances of continuing the war almost indefinitely. This Hopkins report had an enormous effect in shaping American policy towards Russia during the next few months, and, unlike Churchill, who at the time of the Battle of Moscow referred in a telegram to Cripps to "Russia in her agony", Roosevelt did not at any moment consider the Russians' position as hopeless.

The Russian outcry for a Second Front did not become truly vociferous until 1942. In 1941, almost immediately after the German invasion, the Soviet press expressed the hope that there would be one "as soon as possible", and in his more pessimistic moments Stalin cabled to Churchill saying that if the British did not do something "immediately" Russia might well lose the war, and even made some highly unrealistic proposals for a prompt landing in France, the dispatch of British troops or airmen to Russia, and the like. And although the United States was not yet officially a belligerent, some similar appeals were made even to the Americans.

Russian morale, which had been very low during the first months of the war, was largely restored by the successful defence of Moscow and by the subsequent Russian counter-offensive. Also Russia now knew she had allies. Stalin, in his two famous speeches in November 1941, attached the greatest importance to this fact and clearly implied that the Second Front was not far off.

In May 1942 Molotov went to London and Washington. In London the Anglo/Soviet Alliance was signed and Molotov brought back to Moscow the famous "Second Front in 1942 Declaration" which, in the months that followed, was to cause no end of trouble. The Anglo/Soviet Alliance was ratified by the Supreme Soviet on 11 June in an atmosphere of great solemnity. But it did not take long for the Russian people to realize that there would be no "Second Front in 1942" and as pessimism grew, during the Black Summer of 1942, with the Germans driving towards Stalingrad and overrunning the northern

Caucasus, so also did the anger and exasperation over the Allies, and above all over Britain. Molotov had returned from his journey with the clear impression that while Roosevelt, Marshall and many other top Americans were favourable to trying a Second Front in the immediate future, they were meeting with the greatest obstruction from Churchill and the British military. In August, Churchill came to Moscow to inform Stalin that the Second Front was "off".

Meantime, however, there had developed in Britain and America an enormous mass-feeling in favour of the Second Front. It arose for two reasons—an instinct of self-preservation, which suggested to millions of people that if Russia lost the war Hitler would turn his Wehrmacht towards the West, and particularly against Britain; and, secondly, from an acute guilt-feeling, especially in Britain, that millions of Russians were being killed in the common struggle, while Britain was doing "next to nothing". As Sir Bernard Pares said in 1942, a "feeling of nation-wide gratitude" was sweeping Britain, which, thanks to the Russians, was not even being bombed any more. But with this gratitude there also went a genuine desire to help the Russians—even if it cost many thousands of British lives.

This situation produced a strange phenomenon—that of "one-way admiration". The British people, in particular, were filled with the greatest admiration for Russia and for the Red Army; but this feeling was not reciprocated by the Russians. For what was there to admire about the British *as soldiers*? The fighting—notably in Africa—was on only a very small scale, and their casualties were microscopic compared with the millions of men the Russian people were losing. Britain, in short, despite the great popular movement in favour of the Second Front, was sitting back and doing very little to help. And even if the British people had their heart in the right place, their leaders had not, and the Russians very soon convinced themselves that Churchill was determined to win "his" war by making the Russians do practi-cally all the fighting.

This feeling of hostility to Churchill continued practically till the end of the war. The Russian attitude to Roosevelt, how-ever, was entirely different. He was known to have been, even in 1942, much more favourable to the Second Front than Chur-chill; and they also knew that all further delays—right up to the

Normandy landing in June 1944—were to be attributed to Churchill, and certainly not to Roosevelt.

To the Russians, the North Africa landing and the subsequent campaign were no doubt "better than nothing", but they did very little to relieve the German pressure on the Russians. After Stalingrad, it is true, they no longer regarded an early opening of the Second Front as a matter of life and death to themselves, as they often did in 1942, but the unhappy feeling that *they* were bearing the brunt of the war, and that Churchill at any rate thought this quite fit and proper, continued right up to the end of the war with Germany.

So it is not at all far-fetched to argue that, with the exception of the first eight or nine months, the Cold War between East and West continued right through the Second World War. In 1942, it took the form of the angry controversies over the Second Front; and in the Russian view this Second Front was being sabotaged by the "class enemy", above all by Winston Churchill, the old anti-Soviet No. 1 interventionist of 1919–20. At the height of the virulent Russian press campaign against the British "saboteurs" of the Second Front, even Hess was trotted out, with innuendoes to the effect that some highly suspect secret negotiations were going on between the British government and this "plenipotentiary representative of the Nazi government in England", while during the same week Professor P. Yudin, one of the Party's top ideologists, gave a lecture in which he argued that the reasons for the absence of a Second Front were entirely political. Unfortunately, he said, there were still some powerful Munichite influences inside the British government and, although Churchill had the power to eliminate these influences, he was obviously showing no particular desire to do so.★

In 1943, after Stalingrad, the Cold War assumed a different character. Again the clash was most violent of all between Russia and Britain, not between Russia and the United States. This time it was over Poland, with the Soviet Union breaking off diplomatic relations with the Polish government in London, and setting up in Moscow the nucleus of a future pro-Soviet Polish government. If Roosevelt had no strong feelings about it, Churchill had. And it was, indeed, the creation by Moscow in 1943 of a miniature Polish "puppet government" (as it was

★ Cf. the author's *Russia at War*, p. 488.

called in the West) which, once the Red Army had entered Polish soil a year later, became a full-scale "puppet government", which started the process of creating a Russian *cordon sanitaire* along her Western borders, a *cordon* consisting of a series of "socialist states" with governments more or less appointed by the Russians. It was on the day in April 1943 when Stalin set up the "Union of Polish Patriots" (which in 1944 developed into the "Lublin Committee") that he laid the foundation-stone of what later came to be known as the "Stalin Empire" of Eastern Europe. The countries in which socialist regimes were artificially set up by the Russians were Poland, Rumania and Hungary. More spontaneous, that is without any Russian pressure, was the creation of a socialist regime in Bulgaria and Albania; in Czechoslovakia a Soviet-controlled regime did not come into being until 1948, after three years of a more or less normal, Western-type parliamentary democracy. Yugoslavia was the only country which had generated spontaneously her own national revolution, practically without any Russian help, and it was also Yugoslavia, with her acute sense of national independence, which in 1948 was the first to rebel against her status of a Russian "satellite".

The year 1943 was a remarkably significant one in the long history of the Cold War. In April, as we have seen, the corner-stone was laid, as it were, for the *new* Cold War, by the establishment of the "Union of Polish Patriots" in Moscow. A month later, on 22nd May, the corner-stone of the *old* Cold War was demolished, through the dissolution of the Comintern. The coincidence was not fortuitous; if the creation of a Polish "puppet government" spread alarm among numerous Western statesmen, the dissolution of the Comintern a month later was intended to reassure them that the Soviet Union had abandoned its wicked "conspiracy" against the capitalist world.

Having become, soon after the death of Lenin, little more than a Soviet agency for the protection of the Soviet Union and of Stalin's "socialism in one country", which dictated Stalin's will to the foreign communist parties, the Comintern had been almost completely dormant since the German invasion of the Soviet Union, confining itself to routine anti-Nazi propaganda. On Stalin's instruction it simply dissolved itself, declaring the whole organization to be "out of date", and explaining that the war had demonstrated a very important fact:

Whereas in the Axis countries it is important for the working class to strive to overthrow the government, in the United Nations countries it is, on the contrary, the duty of the working class to support the governments' war effort.

Among the leading members of the Comintern who signed the Dissolution Resolution were Dimitrov, Zhdanov, Pieck, Thorez, Togliatti and Anna Pauker. A few days later, Stalin made a statement declaring the dissolution to be "right and timely", since it showed up the Nazi lie that "Moscow" intended to interfere in the lives of other states, or to "Bolshevize" them; it also "facilitated the work of all patriots for uniting all the progressive forces, regardless of party allegiance and political beliefs". This was a clear allusion to the various resistance movements in the Hitler-occupied countries of Europe.

During that week, the American ex-Ambassador, Joseph Davies, of *Mission to Moscow* fame, who had done his utmost in the late 'thirties to explain the Purge trials in a manner most favourable to Moscow, recalled that in those days he had often said to Foreign Commissar Maxim Litvinov that the Comintern—the stick with which everybody beat the Soviet Union—had all along been the source of all the trouble between Russia and the Western Powers.

Now that we have described the birth of the *second* Cold War (the Polish puppet government) and the death of the *first* Cold War (the dissolution of the Comintern), it may be useful to look some years ahead, and to examine two fundamental questions: (1) whether the Cold War was really necessary, and (2) what exactly the purpose was of Stalin's "conquest" of the greater part of Eastern Europe as a result of the Second World War.

Regarding the first question, it is useful to recall that during the immediate post-war years Walter Lippmann, that great Rooseveltian, continually emphasized that the Cold War was "unnecessary", and that President Truman, in departing sharply from Roosevelt's foreign policy, was grossly oversimplifying the issues. But in those days of Cold-War hysteria, his was very nearly a voice crying in the wilderness. Today not only every serious American scholar and historian but even some of the most vociferous cold-warriors of those days admit, either wholeheartedly or reluctantly, that American foreign policy took a dangerously wrong turn almost immediately after the death of

President Roosevelt on 12th April 1945. Not only do scholars like D. F. Fleming in *The Cold War and Its Origins 1917–1960*, William A. Williams in *The Tragedy of American Diplomacy* and James P. Warburg, in his numerous books, and especially in *The United States and the Post-War World* brilliantly demonstrate the futility of the Cold War, but even a cold-warrior like Mr. George Kennan (the "Mr. X" of *Foreign Affairs* in 1947) today admits his error of judgement and the regrettable effect which that policy-shaping article had for several years afterwards. In reviewing Mr. Kennan's last book, *Memoirs 1925–1950* in *The Observer* of 28th January 1968, Mr. A. J. P. Taylor rightly observes that "he was coolly detached from the enthusiasm for Soviet Russia during the Second World War and unmoved by the hysterical anti-communism that followed it". But, for all his "cool judgement", Kennan still wrote these "alarmist phrases" in 1947:

> We of the Anglo-American world were not strong enough . . . to put down all the forces that threatened our existence. We were forced to ally ourselves with a part of them in order to defeat the other. . . . Today we Americans stand as a lonely threatened power on the field of world history.

A. J. P. Taylor rightly remarks that it was nonsense to describe the United States in 1947 as either "lonely" or "threatened". On the contrary, they possessed greater strength and resources than any great power had known before. But—

> When Americans were addressed by the rational Mr. Kennan in these frightening terms, they naturally responded violently. They flung themselves into the Korean War and Mr. Kennan protested in vain that they had learned the wrong lesson. He had meant to preach "containment". Instead, he had helped to launch a crusade.

But the crusading spirit was, in fact, there long before the Korean War. It had been mounting ever since the day Harry Truman took over from Roosevelt on 12th April 1945; and the explosion of the first American atom bombs, first at Los Alamos (at the time of the Potsdam Conference) and then, barely a fortnight later, over Hiroshima and Nagasaki gave tremendous new impetus to this "crusading spirit". And, less than two years later, came the Truman Doctrine.

Taylor begins his article with an important question:

Should foreign policy be a moral crusade or should it be devoted solely to promoting the national interest? English people wrangled over this question throughout the nineteenth century, and Americans have taken up the dispute in the twentieth.

And the Russians? Fundamentally, the whole tragedy of the Cold War stemmed from the fact that, while Roosevelt was convinced that in the post-war years Stalin would put Russia's "national interest" above all else, Truman based his whole policy on the obsolete myth of the Communist Bogey, thus replacing Roosevelt's policy of a no doubt difficult, but still perfectly possible, peaceful coexistence with the socialist world by a crusade against "world communism".

In fact, except on very rare occasions, as under Lenin, every Russian government's prime consideration was the country's security. This obsession with security was never stronger than in the years following the Second World War, which had very nearly destroyed Russia (it had, indeed, been touch-and-go in 1941), and it was security infinitely more than any ideological considerations which determined Stalin to create in Eastern and part of Central Europe a "friendly" *cordon sanitaire*, in place of that hostile *cordon sanitaire* which had been set up by the Western powers at the end of the First World War.

That the methods the Russians used in setting up "friendly" governments in any of these countries—notably Poland—were ruthless and unscrupulous is true enough; but then, with the exception of Czechoslovakia, none of these countries had ever had normal democratic governments in the Western sense; and, significantly, Czechoslovakia was the very last to be placed under strict communist control—three years after the end of the war and only when the Cold War had reached a desperate degree of intensity. Finland, which no longer represented any danger to the Soviet Union after the Second World War, continues to be a Western-type democracy to this day, and so does Austria. It has even been suggested by one American historian that Stalin would have been perfectly satisfied if half a dozen "Finlands" could have been set up in Eastern Europe. But this was scarcely possible in a country like Poland, with its long tradition of Russo-phobia, nor very easy in countries like Rumania and Hungary, once the Cold War, with its challenge to Russia's "sphere of influence", had got going in earnest—which it did from the very moment the Second World War had ended. But, as this book will try to show, much less harsh regimes would almost certainly have been set up in what came to be known as "the satellites" if Roosevelt had lived a few years longer. For Russia had everything to gain after the Second World War from "peaceful coexistence" and "friendly co-operation" with the United States, and would have made important concessions in Eastern Europe to achieve these. But Truman was least of all interested in either friendship or cooperation with Russia.

Roosevelt was a man of the greatest intelligence and he had a profound understanding of history. His approach to Russia was not primitive. As James P. Warburg says:

[he] realized more fully than Churchill and most of his own advisers that Stalin's suspicious and secretive nature, which had made wartime cooperation difficult, had its roots in history.

What were these roots? First, Russia had incurred Western hostility by making a separate peace with Germany in 1918, thus making victory in the West more costly and more difficult. Secondly, the Bolshevik Revolution appeared to be a threat not only to victory, but also "a challenge to the whole ethical and religious structure of Western society, as well as to its economic foundations". Hence the attempt by the Allies and Japan to over-throw the Bolshevik regime in 1918–21. This, in turn, gave rise in Russia to acute resentment and distrust towards the Western powers, as well as Japan, for many years to come. Already in 1914 (not to mention earlier invasions) Russia had been invaded by Germany. During the Civil War of 1919–21 the Allies had, albeit half-heartedly, embarked on a military intervention against the Russian Revolution; and, during the rest of the inter-war period, Russia had remained acutely conscious of the danger represented to her by her "capitalist encirclement", and then became truly alarmed by the staggering growth of a formidable German military power under Hitler. Russia, as a "nation state", which, by and large, she became once again under Stalin after the failure of the World Revolution had had to be recognized, was conscious of having lost some territory to Japan as a result of the Russo/ Japanese war of 1904–5, and, even more, of having been pushed a long way East in Europe through the establishment of an anti-Russian *cordon sanitaire* along her western borders, this area partly consisting of territories that had belonged to the Russian Empire before 1918. Hence the ease with which Roosevelt agreed to the re-annexation by Russia of some of these countries, such as the Baltic States, even though this was contrary to the lofty but unrealistic principles of the Atlantic Charter—a document which, to Churchill, was almost as meaningless as it was to Stalin. Also, at Yalta, Roosevelt conceded Stalin's "pre-eminent interest in having governments in adjacent countries friendly to the Soviet Union and somewhat reluctantly accepted the . . . Churchill/Stalin agreement allotting varying degrees of influence to Russia and Great Britain in the Balkans". But

> in general he accepted the fact that the Soviet Union would have predominant power in Eastern Europe, stipulating only that the East-European States should have freely-elected representative governments. (This vaguely expressed stipulation was subject to conflicting interpretations and seemed . . . wholly unrealistic.)*

So indeed, it was, as already explained, except in Czechoslovakia and Finland.

> As for the Far East, on the assumption that Stalin would enter the war against Japan, as promised, Roosevelt conceded nothing that Stalin would not have the power to seize in any case—the Kurile Islands, Northern Sakhalin, a warm-water port at Dairen and an equal voice with China in the control of the Manchurian railways.

In return, Stalin "agreed to support the government of Chiang Kai-shek as against the Chinese Communists. . . ."

What follows is even more important:

> Shortly before Roosevelt's death, tension between Russia and the West arose over Stalin's high-handed action in imposing a communist-dominated government upon Poland. . . . Nevertheless, until the day of his death on 12th April 1945, *Roosevelt clung firmly to the conviction, which he expressed in his latest message to Churchill, that this matter, as well as all differences between the Soviet Union and the West, could and must be peacefully ironed out.* (My italics.)

Attempts have been made to refute this fundamentally important point, but no one has convincingly done so. That Roosevelt knew that there would be difficulties between Russia and the

* Warburg, op. cit., p. 8.

West is certain; but he did not expect major difficulties, above all for a very simple reason: Roosevelt had in mind that Stalin's position of predominant power in Eastern Europe

was offset by acute economic weakness resulting from the war, and the consequent need for economic aid which only the United States was in a position to extend.

This is a very important point, and is borne out by what happened in Russia between 1943 and 1945. Important American business interests, as represented by men like Donald M. Nelson and Eric Johnson, showed themselves favourable, as early as 1943, to a post-war Reconstruction Loan of 6 or 7 billion dollars from the USA to the Soviet Union, and saw in this, among other things, a useful precaution against a possible post-war slump in the United States.* Not only that: they regarded such a loan as a powerful lever for controlling, to a considerable extent, Russian post-war policy in Eastern Europe. The question of such a loan—which the Russians took very seriously indeed—was raised at both Teheran and Yalta; but while Roosevelt was favourable to the principle of the thing, he thought that conditions for granting such a loan would be more suitable to the United States once the war was over, and the Russian and American leaders could confine themselves to political and economic discussions, without either being in any way dependent on military operations. If such a loan had been granted, it is obvious that the East European countries would have had a much easier time; that Russian reconstruction would have been greatly facilitated; and, above all perhaps, that such a loan, the basis of close Soviet-American co-operation, with a lasting peace in the offing, would have created inside Russia an incomparably freer and more liberal atmosphere than the poisonous Cold-War atmosphere that was to develop in Russia, notably after Churchill's Fulton speech of March 1946 and especially after the breakdown of the Foreign Ministers' Conference of April 1947, which closely followed upon the announcement of the Truman Doctrine and marked the *de facto* splitting of Germany in two.

There is very little doubt that Roosevelt saw all the benefits that could be derived by everybody concerned from such a loan, though, for the above reasons, he refrained from firmly com-

* See the author's *Russia at War*, p. 937.

mitting himself on this point while the war was still in progress. I know, however, from conversations with Averell Harriman, the US Ambassador in Moscow, that he himself was among many of Roosevelt's advisers who favoured small credits to Russia, but were wholly opposed to a huge single loan, equal to more than half of all the Lend-Lease given to the Soviet Union during the war. After Roosevelt's death, Harriman's opposition to the loan became much more vociferous; and his opposition met with the fullest support not only of Truman, but of practically all the new President's advisers—Leahy, Forrestal, Stimson, Byrnes and the rest. Even so, in 1946 and even in 1947 Stalin was still "interested" in the loan, as he stated on numerous occasions.

Looking at it in retrospect, we realize more than ever how such a loan could have prevented the Cold War and reduced it merely to some minor disputes (which Roosevelt, of course, had foreseen). It would also have prevented the progressive super-Stalinization of Eastern Europe, and the ugly Cold-War regime, with its police terror and xenophobia, which was to begin to develop in the Soviet Union in 1946.

By some curious instinct, the Russian people knew that Roosevelt's death was a major disaster to them, and the Soviet government was fully aware of it, too. The Soviet press, announcing Roosevelt's death, appeared with the President's picture on the front page and with large black borders—something quite unprecedented in the case of a foreign, especially "capitalist" leader. Thousands of women in Moscow that day could be seen weeping; they felt that Russia had lost "a real friend". One of the most grief-stricken women in Russia was Fenya, a kindly elderly Russian maid at the Hotel Metropole in Moscow, who had been appointed to Yalta as Roosevelt's personal chambermaid, and who commented on her return, almost with tears in her eyes: "Such a sweet and kind man, but so terribly terribly ill." When Roosevelt suddenly died soon after, not only Fenya, but thousands of other Russian women wept.[*]

Whether in reality, if Roosevelt had lived, the 6 or 7 billion dollar loan would have materialized cannot, however, be asserted with any certainty. Not only Truman's but most of Roosevelt's advisers were violently opposed to it, and what exactly Roosevelt would have done we do not know. That he was much better

[*] *Russia at War*, pp. 972–3.

disposed towards the Russians than Churchill was—let alone Truman—is shown by his attitude at Yalta. The only bit of evidence pointing to Roosevelt's opposition to the loan comes from a somewhat dubious source—Mr. James Byrnes, who quoted the violently anti-Soviet Leo Crowley (the one who hastened to terminate Lend-Lease as soon as Germany surrendered). According to Byrnes, Crowley told him of his conversation with Roosevelt on 1st April, a few days before the President's death:

> Crowley said he told the President about a rumour that the Government was considering a loan to the Soviets of $10 billions [sic], and that he [Crowley] thought it wise to refrain from making any loan until more was known of the Soviets' post-war attitude. He said the President agreed.

This does not prove for a moment that, in Roosevelt's view, the loan was "off". On the contrary the story rather confirms that Roosevelt preferred to discuss the matter after the war had been won. Even W. A. Williams, highly critical of Roosevelt's Russian policy, admits that the Crowley story has to be "evaluated with caution". What is certain, however, is that the atmosphere of Soviet/American relations could never have deteriorated to the extent it did under Truman. It was not until after Roosevelt's death that his anti-Russian advisers, such as Leahy and Harriman, adopted a violently anti-loan attitude, which enormously pleased the new President.

The Russian quest for security after the Second World War has, of course, a long pre-history. It goes all the way back to the Revolution, and even beyond. One need hardly recall that throughout their history the open expanses of European Russia had been tempting to all kinds of invaders. In the seventeenth century (to go no further back) Moscow had been captured by the Poles; in the eighteenth century, the Swedes, under Charles XII, invaded Southern Russia until they came to grief at Poltava; in 1812 Napoleon's *Grande Armée* captured Moscow; in 1914, Russia was invaded by the Germans; in 1920, by the Poles again, who for a short time even occupied Kiev (not to mention all the various foreign troops that invaded Russia in the course of the Civil War); and then came the most fearful invasion of all— that of Hitler in 1941—an invasion that cost the Soviet Union 20 million lives and one-third of her national wealth. Almost invariably these foreign invaders came from the West—mostly through Poland; in 1941 they came simultaneously from several countries of Eastern Europe, all the way from Rumania to Finland.

The inter-war period was marked by two important phenomena which made war between Russia and Germany more than likely. (1) By turning her back on the League of Nations after the First World War, the United States removed the great makeweight that was necessary to keep the peace. (2) Later, the British and French governments turned Eastern and Central Europe over to Hitler at Munich, opening wide his way into the Soviet Union. The "free hand in the East" for Germany was a "doctrine" almost openly advocated by people like Chamberlain and Bonnet, and quite openly by some of their friends.

When Russia was invaded by Hitler's *blitzkrieg* in 1941 she was glad to find friends and allies in Britain and the United States; but the fact remains that the brunt of the fighting was done by Russia, and that she lost forty or fifty times more people than either of them. Until June 1944 Britain and the USA fought, in effect, what was only a peripheral war against Germany. But although the Russians liked Roosevelt, they did not trust Churchill, whom they held primarily responsible for the endless delays in opening the Second Front. They also remembered what Truman had said on 24th June 1941 in favour of playing on both sides, so that the Russians killed as many Germans as possible, and the Germans as many Russians as possible. It was Churchill, too, who wanted to get at the Balkans and Eastern Europe through the non-existent "soft underbelly". But this operation, planned for 1943, had to be abandoned because of the great cost in human lives, which Churchill was unwilling to face; and hence the halfhearted North Africa and Italy campaigns, which were of no great help to the Russians. Not till 1944, when the Germans had already been virtually defeated, did the "real" Second Front open.

In short, although Germany was *the* enemy, the Russians had reason to distrust the Allies even while the Second World War was still on. Churchill's dream of breaking through to Eastern Europe in 1943 came to nothing. But he tried, in 1944, to obtain by diplomatic pressure what he had failed to achieve by force. In other words, the Russians were not at all reassured that Churchill had not abandoned all hope of setting up a *cordon sanitaire* in Eastern Europe, chiefly based on an essentially anti-Russian Poland. Thus, what the Russians sought both during and after the Second World War was security not only against a revived Germany but also against their wartime allies, whose grave concern for a "democratic" Poland they found particularly suspect.

Stalin's very top consideration after the Second World War was security, and not world revolution. Even Louis J. Halle, an important State Department official between 1941 and 1954 (that is during both the war and the Cold War), says in his recent book, *The Cold War as History*, that Stalin was a Russian first, and that any ambition in Moscow to spread communism anywhere was "at best secondary". In a remarkable review of this book by D. F. Fleming, the latter writes:

> For 900 years, fear has been the driving force in Russia. Halle stresses the ever-recurring invasions from all sides of the great Russian plain, and Russian expansionism is explained as a reaction— as a "defence expansion".

This is clearly something with which Roosevelt reckoned and for which he made allowances, as we know from his half-hearted "protection" of countries like Poland and Rumania at Yalta. The great deterioration started under Truman, in this, as in other fields. Thus, in the words of Fleming:

> The great effort of Roosevelt and Hull to organize a new league of nations which would keep the peace in cooperation with the Soviet Union was rejected under Truman and quickly reversed.

Fleming then challenged Halle's assertion that, "in contrast to the catastrophic dismantling of our armed forces", Russia "did not demobilize after the war" but kept in the armed forces 5 to 6 million "battle-hardened" men and never went below that during the post-war period. These figures are dismissed as absurd on Isaac Deutscher's much more reliable estimate: "Before the Truman Doctrine in 1947, the Russians had demobilized their armies so rapidly that they reduced them from $11\frac{1}{2}$ million men at the end of the war to less than 3 millions, but increased this number to around 5 millions after the Truman Doctrine had been proclaimed." As will be shown later, this had a very clear and definite purpose. The United States still held the monopoly

6

of the A-bomb, and the only possible deterrent the Russians could conceive was an enormous land army which could, within a few days, overrun the whole of Western Europe. Nor did they consider the A-bomb an "absolute" weapon then; the United States did not, as now, have 10,000—or is it 50,000?—A-bombs and H-bombs; and even an all-out attack with all the A-bombs she had would not have knocked out Russia. She might have had her main cities destroyed, and lost 5 or even 10 million people; but this loss would not have been decisive. In the long run, the greatest sufferer would not have been the Soviet Union, but Western Europe, possibly even including Great Britain. Hence the great nervousness in Western Europe—except among all-out anti-Red fanatics—over the wild talk in the USA about the great virtues of dropping "A-bombs on Moscow", and the extraordinary success of all the campaigns (though many of them communist-inspired) for "outlawing the A-bomb"—such as the famous Stockholm Appeal, which tens of millions of non-communists signed—in Italy, France, Britain and all West European countries.

The story of the Teheran and Yalta conferences is too familiar to need recalling here. In August 1968, after the Soviet invasion of Czechoslovakia, General de Gaulle said it was a tragedy which was inherent in what he called "the Yalta System", since at Yalta Europe had been divided into two great spheres of influence, and what happened in one half of Europe did not concern the other. There was much angry controversy, especially in the French press, many claiming that de Gaulle did not know what he was talking about, and was merely still feeling resentful, even after nearly twenty-five years, at not having been invited to Yalta to join the Big Three, Stalin, Roosevelt and Churchill. That de Gaulle remembers insults suffered many years earlier is true enough; but those critics who quoted copiously from the Yalta documents to show that no partition of Europe had been agreed upon there were arguing beside the point. Officially, of course, no such partition had been agreed upon, but this partition was clearly *implied* in the decisions taken at Yalta, and even if Churchill violently protested there against anything that savoured of "partition", Stalin and Roosevelt knew perfectly well that the Yalta decisions meant precisely that.

Not that Churchill could have had a clear conscience as regards the principle of "partition" and "spheres of influence". For, only a few months before, in Moscow in October 1944, he had made his cynical partition deal with Stalin, dividing up the Balkans into Anglo/American and Soviet "spheres of influence"—Greece predominantly Anglo/American; Rumania and Bulgaria predominantly Russian; Yugoslavia and Hungary, fifty-fifty. In the case of Hungary, the deal was not observed for long by the Russians, while the Yugoslavs violently objected to any such deal being made behind their backs, and themselves rejected Churchill's 50 per cent by refusing to have anything to do with the Yugoslav royal government and the young king, whom Churchill had wanted to plant on them—as he later forced their own king on the Greeks. Greece being an "Anglo/American sphere of influence", the Russians did not interfere; worse still, they allowed the Greek communist and non-communist resistance to be slaughtered by British troops.

But if Churchill obtained full satisfaction from Stalin in regard to Greece, he received little or none as regards Poland. He continued to raise this question at every conference—at Teheran, in December 1943, in Moscow in October 1944, and again at Yalta, in February 1945; not to mention the endless squabbling over Poland by the diplomats over the validity or non-validity of the Lublin Committee, the Russian "puppet government" in Poland since August 1944, and the like.

Throughout, Churchill took the high-minded line that Great Britain had declared war on Nazi Germany in 1939 to "save" Poland, though in reality not a single British bomb was dropped on Germany to "save Poland" and not a single British life lost in this "Battle for our gallant Polish Allies". And both the Russians and the Poles knew this perfectly well. One of the most significant exchanges between Churchill and Stalin at Yalta concerning Poland was this: Poland, said Churchill, was, to Britain, a matter of honour; to which Stalin replied that, to the Soviet Union, Poland was not only a matter of honour, but also a matter of security. Roosevelt knew precisely what Stalin meant—and also what was at the back of Churchill's mind. In constantly stressing the need of absolutely free elections in Poland, he knew that in Poland, violently nationalist and very largely anti-Russian, such elections could not fail to produce a pro-Western, and essentially anti-Russian, government. His mind was still travelling back to the happy days that followed the First World War, when, with

Russia hopelessly weak, the Western powers had no difficulty in creating a *cordon sanitaire* along Russia's western borders. With the exception of Masaryk's Czechoslovakia, which had genuine democratic traditions, virtually none of the other border states had. For a time a semblance of "Western democracy" was maintained in Rumania, Poland and the three Baltic Republics which had broken away from the old Russian Empire. But this did not last long. After a brief communist dictatorship in Hungary, that country became, with the help of Allied troops, a ruthless right-wing dictatorship; in Poland, "democracy" lasted till 1926, when it became a dictatorship under Marshal Pilsudski, while in 1935 the new Constitution adopted soon before the Marshal's death, turned Poland into a near-fascist regime, the so-called "colonels' Poland", since its real rulers were a bunch of colonels, such as the inglorious Colonel Beck who vanished after the military rout of Poland in 1939, and apparently died in Rumania; it was men like Beck who were primarily responsible for Poland's great military disaster—with his constant flirtation with Hitler★ and his refusal, on any account, to accept Russian help—even when the Germans were on the point of invading Poland. True, this policy of "neither Russia nor Germany" was in the "Pilsudski tradition", but in 1939 it was applied in a manner bordering on sheer insanity. In the end, to save Poland, Beck welcomed the British "guarantee" against German aggression, but would not accept Russian help, which the French at any rate urged him to do—at least when the German invasion of Poland was already virtually imminent. France and Britain, as we have seen, neither could nor would help.

In the three small Baltic states "democracy" did not last very long either; all three, by the early 'thirties, had become virtual military dictatorships, the mildest of them in Estonia, which was ethnically, geographically and traditionally very close to Finland.

In Yugoslavia and Bulgaria, too, dictatorship succeeded ephemeral "democratic" governments very soon after the First World War. Austrian democracy fell in 1934. The Wilsonian dream had proved a myth in the whole of Central and Eastern Europe—with the sole exception of Czechoslovakia, which lasted till the Munich betrayal, and, in a modified form, even

★ Beck had been Polish Military Attaché in Paris in the early 1920s, but was expelled by the French as a German spy.

until the German invasion of Bohemia and Moravia in March 1939. (Meantime, in now "independent" Slovakia, a clerical-fascist regime had been set up.)

So there was, in Churchill's and then in Truman's and Secretary of State James Byrnes' "passionate" pleading with the Russians for the "restoration" of "pure democracy" and for "free, un-fettered elections" in these countries, with the exception of Czechoslovakia, something totally artificial, if not downright absurd. Apart from some very brief and abortive experiments just after the First World War, when Woodrow Wilson's ideas seemed to provide the ideal blueprint for the whole world in pure and parliamentary democracy, none of these countries had had anything, in their whole history, even remotely resembling a Western-type form of government. All they were familiar with was some kind of autocracy or dictatorship. This was true of all of them—Rumania, Bulgaria, Hungary, Albania, Yugoslavia and Poland. The only truly remarkable exception was the newly founded state of Czechoslovakia. Her territory had, for hundreds of years, formed part of the Hapsburg monarchy. Besides having lived side by side with the highly civilized Austrians they had, in the nineteenth and early twentieth century, developed a great national culture of their own—with great names in literature, music and the plastic arts. In the case of music, it is sufficient to mention two of the greatest composers of the nineteenth century, Smetana and Dvořák. In literature Jaroslav Hašek, the author of *The Good Soldier Schweik*, that immortal world-famous Czech classic; or Franz Kafka, who, though writing in German and of Jewish descent, was a Czech living in Prague, or Karel Čapek in the 1920s. In art, Alphonse Mucha, one of the greatest masters of *art moderne* around 1900. Democracy is not, in fact, necessary to produce great art and literature; Poland produced some of the world's greatest music and literature. Less well-known though known abroad, some remarkable music, literature and art were produced in feudal Rumania, not to mention equally feudal Hungary with Liszt and Bartók, to name only these two giants. All these countries were in the mainstream of European civilization, including Russian civilization, before the Revolution.

The greatest tragedy of these East European states after the Second World War was not their Soviet-imported or Soviet-inspired socialism; this, on the contrary, had enormous virtues, above all more or less in "underdeveloped" countries like Rumania, Yugoslavia, Bulgaria, Albania and even under-industrialized Hungary. Much worse was their ideological *gleichschaltung* and the Moscow-type tyranny set up throughout Eastern Europe over all free thought and artistic and literary activity. How supremely important this thought-control was to Moscow was best demonstrated by the Russian invasion of Czechoslovakia in August 1968. As I wrote in the New York *Nation*, on the day of the invasion, it was Russia's "Censorship War". To re-establish the Censorship in Prague, the Soviet Union was prepared to pay an enormous price: the goodwill she had enjoyed in the world for many years as the Great "Peace Factor" (the USA, with her war in Vietnam, being the Great "War Factor"); the friendship (though no longer the old Stalinite obedience) to Moscow of the foreign communist parties (especially the important French and Italian parties); the debunking overnight of the high-minded phrases the Soviet leaders had kept on repeating for years, day after day, such as "sovereignty", "non-interference in the internal affairs of other countries"; each communist party's right to go its own way, in accordance with the country's national interests and traditions (Palmiro Togliatti's famous—and near Titoite—"polycentrism"); above all, perhaps, Russia's well-established reputation for meticulously carrying out the treaties she had signed—especially that "Definition of Aggression" which the *Russians themselves* had got United Nations to adopt, and practically every single paragraph of which had now been grossly violated by the same Russians—in invading Czechoslovakia.★

In Poland, Hungary, Yugoslavia, Bulgaria and Rumania (though not till 1948 in Czechoslovakia) art and literature were

---

★ The tanks sent to Budapest in November 1956 had an entirely different context: there were, in Hungary, very strong counter-revolutionary elements, egged on by Radio Free Europe, and more than encouraged by the powerful Hungarian Catholic hierarchy; moreover, Imre Nagy had threatened to desert the Warsaw Pact, a very serious matter to East European security, and, tech-nically, Janos Kadar, Nagy's successor, *had* formally called in the Russian troops to "fight the counter-revolution"; which is certainly *not* what President Svoboda, Mr. Dubcek or Mr. Cernik would have dreamed of doing in 1968—the Russian tanks being the most effective means of crushing *their* liberal form of socialism. Nor had the Czech leaders ever dreamed of leaving the Warsaw Pact.

subject, immediately the Second World War was over, to the same socialist-realist tyranny from which Russian art and literature had already suffered since about 1930. For a very short time in 1956, first in Hungary and then in Poland, writers and artists made a short but abortive attempt to regain some of their artistic and literary freedoms, but a truly independent weekly like the Warsaw *Po Prostu* lasted barely more than three months in an almost totally emancipated form. After that, Gomulka, "the hero of Poland's October Spring" of 1956, himself enforced a rigid censorship on *Po Prostu* and the other almost equally independent Polish papers that had sprung up in the course of 1956. By far the boldest revolt against the tyranny of thought came in 1968 from Czechoslovakia, when the entire nation, including the working class and the Party leadership, unanimously (except for a few profiteers of the Stalinist régime of the last twenty years) hailed the abolition of the censorship. Economic pressures and other forms of blackmail and intimidation against Prague having failed, the Big Socialist Brother had one way left of destroying Czechoslovakia's freedom—by driving his tanks into Prague.

Yet, in all these countries, other than Czechoslovakia, art and literature thrived under *any* régime—monarchist, feudal, even near-Fascist (as in Hungary), though not in Nazi Germany, where Hitler had his own Nazi equivalents of Stalin's socialist realism.

Compared with the great epochs of Russian literature—the whole glorious nineteenth century, the pre-Revolution decades, and the early years of the Soviet régime—the years of Stalin, apart from a few major but mostly non-conformist writers, are appallingly barren; and compared with the German eighteenth and nineteenth and early twentieth centuries, the Hitler years of German literature are a desert. And although Stalinism, as a partly constructive force, is still vastly superior to Hitlerism, a purely destructive one, one feels with some bitterness—especially if one has lived through the war years in Russia—that there is still some truth in what Nikolai Berdiayev wrote in 1937— "Stalinism is the Russian form of Fascism".

By constantly using Wilsonian "democratic" slogans with reference to Rumania, Hungary, Bulgaria and even Poland, men like Churchill and James Byrnes were being fundamentally absurd, for to the vast mass of the people of these countries, such high-minded words were as good as meaningless. They had never had either "democracy", or parliamentary government, or "free elections". To Rumanians, Soviet-cooked elections were substantially no different from the Antonescu-cooked elections before the Second World War. The same is almost equally true of Poland; if most Poles waxed enthusiastic for a man like Mikolajczyk in 1945-6, it was only because they strongly preferred "the West" to the Russian "East". Churchill and Byrnes thought they could play on this anti-Russian and pro-Western nationalism of the Poles and, by enforcing "free elections", turn Poland away from Russia. This Stalin understood only too well, and that is why he resorted to every kind of trickery in Poland (more than anywhere else) to "cook" the elections. In Hungary he even allowed the first post-war election to be genuinely free, and the majority of that priest-ridden nation naturally voted "against the Russians"; after that, in Hungary too, "Polish" methods had to be enforced. Rumania, another defeated ally of Nazi Germany and one which knew even less than Hungary about "free elections", they found even easier to handle, while in Bulgaria, with its ancient pro-Russian tradition, the Russians had no difficulties at all. All they did, in effect, was to get rid of the "feudal lords", such as Maniu, in Rumania, and the "Fascist colonels" and the very small number of Bulgarian "Manius" in Bulgaria.

The imposition of this stern Soviet control over the East European countries—Poland, Rumania, Hungary, Bulgaria and, by 1948, Czechoslovakia—would scarcely have assumed such harsh, and sometimes brutal, forms but for the acute consciousness in the Soviet Union that a great change had come about in American policy *vis-à-vis* herself since the death of President Roosevelt, less than a month before the end of the war in Europe. No doubt, ever since Teheran, Stalin had made it plain that he intended to pursue a spheres-of-influence policy after the war, a policy which in fact Roosevelt more or less condoned at both Teheran and Yalta. Everything changed when Harry Truman became President. But one of the singularities of the Soviet/American relationship during the months following Roosevelt's death was that while Harry Truman almost immediately adopted a pugnacious, if not downright aggressive attitude towards

Russia, the Russians, feeling economically extremely weak, were in fact to be on the defensive until March 1947 after the announcement of the Truman Doctrine and the subsequent breakdown of the Foreign Ministers' Conference in Moscow which virtually consecrated that partition of Germany which Potsdam, with its ominous reparations settlement, had already foreshadowed.

Apart from clinging at any price to their "zone of influence", or rather, as they themselves called it, their "security zone", in Eastern and Central Europe, the Russians were not guilty of any aggression, and as late as 1947, in his conversations with, or letters to, Western writers and journalists, Stalin preached what is now known as "peaceful co-existence". Apart from the two abortive attempts to "nibble" at Turkey and Iran, the only move that might be called an "act of aggression" (though, juridically, their case was not negligible) was the Berlin Blockade of 1948-9.

FOUR

The Effect of Roosevelt's Death

In *War and Peace* Tolstoy argued that neither the Napoleonic Wars nor the Napoleonic Empire had much to do with the insignificant personality of Napoleon Bonaparte, and that they would have happened anyway, in one form or another. Historians will go on arguing indefinitely whether a single man can, in any circumstances, change the course of history. Some say, perhaps correctly, that even if Adolf Hitler had never been born, something very similar to Hitlerism would have emerged, anyway, in the midst of the great slump of 1932–3 in Germany, with her 6 or 7 million unemployed. Similarly, without Bonnet and Daladier in France, Chamberlain and Halifax in England, there would have been hundreds of potential leaders in both countries to pursue a policy of appeasement and a policy of a "free hand in the East" for Hitler.

The drastic change of American foreign policy after the death of Roosevelt was *not*, however, inevitable. It came as a result of the accident whereby not Henry Wallace but Harry S. Truman stepped into the shoes of Franklin D. Roosevelt. Had F.D.R. foreseen his early death, it is exceedingly doubtful that he would have chosen Truman as his successor. F.D.R. was a great student of history; to Harry Truman, it was as good as *terra incognita*.

The nature of the change in the few days that followed Roosevelt's death has been best described by Professor Fleming in *The Cold War and Its Origins*. He opens his Chapter XI, entitled "After Roosevelt", with the following:

Just before Roosevelt died on April 12th, 1945, he had prepared a radio address. . . . In it he had written that "the mere conquest of our enemies is not enough. We must do all in our power to conquer the doubts and the fears, the ignorance and the greed, which made this horror possible". . . . Then in his last words Roosevelt said: "The only limit to our realization of tomorrow will be our doubts of today. Let us move forward with strong and active faith.' . . .

Fleming continues:

When the strong hands of both Roosevelt and Hull were removed from the helm of the ship of state within a short space of time, it was almost certain to move less surely into the future. Some of their successors meant to carry on their international policies, but others wanted to reverse them, especially the key policy of cooperation with the Soviet Union. After he returned from Yalta, Roosevelt had little time or energy to counsel with the new Vice-President, Harry S. Truman, about post-war foreign policy, and as his strength waned, the risk of a reversal of his world policy constantly increased. It began to materialize two days after his death, when on the way home from Roosevelt's funeral, the new President began to learn of "the status of many serious problems in our foreign and domestic relations" from James F. Byrnes. . . .

The next morning at 9.45, and every morning thereafter, the new President, overwhelmed by the tremendous responsibilities suddenly placed on his head, had a conference with one of the strongest and most impressive personalities in Washington, Fleet Admiral William D. Leahy. . . .

It was Leahy, said Frank Gervasi in an article "Watchdog of the White House" (published in *Colliers*, 9th October 1955) who "tutored Truman on what happened at all the big Four-Power conferences and a lot of others he had attended. . . ." He "coached Roosevelt's inexperienced successor on the significance of Russia's emergence as a major power at the end of World War II and these tutoring sessions enabled Leahy to become 'one of the principal architects of the "tough policy" towards Russia' ".

Leahy obtained results with spectacular speed. As Fleming says:

A week after Leahy's first conference the new President was ready to reprimand the Russians strongly. The occasion came when on the afternoon of April 23rd, 1945, when Soviet Foreign Minister Molotov came to see the President on the way to the San Francisco Conference. Stalin had refused to send Molotov to the Conference until after Roosevelt's death, when he acceded to Truman's request as a gesture of goodwill towards him.

Before the Truman-Molotov meeting there had been a conference attended by Secretary of State Stettinius; Secretary of War Stimson, Navy Secretary Forrestal; Admiral King; General Marshall; Leahy; Assistant Secretary of State James Dunn; Charles Bohlen; Ambassador to Russia Averell Harriman; and General Dean, head of the US Military Mission in Moscow. According to Fleming, "the majority of this group was quite ready to take a tough attitude towards Russia, some from long predilection, others influenced by a series of dispatches during the last three months from Ambassador Harriman in Moscow, recommending such a policy". In this, Harriman was continuing the strong anti-Soviet line he had already pursued (though more discreetly) under Roosevelt. Of all F.D.R.'s advisers, Harriman had been one of those most violently opposed to that 6 or 7 billion dollars' Reconstruction Loan the Russians had hoped to receive from the United States after the war was over.

By far the most moderate of those attending the conference was the Secretary of War, Stimson:

> This most experienced elder statesman in the room reminded the group that the Russian conception of freedom, democracy and voting was quite different from ours, and he "thought that the Russians perhaps were being more realistic about their own security than we were. . . ." He recalled that the Russians had carried out their military engagements quite faithfully and he would be sorry to see this one incident to project a breach between the two countries. . . . Stimson almost seemed to say that, after all, Poland was a matter of desperate concern to Russia and far away from our borders.

Another fairly moderate line was taken by General George Marshall, who was against antagonizing the Russians unduly, since their help in the war against Japan was still badly needed. As against this, Forrestal was "for a showdown with them now rather than later", and (in Fleming's words) "Truman came down heavily on that side", saying that "he felt that our agreement with the Soviet Union had been a one-way street and that he could not continue. It was now or never. He intended to go on with his plans for San Francisco, and if the Russians did not wish to join us they could go to hell" (see *The Forrestal Diaries*, pp. 39–41). "This decision," Fleming concludes, "brings out strikingly the great rapidity with which Roosevelt's policy of working

with Russia was reversed. It may well be that Roosevelt would
have resisted the acceptance of the Lublin government at San
Francisco. The strong probability is that he would have, but
without telling the Russians to go to hell."

A similar point is made by another eminent authority of
American politics, Mr. James P. Warburg.* After pointing out
that Truman was a man "more characteristic of the American
people as a whole than the paternalistic Hudson Valley patrician
whom he succeeded in the White House", he goes on to say that
Roosevelt had a profound knowledge of European history, of
which Truman had none, and that, brought up in the Baptist
religion, Truman had an over-simple view of what was "right"
and "wrong". In short, America in his view invariably represented
Good, and Russia Evil. "If one adds up these characteristics,
plus an almost total unfamiliarity with the world outside of the
United States, one obtains some insight into the factors which
made Harry Truman adopt a simplicistic and . . . distorted
view of the foreign policy problems that he faced when he
became President." Warburg, like Fleming, denies that Harry
Truman ever had any intention of continuing Roosevelt's
conciliatory policy, least of all after Leahy, Forrestal and Harriman
had taken him in hand, barely two days after Roosevelt's death.
As Warburg says:

> The records show that practically all of Truman's advisers
> urged him to modify Roosevelt's conciliatory policy, differing
> only as to the timing of a showdown with Stalin. . . .
> Perhaps because Truman as yet knew very little about what was
> going on at Los Alamos, perhaps because of his native belligerence,
> the new President decided in favor of an immediate showdown.
> When Molotov called at the White House on April 23, he received
> a dressing-down in language which, according to Admiral Leahy,
> had no precedent in diplomatic intercourse. Molotov was shocked
> and dismayed. Churchill, hearing of the interview, was delighted.
> However, neither Truman's tough talk nor his subsequent show of
> force over the Trieste dispute, nor his halting of Lend-Lease
> shipments to Russia caused Stalin to back down. The showdown
> having failed, Truman sent the ailing Harry Hopkins to Moscow
> to persuade Stalin to let Molotov attend the San Francisco
> Conference.

* *The United States in the Postwar World*, New York, 1966, pp. 10–25.

Warburg, quite correctly in my view, dismisses as unsubstantiated the theory according to which the Hopkins mission signified Truman's intention to resume Roosevelt's policy of endeavouring to avoid a break in Soviet/Russian relations. The apparent concessions he made to the Russians, such as not supporting Churchill's demand that the American troops still occupying parts of the Soviet zone in Germany should be left there until further notice, merely denoted what Warburg calls "a strategy of delayed confrontation". Truman was desperately hoping that the A-bomb would be produced before he met Stalin, and that was why he postponed the Potsdam meeting three times. And when the Big Three at last met at Potsdam, Truman, in reality, *"did not wish at this time to reach an agreement on Germany or on any other issue"* (Warburg's italics). In Warburg's view, three major blunders were nevertheless made at Potsdam: the question of Germany's western frontiers remained unsettled, though the new Polish/German frontier had been given *de facto*, even if not *de jure*, recognition; secondly, it was an "incredible blunder" to give France a zone of occupation in Germany and an equal voice on the Allied Control Council, amounting to a veto, without obtaining French signature to the four-power contract under which the four-power government was supposed to operate; finally, it was an error to imagine that at Potsdam the four victorious nations could impose on Germany a political and economic revolution without having reached agreement on what kind of Germany they wished to create.

One might mention another consequence of Potsdam: by telling the Russians in fact to collect all the reparations they could from Eastern Germany and from "German assets" in the rest of Eastern Europe, Byrnes laid the foundations for splitting Germany in two and for strengthening Russia's political and economic stranglehold on her own "sphere of influence". Truman no doubt imagined that all this was a purely temporary arrangement, and that once America had her A-bomb the open-door policy in Eastern Europe, as elsewhere, would come into its own again.

Russia's other experiences in the summer of 1945 were not too happy. Although Roosevelt and Hull had been extremely hostile to Argentina, the last refuge of every kind of Fascist and Nazi riff-raff, the South American Republic was admitted to the UN by a large majority, despite strong protests from Molotov. The fact that Hull, a member of the American delegation, but too sick to attend the conference, phoned Stettinius to protest against the admission of Argentina made no difference.

What also disturbed the Russians was the meteoric rise, since Roosevelt's death, of Senator Vandenberg. He continually demanded "justice" for Poland, and even proposed to Russia an American guarantee against German aggression. The whole idea would have been more attractive if a similar American guarantee given to France by Woodrow Wilson in 1919 had not been subsequently cancelled by the isolationists in the American Senate.

Molotov and the other Russians who went to the UN had the unhappy impression that on almost every issue they would be out-voted; which explains why they clung as desperately as they did to the veto—not that the American Senate would not have supported the veto with equal vigour if American sovereignty were in any way threatened at the United Nations. In short, the Russians felt themselves in a somewhat isolated position at the UN, and, as long as this state of affairs continued, they would above all look upon the UN as a forum for publicizing their own point of view, and for denouncing every kind of "warmongers" and preventive-war enthusiasts.

What had been happening meantime in the first post-war summer of 1945?

FIVE

The Elections of 1946

The Russians did not know how angry Mr. Truman was with Mr. Byrnes after the Big Three Foreign Ministers' meeting in Moscow in December 1945. The Russian press comments on this meeting were favourable, and readers took at their face value the warm thanks for his hospitality that Byrnes and Bevin had cabled to Molotov after leaving Moscow. The Hiroshima bomb had left the Russians with an unpleasant after-taste, but there was still no acute anxiety about the future of East/West relations as the Soviet Union entered 1946, the first post-war year. The New Year editorial of *Izvestia* was a characteristic mixture of melancholy reflections on the human losses and destruction the country had suffered during the war, pride in Russia's military achievements and consciousness of the enormous tasks ahead:

> We are entering this New Year with peculiar feelings. The graves of our brothers and sisters who gave their life for their country are still fresh. On New Year's night millions repeated to themselves the heart-felt words of our leader: Eternal glory to the heroes who died in battle for the honour and victory of our country. Twelve months ago, we were still fighting in Czechoslovakia and in the streets of Budapest. . . . Hitler's Germany was already doomed, but was still bossed by the war criminals now in the dock of the Nuremberg tribunal.

This reference to Nuremberg was also characteristic; it was a reminder that, whatever complications there were, or would be in the future, with the wartime Allies, all were united in their determination to punish the Nazi war criminals. For months afterwards, an enormous amount of space was to be given to the

Nuremberg trial in the Russian press—chiefly, it is true, with reference to the war crimes committed against Russia.

But, having dwelt only briefly on the past, *Izvestia* then spoke at much greater length of the tasks ahead of the Russian people. 32,000 industrial enterprises had been destroyed by the Germans, 1,700 towns had been partially or wholly destroyed, as well as 70,000 villages, and 98,000 *kolkhozes* had been looted. Small wonder that the Soviet Union was now suffering great hardships and privations. But she was now getting ready for the new Five-Year Plan "which will not only restore the pre-war level of production, but surpass it". Already, during the second half of 1945, some progress had been made: in the engineering industry, there had been a 33 per cent increase over the previous half-year; agricultural machinery was now being made again on an ever-growing scale; compared with 1944, there had been a 22 per cent increase in the output of iron and a 13 per cent increase in that of steel. The area under cultivation in the ex-occupied areas had been greatly increased; factory chimneys were smoking again; with the help of the state, thousands of villages were again rising from the ashes; and schools of all types were crowded. "A hard and formidable task is ahead of us, but we shall carry it out."

The Russian civilian population had, in the main, lived on miserably short rations during the war. The "hardships and privations", to which *Izvestia* had referred, were continuing, and the food shortage was still an everyday worry. On the following day the same paper published an "encouraging" interview with V. Zotov, Commissar for the Food Industry, who declared that already twice as much sugar was now being produced as in 1944, three times as many cigarettes, and 30 per cent more vegetable oils; and, compared with 1945, there would be a further 50 per cent increase in these oils, macaroni, canned food, sugar, beer, soap, margarine and tobacco—which, considering the almost complete absence of commodities like sugar in 1944–5, was not altogether reassuring. In fact, by 1947, the food shortage was to become catastrophic.

The great event of January/February 1946 was, of course, the "election campaign", even though there were no competing parties and everybody was expected to vote for candidates of the single "Communist and Non-Party" bloc. The selection of the local candidate from amongst those proposed by various party

7

or trade union organizations was sometimes a fairly long and complicated process, but once the candidate had been agreed upon there was no further problem. The current remark made to Westerners by defenders of the Soviet election system was that only the "worthiest" people were, by this means, elected to the Supreme Soviet, and although the responsibilities and duties were admittedly "rather limited", at least the system made the election of "dud M.P.s" practically impossible. There were, of course, special candidates who were chosen by the constituencies without any rivals; thus, countless constituencies wanted to be represented by Stalin, and many others by other top leaders of the Party, or by some of the most famous generals of the last war. In particular demand were Molotov, Kalinin, Beria, Malenkov, Voroshilov, Zhdanov, Mikoyan, Kaganovich, Khrushchev, Kosygin, Voznesensky and other members of the Politburo, and, among the marshals and generals, Zhukov, Rokossovsky, Konev, Govorov, Malinovsky, Meretskov, Bagramyan, Admiral N. V. Kuznetsov, etc. Those who had been proposed for numerous constituencies published on 9th January a statement saying that, under the law, they could stand for only one place, and declaring in which constituency they were going to "seek election". Thus Stalin, Molotov, Malenkov and Bulganin had chosen constituencies in Moscow; Zhdanov and Kosygin, Leningrad constituencies; Khrushchev, a Kiev constituency, etc. Some were standing for the Soviet of the Union, others for the Soviet of Nationalities, the two "chambers" of the Supreme Soviet.

The truth is that neither the Supreme Soviet (except its presidium) nor the Party's Central Committee (except its Politburo) had been in great evidence during the war. A meeting of the Supreme Soviet had been called in June 1942 to ratify the Anglo/Soviet Alliance and, more important, to take note, as it were, of the Anglo/American "promise" of the Second Front in 1942. Another meeting of the Supreme Soviet was called in February 1944 which amended the Constitution, giving all the sixteen Soviet republics the right to have an "independent" foreign policy, with foreign ministries, embassies abroad, etc. Obviously this was done with a view to securing more seats at the UN. The plenum of the Central Committee hardly ever met, and the last Party Congress had taken place in 1938; the next—the nineteenth—was not to be called until 1952.

The main purpose of the election of the new Supreme Soviet was to rubber-stamp unanimously the hierarchy's new Five-Year Plan. The election to the Supreme Soviet of the most famous Red Army generals was natural enough so soon after the end of the war, though the Party had done its best, since the end of the war, to play down the importance of the *miles gloriosus*.* Typical of this was the speech delivered by G. F. Alexandrov, of the Central Committee, at the usual Lenin memorial meeting on 21st January 1946:

> The military science of the Soviet State was elaborated by Lenin and Stalin in the days of the Civil War and the Foreign Intervention. . . . If we defeated Hitlerism, it is because the Soviet people had at its head the greatest commander-in-chief, Generalissimo Stalin. (Tumultuous cheers.)

There followed a long list of Russian victories, all of them carried out "under the leadership and the military genius of Stalin". Not a single marshal or general was mentioned.

Significantly, too, Alexandrov stressed the fact that Russia had travelled along the very hard road of industrialization, collectivization and the war under the leadership of Stalin, and *without Lenin*. The Soviet Union had taken the only possible right road; the hardships and privations had been great, especially during the war, but now the country could look forward into the future with confidence.

The war had left certain unpleasant hangovers. Some non-Russian nationalities of the Soviet Union had not proved particularly loyal. Also, there had been strong anti-*kolkhoz* moods among the peasantry and among soldiers from peasant families. In an "Address to All Voters" on 2nd February, the Central Committee stressed these two very questions: the "brotherly upsurge" in which all the peoples of the Soviet Union had risen in the hour of danger to defend like one man their Soviet homeland—even the Lithuanians, Latvians and Estonians were

---

* I referred in *Russia at War* (p. 1003), to the nasty little whispering campaign against generals and especially against generals' wives, with their *nouveau-riche* manners and their malapropisms, which the Party began to conduct very soon after V E Day. Similarly, I referred to that widely-publicized poem by Nedo-gonov, *The Flag over the Village Soviet*, published soon after the war, the main theme of which was "If you don't work hard on the *kolkhoz*, we shall spit on all your medals and decorations."

specifically mentioned; secondly, the war had shown that the *kolkhoz* system had "saved" the country:

> Thanks to the *kolkhoz* system the Soviet Union became the country of advanced agriculture. But for the *kolkhozes*, agriculture would have fallen into complete decay during the war, and would have left the army and the country without food. No doubt the *kolkhozes* suffered from great difficulties during the war, and thousands of them were ruined by the Nazis. . . . Now we must re-equip the *kolkhozes*, so that the peasantry can be comfortable and prosperous. Vote therefore for the Communist and Non-Party Bloc!

There were countless "election meetings" all over the Soviet Union in February, but the greatest prominence in the press was, of course, given to the speeches made by members of the Politburo (which were printed more or less verbatim in the press and also appeared immediately afterwards in pamphlet form). Although these speeches by Stalin's "closest comrades-in-arms"—with their extravagant tributes to Stalin and the usual peroration ending with Stalin's name—had much in common, they are still of considerable interest. No doubt some, such as Kalinin's letter to his Leningrad voters (he was, apparently, too ill to go to Leningrad, and was to die a year later), are little more than a string of platitudes, but others made some important points. Several speakers dwelt on the fact that, but for the industrialization and collectivization carried out in the twelve years before the war, this war would have been lost. More specifically, Malenkov, speaking in Moscow on 7th February, declared that if it had not been for the Urals-Kuzbas industrial base created before the war, Russia would, in losing the Donbas in 1941, also have lost the war. Similarly, Voznesensky, speaking to his voters at Gorki, stressed the importance of the thousands of planes and other equipment that had been produced in the new Gorki industries outside the enemy's reach. Kaganovich, speaking in Tashkent, said that it was in fact in the last ten years before the war that the Soviet Union, "thanks to the genius of Stalin", had succeeded in building up an industry which saved her from defeat. (Lip service was occasionally paid to Lenin, but it was under Stalin that Russia had become properly industrialized.) Several speakers stressed that in 1941 Stalin had not been caught unawares by the German invasion—though the subsequent disasters were, somehow, glossed over.

A number of speakers—notably Malenkov and Molotov—justified the 1936-9 purges in retrospect. It was essential in those years, said Malenkov, to

> break the resistance of the most ferocious enemies of the Party and the people. ... We must not forget the importance of our struggle against the Trotskyites, Zinovievites and Bukharinites who were the flunkeys of fascism ... and were doing their utmost to persuade our people not to put all their energy and material resources into our heavy industry. They were also planning the dismemberment of the Soviet Union. ...

When the war had begun, the previous elimination of these traitors, who had done their best to disunite the Soviet people, had proved invaluable. Molotov also said that it had been an essential part of Russia's war preparations "to sweep out of the way those internal enemies, saboteurs and wreckers ... that gang of spies and diversionists in the service of their foreign masters".

On the whole, however, "unpleasant" subjects were avoided, and stress was laid on the solid unity of all the Soviet peoples in the hour of supreme danger, no mention being made of the rather dubious loyalty of the Baltic peoples, or the plain disloyalty of certain Moslem nationalities in the Caucasus, who had, towards the end of the war, been deported *en masse*. Even Beria, speaking at Tbilisi, paid warm tributes to the loyalty shown by the Georgians, Armenians and Azerbaijani, and did not mention those whom his NKVD had deported. He preferred, instead, to speak of the great future of the tea and citrus-fruit plantations in Georgia, of her new steel works and automobile plant. The head of the NKVD made no mention of his department's activities during and since the war, but briefly referred to the need for "vigilance" in future, since reactionary and fascist policies in the capitalist world were not dead yet by any means.

Apart from the ever-recurring eulogies of Stalin as the man who had foreseen the danger and had industrialized Russia in the nick of time, and as "the greatest military genius" (the generals, officers and soldiers were mentioned only in passing), the speeches dealt chiefly with the work of reconstruction lying ahead and with that new Five-Year Plan which was now being prepared.

A beginning had already been made. Voznesensky claimed that even while the war was still in progress 75 milliard roubles had already been put into the restoration of the liberated territories; by now the industrial base there had been restored to the extent of 30 per cent. The rest of the work would have to be completed in the next four years. But, taking the country as a whole, the 1940 level of production would be greatly exceeded by 1950.

Speaking of housing, Kaganovich declared that since the war, in which 25 million people had been left homeless, "several millions" had already been moved from dugouts into reconstructed houses.

> However, the destruction is so immense that it will require an enormous effort and vast financial resources to restore fully our factories, the Donbas, the railways, sea and river transport, *kolkhozes*, State Farms, and urban and rural houses. But we intend to restore everything that has been destroyed during the next five years, but also to exceed the pre-war level of production, particularly in heavy industry—iron, steel, engineering, coal and oil; and also in the textile and light industries.

There were interesting references—or lack of references—in these election speeches to the wartime allies. There was a passing reference in Mikoyan's and Beria's speeches to the victory won "with the help of the allies". Lend-Lease was not mentioned; but insofar as the Soviet Union was not left entirely alone to fight Germany, this (as Beria put it) was due to the greatness and clearsightedness of Stalin's foreign policy. More significant were the fairly frequent mentions of the "disquieting" things that were now happening in the West. Malenkov, Molotov and Zhdanov were the most outspoken on the subject. Thus Malenkov:

> There were cases in history when the fruits of victory slipped out of the victor's hands. This must not happen to us. . . . We must, in the first place, consolidate and strengthen still further our Soviet socialist state. . . . And we must remember that our friends will respect us only so long as we are strong. . . . There is no respect for the weak ones, and the weak ones get beaten.

And Malenkov went on:

> We represent an enormous power. Let us not forget this. And let also those remember it—those who imagine that we shed

our blood, suffered enormous casualties and won our victory so that others may help themselves to its fruits. Let them remember this and stop trying to frighten us. We are not people who are easily frightened. (*Prolonged cheers.*)

Here was clearly an allusion to the atom bomb.

Molotov, for his part, ironically remarked that certain people in the West were not pleased to see that they could not substitute some other party for the Soviet Communist Party in this election; but it so happened that even in the Western countries the Communists were enjoying the widest popular support—

> Which only shows that the earth is not only revolving, but not revolving in vain (*Laughter, applause*) and is also moving forward, towards a better future. (*Cheers.*)

This remark came closest to the "world communism" theme. More important as regards the immediate future was the fact that the Soviet Union was now "a supremely important factor in international life". No serious international problems could be solved today, said Molotov, without the participation of the Soviet Union, or without her voice being listened to. Stalin's presence in international talks was the best guarantee of their being successfully concluded.* Molotov then said that the "reactionary forces" were still strong in the West, and among the "insatiable imperialists" there was a lot of dangerous talk about "a third world war". Fortunately the ally (the USA?) had at last agreed that it was anomalous to maintain in Western Germany, in some form or another, several hundred thousand soldiers of the routed Nazi armies. But in Italy even now there were tens of thousands Polish troops, kept by the Allies, and under the command of the Fascist general Anders, notorious for his hatred for the Soviet Union and capable of any wild adventures against the new democratic Poland.

Similarly, in the Western zones of Austria there was a White-Russian infantry corps under a Colonel Rogozhin which had served under Hitler. "In the interests of peace and friendly

* Was this a reference to Stalin's talks with Byrnes and Bevin in December 1945? As we know, though extremely active as a "diplomat" during the war, Stalin usually refrained from taking a major part in any official diplomatic negotiations after the war.

relations with the Allies, we have asked that this gang of degenerates be disbanded," Molotov said.

It is worth noting that at the beginning of 1946 Russian leaders
still continued to speak of "the Allies". And despite Molotov's
passing reference to the progress of the Western communists, he
undoubtedly wanted "a long period of peace and fully assured
security" if the Soviet Union was to "catch up with the most
advanced capitalist nations and outstrip them in the per capita
output of commodities". She had already started on this process
before the war, but the war had interrupted it. The Soviet
Union's peace-loving policy, Molotov said, was not a transient
phenomenon, but arose from the fundamental interests and
needs of her people. Whether by "lengthy period of peace"
he meant that a new attack on Russia by the imperialists was still
inevitable in the long run was not clear. It would perhaps have
been too much to expect an old Leninist to assume that "peaceful
coexistence" could last forever; for one thing, his contacts with
the West in the last six months had not been too encouraging
for such a belief.

I often wondered during and after the war to what extent these
colleagues of Stalin were popular in the Soviet Union. About
Beria, the NKVD man, there were, of course, no illusions, and
even in his native Georgia he was probably as heartily detested as
anywhere else. It takes Germans actually to *like* their Himmlers.
Kalinin, with his white goatee, who played the part of the
kindly old peasant to whom, as head of the Presidium of the
Supreme Soviet, petitions were sent by people in distress—for
instance by relatives of those deported to camps, etc.—was widely
regarded as rather a fraud, the Father Christmas impersonating the
great benevolence of the Kremlin. In fact he was as tough as any of
the top *apparatchiki*, liked good living, and was even said in his
rather doddery old age to have a young dancer from the Bolshoi
as a mistress. Some, like Voznesensky, Kosygin and even Kaganovich, were respected as good technicians; about Voroshilov, with
his lamentable war record, there were no illusions. The two most
popular men were probably Mikoyan—who seemed good-
natured and human and was associated with consumer goods and
ice-cream—and Molotov, who was regarded, quite rightly, as
a man of enormous ability, and one who had the interests of
the country at heart. People were impressed by the way he had,

since the war, been standing up to the Western diplomats. Malenkov, too, was generally liked; though in reality a very tough *apparatchik* who had spent a long period as Stalin's personal secretary and had very quickly risen to prominence during the war, he cultivated a genial fat-boy exterior. Many years later, in 1956, he made a similar favourable impression during his baby-kissing tour of England. Khrushchev, who was usually in Kiev, was little known in Moscow just after the war. One of the men who usually left a highly unpleasant impression was Zhdanov, with his cruel cat-like face; and this also was true of his pre-election speech in Leningrad on 6th February. He scarcely even alluded to the unequalled tragedy of the city, in which a million people had died of hunger in the blockade. Instead, though knowing that Stalin was not popular in Leningrad, he exalted the military genius of Stalin, who, he said, had "organized" the defence of the city and had planned the military operation of February 1943 which had resulted in the creation of the "Schlüsselburg Gap" in the ring of the blockade. For several years before the war, Zhdanov had been head of the Leningrad Party Organization, and was thus largely responsible for the fearful famine of the winter of 1941–2; for, while there was still time in July/August 1941 to bring in food supplies and to evacuate a large part of the population, absolutely nothing was done in one case, and practically nothing in the other. No doubt, once the ring of the blockade had closed round Leningrad, Zhdanov played his part in organizing the various life-lines across Lake Ladoga, but at the height of the famine between November 1941 and February 1942 he had shown what can only be described as a mixture of helplessness and ruthlessness. Maybe he could later claim to have been the "saviour" of Leningrad—but at what a price! In his election speech he made no personal claims, but attributed the "glorious defence of Leningrad" to the military genius of Stalin. As in many other election speeches by the hierarchy, not a word was said about any general. As for the future of Leningrad, Zhdanov declared that it would again become a great engineering and shipbuilding centre, as well as a great producer of consumer goods, but added that its fuel and raw-material "base" would have to be changed; instead of importing iron and coal from the south, Leningrad would now get the bulk of its iron ore from the less distant Kola Peninsula and its coal from the "Pechora Basin"—with Vorkuta as its centre. Both these recently developed industrial areas were notorious centres of forced labour. Characteristically, like some other speakers in that election, Zhdanov echoed Stalin's special May 1945 tribute to the *Russian* people, "the leading force among the peoples of the Soviet Union", and the nation "who had shown the greatest confidence in our Party, in its Bolshevik Stalinist leadership, and had shown an exceptional clearsightedness, strength of character and patience".

Already in February 1946, when, on the surface, relations with the Western allies still seemed to be reasonably "correct", Zhdanov was more outspokenly hostile to them than most. He was glad that, as a result of the war, the Soviet Union, which now stretched from Königsberg to the Kurile Islands in the Pacific, had consolidated its frontiers; also, the Soviet Union now played an enormous role in the settlement of all international affairs:

> Our aim is to pursue relentlessly the Stalinite foreign policy of peace and international friendship. But it is not easy. . . . The roots of fascism have not been pulled out everywhere. Even amongst the peace-loving nations, there are reactionary elements who are hostile to the Soviet Union. Much will yet have to be done to apply in practice the decisions of Yalta and Potsdam and to consolidate UNO. You follow the press, and you know that our policy of peace and security . . . does not please everybody. No, we can't please everybody, but we've got to be extremely vigilant.

Zhdanov, as we shall later see, was to represent in the Soviet hierarchy the most violently anti-Western current of all, both in his capacity of cultural dictator and in that of the principal Soviet spokesman and moving spirit of the Cominform when it was set up in 1947.

The most important election speech, which was delivered at the Bolshoi Theatre in Moscow on 9th February, the eve of polling day, was of course that of Stalin himself. If his lieutenants were allowed—or even instructed—during the "election campaign" to show distrust, if not downright hostility, to the West, Stalin, on the contrary, sounded remarkably conciliatory. His speech was a broad survey of the past few years, dealing principally with various aspects of the war; only towards the end of his speech did he briefly outline Russia's future course of action.

He began by describing the origins of the Second World War in Marxist terms—"crisis of capitalism", "competition for markets", etc. Significantly, he refrained from mentioning either the "free-hand-in-the-East" tendencies that had existed in the West, or its counterpart, the Soviet/German pact. Instead, completely departing (much to the indignation of post-Stalin Soviet commentators) from the 1939 Soviet concept of this war—of having been at first as much an imperialist war as the First World War—or the even more extreme view expressed in a spirit of opportunism by both Stalin and Molotov in the heyday of the Soviet/German Pact that not Nazi Germany, but France and Britain, were the "aggressors", Stalin now declared that the Second World War was *not* a repetition of the First World War. After an indictment of Germany, Italy and Japan and their anti-democratic and aggressive regimes, Stalin said:

> As distinct from the First World War, the Second World War against the Axis powers assumed *from the very beginning* the character of an anti-fascist war of liberation, one of the purposes of which was also to restore democratic freedoms. The entry into this war of the Soviet Union could only strengthen—as indeed it did— the anti-fascist liberation character of the Second World War.

Hence, said Stalin, the creation of the anti-fascist coalition of the Soviet Union, the USA, Britain and other freedom-loving countries which later played a decisive role in smashing the armed forces of the Axis powers.

This extraordinary tribute to Britain's and America's pure intentions since the very beginning of the Second World War— though wholly contrary, as we have seen, to the earlier "Marxist" and Comintern interpretations of the origins of the war—could only be regarded as a demonstration of continued friendship towards the wartime allies and as an appeal to them to preserve the Coalition after the war.

The war, Stalin went on to say, had been the hardest and cruellest of all wars Russia had experienced; but it had also proved a remarkable test of the Soviet social system and of the Soviet state structure. In particular, it had shown that, unlike pre-1914 Austria-Hungary, the multinational Soviet state was perfectly viable. (Stalin refrained from mentioning some of the black— or grey—sheep.) Thirdly, the war had revealed the magnificent qualities of the Red Army, an army which in the end smashed that German war machine which had previously spread terror throughout the whole of Europe. He paid a warm tribute to the army and its leaders, and enumerated some of the most famous Russian victories. But, he added, unequalled though the soldiers' courage was, courage alone would not have secured victory. What was also needed was first-class equipment in sufficient quantities, well-trained officer cadres and a good supply service. Without sufficient quantities of metal, fuel, cotton and food the war could not have been won. In 1941, Stalin said, the Red Army had at least "the indispensable minimum" (a rather modest way of putting it!) to fulfil its needs. This "minimum" had been achieved as a result of the three pre-war five-year plans. In 1940, Russia was in a better position to face a major war than she had been in 1913. With over 15 million tons of pig-iron, 18 million tons of steel, 166 million tons of coal and 31 million tons of oil she was producing between three and a half and five times more of these commodities than in 1913. There had also been a three-fold increase in cotton and a two-fold increase in grain. In thirteen years—between 1928 and 1941—a backward country had been turned into an industrial country.

> Our friends abroad spoke of a "miracle"; our enemies described the Five-Year Plans as "Bolshevik propaganda" or as "tricks of the Cheka". But there are no miracles in this world, and the Cheka is not powerful enough to cancel the laws of social development.

Stalin then defended the top priority that had been given to heavy industry, and also the collectivization of agriculture. This had been successfully carried out despite much resistance "not only from backward people dreading anything new, but also from prominent members of the Party who were trying to drag the Party back to the 'usual' capitalist forms of development". The anti-Party machinations of the Trotskyite and right-wing deviationists, he said, aimed at sabotaging and slowing down the process of industrialization and collectivization which saved the country during the war.

Without dwelling on the military disasters during the first year of the war, apart from commenting that "during that year the output of our military industry was slowed down by the evacuation of the war plants to the East", Stalin enumerated all that the war industries had produced in the last three years of the war: an average of 30,000 tanks, self-propelled guns and armoured cars a year; 40,000 planes a year; 120,000 guns a year, 450,000 machine guns, over 3 million rifles, 2 million tommy-guns and 100,000 mortars a year. In 1944 alone 240 million shells and over 7 milliard cartridges were turned out. Also, the Red Army had plenty of food and clothing. (No mention was made of Lend-Lease.)

Turning to the future, Stalin said that the immediate programme was contained in the new five-year plan to be submitted to the Supreme Soviet. In the next five years the war-devastated regions would be fully restored and the overall output of the country would exceed the pre-war level. In the very near future, Stalin said, amidst loud cheers, rationing would be abolished and there would be a progressive lowering of prices of all consumer goods. Stalin then alluded to the atom bomb:

> I do not doubt that if we give the necessary help to our scientists, they will not only catch up with, but outstrip in the very near future the achievements of science beyond our borders. (*Prolonged cheers.*)

It is curious that, in discussing the long-term economic development of the Soviet Union, Stalin should have fixed remarkably modest targets—50 million tons of pig-iron a year, 60 million tons of steel, 500 million tons of coal, 60 million tons of oil. To achieve these targets, "three five-year plans will no doubt be required, if not more"—that is, roughly, between 1960 and 1965.

In reality, these figures were to be exceeded by 1960 and vastly exceeded by 1965. Thus steel production was 65 million tons in 1960 and (a remarkable jump) 91 million tons in 1965; oil production, 148 million tons in 1960 and 243 million tons in 1965. He was careful, however, not to attempt any long-term forecasts on agricultural output—that most doubtful link in Soviet economy.

In conclusion, Stalin gave his views on the concept of the "Communist and Non-Party Bloc" for whom everybody would be expected to vote. The difference between the "party" and "non-party" men and women standing for election was "purely formal". Suggesting that there was no longer any class war in the Soviet Union, he said that the non-party people were now "separated from the bourgeoisie by that barrier called the Soviet system". The meeting, needless to say, ended with the usual ovation, with cries of "Glory to Great Stalin!", "Glory to Stalin, the Maker of all our Victories!", etc.

Polling-day was on 10th February. With Moscow decorated with countless banners and slogans and queues outside the numerous polling-stations, it had the appearance of a major public holiday. Propaganda impressed on Soviet men and women their great civic responsibility in voting for the Bloc. Everything was done to avoid abstentions; even in hospitals, the sick and dying could vote, thanks to the portable ballot-boxes that were taken round. There is literally no means of knowing whether the figures published corresponded exactly to the number of votes cast. They showed that in the country as a whole there were 101·7 million registered voters, that 101·4, or 99·7 per cent, had taken part in the vote, and that 100·6 million had voted for the Bloc, that is, 99·2 per cent. But, singularly, 819,000 adverse votes had been cast, or 0·8 per cent. The highest number of abstentions and hostile votes were in two of the Baltic republics: in Estonia, 98·7 per cent took part in the voting, but only 94·6 per cent voted for the Bloc; in Lithuania the respective figures were 91·8 per cent and 95·3 per cent. Thus, there was a nearly 10 per cent abstention in Lithuania. Lithuanians later told me that in fact the number of abstentions, especially in the villages, was much higher, and they assumed that if in the official election statistics even so "low" a figure as 91 per cent was given, it was because a 98 or 99 per cent figure would simply have looked too improbable.

The Supreme Soviet—first the Soviet of the Union, then the Soviet of Nationalities—met in a festive atmosphere in the Kremlin on 12th March. It was an even more colourful gathering than usual. Not only were many of the Asian male and female deputies wearing their bright national costumes, but many others were in military uniform, most of them with dazzling rows of decorations. A speaker later noted that of the 657 deputies of the Soviet of Nationalities 496 were men and 161 women, 34 per cent were "workers", 30 per cent "peasants", 36 per cent "employees and intellectuals"; another speaker said that in the Soviet of the Union there was a higher percentage of "workers" (42 per cent); of the 682 members of this Soviet, 116 were women. In both Soviets there were numerous representatives of the armed forces, among them 102 Heroes of the Soviet Union, including 11 "double" and 2 "treble" Heroes; there were also numerous "Heroes of Socialist Labour", Stalin Prizewinners, famous scientists, industrial and agricultural shock-workers, particularly successful *kolkhoz* chairmen, etc. About 18 per cent were non-Party, the rest were party members. Watching all these 1,300 very different, but each in his or her own way very distinguished, people, one had the feeling that here was assembled the real élite of the country and the regime—with a strong emphasis, however, on the Party élite. Some of them—for by no means all were people of high education—had been elected and brought to the Kremlin as samples of conscientious and devoted work—the good *kolkhoz* chairmen, the record-breaking milk-maid, etc., or—and the native costumes were important—as illustrations of the equality and friendship among the numerous nationalities of the Soviet Union. It was many of these colourful Asiatics who constituted a large part of the non-Party minority.

The proceedings began, of course, with an ovation in honour of Stalin, as—looking a little older, greyer and fatter than a year before—he appeared in the hall, together with Molotov, Kalinin, Voroshilov, Beria, Khrushchev, Malenkov and the rest of the party hierarchy. The meetings of this session of the Supreme Soviet went on for a week, but Stalin was present only at the first two meetings. A number of laws were rubber-stamped by the Supreme Soviet, among them a curious one changing the name of People's Commissar to "Minister" and that of People's Commissariat to "Ministry". But the main purpose of this session of the Supreme Soviet was to approve the first post-war five-year plan of 1946–50. This was presented to the Assembly on 15th March by the head of the Gosplan, N. A. Voznesensky, that very Voznesensky who was to be executed in mysterious circumstances four years later.

Voznesensky spoke for about three hours, and the 1946–50 Five-Year Plan law adopted by the Supreme Soviet runs to 100 pages. The two documents constitute a remarkable programme for post-war reconstruction in a country that had suffered appalling human losses in the war, and a large part of which had been devastated.

The primary purposes of the new five-year plan, Voznesensky

said, were (a) to restore the war-devastated areas, (b) restore the pre-war level of production in industry and agriculture and then (c) to exceed it—all within these five years. Compared with 1940, industrial production would have to be increased by nearly 50 per cent; top priority would be given to heavy industry and railway transport; in 1946 alone the conversion of numerous war industries to peaceful needs and other reorganizations of the national economy must be completed. Voznesensky also stressed the need to increase the output of agriculture, and though he also mentioned consumer goods he was less emphatic about them. The low targets in consumer goods may be measured from the example of leather footwear—only 240 million pairs of shoes in 1950, or not much more than one pair per head of population. Apart from a reasonably high output of cotton fabrics (4·6 milliard metres, or about one-half the 1966 output), the targets of other textiles were still very low.

The plan also provided for the supply to the armed forces of "the most modern" equipment (implying atomic weapons); for a high degree of capital accumulation and capital investments; for the development and modernization of the building-materials and housing industries; for the restoration of the devastated cities, towns and villages, and a general increase in housing; for an increase in labour productivity; for an early abolition of rationing; and for a very large extension of the schools, higher educational establishments and the medical services. Compared with 1965, some of the industrial 1950 targets even in heavy industry were still modest—pig-iron 19·5 million tons (15 million tons in 1940); steel 25 million tons (18 million in 1940); oil 35 million tons (31 million tons in 1940). But there was now to be a revival of the tractor and agricultural machinery industry and an expansion of the automobile industry (mostly trucks), with about half a million vehicles a year (during the last three years of the war most motor vehicles had come from the USA); electric power was to be increased, compared with 1940, by some 70 per cent (82 md kwh. in 1950—a still negligible figure compared with the 578 md kwh. in 1965).

The Five-Year Plan provided for an overall agricultural increase in 1950 by 27 per cent compared with pre-war, the target for 1950 being 127 million tons of grain (119 in 1940), with an average hectare yield of 12 quintals (1·2 tons); a major effort was also to be made to increase substantially the output of sugar beet (26 million tons), cotton (3 million tons), flax and sunflower seed; a 39 per cent increase of cattle and a threefold increase of pigs was also planned. The plan also spoke of various irrigation and drainage schemes, the construction of numerous canals and reservoirs, the planting of protective forest-belts, etc. Significantly, it was also emphasized that the strict delimitation of the private plots and the *kolkhoz* land proper be observed, and that no further violations of the farm cooperative statutes be tolerated (during and since the war there had been a tendency among the *kolkhoz* peasants to help themselves to large portions of the collective land).

There was also to be an intensified development of education at all levels—by 1950 the number of pupils of elementary, seven-year and secondary schools was to be increased to 31 million; that of universities and high-education schools to 674,000; and that of special secondary schools to 1·2 million; in the five years, the former category of schools were to turn out over 600,000 young specialists, and the latter over 1,300,000. Much attention was also given to hospitals—there were to be nearly a million hospital beds in 1950, as against 700,000 in 1940; sanatoriums and rest homes destroyed during the war were to be restored and extended; there were to be 47,000 "cinema installations" in 1950 (nearly double the 1940 figure); the number of kindergartens also was to be doubled, and all children who had lost their parents during the war would be kept by the state. There were also provisions for state grants to mothers with large families, for the maintenance by the state of "illegitimate" children unwanted by their mothers (in accordance with the curious wartime family law of 1944, described in *Russia at War*), pensions to war invalids, etc. The new housing being planned in terms of square metres (72 million), it is difficult to assess the exact number of restored and new houses provided for under the Five-Year Plan, but it appears to amount to between $1\frac{1}{2}$ and 2 million houses in the towns and cities; and over 2 million houses were to be built in the rural areas. Medicines and medical equipment to be produced in 1950 was nearly double the 1940 figure.

Life for the Russian people after the war continued to be very hard; resources were limited, and if an effort was made to give

8

top priority to heavy industry, and to give preferential treatment to the industrial worker, the peasants were expected to work for as little as possible. The everyday hardships were to be further aggravated by the disastrous drought that struck vast areas in 1946; but paradoxically, for purely political reasons, as we shall see, the Soviet government had to export grain to certain foreign countries, notably to France and Czechoslovakia. Khrushchev was later to claim that as a result of these exports many thousands of people died of hunger in the Kursk province and other places in 1947.

Still, by March 1946, the machinery of post-war reconstruction and development had been set in motion. It is certain that, by and large, Russia was moving in the right direction—though the hard way, the Stalinist way. The last thing the Soviet people—with all this work on their hands—were interested in was conquering the world. Yet never since the war was the international tension between East and West to be more bitter and violent than during the next few years. . . .

SIX

The Hardening of the Regime

One of the outstanding characteristics of the Soviet people's war against the Nazi invaders was that it was a national and not an ideological war—a war first for national survival and then for national victory. The regime came into it only incidentally and during the earlier stages of the war almost shamefacedly. Almost from the start the Party had not only to adapt itself as best it could to this essentially national "people's war", but also to encourage by every possible means at its disposal this national upsurge against the German invaders.

From the time of his famous broadcast of 3rd July 1941, twelve days after the German attack on Russia, right up to the end of the war, Stalin exalted the greatness of the Soviet, and particularly the *Russian* people, appealed to their national pride and national sentiment, recalled on almost every occasion the "great ancestors" —Alexander Nevsky, who routed the Teutonic Knights in 1242; Dimitry Donskoy, who routed the Tartars in 1380; Suvorov, who fought Napoleon; and Kutuzov, who routed the *Grande Armée* in 1812. Lenin was mentioned much less frequently than these military heroes of a distant pre-Revolution past. Absolute national unity was aimed at; Stalin did all he could to enlist the wholehearted cooperation of the Church, which was all the more important, since a large proportion of the rank-and-file soldiers in the army came from the countryside, where religious traditions were still strong.

In 1941–2, when many non-Russian parts of the country, including most, and then the whole, of the Ukraine had been overrun by the Germans, and Stalin had primarily only Russia proper to depend on—that Russia whose two principal cities, Moscow and Leningrad, had been saved in the nick of time— he chose the Russian people for special praise for all the bravery and loyalty they had shown. When the war was over, he made a famous speech at the Kremlin in which he praised the Russian people even more emphatically as the people of the Soviet family of nations who were most remarkable of all, and who had, moreover, shown more patience and endurance than any other, and had never lost faith in the Soviet government and the regime. This Great-Russian nationalism reached its peak in the speech Stalin delivered soon after Germany's capitulation.

This patriotic and nationalist propaganda made an enormous appeal to the ordinary citizen, even though it may not have entirely pleased certain members of the Non-Russian nationalities. Some months after the war it was somewhat toned down, though, as we have seen from some of the election speeches made in 1946, there were still some echoes of it.

One of the very big question-marks of history is whether the Stalinist regime had any intention of liberalizing itself after the war. There is no doubt that while the war was on there were some definite signs of liberalization and, more important, there were deeply cherished illusions both among civilians and soldiers that "as a reward for the bravery with which they had fought the enemy, and for the deep loyalty they had shown Stalin", the regime would become much "softer" after the war. The peasantry, including the millions of peasant lads in the army, entertained the hope that the *kolkhoz* system would be, if not abolished, at any rate radically changed, so as to give every in- dividual peasant family greater freedom and, above all, prosperity. In my talks during the war with dozens of soldiers, this problem, especially towards the end of the war, was almost invariably raised.

Secondly, there was the question of "intellectual liberalization". The seemingly cordial contacts Stalin was maintaining with Churchill and Roosevelt since 1943, the frequent compliments— after the "Second Front" storm of 1942 had subsided—he paid to "our glorious allies", and the way he had of lumping together the USSR, Britain and the United States as "the three great democratic and freedom-loving countries" had much to do with this. Russian public opinion had, needless to say, very mixed feelings about the Allies who were not pulling their weight in the common struggle and were delaying the Second Front.

The touching illusions that there would be after the war what is known today as "ideological coexistence" were never so strong as in 1943-4. Especially in 1944 the idea of "relaxing" after the war was making rapid headway. In the Party itself there were a growing number of what were called "softies". Thus, in the summer of 1944 a party member like the writer Vsevolod Vyshnevsky made a speech at VOKS, the Society for Cultural Relations with Abroad, in which he drew this glowing picture of "cultural coexistence" after the war:

> When the war is over, life will become very pleasant, A great literature will be produced as a result of our experiences. There will be much coming and going, and a lot of contacts with the West. Everybody will be allowed to read whatever he likes. There will be exchanges of students, and foreign travel for Soviet citizens will be made easy.

All kinds of other "Western" ideas were being toyed with— for instance a project for publishing "escapist" literature, including a series of hundreds of thrillers and detective stories, translated from the English, and published under the general editorship of that great lover of thrillers, Sergei Eisenstein. A lot of light and entertaining books, plays and films would also be produced. Already in 1944 there were signs of "decadence" in Moscow— amusingly "escapist" films with frivolous songs by Nikita Boguslavsky, and even concerts of highly "decadent" songs sung by Alexander Vertinsky, who had returned to Moscow after years of exile, and now made himself immensely popular, not least with army officers. The opening of "commercial shops" and "commercial restaurants", though hideously undemocratic, since in the main only the rich could shop and feast there, was still regarded as a small beginning of a "return to normal".

It did not take very long for the Party to grow alarmed by these escapist and frivolous moods. In 1944 the official party magazine, *Bolshevik*, published a violent diatribe against "frivolous" and "amusing" forms of entertainment, and against the general—and widely accepted—view that after the war art and literature would follow the "easy road". This, *Bolshevik* stressed, was in flat contradiction with the Leninist/Stalinist concept of art and literature being powerful weapons of agitation and education among the masses. Artists were warned against "aping Western models". However, this was still only a small beginning, and the journal even went out of its way to give the highest praise to composers like Prokofiev and Shostakovich, who were to become Zhdanov's principal targets in his music purge three and a half years later.

All the evidence shows that, while towards the end of the war there was a certain hardening of the regime, it did not become completely ruthless until the Cold War had begun in earnest.

Nevertheless, there were growing signs of certain tensions between the army and the Party as early as the end of 1944. Also, the entry of millions of Russian soldiers into Eastern and Central Europe, and the coming repatriation of millions of Soviet citizens who had been deported to Germany and of the Russian war prisoners who had survived German captivity, created for the Party a number of new ideological problems. Another one was the state of mind of the population in the liberated parts of the Soviet Union, including such "dubious" parts as the Western Ukraine and the three Baltic republics—Estonia, Latvia and Lithuania.

The latent conflict between the Party and the army is, of course, a highly complicated one, since obviously no clear dividing line can be traced between the two. There were, for one thing, millions of party members in the armed forces, but many, indeed most, of the military Party members had entered the Party during the war, not because they were ideologically trained communists, but because they had distinguished themselves in battle. In the grim days of 1941, there was one way the Party had of closely identifying the army with the Party—and that was to throw the Party open to as many soldiers as possible. Two famous decrees, one of August 1941, the other of December 1941 (the latter issued at the height of the Battle of Moscow), made it possible for any soldier "who had distinguished himself in battle" to join the Party with the minimum of formalities and after only a three months' candidate stage; in other words, he could become a candidate member almost automatically and a full member in a much shorter time than usual. No serious ideological training was expected from him—in fact, practically none at all; the only condition was that he should be a good soldier, and love his country and Stalin. The influx of fresh forces into the Party since the very beginning of the war went on *crescendo*. In the second half of 1941 198,000 candidate members and 145,000 full members were accepted into the Party; in 1942, 1,368,000 candidate members and 574 full members were accepted; between 1942 and 1944 the monthly average was 125,000 new members, of whom 25,000 joined the territorial (that is, civilian) party organizations, and 100,000 the military ones. The highest peak of admissions to the Party was to be reached in August 1943, when 201,000 candidate members and 110,000 full members were admitted. The date is significant: in August 1943, just after the great victory of Kursk, the patriotic pride and fervour of the soldiers had reached the highest pitch.

But this was wartime, and the human losses among Party members, especially the new ones, were extremely heavy. The influx continued, at least until the end of 1944, almost unabated, and, although at least 2 million communists had been killed in the fighting, the Party, which had nearly 4 million members at the beginning of the war, including 579,000 women, totalled in January 1946 over $5\frac{1}{2}$ million members, including a million women.

With its August and December 1941 decrees, which encouraged soldiers to enter the Party with practically no formalities or ideological training, the Party strove to create an "organic unity" between itself and the army, just as "organic unity" was sought in everything else—even between the Soviet state and the Church! The arguments used by Party propaganda for persuading soldiers to join the Party were to the effect that "during the country's hardest ordeals, every man entering the Party proved his devotion to the Country in the midst of the deadly fighting". "The Party called into its ranks all those ready to give all their strength and even their life in the defence of the Homeland."[*]

Admission was facilitated to such an extent that even young soldiers "of Comsomol age", that is up to the age of 24, were admitted *en masse*, and by the end of the war there were over a million members of the Party under 24, that is about 18 per cent of the total membership. This was a percentage increase from some 8 per cent before the war. By the end of the war, 18 per cent of the Party members (twice as many as before the war)

[*] *IVOVSS*, vol. VI, p. 366.

were women. The explanation given is that women played an exceptionally important part during the war in running industry and agriculture.

One of the peculiarities of the Party during the war—and this is an ever-recurring theme in post-Stalin studies on the Party in wartime—is that the "personality cult", which had done the Party so much harm before the war, no longer played quite the same pernicious part. Although the plenitude of power was, in theory, concentrated in the hands of the State Defence Committee, with Stalin at its head, there was in reality a singular process of Party decentralization during the war, both in an administrative and a territorial sense. Thus, not only did every member of the Politburo and indeed many other members of the Central Committee enjoy a certain autonomy in the economic sector that had been entrusted to him, but also local Party secretaries had greater scope for exercising their own personal initiative so as to obtain the best possible results in the territory under their jurisdiction. Thus, what Mr. Z. K. Brzezinski* describes as the not ineffective establishment of local Party "satrapies" during the war, post-Stalin Soviet writers prefer to describe as a "democratization" of the whole Party structure. The post-Stalin official history of the war says that "Stalin's autocratic actions were strictly limited by the independent decisions taken by members of the Central Committee who headed distinct sectors of the state, economic, political and military work, and also by the vital activity of local party and Soviet organizations" (*IVOVSS*, vol. VI, p. 335).

During the war, the Party had done everything to identify itself with the army, which was immensely popular in the country. It is, of course, significant that after Stalingrad Stalin should have assumed the rank of Marshal of the Soviet Union and, after Germany had been defeated, even the archaic Suvorov title of Generalissimo. Similarly, top party *apparatchiki* were eager to hold high military ranks: Khrushchev was a Lieutenant-General, Beria a Marshal, and so on. Nevertheless, as the war was nearing its end, there was growing anxiety among the older Party members at the thought that the Party had been diluted by millions of patriotic young soldiers with no ideological training to speak of. At the end of 1944 angry articles began to appear in

* *The Permanent Purge* (Harvard U.P.) p. 139.

the Party press, notably in *Bolshevik*, declaring that abuses had been committed by the army's Party organizations in admitting anybody to the Party for the mere asking—even many soldiers who had never fired a shot. As we shall see, these young soldier-Party-members, on being demobilized, would return home in large numbers and demand to be integrated in the local Party organizations; even though not all were incorporated the general "ideological" level of these organizations sharply declined in many cases after the war as a result of this influx.

The ideological training of these young people both during and immediately after the war was to be severely criticized in the post-Stalin *History*:

> The party achieved excellent results with its ideological work. Nevertheless, the real trouble was that, in wartime conditions, there was an excessive glorification of Stalin's articles and speeches, whereas the great theoretical heritage of Marx, Engels and Lenin, as well as the collective thought of the Party, were sorely neglected. (*IVOVSS*, vol. VI, p. 363.)

Towards the end of 1946 there came an avalanche of Central Committee resolutions criticizing the functioning of the Party organizations and severely tightening up the rules of admission to the Party. Higher party officials subjected to criticism from Moscow frequently retorted that they had been flooded by incompetent young members admitted to the Party during the war. In the years that followed, there were, if not purges, at any rate very frequent demotions of young Party members from responsible jobs that had been given them just after the war.

But to return to the end-of-the-war period. There were many ideological, psychological and economic problems with which the Party was faced. One of them arose from the entry of hundreds of thousands and even millions of Soviet troops into Eastern and Central Europe. The Party seemed at first rather worried by the effect of the better living and housing conditions the Russian soldiers would see in these foreign lands. In the autumn of 1944, *Pravda* ran a series of articles asking soldiers not to be over-impressed by the "tinsel" of Bucarest and its department stores; this was only the outward façade, and behind it were the millions of wretched, exploited and illiterate Rumanians. In fact, except perhaps for Czechoslovakia, the Russian soldiers were not vastly impressed by the countries they had gone to subdue or liberate; none of them, in 1945, was exactly an economic paradise. Particularly curious was the Russian soldiers' reaction to Germany, which had, of course, also been severely devastated by allied bombings. But what remnants there were of past wealth and opulent living usually aroused nothing but anger among the Russian soldiers: "Why should these rich parasites have had to come to invade *us*?"

Similarly, the nearly 5 million Soviet citizens (mostly Belorussians and Ukrainians) who had been deported as slave labour to Germany, and had worked there in ghastly, near-concentration-camp conditions, were not favourably impressed by Germany either, and most of them came home, often in very poor physical condition, but only too glad to have seen the last of Germany. Nevertheless, the Party—perhaps under the influence of an ever-suspicious Stalin—was anxious not to leave anything to chance. As the post-war *History of the CPSU** says:

> [It was important during the post-war years] to give greater attention to educational and ideological work. During the war, tens of millions had lived in territory temporarily occupied by the enemy. Millions had been deported to Germany by the Hitlerites. ... They had subjected all these people to assiduous propaganda. ... A large part of our army found itself on the territory of capitalist countries, and reactionaries tried in various ways to influence them.
>
> In the Western Ukraine and Western Belorussia and in the Baltic republics, bourgeois nationalist groups left behind by the Hitlerites carried on anti-Soviet propaganda among the population. ... The mass of the people scornfully rejected [this]. ... but a section of the population showed ideological instability.

It is more than doubtful whether many Russian soldiers were in any way influenced by "reactionaries" in the capitalist countries, and whether serious attempts were made to influence them. Nor were the slave-labourers much interested in propaganda coming to them from the Nazis, even if the latter seriously tried to convert them—which is doubtful. For all that, the slave-labourers, on their return to Russia, still went through some fairly strict police check.

* English translation, Moscow, 1960, pp. 628–9.

It does not seem that many of the repatriated slave-labourers were made to suffer for their forced deportation, but they were, nevertheless, often treated "with suspicion". Much more tragic is the case of the repatriated war prisoners—the $1\frac{1}{2}$ million or so who, out of a total of 5 million captured by the Germans since 1941, had survived German captivity. The fact that a soldier had at some stage surrendered to the Germans was, *ipso facto*, a black mark against him. The post-Stalin *History* has some bitter things to say on the subject:

> All these people, having survived the horrors of Nazi captivity, were eager to return home as quickly as possible, to take part in the people's creative work of reconstruction. Where this work had already been organized, these repatriates, on coming home, immediately joined in it. However, in the conditions of the Stalin personality cult, there were serious hitches. Many of those who had returned from Nazi slavery were treated as suspects, and a part of the former prisoners-of-war were declared to be traitors to their country and subjected to unlawful punishment.[*]

The *History* does not say what proportion of former war prisoners were sent to labour camps, but certainly practically all those who, in one way or another, had got into the Vlasov Army and were sent back to Russia were deported; but so also were some of the other ex-war prisoners. Many died in Russian camps; others were not released until after Stalin's death. This ill-treatment of a high proportion of the Russian soldiers who had—often in the most tragic circumstances—been captured by the Germans was one of the ugliest episodes in the last years of Stalin rule.

In Belorussia, the greatest of the partisan areas during the war, there had been the most widespread resistance to the Germans; but, even so, as early as the autumn of 1944 the Central Committee expressed some anxiety about the effects of German propaganda among the Belorussian people—propaganda in favour of private trade and against the *kolkhoz* system. All this was gradually put right, but not without much difficulty. In Belorussia, there had been only a small Party organization before the war. Now it was considerably larger, but two-thirds consisted of young ex-servicemen, with little or no Party-work experience.

[*] *IVOVSS*, vol. VI, p. 359.

The same was true in the Ukraine, where the ex-soldiers represented more than two-thirds of the post-war Party. In both countries, and especially in the Ukraine, there were serious difficulties with peasants, who, towards the end of the war, had helped themselves to large slices of the communal land of the *kolkhozes*. In September 1946 the Government and the Soviet and Ukrainian Central Committees issued a decree imposing heavy penalties on those who had broken the *kolkhoz* laws. But the trouble was not yet remedied, and the rural party organizations in both Belorussia and the Ukraine were weak, inefficient and perhaps half-hearted in imposing strict discipline on the *kolkhoz-niks*; after all, many of the young communists were peasants themselves.

Much more serious was the situation in the Western Ukraine. This part of the country, with Lwow (Lemberg) as its main city, had been part of the Austro-Hungarian Empire until 1918 and part of Poland between the two wars, and had not been incorporated into the Soviet Union until 1939. It was a hotbed of Ukrainian nationalism of a particularly virulent kind—anti-Russian, anti-Polish and, of course, anti-semitic. Here were numerous Bandera, Melnik and Bulba bands, though it is uncertain whether these three Ukrainian nationalists, who were still in Berlin almost till the end of the war, actually took part in the West Ukrainian guerrilla war of 1945–7.* But what is certain is that these Ukrainian guerrillas had a large number of German SS officers to command them. Like all guerrilla wars, it was one of great savagery and brutality. The Russians sent there some of their toughest NKVD troops. There were heavy losses on both sides, and when the Ukrainian guerrillas were finally defeated many of the soldiers, including a number of German SS-men, were shot, while thousands of others were deported to Russian labour camps. In the course of this war, the Russians also had to fight Polish *Armija Krajowa* guerrillas along the Polish/Ukrainian border—last-ditchers of the anti-Russian Polish underground army.

In the Baltic republics, the Russians met with no armed opposition, though the population received them with somewhat mixed feelings. Here also there were plenty of "bourgeois

---

* In any case, Bandera later settled in West Germany, and Melnik in Luxembourg. Later still Bandera was assassinated, probably by Soviet agents.

nationalists", though what made things easier for the Russians was that most of the Baltic bourgeoisie, as well as the officials and others who had most closely collaborated with the Germans—including the SS and the Gestapo—had fled to Germany, and now were crowding DP camps in the Western zones. Nevertheless, an unspecified number of Estonians, Latvians and Lithuanians were deported to the East in 1945-6.

In its Marxist jargon, the *History* describes the situation as follows:

> The Party had to keep an unusually close watch on the Baltic republics, where the situation had some special peculiarities. Here the exploiting classes had not yet been liquidated, and a large part of the intelligentsia had not yet shaken off its bourgeois ideology. The peasantry had not yet been taken the road of collectivization, and the *kulaks* were still actively agitating against the Soviet system. . . . Carrying out the instructions of the Central Committee, the Party organizations began actively to enlist the intellectuals into socialist construction work. It was important to give a Marxist/ Leninist training to the local communists and, above all, to their leading cadres. . . .

An important educational and propagandist campaign was organized throughout the Western Ukraine and Belorussia, as well as the Baltic republics. These were soon to be subjected to collectivization, and also to substantial industrialization. In Estonia and especially in Latvia there was a fairly large working class which was not unfavourable to the Russians. But the peasantry and what was left of the middle class were mainly hostile.

But the Russians had of course reason to hope that, since people have to live, and there was for the Baltic republics no alternative anyway to forming part of the Soviet Union, things would gradually sort themselves out. Before the Supreme Soviet in March 1946, the three countries had their speakers, the aged Professor Kirchenstein, the "father of the house", who opened the proceedings, Y. E. Kalaberzin speaking for Latvia, Y. Y. Nuut for Estonia and M. A. Gedvilas for Lithuania. They said all the right things. Without touching on the various awkward human and political problems in the Baltic countries, they dwelt on the weaknesses of the "bourgeois order" that had prevailed in these countries between the two wars, when they were dependent, for their butter, bacon and timber exports, mainly on the German and British markets, and were exploited by foreign and local capitalists, which resulted in a "general pauperization" of their people. There had been no effort to develop industry. Although as a result of the German occupation there had been a disastrous loss in livestock, the Soviet Five-Year Plan provided not only for a full restoration of the agriculture and stock-breeding of the three countries, for which the whole Soviet Union would constitute a "natural" market, but also for a development of industries and power-stations in all three, including the hitherto almost entirely rural Lithuania.

In March 1946 the situation was still far from being very tense. The Russians were, in the main, living badly—as badly, or almost as badly, as during the war. The new five-year plan meant very hard work for everybody, with more privations and more austerity; but, on the whole, the mood was fairly optimistic. Ugly things were, of course, happening. The deportation to camps of many ex-war-prisoners and of many people who had, or were supposed to have, compromised themselves during the German occupation, particularly in the Western Ukraine and the Baltic republics. In the Western Ukraine a guerrilla war was going on. Rumania and Hungary were, for the present, rather cowed and subdued. Poland, though firmly held together by the Red Army and the new state and Party machinery that had been built up, was still in a restless state and, below the surface, a little civil war was continuing in some parts of the country. On the other hand the Polish people were united on at least two issues: whether they liked the new regime or not, they were enthusiastic about the reconstruction of the country, and particularly of Warsaw, which was rapidly beginning to rise from its hideous ruins; and, secondly, every Pole, whether pro-Russian or anti-Russian, was delighted with the Oder/Neisse frontier; at least *that* could be put to the Russians' credit, and it was even a strong argument for not quarrelling with them, since the West were much less wholehearted about that frontier. Czechoslovakia, more pro-Russian than any of the other satellites, and continuing, with its broad coalition government, to be the almost perfect shop-window of East/West coexistence, was giving no trouble. Germany was in a state of prostration; the German peace treaty was still in the future, though those with Italy and the other

German satellite states were now on the point of being taken up seriously by the victorious powers. Relations on the Allied Control Council in Berlin were showing signs of strain, but nothing very serious had yet happened, and the Nuremberg Trial of the major Nazi war criminals continued to symbolize, as it were, at least an outward unity between the Soviet Union and the great Western powers.

No doubt there were difficulties. In the early months of 1946, Iran was on the face of it the worst point of East/West friction. Whatever happened about Iran—and the Russians had no very strong feelings about it—there was a widespread impression that although some of the Western statesmen were being difficult they had more or less accepted the *fait accompli* of the Oder/Neisse frontier and the extension of the Russian "sphere of influence" to Poland, East Germany, Rumania, Bulgaria, Albania, Hungary, Yugoslavia and Czechoslovakia. In these countries, oddly enough, the most extreme and aggressive-sounding communist regime was to be found in Yugoslavia; and it was not a regime in any way imposed on the country by the Russians, but one that emerged from the country's own immense resistance movement during the war.

Although the Soviet press in 1946 (and in 1947, for that matter) was full of rapturous articles about Yugoslavia, which appeared to be by far the most wholehearted and dynamic of the new socialist states, some strange whispers could be heard in Moscow immediately after the war, and even while the war was still in progress. Thus, Ralph Parker, who, through his Russian wife, had some singularly good contacts in the top Party spheres, remarked to me during Tito's visit to Moscow towards the end of the war: "There's a pretty strong impression *up there* that Stalin doesn't like Tito." It was obvious why: Tito was showing no servility to Stalin; he tended to throw his weight about, and to suggest that Yugoslavia had liberated itself by its own forces and with only a minimum of help from the Red Army, and was generally showing signs, if not of bourgeois nationalism, at least of socialist nationalism. Equally important was the fact that of all the satellite leaders Tito was the only truly striking personality in his own right. Stalin preferred stooges like Bierut, Dimitrov, or Gheorgiu-Dej (at least as he then was).

Even so, Yugoslavia had not yet become a problem by 1946,

and from the Russian point of view things seemed to be moving more or less in the right direction.

And then, in the middle of March, came Churchill's speech, delivered in the presence of an applauding Harry Truman, at Fulton, Missouri—the famous "Iron Curtain" speech. The contents of the Fulton speech can be summarized thus: An Iron Curtain had descended on Europe between Stettin in the north and Trieste in the south; and the world was thus divided into two blocs, one capitalist, the other communist. To check the expansion of the communist bloc, the English-speaking peoples must form a union and must, indeed, immediately form a military alliance. They must lead "Christian civilization" in an anti-communist crusade, and must on no account part with the secret of the atom bomb, for only thus could war be averted, since there was nothing the Russians respected as much as strength. In fact, Churchill was asking the USA to underwrite the British Empire, India and all, and the important thing was to scare the Russians. Many read into the Fulton speech a suggestion that they could be scared back to their 1939 frontier.

It so happened that I had gone, during that week, on a visit to Finland. I found the Finns pleasant and friendly. I was received in audience by President Paasikivi, that great Finnish realist, who, though originally a highly conservative businessman, considered it in Finland's interests never to quarrel with the Russians. He said he had done his utmost, in November 1939, to meet the Russians at least half-way, since he regarded their demand for a frontier rectification north-west of Leningrad "understandable and reasonable" in the tense atmosphere of the Second World War, which had already begun. He (Paasikivi) was prepared at the time to make concessions to the Russians, but he was overruled by the Finnish government. The Russians had, of course, been very foolish to set up their "Terijoki" puppet government under Kuusinen, but before long had had to recognize their mistake. It had also been a mistake on the part of the Russians not to content themselves with the original "frontier rectification" they had proposed, but also to grab Viipuri once the Winter War was over. This had created very strong feeling in the country against the Russians, and had in the end played into Hitler's hands. And if it came to a war between Russia and the West, Paasikivi said, Finland would *have* to be on the

Russian side, at least as a neutral, if not as an active belligerent. The alternative would simply be to be wiped out by the Russians. In the hospitable house of Mr. Tuomioja (later in the year Finland's representative at the Paris peace conference and, later still, her spokesman at the UN) I met the future President of Finland, Mr. Kekkonen. Kekkonen's line was very similar to Paasikivi's: Finland had to be realistic; the Finnish Government of 1939 was wrong to have dug in its heels; but although the Russian armistice terms—particularly the 300 million dollars in reparations—were pretty tough, Finland was lucky not to be occupied by Russian troops and the most important thing for her was to maintain good-neighbourly relations with Russia and to remain strictly neutral. The Finns, he said, were happy to have remained masters in their own house. Needless to say, a good deal was said about the Fulton speech; nobody present was happy about it. On the contrary, as Kekkonen said, it was going to poison the international atmosphere. This kind of thing, he remarked, would do nobody any good, and Finland was frankly worried about it, for it might provoke the Russians who until then had been "pretty reasonable" in their relations with the Finns. He did not think the Russians would occupy Finland, or that the Finnish communists would try on a *putsch*, but the Fulton speech had created the kind of unhealthy climate in which anything was possible—if things went from bad to worse.

I also remember that week attending a dinner party given by the British head of the Allied Control Commission in Helsinki, when I happened to be seated next to a Russian general. Usually, on such occasions, Russians are jovial and exuberant, but my neighbour looked angry, glum and depressed, and could speak of nothing but the Fulton speech, taxing Churchill with "monstrous ingratitude" for all that the Red Army had done to defeat the Nazis, and wondering whether his ideas were shared by the British and American governments. He particularly disliked the idea that the speech should have been delivered *pod pokrovitelstvom Trumana* (under Truman's patronage). And if, he said, Churchill wanted to rearm Hitler's army and "liberate" Poland and set up atom-bomb bases there, he had better think again. Absolutely nobody in the Soviet Union wanted war. If Churchill wanted it, he could have it, but he'd be sorry—atom bombs or no atom bombs. The violence of this Russian general's

9

reaction struck me as extremely significant. I had never heard anything like it since the war, even after the shock of Hiroshima and all the unpleasantness that had accompanied the diplomatic negotiations, especially in October 1945 in London. But this still tended to be regarded as routine horse-trading. The Fulton speech was a real challenge—something quite different.

Our British host seemed embarrassed, and pointed out to the general that Churchill had spoken as a private individual. "Yes, with the blessing of Truman," the general muttered. He left immediately the dinner was over, coldly remarking that he had some urgent work to do.

I returned to Moscow a few days later and found people badly rattled by the talk about "the next war" to which the Fulton speech had given rise. *Pravda* and other papers had published angry editorials. Then, on 13th March, *Pravda* published an interview with Stalin—the first of a long series of interviews he was to give during the next few years. He was obviously quite aware of the anxiety the Fulton speech had caused in Russia, and of the controversy it had aroused in the world press. He declared Churchill's speech to be "a dangerous act", and that it was causing "great damage to the cause of peace and security". "In effect, Mr. Churchill has taken up the position of a war incendiary," he said, adding pointedly: "And Mr. Churchill is not alone—he has friends not only in England, but also in the United States."

After referring to Churchill's "English-speaking world" as something very similar to Hitler's concept of the German *Herrenvolk*, Stalin then bluntly declared that the speech was nothing less than "a call to war against the USSR". This, said Stalin, was of course incompatible with the existing Anglo-Soviet alliance, so, to pull wool over people's eyes, Churchill was now proposing to extend the alliance by fifty years. But he could not have it both ways; if he advocated war against Russia, then his fifty-year alliance could be nothing but a scrap of paper.

Without mentioning Churchill's "Iron Curtain" phrase, Stalin dwelt instead on his charge that the Soviet Union had "expansionist tendencies". It was not true that Berlin and Vienna were under Russian "domination"; in both cities there were allied control councils, on which the Russians had only one-quarter of the votes. As for Churchill's lamentations over the fate of the other neighbouring countries, Stalin said that the

Germans had invaded Russia through Poland, Hungary, Rumania, Bulgaria and Finland. They had been able to do so because in all these countries there were governments hostile to the Soviet Union. As a result of all this, Russia had lost 7 million of her people*—incomparably more than either Britain or America had lost in the Second World War. Russia could not forget these sacrifices, even though some people abroad may have been trying to do so. There was nothing surprising in the Russians' desire to see in these countries "governments with a loyal attitude to the Soviet Union". But Churchill was trying to sow discord between Russia and Poland, as he had already done in the past. Stalin then asserted—without mentioning Western reservations—that Poland's western frontier had been approached at Potsdam by all the Big Three. He also denied—and this was characteristic of 1946—that there were "totalitarian police states" in the East European countries—Poland, Rumania, Yugoslavia, Bulgaria were governed by "a bloc of several parties, ranging from four to six, and the more or less loyal opposition parties can take part in the government".

Obviously, Stalin was not on very solid ground here, but to keep in with the West he had been anxious since the war to meet the Western powers at least part of the way. He had not—not yet—tried to impose all-communist governments on the Eastern countries, and at that time he valued the East/West coexistence as symbolized by Czechoslovakia and Finland. Bulgaria, Rumania and Hungary, as ex-fascist powers, had to be dealt with rather more "vigilantly", but even here pro-forma appearances were still being kept up, as they were in the very special case of Poland. If Yugoslavia was the most extremely communist country of the lot it was, in fact, against Stalin's wishes.

As we shall later see, Tito was later blamed by the Russians for being too "provocative" to the West. But at the beginning of 1946 Stalin still sounded very outraged by Churchill's charges about the "totalitarianism" imposed by Russia on all the satellite countries. No doubt, he said, Mr. Churchill would much prefer Poland to be run by Anders and Sosnkowski, Yugoslavia by Mihailovic and Pavelić, Austria and Hungary by some Hapsburg

* That was the then official figure; that of 20 million was not officially admitted until the late 1950s.

king. To Mr. Churchill it was these backyard fascists who represented "genuine democracy". After paying a tribute to the increasingly influential communists of Western Europe, where they had boldly resisted the fascists and the German invaders, Stalin recalled that Churchill had already tried, with the help of fourteen countries, to invade the Soviet Union after the First World War. He was now planning another crusade against "Eastern Europe". It was doubtful whether he and his friends would succeed in this, because there were millions of "ordinary" people who were determined to defend peace. But even if they did succeed in bringing about another war, they would be beaten, just as they were twenty-six years ago—that is, at the time of the intervention.

In reality, of course, as every Russian understood, the intervention of the "fourteen countries" during the Russian civil war was a feeble and half-hearted affair, and not comparable to the threat of an atomic attack on Russia now. What is significant is that already in 1946 Stalin strongly reckoned on the anti-war feelings of "millions of ordinary people" both in Eastern and Western Europe. This anti-war sentiment, especially in countries like France, was to prove of the greatest help to Russia when the Cold War reached its most dangerous stage in 1947–8.

If we have dealt here at some length with Churchill's "Iron Curtain" Fulton speech (delivered, let it be repeated, in the presence of President Truman) it is because this was unquestionably a major landmark in the rapid deterioration of East/West relations. Psychologically, it was also very important in causing very genuine alarm in Russia.

Not that East/West relations had yet reached breaking-point. The year 1946 was marked by interminable diplomatic negotiations in connection with the satellite peace treaties, by two stormy UN Assembly sessions and by a major crisis over Iran— an unpleasant episode from which the Russians emerged badly and which, therefore, was not given much publicity in the country, at least not during its later stages.

SEVEN

The Troublesome Year of 1946

As early as 1943 the question arose whether the United States had any clear and coherent post-war policy in relation to Russia. For fighting the Germans, the Russians were of the greatest value to both Britain and the United States. It was they who, in Churchill's 1944 phrase, were "tearing the guts out of the German army". Until the end of 1942 the Russians were deeply discouraged by the very parsimonious help they were getting from the Western allies; hence the fury of the Russian press campaign against Britain at the time of Stalingrad in the autumn of 1942. But, disappointed though the Russians were by the North Africa landing in November that year—for it was not the Second Front they had hoped for—Stalin still gave it the highest praise in the press statement he made a few days later. This in itself suggested that his suspicions that the Western powers might do nothing important to help Russia had been largely allayed. In 1943 Lend-Lease shipments were stepped up in a spectacular way and were of considerable help to Russia, though to say, as Harry Truman was to say in 1945, that without them Russia "would have been ignominiously defeated" is, of course, more than questionable. By the time Lend-Lease began to arrive in large quantities, the Russians had already won the Battle of Stalingrad. The heavy armaments shipped under Lend-Lease did not amount to more than 10 or 15 per cent of what the Russians were themselves producing. And when one considers that the Second World War cost the United States 400 billion dollars, of which only 11 billion dollars' worth went to Russia as Lend-Lease, one realizes that, by American standards of expenditure, this help to Russia was not an overwhelmingly large item.

The Russians were, however, interested in Lend-Lease not only for what it represented in immediate benefits, but also for what it might signify as a precedent for the future. The defeat of Germany had become a foregone conclusion by the beginning, and especially the middle, of 1943, but the Russians knew perfectly well that they would be faced after the war with a gigantic problem of reconstruction. Would they have to depend entirely on their own resources, or would they obtain financial help from abroad— that is, from the United States, the only major country that had grown enormously rich during the war? The Russians knew, of course, that many American business leaders were worried by the thought of a post-war depression in the United States, and thought that, to survive and prosper, the American economic system needed a constantly expanding foreign market. Men like Donald M. Nelson and Eric Johnson were convinced, as Eric Johnson himself said after a lengthy visit to the Soviet Union, that Stalin's primary concern was to "rebuild Russia". During the Foreign Ministers' Conference in Moscow in October 1943 Stalin discussed the matter with Cordell Hull, and the question was again raised by the Russians at Teheran a month later. But neither at Teheran nor at Yalta, despite all the outwardly friendly atmosphere of these meetings, were the Russian overtures concerning a large American post-war loan for reconstruction seriously taken up. Already before Yalta, Stalin had made a request for an American loan of $6 billion; but Harriman, the US Ambassador, reacted highly unfavourably to the idea. His response to the Nelson/Johnson school of thought was that although he agreed that "the question of long-term credits represents the key point in any negotiations with the Soviet Government", he also shared the State Department's view "that the lever provided by Russian weakness and devastation could and should be used to insure a predominant role for America in all decisions about the post-war world".

Admiral Standley, who had been US Ambassador in Moscow in 1943, took a more charitable, and indeed, as it turned out, more realistic, view in a speech he delivered in November 1944:

> Some kind of tension with the Russians will be unavoidable after the war, because they will be the only major victorious power on the continent of Europe. But the tensions can be kept within bounds. . . . We must assume two important premises. First, that

Russia's security is vital to her, and that she cannot turn to industrialization and development of her raw material resources unless
she has that security. After victory, security is her next consideration. And unless we help establish it, the Russians will have to proceed on their own to provide it.*

At Yalta, a few months later, the Russians raised the question
of a big post-war loan, but met with only evasive answers, and
Roosevelt never took up the matter seriously. The Russians were
up against two things: the traditional American open-door
policy and the American desire (idealistic in some cases, and
extremely hardheaded in others) to act as the protector of "democracy" in all the countries of Eastern Europe. This, especially
in the case of Poland, clashed with Russia's primary security
considerations. By the time Roosevelt died, the hostility to
granting the Russians a large post-war loan became even more
explicit. "I am opposed to [it]," Harriman said in May 1945. "I
would apportion that credit out piecemeal, demanding in return
concessions in the political field."

Having obtained no response to his overtures concerning a
large post-war loan during the Yalta talks, Stalin saw that for
the purposes of reconstruction the only alternative was to obtain
large reparations from Germany. At Potsdam, as we know, the
Russians fought hard for a whole week to get these reparations on
an all-German basis, and then, in the face of American opposition,
had to content themselves with obtaining them mainly from
the Soviet Zone and, as far as possible, from the rest of Eastern
Europe. By the beginning of 1946 even what little they were
still getting from Western Germany was stopped on the initiative
of General Lucius Clay.

It will remain a matter of speculation what American policy
towards Russia would have been had Roosevelt not died in
April 1945, but there is good reason to suppose that there might
well have been fruitful negotiations and compromises with the
United States, and that the virulence of the Cold War might have
been avoided. Roosevelt's personal prestige in Russia was very
high. To the Russians it was clear from the start that Truman
was "the enemy", though at least until 1947 they still hoped to
arrive at some kind of *modus vivendi* with the United States. But
Truman was having none of it. The Russians knew, of course, that

* Cf. W. A. Williams, *The Tragedy of American Diplomacy*, p. 221.

a day or two after the Germans had invaded Russia Truman had openly declared that "if we see the Germans winning, we should help the Russians, and if we see the Russians winning, we should help the Germans, so that as many Russians and Germans as possible are killed". When Molotov went to Washington a few days after Roosevelt's death, he was shocked by the new President's sharp hostility towards him. The American "ideology", that there was nothing to choose between Hitler and Stalin, was already rapidly crystallizing. Some influential leaders, like John Foster Dulles, who had courted Hitler until almost the outbreak of war and was, even during the war, advocating a "Christian peace" with Germany, thought the Russian communists fundamentally much more evil than the Nazis.

The flaw in America's self-righteous (and often even sincere) indignation at the idea that the Russians were establishing "communist dictatorships" in Eastern Europe could, of course, be demonstrated by her readiness to tolerate and, on occasion, even to encourage right-wing dictatorships in the Western Hemisphere and elsewhere, for instance in that Greece which Stalin had "abandoned" to Churchill under their spheres-of-influence deal in October 1944. It was this strange agreement which, in the case of countries other than Greece, American policy after the war was determined, if possible, to cancel.

The explanation put forward that settlement under the Potsdam reparations which gave Russia a completely free hand in Eastern Germany and Eastern Europe (not only economically but in effect also politically) was only a temporary expedient seems highly plausible. It went contrary to the traditional American open-door policy, but now that the United States had the atom bomb and could speak to the Russians from positions of strength, this policy, though ostensibly abandoned for a time, could come into its own again with renewed vigour. American policymakers knew perfectly well that determination to create a security perimeter in Eastern Europe was not the same as trying to conquer the whole capitalist world, but, in propaganda, the distinction became singularly blurred. Much more stress was laid on Russia's "revolutionary mission" than on the fact that in 1945 she was in a desperately weak economic position and required, as everybody knew, long years of reconstruction.

Neither Byrnes nor Truman would even consider a reconstruction loan to Russia. Not that it was necessarily bad for American business—on the contrary, it might have been highly rewarding—but it ran contrary to the "Stalin, the new Hitler" cliché. America was overwhelmingly strong economically and, since the atom bomb, also militarily, and Truman was an enthusiastic advocate of American supremacy in the world. If the appeasement of Hitler in the 1930s was now recognized to have been a mistake, this mistake would not be repeated—even though in fact the alleged "expansionism" of Russia had nothing in common with the Nazi bid at world domination. Truman's faith in the power of the United States was such that he thought, especially after Hiroshima, that he could force the Russians to accept all American proposals without much risk of war.

As early as 23rd April 1945 he told the Cabinet that he felt that "our agreements with Russia have so far been a one-way street. And if the Russians did not want to join us at San Francisco, they could go to hell." At Potsdam, even though he did play to Stalin Paderewski's Minuet, his favourite party piece, he left the Russians in no doubt that they were up against a very tough opponent. And when the conference was over, and the atom bomb had been duly dropped on Hiroshima, he declared that Eastern Europe "was not to be the sphere of influence of any one power". As Byrnes later openly admitted, the future of Eastern Europe had much to do with the decision to drop the bomb—or rather bombs—on Japan. The Potsdam reparations agreement was a temporary expedient; it was intended to avoid any indirect American financing of Soviet recovery. The bomb was expected, in the end, to re-establish the open door in Eastern Europe and to set up pro-Western governments there.

Such was the situation at the end of the war. The Russians were well aware of what was happening, though, while determined at any cost to cling to Russia's security zone in Eastern Europe, Stalin tried at first not to allow relations to become unduly envenomed. Even as late as the end of 1946 Stalin still said, in reply to a question by Hugh Bailey, that he *was* interested in an American loan. And that was long after the Russians had already decided on their first post-war five-year plan. Not that he could have had any serious illusions by then that such a loan was likely to be granted, since none had materialized even while Roosevelt was alive.

The Russians—and Stalin in particular—were very upset over the way they had been treated at the time of the Japanese capitulation. They were given no occupation zone, and were not even allowed to send a token force to disarm the Japanese in Hokkaida. Soon after the Japanese capitulation, Truman even proposed that some of the Kurile islands be given to the USA as an air base.

We saw in an earlier chapter how badly the first East/West negotiations after the war went when the Foreign Ministers met in London in September 1945. Things were rather better at the Big Three meeting in Moscow in December, when an important agreement was reached about preparing the satellite peace treaties, and the Russians made minor concessions about Rumania and Bulgaria. But even then Truman (at least according to himself) was furious with Byrnes for not having been tough enough with the Russians. He was particularly furious (again according to his own story) because Byrnes had obtained nothing but vague promises from the Russians about withdrawing their troops from Iran.

Iran and Turkey hold an important place in the great Soviet/American conflicts of 1946–7. It is no exaggeration to say that if Stalin was not fundamentally interested in a world revolution, and never seriously thought of even extending Soviet influence to Western Europe, in many respects he followed the Tsarist tradition. Nothing is more curious than the pride with which he announced that in recovering southern Sakhalin, Port Arthur and other territories and interests lost to the Japanese in the Russo/Japanese war of 1904–5, he had "erased that blot of shame" from which "men of his generation" had suffered for forty years. In other words, Stalin had recovered what the inept Nicholas II had lost. The Tsarist governments of the past had also always been interested in Persia (Iran) and even more so in the Turkish Straits, that narrow bottleneck of the Black Sea which presented such obvious military disadvantages to Russia and the other Black Sea powers. During the First World War, the Russians had been "promised" Constantinople and the Black Sea Straits, and even as late as 1917 Foreign Minister Paul Milyukov of the first Provisional Government regarded this promise as a particularly valid reason for continuing the war on the side of France and Britain. Stalin was not proposing to "take over Constantinople", but he proposed to the Turkish government a joint Soviet/Turkish control of the Straits. With the Cold War growing in intensity, Stalin was, moreover, increasingly conscious of the vulnerability of Russia's southern frontier, with Turkey and Iran becoming potential springboards for an Anglo/American attack. As we have seen, he told a startled Byrnes in December 1945 that the Persian border was dangerously close to Baku, and he told Ambassador Bedell Smith a few months later, in April 1945, "I have been told by Beria and others that saboteurs (from Iran) or even a man with a box of matches could do us untold harm."*

Stalin had, in fact, a triple interest in Iran—ideological, insofar as there was a strong pro-Soviet party, the Tudeh, in the country, and a pro-Soviet autonomist movement in Iranian Azerbaijan; economic, since Russia was greatly interested, especially in 1945, with her own sources of oil badly depleted or wrecked during the war, in obtaining additional sources of oil in Iran; and, finally, strategic, for the reasons already mentioned.

In the early years of the century, Persia had been the scene of sharp rivalries between Tsarist Russia and Great Britain, especially since in 1901 the powerful Anglo/Persian Oil Company had established itself there. However, in view of the growing German threat, Britain and Russia reached a compromise by 1907, whereby the country was divided into two spheres of influence. After the Revolution, the new Soviet government repudiated its "imperialist" treaty of 1907 but at the end of the civil war also recovered Transcaucasia, including Russian Azerbaijan, with Baku as its capital, which (like the neighbouring Georgia) had proclaimed their "independence"—with the help of British occupation troops. About the same time Persia tried to shake off British domination; the Majlis refused to ratify the Anglo/Persian treaty signed shortly before, and a nationalist leader, Reza Khan, seized power and became Shah. Like Kemal Pasha in Turkey, Reza Khan signed a Friendship Treaty with Soviet Russia, under which the latter renounced all claims on Persia, but reserved the right to intervene militarily if she felt that Persian territory was being used against her by any hostile power. It was on the basis of this 1921 Treaty that Iran (at that time infested by German agents) was jointly occupied by British and Soviet forces in 1941.

* Bedell Smith, *Mission to Moscow*, 1949, p. 12.

Having been unable to dislodge the powerful Anglo/Iranian Oil Company, Reza had grown increasingly anti-British, which would explain his flirtation with Nazi Germany. Thus he constituted a danger to both Britain and Russia, and in September 1941 he was dethroned and succeeded by his son. Later in the war, as we know, Persia was to become an extremely important route for British and American supplies to Russia. In 1942 and again in 1943, Britain and the Soviet Union promised to evacuate their troops within six months after the end of the war, and a similar undertaking was given by the United States. It was during the later stages of the war that various complications arose. The Russians, though suffering from great shortages at home, spared no effort to make a good impression in Iran during the war. Thus, they set up a free hospital in Teheran for the diseased Persian multitudes,* gave great encouragement to the left-wing Tudeh Party, and, more important still, helped to organize strong autonomist movements among the Azerbaijani and Kurds of northern Iran.

The British and American oil companies were not caught napping. In September 1944 Anglo-Iranian and Standard Oil made an agreement for joint oil prospection in large parts of Iran. The Russians then proposed to the Iranian government the establishment of a joint Soviet/Iranian company for oil prospection and development in northern Iran, in the area roughly corresponding to that occupied by Soviet troops, and practically all the way from the Turkish to the Afghan border of Iran—a zone of a depth of 100 to 200 miles—besides the whole province of Iranian Azerbaijan in the north-west, with Tabriz as its capital. Not without some British pressure, the Iranian parliament rejected the proposal in December 1944. Stalin was highly displeased with this. At Yalta he complained of British intrigues, and at Potsdam he agreed to no more than an early evacuation of Russian troops from Teheran, leaving the rest of the problem for the Foreign Ministers to settle. In September 1945 the latter agreed, in view of persistent Persian demands, that all Russian, British and American troops would leave the country by 2nd

---

* This turned out to be a tragi-comic experiment; the demand for free hospital treatment was so immense that, to limit the number of patients, first a moderate fee and then a much higher fee had to be charged, with the result that the very poor were soon debarred from using the hospital.

March 1946. But here new complications arose. While the British and American oil companies were firmly hanging on to southern Iran, the Russians were anxious not to be dislodged from the north of the country. In October 1945 a "democratic autonomist" party was established in Iranian Azerbaijan which entered into an alliance with the local Tudeh party, and a month later Pishewari, the head of the "democratic autonomists", proclaimed at Tabriz an autonomous republic. Pishewari had been head of the ephemeral Caspian Soviet Republic back in 1920. Though regarded by the Western powers as merely a Russian stooge, Pishewari, as well as the local Tudeh leaders, nevertheless represented a progressive anti-feudalist and nationalist movement. A similar autonomist movement developed simultaneously among the Kurds of north-west Iran, under the leadership of Mullah Barzani, the veteran Kurdish freedom fighter.

The 1,200 Iranian soldiers sent by the Teheran government to "restore order" in Iranian Azerbaijan were turned back by Russian troops. It was at this stage that the pro-British Iranian premier Hakimi asked to be allowed to come to Moscow to report to the Foreign Ministers' Conference meeting there in December. The Russians rejected his request, confined themselves, as we have seen, to vague promises about evacuating their troops from Persia, while Stalin pointedly stressed to Byrnes the dangers that saboteurs from Persia represented to the Baku oilfields. Hakimi resigned on 26th January 1946, but before doing so submitted the Soviet/Iranian dispute to the Security Council. It was here that the first violent clash occurred between Bevin and Vyshinsky. It is characteristically described as follows by Mr. John Foster Dulles:

> The plea of Iran was strongly supported by the United Kingdom, with which it had close political and economic [!] relations. . . . As a countermove, the Soviet Union made a request that British troops be withdrawn from Greece. . . .
>
> Mr. Bevin and Mr. Vyshinsky went for each other, hammer and tongs. It was a frightening beginning for the Security Council. The outcome was that the Soviet troops were withdrawn from Iran on 21st May 1946, and that British troops remained in Greece.

After a discourse on how wrong it was for the Russians to stay in Iran and how right it was for the British to stay in Greece, both of which had been demonstrated to "world opinion" by the Security Council, Dulles concluded that "moral power prevailed".*

But many things actually happened before the Russians pulled out of Iran. The Security Council had recommended bilateral Soviet/Iranian talks, and the new Iranian premier, Qawam-es-Saltaneh, a wealthy old man who was reputed to be more pro-Russian than his pro-British predecessor, set out for Moscow. He stayed there from 19th February to 6th March, saw Stalin several times and was treated with the greatest consideration. The joint communiqué, published on 8th March, spoke of the "atmosphere of friendship" in which the talks had been conducted, and promised to develop still friendlier relations in future, "with the appointment of a new Soviet Ambassador to Iran", which rather suggested that the previous one had been too high-handed with the Persians.

This is where serious trouble started. Qawam had obviously not given the Russians full satisfaction, least of all about Azerbaijan. There were some ominous Soviet troop movements in Iran. The Iranian government again appealed to the Security Council, declaring the presence of Soviet troops on Iranian soil to be a "threat to peace". The US government was determined to have Iran put before the Security Council, even if the Iranian government did not persist. On 27th March Gromyko declared that he would not take part in any further discussions on Iran on the Security Council. Was this merely a face-saver? The Russians realized that both Britain and the USA were ready to pick a major quarrel with them over Iran. On the previous day, 26th March, the Russians had published a very strange communiqué which, after enumerating the places from which Soviet troops were now being evacuated, concluded on the disturbing note that "the complete evacuation of Soviet troops will be completed within five or six weeks *if nothing unforeseen happens*". The American reaction to this may be well imagined, and Gromyko was fully conscious of the seriousness of the situation.

On 4th April a joint communiqué was signed in Teheran by the new Soviet Ambassador, I. Sadchikov, and Prime Minister Qawam. This stated that Soviet troops would be withdrawn from Iran within six weeks of 24th March; that, in not more than

* John Foster Dulles, *War or Peace*, London, 1950, p. 43.

seven months from the same date, the appended Agreement on the creation of a Soviet/Iranian Oil Company would be submitted to the ratification of the Mejlis. The last paragraph of the communiqué was very strangely worded:

Insofar as Azerbaijan is an internal Iranian matter, the Iranian government and the population of Azerbaijan will find peaceful means of carrying out the reform in accordance with the existing laws and in a spirit of benevolence towards the Azerbaijani population.

This looked no more than an appeal by the Russians to treat the Azerbaijani gently. If the Russians warned the Iranian government against destroying the autonomous republic, they did so verbally, but not in writing. To the communiqué were appended the letters of Qawam describing in detail the oil agreement to be drawn up and submitted to the Majles for ratification, and the Soviet Ambassador's answer approving of the terms. Under the agreement Iran would hold 49 per cent of the shares and the Soviet Union 51 per cent during the first twenty-five years, and 50 per cent each during the second twenty-five years. Iran would supply the labour for oil prospection and development in northern Iran; Russia would look after the various expenses, supply the equipment and pay the salaries and wages. Qawam undertook not to grant any concessions to the area in question "to foreign companies or Iranian companies in which foreigners participated or which had the use of foreign capital"— obviously meaning British or American capital. At the end of the fifty years the Iranian government could buy the Russian shares of the company.

It must well have crossed the Russians' mind that, encouraged by the British and Americans, Qawam was double-crossing them. The obvious thing for the Russians to have done was to get the oil deal ratified before pulling out their troops; by reversing this order they were exposing themselves to the worst disappointments. And, as regards Azerbaijan, they had obtained from Teheran nothing but the vaguest assurances—if that.

On the face of it, Qawam was playing a highly tricky game. Very soon after the Russians had withdrawn their troops, in May, there were riots among the workers of the Anglo-Iranian. Bevin attributed these to the Tudeh Party and to the Russians, and he sent troops to Iraq, in the neighbourhood of the Abadan refineries. Qawam thereupon brought members of the Tudeh into his cabinet, proclaimed martial law in Teheran and had several pro-British, as well as pro-Russian, politicians arrested.* There followed a rebellion of southern tribes, apparently instigated by the British, and Qawam was forced to get rid of his Tudeh ministers. The Russians became increasingly alarmed, and demanded a quick ratification of the Soviet/Iranian oil agreement. Qawam retorted that this could not be done as long as the Azerbaijan authorities were making the fair election of a new parliament impossible. Britain and the USA were meanwhile adopting an increasingly threatening tone. And when Qawam, in the autumn of 1946, decided to "reconquer" Azerbaijan, the Russian troops on the Soviet/Iranian frontier did not budge, despite the stern warnings given by Moscow to Teheran.† The autonomous regime of Azerbaijan collapsed in a few days. There followed a ruthless massacre of the "autonomists". All their leaders, except a few who had succeeded in escaping to the Soviet Union, were publicly hanged. Soon afterwards there was produced in Russia a documentary film dwelling on all the great democratic and social reforms that had been carried out in autonomous Azerbaijan (health services, anti-illiteracy campaign, land reform, etc.), ending with some gruesome shots of the hanged leaders, and with the promise that freedom and democracy would yet triumph in Azerbaijan.

Needless to say, when the new Majles met in July 1947, it rejected the Soviet/Iranian oil agreement. Qawam, though not enthusiastic about the agreement, resigned, and was replaced by the pro-British Hakimi at the head of the government.

The ephemeral Kurdish "People's Republic" at Mahabad, on the borders of Iraq, was also ruthlessly stamped out by the troops of the Iranian government, and their leader, Mullah Barzani, at the head of 1,000 men, fought his way to the Soviet Union through the Kurd-inhabited parts of Iraq and Turkey.‡

Thus, the Soviet Union's attempt after the war to expand politically and economically into Iran ended in complete failure. She was faced not only with the sharp opposition of British and

* André Fontaine, *History of the Cold War.*
† ibid.
‡ Fontaine, op. cit.

American oil companies in Iran, notoriously skilful at protecting their interests by every economic and politic means, but also by the British and American governments, who, regardless of the "principles" of their own oil companies in Iran, came forward, in the case of that country, as the defenders of the rights of small nations. We know with what virtuosity, a few years later—in 1953—the CIA got rid of Prime Minister Mossadegh, who, adopting a strongly nationalist policy, had had the temerity to nationalize the Anglo-Iranian, and had even threatened to blow up the Abadan refineries if he met with any opposition.

It is quite clear that, in 1945-6, the Russians were anxious to gain a foothold in Iran, (a) in order to prevent at least the northern part of that country from becoming, either economically or strategically, an Anglo/American sphere of influence; and (b) in order to secure an additional source of oil. An "autonomous" Azerbaijan was to act as a kind of buffer state between the Soviet Union and Iran proper, and Russia had, in the Azerbaijan autonomists and the Tudeh Party in Persia itself, some more or less genuine supporters. Iran was, in fact, the scene of some hard-headed "colonial" competition between the Russians and the Anglo/Americans, and if in May 1946 the Russians withdrew their troops without having first secured any of the economic advantages thay had sought, it was because a war with an atom-bomb-holding America was not worth risking for Iran. And even if the risk of the "atom bomb on Moscow" may have been negligible, it existed all the same. But there was a perhaps more important reason why the Russians should have surrendered Iran—for it was nothing short of surrender. That was that the satellite peace treaties were in the process of being debated, with negotiations for a German peace settlement to follow, and it seemed a very wrong moment for exacerbating East/West relations to breaking point. Iran could, at least temporarily, be put in cold storage. The fiasco was humiliating to Russia, but, though no doubt feeling it keenly, Stalin continued throughout 1946 to make highly conciliatory statements for the benefit of Western public opinion, if not the Western governments—for he had no illusions about the real dispositions of men like Bevin and Truman.

The fact that the USA and Britain forced the Russians out of Iran by means of the UN Security Council produced some bitter and even plaintive comments in the Soviet press. On 6th May 1946—that is, before the final evacuation of the Soviet troops—*Pravda* recalled that up to February Hakimi had stood at the head of the Iranian government, and he was the man who, in 1919, had attempted to capture Baku. There was good reason why Soviet troops should stay in Iran; there was now a strong democratic movement in the country, particularly in Iranian Azerbaijan; hence all the screaming about "Russian interference" in Iranian internal affairs. But when Bevin proposed to send a three-power committee to Iran, was not *he* interfering? Even Hakimi had been forced to say no. But then Britain and the USA took the matter before the UN, and, regardless of the good relations that had developed between Moscow and Qawam-es-Saltaneh, they had tried to force the issue. The trouble, *Pravda* said, was that the Russian agreement to evacuate Iran was now being represented in the American press as a great success for the United Nations. In reality, the whole sorry business showed that Britain and the USA were trying all the time to turn the UN into the obedient tool of their policy. Yet these two countries had bases in dozens of countries—in Greece, Indonesia, Egypt, Iraq, Syria, Lebanon, Transjordan, Palestine, the Azores, Iceland, etc.; and now they got terribly impatient and self-righteous about Soviet troops being in northern Iran, in the immediate proximity of Baku.

However, less than three weeks later, on 24th May, the Soviet press published a short statement saying the evacuation of Soviet troops from Iran had been completed.

The possibility of obtaining a large oil concession in northern Iran was, in reality, of secondary importance to the Russians, though they were anxious to keep the Western oil companies out. Soviet oil output at the end of the war had fallen very low. Maikop, in the northern Caucasus, had been "scorched" and temporarily put out of action by the Russians before the Germans captured it, while Grozny and Baku had both suffered from German air-raids. But the "second Baku" in the Urals and Bashkiria had already given very promising results during the war, and under the new five-year plan other oil areas—on the Volga, in Uzbekistan, Kazakhstan, Sakhalin, etc.—were to be developed, so that by 1950 the overall oil output was to reach $35\frac{1}{2}$ million tons, a 10 per cent increase over the 1940 output.

This was only a small beginning, but the Soviet Union had almost unlimited oil resources. By 1960 she was, indeed, producing 148 million tons, and by 1965 243 million tons. Fundamentally, her interest in Iranian oil was strategic and political, not economic.

Concerning the Black Sea Straits, there had already been some heated exchanges at Potsdam between Stalin, Churchill and Truman. Despite pressures from all sides Turkey had succeeded in staying out of the Second World War; but once the war was nearing its end and East/West relations were showing signs of deteriorating, Stalin sought to reach a bilateral agreement with Turkey on the joint control of the Straits. After the Russian denunciation, in March 1945, of the Soviet/Turkish Pact of 1925, the Turkish government, alarmed by what might come next, proposed to the Soviet Union a Soviet/Turkish alliance along the lines of the Anglo/Soviet alliance of 1942. After the German capitulation, the Russians replied that they agreed in principle to such an alliance, but the Montreux Convention of 1936, giving in the Russian view excessive freedom to other powers to use the straits, should be revised. Moreover, the Russians asked for a permanent military base on the Dardanelles and the return to Russia of the two provinces of Kars and Ardahan, which the Turks had annexed in 1921. One, as the Russians put it, "rightfully belonged" to Soviet Armenia, the other to Soviet Georgia. The Turks, encouraged by Britain and the USA, found this too high a price to pay for the alliance they had proposed.

At Potsdam Churchill challenged the Russian idea that the Black Sea Straits concerned only them and the Turks and was not impressed by Molotov's reply that such bilateral treaties had been signed in 1805 and 1833. On the following day, 23rd July, Stalin declared that the Montreux Convention was inimical to Russia, since it enabled Turkey not only to block the straits if she was at war but also to do so if she thought there was a threat of war. Thus, "a small state supported by Britain held a great state (Russia) by the throat, and gave it no outlet."* Truman, for his part, tried to drown the problem in a much more general proposal for free international waterways "everywhere":

> I was offering as a solution to the Straits problem the suggestion that the Kiel Canal in Denmark [sic], the Rhine-Danube waterways ... the Black Sea Straits, the Suez Canal and the Panama

* Truman, op. cit., vol. I, p. 304.

Canal be made free waterways for the free passage of freight and passengers of all countries. (ibid., p. 304.)

Churchill agreed that under the revised Montreux Convention Russia should have freedom of navigation in the straits by merchant and warships alike in peace and war, but supported Truman's proposal that "the great powers and the powers interested" should guarantee the new arrangement; this would be much better than a Russian base in close proximity to Constantinople. The proposed "internationalization" of the Danube pleased the Russians no more than that of the Black Sea Straits, and they began to hit back.

> Molotov asked whether the Suez Canal was under the same international control as was proposed for the Black Sea Straits.
> Churchill observed that the question had not been raised.
> Molotov retorted: "I'm raising it." If it was such a good rule, why not apply it to Suez?
> Churchill explained that the British had an arrangement with which they were satisfied and under which they had operated for some seventy years without complaints.
> Molotov charged that there had been a lot of complaints: "You should ask Egypt," he said.

The Russians were also worried by Truman's statement that an international guarantee of the freedom of the Straits meant that any nation had free ingress *for any purpose whatever*. However, on 2nd November 1945, the US government, in their open-door proposal, specified that no non-riparian states could send warships into the Black Sea without the approval of the riparian states—or the United Nations. The Russians did not answer this note, and nothing more happened about Turkey until August 1946 (by which time the Russians had already suffered their serious fiasco in Iran), when they presented a note to Turkey in which they charged the Turks with having violated the Montreux Convention during the war when, they alleged, German and Italian warships had been allowed to enter the Black Sea through the straits; the note alleged that several such violations had taken place between 1941 and 1944. Thus, the note argued, the Montreux Convention had proved ineffective in protecting the Soviet Union against the penetration of enemy ships into the Black Sea. Since the Soviet Union, Britain and the USA had agreed at Potsdam that the Montreux Convention called for revision, the Soviet government, for its own part, was therefore proposing that the straits be free at all time to all merchant ships; that they be always open to the warships of the Black Sea powers; that the passage of warships of other powers could be allowed only in exceptional cases, to be specified; that the regime of the straits should come under the sole competence of Turkey and the other Black Sea powers; and, finally, that

> Turkey and the Soviet Union, being the powers most closely interested and most capable of safeguarding the freedom of merchant shipping and the security of the Straits, should jointly organize the defence of the straits so as to prevent other states from using them with aims hostile to the Black Sea powers.*

Truman sharply reacted to this note (a copy of which the Russians had sent him). Already in April the battleship *Missouri* had made its appearance at Istanbul. Now Truman sent the giant aircraft carrier the *Franklin Roosevelt* into the Eastern Mediterranean, along with four cruisers and several other warships. Secretary of the Navy James Forrestal and Under-Secretary of State Dean Acheson were in a particularly fire-eating mood, and Truman was only too happy to oblige.

The mutual distrust between the Soviet Union and the United States had reached a dangerous pass. But there was this important difference: if the Russian people and the Russian leaders were genuinely alarmed by the Cold War fervour of the US government (hence their feeble attempt to bludgeon Turkey into giving them a base on the straits), American opinion was perhaps genuinely alarmed by Russian "expansionism". But the US government must have known perfectly well that Russia was not in a fit state, still less in the mood, to start a war against the United States, then enjoying the monopoly of the atom bomb. Nevertheless, the US government pretended, or perhaps even succeeded in convincing itself, that Russia was terribly dangerous. Harry Truman wrote:

> If Russian troops entered Turkey with the ostensible purposes of enforcing joint control of the Straits, it would only be a short time before these troops would be used for the control of all of Turkey. ... To allow Russia to set up bases in the Dardanelles would result

* *Vneshnyaya Politika Sovetskogo Soyuza, 1946*, Moscow, 1947, pp. 168–9.

... in Greece and the whole of the Near and Middle East falling under Soviet control. .... The Turkish government, encouraged by the American attitude, rejected the Soviet demands.[*]

What the Russians were, in fact, scared of was the appearance in the Black Sea of, say, an American aircraft carrier with atom-bomb-carrying planes. On 24th September the Soviet government sent Turkey a further note, answering Turkey's rejection of the August proposals for the "joint defence" of the Straits, and warning her against "taking any military measures in conjunction with certain non-Black-Sea powers" which would be "in direct contradiction to the security interests of the Black Sea powers". However, the note ended in a conciliatory tone, proposing a thorough revision of the Montreux Convention and urging detailed preliminary discussions on the future regime of the straits. The note denied that Russia had any designs on the "sovereignty of Turkey", and protested against the "quite unfounded suspicions totally incompatible with the dignity of the Soviet Union". No reference was made in this note to Kars and Ardahan.[†]

Strictly speaking, the Russians had some very good reasons for asking for a thorough revision of the Montreux Convention, though in their 1946 negotiations they seem to have been nervous about admitting just *why* they wanted it revised. For one of its most essential provisions was this: non-Black Sea countries (such as the USA) could enter the Black Sea through the Turkish Straits *provided they did not carry guns with a calibre of more than eight inches.* But between the time the Montreux Convention was signed in 1936 and 1946 the whole nature of armaments had changed. In signing the Convention in 1936, nobody was thinking in terms of missiles, and by 1946 gun calibre was an outdated and, in fact, an inapplicable measure of a warship's power. What relation, for instance, was there between the maximum calibre of a gun, as allowed by Montreux, and the power of an American aircraft carrier, supplied with atom bombs, the appearance of which in the Black Sea was one of Stalin's worst fears in 1946?

Foe a long time nothing more happened, but the Turks kept a large army mobilized. At the end of 1946 the US Ambassador

[*] Truman, op. cit., vol. II, pp. 119–20.
[†] *Vneshnyaya Politika . . . 1946*, pp. 193–202.

in Ankara reported that Turkey would not be able "to maintain indefinitely a defensive posture against the Soviet Union. The burden is too great for the nation's economy", while in January 1947 Bedell Smith reported from Moscow that he had no doubt that the Kremlin would resume its efforts to encroach upon Turkish sovereignty and that if Britain and the USA did not help, "Turkey had no hope of surviving".* One cannot help wondering whether these are just the kind of reports from Ankara and Moscow that Truman *wanted* to get. In the winter of 1946-7, as a result of the 1946 drought, Russia was in a desperate economic plight, and nothing appealed to her less than the prospect of a war over Turkey. But Truman needed as many arguments as possible for launching, a few months later, what came to be known as the "Truman Doctrine"—which, as it happened, was first applied to Turkey and Greece. We shall have occasion to deal with Greece later. Here it is sufficient to say that it was quite clear to me, from conversations with disgruntled Russian officials and diplomats, that long before the announcement of the "Truman Doctrine" they had become reconciled to the fact that their nibbling at Iran and Turkey had not come off. There had been "no harm" in trying, but neither Iranian Azerbaijan and an oil concession in northern Persia nor a military base in the Black Sea Straits was worth fighting for. When I spent several weeks in the Caucasus—including Batum right on the Turkish border— in the summer of 1946, nobody mentioned a war with Turkey as even the remotest possibility. There is no doubt, however, that the untimely proposals about a base on the Dardanelles— and the Russian hope of receiving any satisfaction had always been practically nil—played into the hands of the get-tough-with-Russia people in the USA, beginning with Truman himself. It is all the more startling that this get-tough line should have reasserted itself with particular vigour in the winter of 1946-7, *after* the Russians had in fact admitted defeat both in Iran and in Turkey, and just as the signing, on 10th February 1947, of the Paris peace treaties with the satellites—Italy, Rumania, Hungary, Bulgaria and Finland—suggested that a great stride had been made towards peace in Europe.

But the satellite peace treaties were one thing, and Truman's get-tough-with-Russia policy was another. In the case of the

* Truman, op. cit., vol. II, p. 120.

satellite states there was no major clash of interests between the USSR and USA, and although it might have been more logical to start with the major problem of the German peace treaty (and the Austrian peace treaty), it was clear to both parties that any discussion of Germany would last a very long time, and might well lead to a complete deadlock. It was therefore wiser to clear the satellites out of the way first. After all, the satellites had all, at some stage of the war—though often very late—dissociated themselves from Germany, and so deserved, as it were, to get back to peace conditions as quickly as possible.

So we were to see, in 1946, two curious parallel developments: on the one hand, an intensification of the Cold War and violent clashes between the USA and the USSR at the UN Assembly and the Security Council, as well as in their diplomatic (or rather, undiplomatic) exchanges over Iran and Turkey; and, on the other hand, the fairly mild and reasonable negotiations over the satellite peace treaties. Not that these went very smoothly. All the same, by the end of the year, full agreement was reached, and the peace treaties were signed on 10th February 1947. These relatively businesslike discussions sharply contrasted with the verbal violence at the UN—with Vyshinsky and Gromyko as the principal Soviet spokesmen—on questions like Turkey, Iran, Greece, Indonesia, Spain, the Middle East, etc. Equally unsatisfactory were the negotiations on the Atomic Energy Control Council, while East/West relations became increasingly strained on the Allied Control Council and the Coordinating Committee in Germany, the Allied Council in Austria, the Joint Soviet/American Commissions in Korea, etc. Relations in Germany became particularly poisonous, especially after General Lucius Clay had decided, in the course of the years, to stop reparations deliveries to Russia from Western Germany. But, paradoxically, a certain semblance of "allied unity" could still be seen here and there, notably at the Nuremberg Trial, which was not concluded until October 1946. True, the Russians were dissatisfied with the relatively light sentences passed on some of the accused and especially with the acquittal of Schacht and Papen, those typical representatives of West German Big Business whom certain American business interests—if not the US government itself—regarded once again as their natural friends and allies.

The drafting of the five satellite peace treaties was, in the main, the work of the Foreign Ministers and of their deputies, and the work began as early as January 1946. The Paris Peace Conference of the 21st, which did not meet until the end of July (though it had originally been scheduled to meet about 1st May), was empowered to make recommendations only, and the final text of the treaties was then to be agreed upon by the Big Four. There was a significant change in the Russian attitude towards France. If, in London in September 1945, the Foreign Ministers' Conference broke down because of Molotov's objections to the presence of the French (and Chinese) Foreign Ministers, the Russians decided before long that it would be to their advantage to have M. Bidault, the French Foreign Minister, taking part in the satellite peace treaty negotiations. So in April the Big Three agreed that Bidault would take part in the talks, though without a vote except in the case of the negotiations on the Italian treaty. Belatedly, Molotov had realized that Bidault tried to hold a sort of "intermediate" position between East and West, and often suggested compromises which, if not really acceptable to Russia, nevertheless provided her with face-savers. This was particularly true in the case of Venezia Giulia and Trieste, over which one of the sharpest clashes arose between the USA and the Russians: the Russians wanted everything to be given to Yugoslavia, including even Monfalcone, west of Trieste, while the Americans wanted to give Yugoslavia only a small part of Istria. The compromise finally reached, which provided for the establishment of a Free Territory of Trieste, was based on a French proposal. The Yugoslavs were, of course, furious, and particularly Mr. Kardelj, who had come to argue with the four ministers and had drawn on the map of the contested area a line which was even more generous to Yugoslavia than the Russian line was. Throughout, relations had been particularly poisonous between the Americans and the Yugoslavs. Looking back on it, it is odd to think that, to the Americans, the Yugoslavs were "even worse" than the Russians. Shortly before, two American aircraft had been shot down over Yugoslavia, and, not without some pressure from the Russians, the Yugoslavs finally—and most reluctantly —agreed to pay compensation to the families of the airmen who had been killed.

There were several Foreign Ministers' sessions before the Paris

Peace Conference finally met on 29th July. After the May session held in Paris, Molotov explained why this preparatory work was taking so long. It was essential, he said, to avoid a situation in which, as a result of serious disagreement between Russia and the three others, two distinct draft peace treaties— particularly with Italy—were submitted to the peace conference— a Western draft and a Soviet draft. Such an absurd situation would seriously undermine international peace. The American proposal that the peace conference of the 21st be called on a fixed date whether the Foreign Minister had come to an agreement or not was totally unsound. Molotov was glad to say that there were no serious disagreements concerning Bulgaria, Rumania, Hungary and Finland. But Italy presented serious difficulties; the very modest reparations (300 million dollars) that Russia was asking for herself, Yugoslavia, Albania and Greece were meeting with objections from the USA and Britain, even though the latter were charging Italy huge sums in occupation costs. As regards the Italian colonies, Russia (no doubt in view of all the screaming from Mr. Bevin) had renounced her claim on Tripolitania (to be governed either by her independently, or jointly with Italy). Now there was disagreement between the French, who wanted the former Italian colonies placed under Italian trusteeship, and the British, who, with "the usual American complicity", were proposing to turn Tripolitania and Cyrenaica into a so-called independent "Kingdom of Libya", which would to all intents and purposes be nothing but a British crown colony. The British also wanted, in effect, to take over Italian Somaliland and Eritrea.

So no agreement on these questions had been reached, any more than on Venezia Giulia and Trieste. In all these cases the USA and Britain were conducting not, as they claimed, a "peace offensive", but quite blatantly an offensive against the Soviet Union. In the same statement Molotov also dealt with the "great new difficulties Mr. Byrnes was now creating over Germany, and with the vast network of air and naval bases the United States, with British complicity, were setting up all over the world. Of what "defensive" value to the security of the USA were, for instance, air bases in Iceland? Certain American congressmen were openly preaching preventive war against the Soviet Union, and even on the official level of the Foreign Ministers' meetings there was a marked desire to push the Soviet

Union out of her well-earned place of honour in international affairs and to undermine her international prestige".*

However, some serious progress was made at the next session of the Foreign Ministers which opened in Paris on 15th June. Agreement was reached on most points, even on the creation of a Free Territory of Trieste, and invitations were sent on 2nd July to the seventeen other powers, though not without much haggling over the wording of the invitations. The Peace Conference of the 21st met at the Luxembourg Palace on 29th July.† M. Bidault, who had done so much to iron out differences at the last Foreign Ministers' session, was acting as host to the peace conference.

The peace conference did not go well from the Russian point of view. The long arguments on whether resolutions were to be voted by a simple or a two-thirds majority were largely irrelevant, because Britain and the USA "commanded" in fact more than two-thirds of the votes. Whenever there was any point of disagreement between the Russians and the USA, the vote at the conference went against the Russians. As Molotov rather bitterly remarked on 14th October, on the eve of the closing session, the Foreign Ministers had, before the conference, coordinated their views on most questions, but a few questions on which no agreement had been reached were submitted to the conference.

The results of the Conference cannot be regarded as satisfactory. In most cases the articles of the treaties on which the Foreign Ministers had reached no agreement before the Conference have remained uncoordinated. Yet it should have been remembered that *international conferences meet not in order to demonstrate disagreements, but in order to find ways and means of finding solutions acceptable to all. . . . Our experience has shown that the dominating group, with Britain and the USA at its head, did not aim at this, and, having a majority, was content merely to push through its own point of view.*

The Soviet delegation, Molotov said, being in a minority, still tried to appeal to the delegates' sense of objectivity, and to

* *Vneshnyaya Politika . . . 1947*, pp. 124–39.

† Apart from the Big Four the following were invited: Australia, Belgium, Brazil, Canada, China, Ethiopa, Greece, the Netherlands, India, Norway, New Zealand, Poland, Belorussia, South Africa, Czechoslovakia, Yugoslavia and the Ukraine.

promote the cause of international cooperation. But even its weightiest arguments had very little effect. The use of persuasion was unpopular if it concerned anything with which the American or British delegation disagreed. Molotov also cited cases when a British delegate who had voted together with the Soviet Union at the Foreign Ministers' meeting abstained during the plenary meeting together with eleven others, as a result of which a question like the Greek/Bulgarian frontier now remained among the questions on which no formal agreement had been reached by the conference. Consequently, said Molotov,

> the Council of Foreign Ministers will have to assume very great responsibility regarding the final decisions, on which the signing of the peace treaties will ultimately depend.

The Paris Peace Conference went on for over two months, and there can be no question of summarizing here even briefly the almost innumerable speeches made at it by Molotov and Vyshinsky, not to mention the Ukrainian and Belorussian spokesmen. They concerned procedure, the question of inviting Albania to the conference table (the argument centred round the question whether, as Tsaldaris, the Greek representative, asserted, the Albanians had "collaborated" with the Axis powers or whether, on the contrary, as the Russians asserted, the Albanians had a magnificent Resistance record) Italian reparations and de Gasperi's "unjustified claims" on Venezia Guilia and the greater part of Trieste. Even though Trieste was economically essential for Yugoslavia, and some of the territory claimed by the Italians was inhabited by Slovenes and Croats (here in Paris Molotov no longer tried to argue that most of the population of Trieste, though Italian, would prefer their city to be given to Yugoslavia, as he had previously done); and various other aspects of the five peace treaties. Frequently Molotov complained of the tendency on the part of certain delegates—for instance the Australian one—to forget, barely a year after the end of the war, "the role the Soviet Union had played in the routing of our common enemy, and the enormous sacrifices she had made". Although the reparations the Soviet Union was demanding from the satellites were only a small fraction of the damage they had caused her, there were still some who thought her "grasping". Some Western papers were deliberately inventing stories to stir up anti-Russian feeling: for instance the story that Russia was demanding from Italy not 300 million dollars in reparations (to be shared with Yugoslavia, Greece and Albania) but 3 billion dollars. In reality, the 100 million dollars the Soviet Union was claiming for herself represented only 4 to 5 per cent of the damage caused by the Italian Fascist troops in the Soviet Union.★ Molotov also attacked the Western "demogogy" which consisted in giving all-out support to Finland, and to ignore completely the sinister part Finland had played, for instance, in the tragic blockade of Leningrad.

It is impossible here to summarize all that the Russians said about Rumania, Hungary and other countries. Of much more lasting and fundamental interest was Molotov's speech on 10th October on what might be called the balance of power in the world. In his attack on the "equal opportunities" principle supported by the USA, he said a double standard was being used. Much had been said by the Americans and their supporters of the "equal opportunities" all should enjoy on an "international waterway" like the Danube. Would the same "equal opportunities" apply to the Suez and Panama canals? Obviously not, Molotov argued, and he saw in the interest shown by Britain and America in the Danube an attempt at economic penetration of the riparian countries. All this, Molotov said, was linked with "dollar diplomacy".

> The national income of the United States (and anyone in Paris can buy the *World Almanac, 1946* giving these figures) has increased from 96 billion dollars in 1941 to 160 billion dollars in 1944. . . . We are all grateful for the part of the USA has played in the last war . . . and we are very happy that our ally should not have suffered what other countries have suffered—I mean my own country and also the riparian states of the Danube basin. But the fact remains that the USA is virtually the only country that has grown rich in the last war.

And here, significantly, Molotov already protested in advance against American penetration into Eastern Europe and, in effect, to what later became the Marshall Plan. How, he said, could there be "equal opportunities" between America and countries like, say, Rumania or Yugoslavia that had been fearfully weakened

★ *Vneshnyaya politika . . . 1946*, p. 307.

by the war? If American capital were, in the name of "equal opportunities", given a free hand, what would be left of Yugoslavia's or Rumania's national industries? American capital would simply buy up all the more interesting industries in these countries and become sole master there. Radio and cinemas would all be in American hands. And he quoted Senator Thomas as saying that "the dollar is an instrument of our foreign policy", and that "our dollar is of the greatest help to the State Department". The same Senator had explained, Molotov said, how important it was for the United States to have granted the last big loan to Britain and how essential that large loans should be granted to France, China, etc. The Senator was also in favour of lending money to Poland "on certain conditions", and, altogether, believed in the "unlimited possibilities" of this dollar diplomacy. Clearly, Molotov said, this "dollar diplomacy" aimed at cashing in on the enfeebled economic state of numerous countries in the world during this immediate post-war period. But no self-respecting democratic country, realizing what all this meant, could work up any enthusiasm for such expansionist plans.*

Here, nearly a year before the Marshall Plan, was Molotov's warning against "enslavement by the dollar". Particularly sharp was the warning he gave to the East European countries against being tempted by American offers of "conditional" economic help. At the same time, one could not but read into Molotov's analysis a singular Russian confession of weakness in the face of a rich and expansionist America.

How weak Russia felt at the end of 1946 may be seen from the fact that during the Foreign Ministers' session that met in New York in November, that is, after the Paris Peace Conference, Molotov accepted practically all the "recommendations" that this Peace Conference had adopted on a majority vote. He even accepted the Western proposal concerning the powers of the Governor of Trieste, much to the annoyance of the Yugoslavs, who were still agitating for the plain annexation of Trieste, even though the Russians had long before accepted the principle of the Free Territory. At the New York session Molotov also agreed to calling an international Danubian Conference. Whether he had already firmly made up his mind that the Western powers were to be excluded from the Danube Commission controlling

* *Vneshnyaya politika . . . 1947*, pp. 373-6.

the navigation on the Danube—as they were to be at the Danubian Conference in Belgrade in 1948—is not quite certain, but it is highly probable in the light of his speech of 10th October in Paris. At any rate, by 1948 the Cold War had become even more intense than it was in 1946.*

Not that relations with the United States were easy in 1946 in any sphere. We shall deal later with the central problem of Germany, and with the angry Russian reactions to General Clay's decision to suspend reparations deliveries to Russia from Western Germany, to Byrnes's Stuttgart speech (which, for slightly different reasons, greatly upset the French), and to the American twenty-five-year plan for the demilitarization of Germany, in which the Russians saw an attempt to drive their troops out of Eastern Germany and Eastern Europe generally. The Russians had plainly suffered defeat in their attempts to nibble at Iran and Turkey, and her leaders—if not the general public—were acutely conscious of it. And even in smaller matters Truman and his assistants did not spare the Russians a variety of pinpricks. On 22nd January TASS quoted Under-Secretary Dean Acheson as saying at a press conference that under the Yalta Agreement the Soviet Union had been allowed to occupy the Kurile Islands, but this did not mean that they were permanently handed over to the Soviet Union, "though I may be wrong there". TASS angrily said that Acheson was, indeed, entirely "wrong", and quoted in support the secret Yalta Communqué.

Several other documents also show that, in the Russian view, Mr. Barnes, the American representative in Bulgaria, was egging on the "reactionary opposition" to make it as difficult as possible to carry into effect the decisions reached at the December 1945 Foreign Ministers' Conference concerning the constitution of a government "acceptable" to the USA; that the Russians regarded Mr. Bliss Lane, the US Ambassador in Warsaw (and, for that matter, the British Ambassador Mr. Cavendish Bentinck), as the unofficial leaders of the Polish anti-government forces in the country; that the US government was blaming the Soviet Union for the economic difficulties of Hungary; and so on. Another pinprick was Truman's request to Stalin that the Soviet Union should contribute grain to UNRRA; Stalin's reply to Truman's proposal, coming in the middle of May, when Russia's grain

* Cf. André Fontaine, op. cit.

reserves were at their lowest, was most untimely, all the more so as the Soviet Union had only recently sent 400,000 tons of wheat and 100,000 of barley to France, and 100,000 tons each to Czechoslovakia and Finland.

With no prospect of a loan from the United States, where, on the contrary, a violent campaign had been launched in favour of hampering Russia's and East Europe's economic reconstruction, the Russians noted the fury with which the news had been received in America that a five-year one-billion-krone credit agreement had been reached in October 1946 between the Soviet Union and Sweden. Under this agreement Sweden was to supply a great variety of electrical machinery, mining, building, timber-cutting, laboratory and other equipment, locomotives, trawlers, complete electric power-stations, and much else. Many American commentators were now saying that Sweden had "betrayed the Free World".

In 1946 Stalin still seemed convinced that a Third World War could be avoided, and in the public statements he made he tried to minimize the great difficulties that had been besetting the Soviet Union since the end of the war. In September, after Russia's fiascos in Iran and Turkey, after Churchill's Fulton speech, after all the angry East/West exchanges at the UN, on the UN Security Council and at the Paris Peace Conference, I sent Stalin a questionnaire, in which I asked some pointed questions. His answer was the famous "no war" statement, with its assertion that atom bombs could not be decisive in a new war and that the American monopoly of the bomb would not last long, anyway. Here are the principal questions and answers:

Q. Do you believe in the danger of a "new war" concerning which there is so much irresponsible talk throughout the world? What steps should be taken to avert it if such a danger exists?
A. I do not believe in the danger of a "new war". Those who are clamouring about it are chiefly military-political intelligence agents and their few supporters among the civilian officials. They want to (a) scare certain naïve politicians ... with the spectre of war ..., (b) to obstruct for a certain time the reduction of military budgets, (c) to put a brake on demobilization, which would produce a rapid growth of unemployment. .... One should strictly differentiate between the hue and cry about a "new war" and the real danger of a "new war" which does not exist at present.

Q. Do you believe that Great Britain and the United States are consciously creating a "capitalist encirclement" of the Soviet Union?

A. I do not think that [their] ruling circles could create a "capitalist encirclement" of the Soviet Union, even if they so desired, which, however, I cannot assert.

Here, of course, was a clear hint that in setting up bases all round the globe and in trying to turn Iran and Turkey into their sphere of influence they were, indeed, trying to "encircle" the Soviet Union. In his next answer, to a question on Germany, Stalin maintained that there could be no question of Russia's trying to use Germany as an instrument of Russian ambitions against Western Europe. What mattered, Stalin wrote, was that the Anglo/Soviet and Anglo/French mutual assistance treaties and the Potsdam agreements—to which the USA was a party— should be strictly adhered to; what was most important was the demilitarization and democratization of Germany.

In reply to my next question, Stalin said that he absolutely believed in the possibility of friendly and lasting cooperation between the Soviet Union and the Western democracies in spite of the existence of ideological differences. He also believed in that "friendly competition" which Henry Wallace had mentioned in a recent speech.

Stalin said that he was "really certain" of the possibility of friendly relations with Great Britain, and he advocated the strengthening of "political, trade and cultural ties" between the two countries. Two further important questions and answers followed:

Q. Do you believe that virtual monopoly by the USA of the atomic bomb constitutes one of the main threats to peace?

A. I do not believe the atomic bomb to be as serious a force as certain politicians are inclined to regard it. Atomic bombs are intended to intimidate the weak-nerved, but they cannot decide the outcome of war, since such bombs are by no means sufficient for this purpose. Certainly monopolist possession of the secret of the atomic bomb does create a threat, but at least two remedies exist against it: (a) Monopolist possession of the atomic bomb cannot last long and (b) the use of the atomic bomb will be prohibited.

Q. Do you believe that, with the further progress of the Soviet

Union towards communism, the possibilities of peaceful cooperation with the outside world will not decrease? Is "communism in
one country" possible?

A. I do not doubt that the possibilities of peaceful cooperation,
far from decreasing, may even grow. "Communism in one country"
is perfectly possible, especially in a country like the Soviet Union.*

What, one may ask, was Stalin's purpose in replying to these
(and) later questions? It seems to me that the answer is fairly
obvious. In the tense and anxious atmosphere of 1946 this "interview" (published on the front page of every Soviet newspaper)
was calculated to reassure Soviet public opinion; secondly, it was
addressed to foreign public opinion over the heads of the Trumans, Bevins and the other get-tough-with-Russia enthusiasts,
not to mention the plain preventive-war advocates. Maybe the
atom bomb was not, as Stalin said, "decisive" as a weapon in
the "next" war, though it is only too clear that it had proved a
weapon of some pretty formidable diplomatic pressure, for
instance in the quarrels over Iran and Turkey. The Russians were
fully conscious of it, and if Stalin now said that the American
monopoly of the bomb would not last long, it was because he
knew that that was precisely what the Russians wanted to hear.
Besides, he had some genuinely good reasons for saying so. There
also seems no doubt that he was quite sincere in wanting "friendly
competition" and "friendly and *lasting*" cooperation with the
outside world. The effect was not wasted on wide sections of
public opinion, and although there was a certain amount of
snarling in a few papers, the statement had to be answered in a

* The sending of questions to Stalin had become a routine matter among
correspondents, especially since September 1942, when he answered Henry
Cassidy's letter about the Second Front. Some correspondents sent such
questions almost every week and many never received an answer. But very
occasionally he did answer when he thought it useful to do so. In 1943 he
answered a question about the future of Poland, and another about the dissolution of the Comintern. In 1946 he briefly answered a question about the Soviet
Union's attitude to the UN. Mine (apart from his statement to *Pravda* on
Churchill's Fulton speech) was the first of the long "interviews" he gave after
the war; when I wrote him on 17th September at the suggestion of the *Sunday
Times* he happened to be on holiday in Sochi, and his answer was cabled or
telephoned to Moscow. The text was given me by Mr. Dekanozov, the
Deputy Foreign Minister—who was later to be liquidated as one of "Beria's
accomplices" soon after Stalin's death.

more or less friendly spirit by responsible leaders. Bevin said
that he agreed with Stalin that a "further war" was "not likely
at present", adding, however, that "he did not know anybody
working for war". Eden declared that the statement was "of
outstanding importance", adding:

> At the least it offers a new opportunity, which we all welcome,
> for allied diplomacy. I am confident that this opportunity will be
> seized. . . . I believe that with perseverance and good will the
> difficulties can be overcome.*

But the effect of the interview did not last, least of all in the
USA, and Stalin felt it necessary to give another one, barely a
month later, this time to Mr. Hugh Bailey, the President of UP.
What marked this statement was a more pessimistic and at times
more petulant note. Bailey's first question and Stalin's answer
set the tone of the interview:

> Q. Do you agree with Byrnes's statement about the growing
> tension between the USSR and the USA?
> A. No.

And then:

> Q. Do you consider that the present negotiations will lead to peace
> treaties which will establish cordial relations among the former
> allies . . . ?
> A. I hope so.
> Q. What is your opinion of Yugoslavia's refusal to sign the peace
> treaty with Italy?
> A. Yugoslavia has good reason to be dissatisfied.

Stalin said that the greatest threat to peace came from the war
incendiaries, in the first place Churchill and his followers in
Britain and the USA. In reply to the question whether Stalin
thought the UN provided reliable guarantees for safeguarding
the integrity of small nations, he merely replied: "It is still hard
to say."

On Germany, he declared that what was necessary was both
the political and the economic unity of Germany and that he
favoured central German administrations under Allied control.
Thus the Foreign Ministers could prepare a German peace treaty.
He was not sure, however, whether Germany as a whole was

* *The Times*, 26th September 1946.

developing along peaceful and democratic lines. However, he saw no objection to the industrial level of Germany being raised. On the other hand, he was not at all sure that the democratization of Germany was being carried out in accordance with the Potsdam decisions.

Regarding the UN, he considered that the complaints made about Russia's excessive use of the veto were unjustified.

He said that there were now sixty Soviet divisions in Eastern Europe and Germany (not two hundred, as Churchill had claimed) and that these divisions—most of them incomplete—would soon be reduced to forty under the latest demobilization measures taken.

Among the other significant questions and answers were those concerning foreign aid to Russian reconstruction. The billion-krone credit agreement with Sweden, Stalin said, was an important contribution to international economic cooperation. And when asked *whether the Soviet Union was still interested in receiving a loan from the USA*, he replied: "*Yes, she is interested.*"

More friendly and conciliatory in tone was the interview he gave Elliot Roosevelt, the son of the late President, whom he received personally on 21st December 1946. The interview was published in *Look* magazine.

Stalin stressed that he considered peaceful coexistence with the United States, without the two countries interfering in each other's internal affairs, not only "perfectly possible", but also highly reasonable. If the difference in their regimes did not prevent them from cooperating during the war, the same should be true in peace-time. He entirely agreed with Elliot Roosevelt that extensive trade between the USA and the USSR would be a valuable contribution to peace, as would be a great development of international trade generally.

Asked about his views on popular trends in the United States, as revealed by the November election, Stalin said that he thought the present government of the USA was "squandering the moral and political capital accumulated by the late President". He did not think there had been any deterioration in the relations between the American and Russian people, but he did think inter-government relations were not good. There had been many misunderstandings, but he did not worry unduly about fears of a further deterioration in Soviet/American relations. It would not come to war, for, even if any government of a great power wanted war, no people in the world wanted it. The people of the world were tired of war. Anyway, what intelligible war aims could there be? The threat of a new war was thus unrealistic.

Sounding increasingly conciliatory, Stalin said he favoured cultural and scientific exchanges between the two countries and long-term American/Soviet cooperation in helping the peoples of the Far East. He was also entirely in favour of American loans and credits to the Soviet Union, which as Elliot Roosevelt had suggested, would be mutually beneficial.

It is significant that in the last four months of 1946 Stalin should have taken the trouble of making three long statements which were like so many appeals to the United States and Britain to adopt a policy of "peaceful coexistence" and economic collaboration, and that he should have dismissed as unfounded and "unrealistic" the talk of a Third World War.

But Truman and the State Department looked upon all this as so much soft soap, and in 1947 they persisted in their idea that Russia was out to conquer Europe, if not the whole world. There came, in March 1947, the Truman Doctrine, followed by the disastrous Foreign Ministers' Conference in Moscow, and then the Marshall Plan, itself closely followed by Kennan's "containment" doctrine. In April 1947 George Kennan published in *Foreign Affairs* an article containing this famous doctrine. The Russians were furious about it though, in reality, it was milder than the anti-Russian fury that was being whipped up in the United States with direct encouragement from Harry Truman and his advisers.

EIGHT

Inside Russia, 1946

No one who lived in Russia in 1946 and 1947 could take the threat of Russian "aggression" seriously. Not only did the country have ahead of it a vast reconstruction programme which it had to carry out without much outside help; but living conditions were getting not better, but worse than they had been during the last stages of the war and in 1945. The 1946 harvest, as was already becoming apparent by the middle of the summer, was going to prove a major disaster. By 4th September 1946, as we shall see, food consumption was drastically tightened up.

In the summer of 1946 I had the opportunity of visiting the two UNRRA missions in the Soviet Union—that in Belorussia and, later, that in the Ukraine. UNRRA (United Nations Relief and Rehabilitation Administration), it will be remembered, had been set up on Roosevelt's initiative as early as 1943, and its purpose was to provide important emergency relief to a large number of countries that had suffered most from the war. Standing on their dignity and perhaps also for fear of "spies", the Soviet government had declined UNRRA help for the parts of the RSFSR (that is Russia proper) that had been devastated by the war, but it accepted it with fairly good grace in the case of Belorussia and the Ukraine. I went by train to Minsk to see the Belorussian UNRRA mission there. A startling sight at Belorussian railway stations were the youngsters who were selling for the modest sum of ten roubles cans of UNRRA grapefruit juice. It was a little black market in the kind of UNRRA food which to them was unfamiliar and "useless". On the other hand, the population greatly valued and appreciated the lard, butter, meat and flour that UNRRA had brought to Belorussia, and none of that ever got into the black market.

The large city of Minsk was still a scene of fearful devastation. Two-thirds or three-quarters of the city had been destroyed. The UNRRA mission, headed by a New York businessman, had its headquarters in a country house outside the city, to which the small party of correspondents who had come were invited to lunch by the UNRRA mission. There were also a number of Belorussian officials, the mission's "contact men", present. One comic episode struck me as significant. The head of the mission began by proposing a toast to Generalissimo Stalin—which, in those days, was the correct thing to do at any such functions. And then the head of the Belorussian group got up to reply: "I want to drink the health," he said, "of the greatest statesman of our time, the late President Roosevelt." The Americans looked slightly startled, but made no comment. Later I talked to the head of the mission and asked him what he thought of this toast.

"Pretty crazy," he said, "but perhaps it's hardly to be wondered at. These guys know that Fiorello LaGuardia (the head of UNRRA) is doing his damnedest to help us in every way. But he's meeting with a good deal of obstruction back home. And they also know that the President is not at all keen on keeping UNRRA going—least of all in the Soviet Union. LaGuardia is having a lot of difficulty in getting us supplied with tractors and agricultural machinery. The Belorussians appreciate the food that's added to their miserable rations, and we are doing our best to feed the kids, most of whom lived through the war here and are in a very poor physical state. . . . But we've got to pack up in 1947, though this country will be short of food for years yet. . . ." And he added that the harvest prospects were not good. This was still at the beginning of summer, and the weather might yet improve, but it had not rained for a very long time.

A couple of weeks later I went to Kiev to see the UNRRA mission there. A large part of Kiev was also in ruins, including the Kreshchatik, its famous main street. The man in charge here was Mr. Marshall McDuffie, a New York lawyer. $180 million, $112 million of it in food, may seem a lot of money, but the Ukraine, with a population of nearly 40 million, was an enormous country. The UNRRA food allocation amounted in fact to less than $3 per head of population, though naturally a higher proportion was provided for the urban than the rural population. Marshall McDuffie had established good personal relations with the Ukrainian officials, and had even met Khrushchev, then head of the Ukrainian government, on a few occasions. In a book he later wrote, McDuffie described one of his meetings with Khrushchev:

> At the end of the war he reportedly had the task of punishing collaborators in each recaptured town in the Ukraine. . . . When I arrived at the head of the UNRRA mission just after the war, Khrushchev was the undisputed head of that breadbasket region. . . . In 1946 I had the impression that [he] wasn't used to meeting foreigners; he stared at me quizzically and with great curiosity, like a man studying a bug on a rock. . . . He had a great sense of humour. Pointing at Starchenko, a man of 5 ft. 4 ins. and weighing 250 or 300 lbs., Khrushchev said: "I must have been crazy to send *him* to the United States to ask for more food for the Ukraine!"

When McDuffie met Khrushchev in Moscow many years later, the head of the Soviet government said: "I appreciate what UNRRA did for us in the Ukraine. I remember particularly the help of Fiorella LaGuardia in obtaining special articles for us against certain obstacles." Khrushchev then attacked—he had a long memory—a member of the UNRRA mission who had written a best-selling and poisonously anti-Soviet book in 1946,[*] after spending two months in the Ukraine: "He wanted to make money and he got his money. Anyway, he probably worked for intelligence purposes more than for UNRRA."

Distrust of UNRRA (in this particular case justified) was, of course, fairly typical of the Russian authorities, but McDuffie certainly established the best possible relations with them in Kiev, and had on the whole the good LaGuardia approach, rather than the bad Truman one, to the whole venture. From the Ukrainian officials to whom I talked I received the impression that they liked McDuffie, who indeed later wrote:

> We held out the hand of charity and good faith. To have assumed automatically that our allies were no longer our friends would have been contrary to our character and Christian civilization.[†]

His was not unlike LaGuardia's own attitude at a time when

[*] McDuffie, *The Red Carpet*, New York, 1955, p. 198.
[†] McDuffie, op. cit., p. 4.

UNRRA was about to be wound up, to be superseded by the much more "political" Marshall Aid. In 1946 he proposed that UNRRA's work be continued by an internationally administered food fund. Having met with no response, he asked: "Does the Government of the United States intend to adopt a policy which will make innocent men and women suffer because of the political situation which makes their government unacceptable to the United States?" To which Truman replied: "Yes."*

Not that UNRRA aid in the Ukraine amounted to very much. The same officials who praised McDuffie still thought the help was "*dovolno miserno*" ("pretty miserable") in view of the country's enormous needs. There is, indeed, an entertaining and significant passage in McDuffie's own book about the particular trip which took me to Kiev. He thought the "Russian foreign office dope" who would take us round would do a "Potemkin village" on us.

> My Canadian agricultural adviser was upset when he heard that a group of Western correspondents were coming to the Ukraine to report on UNRRA activities. "This show-off foreign office dope," he said, "will take them to the best farm I've seen in the Ukraine, with artificial insemination, electrical milking, etc. And when the boys ask if it's an average farm, he will tell them 'It's less than average.' ... So they'll get the idea that UNRRA has been duped into importing food when there are tons of meat from rich farms flooding the free market—which I can swear they do not" ... I almost had to slug Khomyak [McDuffie's chief Ukrainian contact man] so that he saw my point. Finally we got the reporters, a disgusted group as they saw their story fade [i.e. the story that UNRRA had been brought to the Ukraine on false pretences] into the markets, and in the whole city of Kiev they found less than a pound of fresh meat.

Funnily enough, it is quite true that the "foreign office dope" did take us to a model *kolkhoz*. We were also given a huge feed with roast chicken and duck and various Ukrainian specialities— and some pretty horrible home-brewed lilac-coloured *samogon* (hooch) which passed off as vodka. It did not, however, escape our attention that the soil was parched and cracked with the fearful drought, and that the wheat had grown barely an inch above the ground, and was already turning brown with the

* James P. Warburg, *The United States in the Post-war World* (New York, 1966), p. 34.

heat and lack of rain. It was the beginning of the great tragedy of the 1946 drought, the worst drought Russia had known since 1891. The villagers were morose and disgruntled.

The UNRRA funds came from contributions by member states (and, in the first place, the United States) which had not been invaded and occupied. In 1947, at the second session of the UN General Assembly, UNRRA was liquidated on the initiative of Britain and the USA.

In August 1946 I had the good fortune of being the only Western correspondent to be authorized by the Soviet Foreign Office to go on a trip to Southern Russia, the Caucasus and Transcaucasia. My only companion was a friend, the brilliant young Polish journalist Ziemowit Fedecki. There was much angry grumbling about such "favouritism", not only among the Western correspondents, but also among the "people's democracies" correspondents. Both Fedecki and I were accused of consorting with the "enemy camp". The foreign office press department made arrangements for us to be met at Rostov, Kislovodsk and Tbilisi. Between these three points we had to look after ourselves. This allowed us really to see life in the raw.

Our arrival by air at Rostov was marked by a slightly embarassing touch of comedy. Rostov is off the beaten track as far as foreign visitors are concerned, and the head of the city soviet must have thought, when he received the news from the foreign office of our arrival, that we required VIP treatment. We knew nothing about it. It was very hot, and we both wore pretty grubby clothes, shabby old short-sleeved shirts and, of course, no tie. At Rostov, we were met by the president of the Gorsoviet in person, wearing a perfectly pressed ceremonial black suit, and by his wife, clad in a rather fancy black dress with all kinds of frills and an elaborate black hat with feathers. They could hardly believe their eyes when they saw us, and the lady acidly remarked, as she surveyed our scruffy get-up, that the last foreign visitor she and her husband had received at Rostov was Mrs. Churchill. "And we thought . . ." she said, without ending her sentence. However, we were taken to the "guest house", and stayed in the very room that "Clemmie" had inhabited some months before. After that we were left to ourselves, and we never saw our hosts again. We were given no meals, and had to fend for ourselves. Finally, at the end of the third day, somebody from the Gorsoviet brought us our railway tickets for Koslovodsk, for which we had to pay there and then.

Like Kiev, Rostov was about half destroyed. It had changed hands four times during the war. For all that, there was southern gaiety in the air; in the acacia-lined main avenue, there were crowds of young people, singing, laughing and making a lot of noise. The girls, in their summer dresses, seemed prettier than in Moscow. Although half the city was partly in ruins, there were bands playing in the public parks, with their fountains and the newly erected plaster statues of athletes which were floodlit at night. Everybody one talked to shook his head about the drought from which the Don country was suffering, and people dreaded what would happen during the winter and "next year". Even so, there were plenty of vegetables, and apricots and cherries and plums in the market, and all of it much cheaper than in Moscow. This market was altogether a great centre of social life in Rostov. Here also was a side-show where, all day long, a Georgian magician wearing a strange oriental costume and calling himself Draga Khan was performing all sorts of marvellous tricks—like making a Chinese lady in a trance lie in a coffin suspended in mid-air, and then sawing her and the coffin in half. But a bill outside the barracks explained in "scientific" language that although elsewhere Draga Khan's tricks would pass off as magic and as miracles, the show was in fact "strictly scientific and based solely on skill". And it added that there was no room for "miracles" and "magic" in the Soviet Union. This made Draga Khan's skill all the more remarkable!

Another centre of life in Rostov was the badly destroyed and now barely patched-up railway station. Once a day the great Moscow/Tbilisi luxury express—with barbers' shops, shower-baths, dining cars, etc.—passed through Rostov. But that railway transport was still at a low ebb in the Soviet Union in 1946 could be seen from the fact that only twelve long-distance trains a day left Rostov or arrived there, and only fourteen local trains. The shortage of rolling stock was still very serious, and accounted for many economic difficulties, among them the very slow progress in the reconstruction of Rostov. It had had 550,000 inhabitants before the war, but now there were 420,000, though with only half the pre-war dwelling-space available. Half the houses and practically all the public buildings had been destroyed by the retreating Germans, among them the enormous theatre built in 1935. Rostselmash, the biggest agricultural-machinery plant in the USSR, had been the largest single Rostov industry, employing 30,000 people; but most of the machinery and workers had been evacuated to the East in 1941. Now it was still a scene of desolation. Only one-tenth of the workshops had been restored. For the rest, most of the work at Rostselmash consisted in clearing away the rubble, and for this work mostly German and Hungarian war prisoners were being used. However, the Hungarians, like the Rumanians before them, were about to be sent home. We talked to some of them. The Hungarians were happy at the thought of being sent home "soon"; the Germans, though in reasonably fit state, looked miserable and wondered if they would *ever* get home.

Nearly all the workers' houses round Rostselmash had been burned out. In the few restored workshops the machinery was either new Russian machinery or German "reparations" machinery. Nearly all the workers were new. Most of the old workers, especially the skilled ones, who had been evacuated to the East, would stay there. In due course, Rostselmash would be "doubled"—the "old" Rostselmash staying in the East, together with the old workers and mostly old machinery, and the "new" Rostselmash being rebuilt in Rostov, with mostly new machines and new workers. But one of the engineers who told us about all this said that this "doubling" was still only on paper. He thought the main work would continue to be done in the East. Altogether, we found that there was still, in 1946, a good deal of pessimism about the reconstruction of Russia. The Rostov city architect said it would take five or six years to "patch up" the city, and perhaps fifteen years or more before the "new architectural ensembles" were completed and before it became a "really new city" again.

We got a little whiff of the Rostov underworld one afternoon. We wanted to bathe in the Don, but the main bridge near the centre of the town had been blown up, and we had to walk a couple of miles before reaching a temporary wooden bridge, and then, crossing it, had to walk another couple of miles to reach the somewhat primitive little sandy beach on the south bank of the Don. We had had our swim, but it was getting dark and we did not feel like walking four more miles back.

Luckily there was a man in a rowing boat who offered (for a consideration) to take us across the river to the centre of Rostov. We talked about this and that, and he said (he looked like a docker, or something like that): "You must be pretty bored here, knowing nobody. Would you like me to arrange a little party for you tomorrow night—vodka, zakuski, of course. And would you like a couple of girls? What about a couple of nice *militsionerki* (police girls) in uniform?" He grinned. "Won't cost you much— not very much." We thought it a rather exciting offer, but said we'd better let him know the next morning—we might have to leave tomorrow for Kislovodsk. Well (fortunately or un- fortunately), the man with the railway tickets arrived that same night, and we had to leave early the next morning.

Our chairman of the Gorsoviet not being as hospitable with us as he no doubt had been with Mrs. Churchill, we had to feed on the odds and ends we bought in the market, and once a day we ate at a hideously expensive "commercial restaurant", a very so-so meal costing 100 or 150 roubles, or—even at the preferential exchange rate—about £2 or £3. *Militsionerki* should have been thrown in free, but they weren't.

This was the beginning of August 1946, and for the first time since 1940 there was a tremendous holiday rush all over the Soviet Union. We were lucky the Rostov Gorsoviet got us on the special *Kurortnyi* (health-resort) train that went to Mineralnye Vody, Piatigorsk and Kislovodsk, in the Caucasus foothills. The woman-guard in our carriage said the crowds at the station in Moscow were something quite incredible. "Travelling permits are no longer required, as they were during the war, and now everybody tries to get to the south, and there just aren't enough trains, not by a long way, and the militia have a hell of a job stopping people from storming the trains, no matter how crowded. However, for the Kurortnyi only people with reserved seats can get on—that's why we haven't got thousands standing in the corridors."

Here, in the second-class compartment with four bunks, we had only two other people—a very fat woman who slept most of the time and who was going to Kislovodsk for a slimming cure, and a jovial little man, a party official from Kurgan in Siberia, who had already been travelling for over a week and who was also on his way to a twenty-six-day "cure". We walked down the carriage. It was very hot, and although all the windows were open nearly everybody was half-undressed, some of the men stripped to the waist. Bataisk, Tikhoretsk and other places we passed had names which were only too familiar from the 1942 war communiqués; for it was along this railway line that the Wehrmacht had for the last time in its career advanced in true *blitzkrieg* fashion across the fertile plains of the Kuban, on to the Caucasus, on to Baku—as they thought—and into the Middle East. This country south of Rostov was, indeed, fertile and beautiful, with its orchards and its immense wheat fields, and tidy Cossack villages with whitewashed huts, and children bathing in the numerous little rivers we crossed. We would then pass through miles of sunflower fields under a radiant blue sky—one of the fairest sights in nature. "They are lucky here," said the little man from Kurgan. "On the other side of Rostov, at Kursk, Voronezh, nothing is growing, everything is burned out.... And in the East, in the Volga country, it isn't much better. People are very worried." And he muttered one of the most fearful words in Russian: "*golod*". *Golod* means hunger; and Russia was threatened with *golod*, barely a year after the war had ended.

But the Kuban country was a lucky exception. Most of the railway stations were wrecked, and here and there a wrecked rusty railway carriage or armoured car still lay alongside the railway line. Some towns had been bombed, others burned out by the retreating Germans, but the villages were mostly intact, and there were a great number of cattle in the fields. At the stations where we stopped chatty buxom Cossack girls were running large markets for the passengers' (and their own) benefit, and the long wooden stalls were piled high with loaves, fruit, cheese, butter, roast chickens, and jars of milk and cream. Everything, except bread, was much cheaper than in Moscow. Flour, they said, would be short till the next harvest. The girls were not very communicative about the German occupation; they said merely that they did not see much of the Germans, except at the end when they set fire to the towns and skedaddled out of the Kuban in a frantic hurry. "They said they would soon be back, but we didn't believe them—we knew quite enough about Stalingrad by then."

The next morning we were in the Lermontov country—first

Piatigorsk, which had been badly wrecked by the Germans (it was here, outside Piatigorsk, that Lermontov was killed in a duel in 1841, aged twenty-six), and then Kislovodsk, the most famous of all Russian health resorts, with its Narzan springs and Narzan baths. It had greatly changed since I had last seen it as a youngster in 1916, just a couple of months before the Revolution. It was then still rather like Lermontov's Kislovodsk, full of riding-horses that took you along rough mountain paths to Bermamyt and other famous beauty spots whence you could see the Caucasus mountain range, and also rich in romantic adventures. Now Kislovodsk was different—a huge health-factory, with some sixty big sanatoria. The Germans, afraid of being trapped there, had pulled out in a hurry, and had had time to burn down only two. Thanks to the foreign office press department, Ziemowit and I were put in the "Ukrainian Railwaymen's Sanatorium", a pretty sumptuous-looking affair, run with the neatness and efficiency of a first-class Swiss hotel. Sir Walter Citrine's "bath-plugs that didn't fit"—his symbol of Russian inefficiency—were inconceivable here.

Since we were in Kislovodsk, we were automatically treated as "patients". We were given a check-up by a woman-doctor, who warned us against smoking too much, and said we could have Narzan baths, but only up to the waist, and never longer than twelve minutes. At the sanatorium we had to follow a strict routine—everything was severely regulated: the meals, every hour of the day, including the after-lunch siesta, the 8 p.m. cinema show, and even the glass of sour milk which the immaculate nurse brought to your "ward" (even a single room was never called a room, but a ward) at 10 p.m. Of course, you got the sour milk only if the doctor had ordered it. At 11 p.m. all lights were out.

The famous old Poplar Alley of 1916 had gone, and now, in the once-romantic park of Kislovodsk, round the Narzan springs where you "took the waters", there were arrows pointing to the different paths that patients were to follow on their morning walks. It was all hideously unromantic.

During the few months they were there, the Germans had turned many of the Kislovodsk sanatoria into military hospitals, and two-thirds of them had remained military hospitals when the Russians returned at the end of 1942. Now there were still, among the patients, a few men severely wounded during the war, but three-quarters of the hospitals were back to sanatorium status, and medically the whole place was remarkably well supplied with X-ray equipment, electric massage and mecano-therapy equipment, and whatnot. I had never seen anything quite like it in Moscow. In 1939, 150,000 people had come here for "cures"—the chief complaints being heart and gastric troubles and abnormal obesity. Others simply came for rest cures.

The lucky people who, for 800 roubles, railway fare included, could get a twenty-six-day *putyovka*—an all-in holiday ticket—to Kislovodsk were selected by the medical boards of trade unions or government departments. Health, needless to say, was not the only criterion; a man's (or woman's) value as a worker was also taken into consideration. Therefore, the proportion of directors, engineers and foremen was much higher than that of "ordinary" workers. Among the latter, preference was given to stakhanovites and other exceptionally valuable workers. No doubt there was also some wangling in getting *putyovki* to Kislovodsk—especially for perfectly healthy wives or even "secretaries". But given the still rather limited possibilities, the system seemed to be working fairly enough.

The director of our sanatorium—a man with an impressive row of military decorations—said that by 1949 there would be 200,000 people coming for cures and rest cures to Koslovodsk. Now there were only 100,000. But by 1949 there would be, in *all* the health resorts of the Soviet Union, several million "patients". "We had a hell of a time during the war," he said. "Now we are getting back to normal at last. Only I ask you: why can't all these Trumans and Churchills leave us alone?"

We managed—for a consideration—to get a lift in a car going from Kislovodsk to Nalchik, where, on the northern fringes of the Caucasus, an archipelago of mountains rose from the steppe. Between the mountains there were wide stretches of fair and fertile land, tilled, around Piatigorsk, by the descendants of Cossack settlers and, further south, nearer Nalchik, by Kabardinians, who in the last hundred years or so had tended to come down from the mountains and settle in the plain. The road from Piatigorsk to Nalchik, passing through orchards and rich fields of wheat and sunflower, and with the snowy twin pyramid of Mount Elbrus on the right, was the very road along which the

Germans had tried, back in 1942, to penetrate deep into the Caucasus.

Now and then we passed a Kabardinian on horseback wearing an immense sheepskin cloak and a wide sombrero-like hat made of white felt; but we had not yet reached the romantic mountain country proper, and a more common sight was a crowd of road-mending German war prisoners.

Nalchik was the last large town in the Caucasus to have been occupied by the Germans. Though partly burned out, the town, standing on the banks of a mountain torrent—a most exciting place to bathe in—was packed almost beyond belief. Where had all these people come from? Apparently they were Russians—most of them from Gorki, Kuibyshev and other Volga areas. I later learned why they had come here. Nalchik, with its great public gardens, and its modern "Soviet" west end and "oriental" east, was the capital of the Karbardinian Autonomous Socialist Soviet Republic. It had its own Council of Ministers' building and other government departments. At night the public parks were crowded, especially the two large open-air dance platforms. Most of the young people here were Russian working-lads and working-girls, and they had arrived during the last month, attracted by the good food, the good climate, and the work available in the various small factories springing up in the neighbourhood. And again, talking to some of these people, I heard the word *golod*; the Volga country was threatened with *golod*, and these young people were part of that extensive migration of 1946 from the north and east to the Caucasus—a migration from a drought-stricken part of the country to the happier south. Besides these migrants, there were many regular holiday-makers at Nalchik.

With much difficulty we got two beds in a hostel dormitory. The hostel was the patched-up part of a burned-down hotel. In the hall stood a huge silver-painted plaster statue of Lenin holding out a large welcoming paw. We had to share the dormitory with fourteen other people, among them officers passing through the town, government officials and workers who had come here for a rest cure. This dormitory was all right, except that two officers would come in at 3 a.m., turn on all the lights, spread out their supper and proceed to eat it; also, it was terribly hot, but the people in the dormitory would not allow

12

the windows to be opened—the room was on the ground floor, and "there were a lot of robbers and thieves about".

One of the strangest sights at Nalchik was a shed on the edge of the park where there was a—at first sight—macabre collection of plaster torsos, arms, legs and heads. They were the statues of Lenin and Stalin smashed up by the Germans and now brought here from over a wide area for restoration and reassembly. We watched a couple of workers sticking a Stalin head on to a Lenin torso and then unsticking it after they had realized their mistake.

The centre of the picturesque "east end" was the market. Here plenty of fruit and dairy produce and meat was sold by Kabardine women wearing large black shawls and by Kabardinian farmers with large white tasselled sombreros, and talking a strange guttural language. The food here was more plentiful and cheaper than almost anywhere else in Russia. And, as oriental markets go, it was different from those found in Persia or the Middle East generally—less vociferous and less squalid. Apart from the innate dignity of the Caucasian peoples, especially the mountaineers, there is also a certain minimum of health and cleanliness about such places which is not found in Bagdad or Teheran, with their children with suppurating eyes, their crowds of cripples and invalids kept half-alive by begging. Come into the Soviet Union from Stockholm, and you think it pretty miserable (I am speaking of the immediate post-war years); but come in from Iran, and you are impressed by its relative orderliness and comparative lack of squalor. Coming from the Middle East to Baku or Tbilisi, you almost have the feeling of being back in Europe. . . .

Ziemowit and I spent quite some time in the *dukhan* in the market square of Nalchik drinking wine and eating oriental pastries. We fell into conversation with an elderly Kabardinian. He told us about the German occupation, and about the deportation at the end of the war of the entire population of the Chechen, Ingush and Balkar countries. It was, he said, a pretty terrifying business. Men, women, children, old people—everybody was packed into trains by the NKVD and sent God knows where.

"As you know," he said, "the Supreme Soviet of the RSFSR announced that this had been done because too many people had collaborated with the Germans," and, "as a whole, the population had not opposed this treasonable collaboration with the enemy. Don't repeat what I said," he remarked, "but do you think it's just to treat people like that—children, women, everybody, yes—even komsomols and party members? The NKVD made a terrifyingly efficient job of it; everybody packed off in a couple of days. Of course," he said, "the Chechens are mountaineers, Moslems, undisciplined, with a dislike of the Russians and of the Ossetins."

"Yes," I said, "cut-throats, but rather splendid cut-throats, as Lermontov wrote, and much more admirable than the lazy Ossetins."

"Quite true," said our friend, "but the Ossetins were careful not to compromise themselves with the Germans—maybe because the Germans never got very far into Ossetia."

"And what about the Kabardinians?"

Our friend winced. "We were comparatively lucky. The Germans were here at Nalchik for only a few weeks, and nothing much happened. But it was touch-and-go. There was a Kabardinian prince living high up in the mountains who could think of nothing better than to send a splendid white charger as a personal gift to Hitler. . . . So we got away with a few bumps and bruises."

"And the prince?"

"Oh, he seems to have run away with the Germans."

"And what bumps and bruises?"

"Well, a few people—perhaps a hundred—were packed off by the NKVD, but otherwise we are all right."

"Well, you're lucky," I said, "and you have such a beautiful country."

He shrugged his shoulders: "Yes, it's so beautiful that the Russians come here like a lot of flies buzzing round a pot of honey. . . . Thing is that they're hungry and scared of the drought in their own parts of the country." And he reflected: "We were lucky, I suppose, not to have annoyed Stalin more than we did, or we would have shared the fate of the Chechens. A Georgian? A Caucasian? He's the Tsar of Russia all right, Ivan the Terrible— and he *can* be terrible once you get under his skin. . . . I suppose, when one comes to think of it now, that he did a good job during the war, but I can tell you we weren't so sure about anything when the Germans were at Kislovodsk and made a great song-and-dance over having planted the swastika flag on top of Mount Elbrus."

"But how did they behave when they were here?"

"They had been given strict instructions to behave very well, not to loot, not to pester our women; in short, to make friends with the people of the Caucasus. But then, of course, before pulling out, they burned down half of Nalchik; so that spoilt the whole effect. . . ."

Vladikavkaz—"Rule-the-Caucasus"—is at the north end of the Georgian Military Highway and is familiar to every student of Russian literature, particularly of Lermontov. Vladikavkaz is the scene of "Maxim Maximych", one of the most famous episodes of *A Hero of Our Times*. Built on both sides of the tumultuous Terek, and with a superb view of the Caucasus mountain range, dominated by the rugged white peak of Mount Kazbek barely fifty miles to the south, Vladikavkaz used to be, before the Revolution, a favourite retreat for retired army colonels and generals, who had come to love the Caucasus the way some Anglo/Indian colonels loved India. Now it was a city—half-European, half-Oriental—of some 120,000 people and was the capital of the Autonomous SSR of Northern Ossetia. Having had its name changed from Vladikavkaz to Orjonikidze— one of Stalin's "trusted lieutenants" who had been driven to suicide at the time of the purges—it was now, in 1946, called Dzaodjikao, the original Ossetin name of the town.* A final German push in the Caucasus in November 1942 had brought them within five miles of Vladikavkaz, but here they were driven back to Nalchik with heavy losses, and there were still quite a few wrecked German tanks to be seen near the city. It had some fairly important industries and a large hydro-electric plant, but above all it was the centre of a rich agricultural and sheep-farming area. It looked a busy city, with its tramcars, the first I had seen in the Caucasus. Around the oriental market place there were numerous *dukhans*, rather dingy eating and drinking places. The Ossetins did not seem to have changed much since Lermontov's days—though the *dukhans* were part of the municipal network of catering establishments, the Ossetin management shamelessly overcharged you if you let them.

We decided to pay a visit to the Council of Ministers of the

* Later it was changed back to Orjonikidze.

North Ossetia Autonomous SSR. At first we had no luck; the Ossetin Prime Minister was not available, but we were told to return in a couple of hours, when we would be received by the Deputy Prime Minister. This one turned out to be not an Ossetin, but a Russian, by the name of Comrade Bobkin. He said the Ossetins were very fine people, but they still needed "guidance", and scarcely made any secret of the fact that not the Ossetin Prime Minister, but he, Comrade Bobkin, was the real boss there. He was a fat man of about forty, full of bluster and self-assurance. After describing to us the economic structure of Northern Ossetia, and telling us that if before the Revolution 85 per cent of the people of the region were illiterate, now nobody was, except the very old, that everybody now went to a seven-year school, and enumerating the teachers' training colleges, agricultural and technical colleges and various scientific institutions in the Republic, he said he would take up to "a typical wheat-and-sheep *kolkhoz*" the next day. In the colleges he had mentioned 80 per cent of the students were Ossetins, and although Ossetin was "the first official language" of the Republic the war had delayed the publication of school and college textbooks in Ossetin, so most of the teaching still had to be done in Russian. Anyway, he added, it wasn't a language particularly well suited to modern scientific books, even though in its written form it had adopted the Russian alphabet.

"It's a pity the Ossetin National Theatre is closed in August, but it's a remarkable theatre, and it produces both original Ossetin plays, and others translated from Russian and other languages." Last winter he had gone to see an Ossetin performance of *Macbeth* by Vilyam Shekspir.

"You speak Ossetin?" I ventured to ask.

"I can understand it," he said a little evasively. "It's not an easy language, but I can speak it—more or less," he conceded.

The Council of Ministers of the Autonomous Republic was, strictly speaking, not very different from an *oblispolkom* (a provincial executive committee) in other parts of Russia, but Comrade Bobkin loved his title of Deputy Prime Minister. We never were given a chance to meet the Prime Minister himself, though we had a few words with him on the phone, after which he handed it over to Bobkin. The Prime Minister's Russian was, indeed, extremely "Caucasian"—the kind of accent in which from time immemorial "Armenian anecdotes" have always been told.

The excursion to the *kolkhoz* the next day was really something. Bobkin took us there in a rather posh German car, complete with chauffeur. The Ossetin *kolkhoz* had been warned of our arrival; not only was a sumptuous lunch served consisting mainly of roast lamb and all kinds of salads, and unlimited quantities of wine, but Comrade Bobkin also suggested that the Ossetin women perform several folk dances, while the men did the singing. Comrade Bobkin was the little local satrap all right. He peppered his Russian with Ossetin words, which he then translated for us—"very good", or "your health", or "good morning, good evening"—and the Ossetins were very obsequious in their manner. I doubt whether they really liked Comrade Bobkin, though they assured him that everything was going reasonably well at the *kolkhoz*; but they complained, all the same, of the shortage of fertilizers and various agricultural implements. Bobkin, who was helping himself generously to the wine, was growing more and more exuberant as the afternoon wore on. He said to the Ossetins that they were wonderful people, that their national poet Hetagurov, who had written in both Ossetin and Russian about fifty years before and whose gilded statue adorned the public park at Djaodjikao, was a very great poet, but that they still did not appreciate sufficiently all that the Soviet Power had done for them, and were always grumbling about something. "It's only a year since the war ended, and you keep grumbling you can't get this and that. We Russians have a much harder time than you chaps living in a land of milk-and-honey. You've just got to wait a bit till the new Stalin five-year plan gets into its stride; and it won't take long till we outspit (*pereplyunem*) America." Then he got very abusive about Truman and "that old interventionist Churchill", but they couldn't strangle the Soviet Union, with their economic blockade, and they could go to the devil's mother. And they had better not try any nonsense with their atom bomb. "*We*'ve already got the atom bomb," he suddenly said, "though we are not talking about it. But *you* can tell them," he suddenly snapped at me.

After the lunch, which, with its elaborate toasts, singing and dancing, had gone on for a good four hours, we went round the *kolkhoz*. When I took a photo of a child with hardly any clothes on (it was a hot day), Bobkin said: "Very wrong of you to have taken that photo; I suppose you'll send it to your paper, and the people in the West will say that the Ossetins haven't any clothes to wear and walk about naked." I told him not to be so suspicious. "Suspicious!" he cried, "you'll be telling me next we have *no reason* to be suspicious!"

However, he suddenly mellowed, and then, already pretty drunk, insisted on taking us in the car to the famous Daryal Gorge, a long way down the Georgian Military Highway. The mountainside was studded with pill-boxes, so it was clear that the Russians had taken every precaution to stop the Germans in case they tried to break into Transcaucasia along the Georgian Military Highway. I need not describe the extraordinary beauty of this wild mountain country and the famous Daryal Gorge, with the Terek roaring through it. Bobkin insisted that we drive to the southern end of the gorge and climb a couple of thousand feet up to the "Castle of Queen Tamara". Actually, there is no castle there—the name is that of the mountain-peak. However, it had grown almost completely dark, and we said we would rather not climb the uncertain pebbly path. But Bobkin was now in an enterprising mood, and crossing the Terek on a cable ferry he vanished into the twilight. We and the driver had to wait over an hour before he returned. We had got really anxious, for he was not very steady on his feet and might well have fallen off some cliff—and, worse still, we might then be accused of having murdered the Deputy Prime Minister. I do not know how far he had climbed, but he claimed to have got to the very top. It was nearly midnight before we got back to Dzaodjikao.

In 1946 the pre-war bus service along the Georgian Military Highway from Vladikavkaz to Tbilisi, the capital of Georgia, had not yet been restored, and (again for a consideration) we had to get a lift from an army truck. We had seen in Intourist officers large pre-war posters advertising the "Glorious Journey along the Georgian Military Highway", with a picture of enormous mountain peaks and a large luxurious-looking bus travelling along the road down below. Nothing like that now. However, we discovered at Vladikavkaz that an empty army truck was going back to Tbilisi. Although not intended for passengers, it had been fitted with benches which could be used when the truck was not carrying oil barrels or timber. The driver made a tidy pile of banknotes out of every "empty" trip. At first there were only five or six passengers. Just outside Vladikavkaz, an official on the road waving a little red flag and some kind of document stopped us, intending to inflict on our Armenian driver four cows which he was "obliged by law" to transport to Tbilisi for a nominal charge. However, after a long parley on the roadside (in the course of which I noticed a bundle of notes changing hands) the driver argued the official out of the project, and we were able to travel in more pleasant and communicative company. Before long the truck was packed with a mixed and picturesque crowd of passengers—some aged white-bearded mountaineers in sheepskin hats, Georgian women in bright embroidered dresses, with their children, and half-a-dozen Red Army men who were going back to their barracks on the high crest of the road, 8,000 feet above sea-level. Here the cottages were like Russian peasant huts, and birch trees grew outside, whereas an hour later, in the Aragvi valley, the cypresses grew.

The main stopping place along the road was the village of Kazbek, 4,000 feet up, a large Georgian village with high wooden verandas and with a superb view of Mount Kazbek only a few miles away. Between Kazbek village and Kazbek mountain, on the crest of a hill, was an old monastery with typically Georgian conical towers. Sheep and pigs were wandering about the village streets, and here our truck was joined by one of the local worthies, a jovial middle-aged Georgian farmer, who introduced himself as "Irakli Abashidze, a former *kulak*"—*byvshi kulak*. He entertained several of us to cream cheese pies, kept the company merry with his jokes and jests, and even invited Ziemowit and me to stay with him at Kazbek, where he was a member of a sheep *kolkhoz* and had several sheep of his own, and three children. "Just ask for Irakli; everybody knows Irakli at Kazbek." He had a stubble chin and a large laughing mouth and from time to time he would burst into a sort of chant or drinking song. He seemed to regret his *kulak* days, but was philosophic about it. Only when, at one point, the truck was stopped for a "check of documents" by three NKVD guards, did Irakli suddenly grow bitter. "NKVD," he said as soon as we resumed the journey, "*ne ludi a volki*: not people, but wolves." And he added in a semi-whisper: "I'm an old *kulak*; I know."

After passing in the twilight the ancient Georgian capital of

Mskhet at the point where the Kura and the Aragvi meet—a town with the conical towers of its churches and monasteries standing out against the hot blue summer sky—we drove into Tbilisi at nightfall. Surrounded by hills, the great city, with its thousands of lights, was an impressive sight. Up the slopes of St. David's Mount, the lighted funicular was running up to the amusements park on top of the hill. Irakli offered to explain the mechanism of the funicular: "Do you know how a funicular works? Well, one carriage goes up, the other carriage goes down. Understand?" That's as far as he could get. Having reached Tbilisi, we took leave of Irakli, who made us promise to stay with him at Kazbek next time we were in these parts. "Just ask for Irakli".

At Tbilisi, for the first time since we had left Moscow, we fell into the clutches of Intourist. This at least had the advantage of providing us with something better than the Nalchik dormitory— a regular hotel room, bath and all. But now our freedom seemed threatened. The charming Georgian Intourist girl announced at once: "Tomorrow you will see the churches of Tbilisi." We said we weren't interested in churches. She took it quite well and merely said that we were not typical "intourists". We said we were not, and did not intend to be. But would she, instead, join us for supper the next night at the celebrated Dukhan Simpatia, which we were going to explore anyway? A little hesitatingly she agreed.

With half-a-million population Tbilisi was a capital city right enough, with its enormous government buildings, nearly all built in the last ten or fifteen years, its magnificent tree-lined squares and avenues, like the famous Rustaveli Avenue, its national museums, its university and numerous other higher-education schools, its theatres and superb Botanical Gardens, its enormous Beria Square and Beria Gardens along the river (as they were *then* called). Oriental colour and a certain squalor were provided by the old town of Tbilisi, its church domes and minarets reflected in the muddy yellow waters of the Kura. It was now said that much of this old town would soon be demolished, though a small section of it would be preserved "for historic interest". The old city was now largely inhabited by Armenians, Jews and Moslems, most of these the rather down-at-heel descendants of Turkish and Persian invaders of old.

Tbilisi was not Russian. The Georgians prided themselves on

their old culture and their high standard of education, and said Georgia required no Russian guidance, unlike" primitive" places, such as Kabardia and Ossetia.

In the next few days we explored various Georgian ministries and found, indeed, that with very few exceptions all the officials, including the highest, were Georgians. For all that, they all spoke almost perfect Russian, usually without even the trace of a "Caucasian" accent—which was more than Stalin himself had achieved! In Tbilisi most of the films shown were Russian; nearly everybody spoke Russian. Some of the theatres were Russian, too, but the Georgians prided themselves on their Georgian theatre, and especially on Horava, the Shakespearean actor, and one of the most famous actors in the Soviet Union. In fact, as we soon discovered, the "Russianism" of Georgia was more superficial than appeared at first sight, and few people in the Soviet Union were more nationalist than the Georgians. Thus, I picked up a history book of Georgia, as used in secondary schools, and found that it wallowed in the Georgian people's struggle for their independence since time immemorial, and glorified such medieval heroes as the great Queen Tamara and the hero of an interminable three-part Ivanhoe-type film, the valiant Georgi Saakadze. Georgia had to fight for centuries against the Turks and Persians, and if, in 1801, she allowed herself to be "incorporated" into Tsarist Russia, she did so as a means of escaping conquest by Turkey or Persia. It was thus a "progressive" step. There was, of course, in the final chapters, a glorification of Stalin, the greatest Georgian of all times, etc.

Georgia, the ancient Colchis, the land of the Golden Fleece, the "most beautiful country in the world", had been relatively lucky in the war. It had not been invaded by the Germans, and the only direct damage caused by the war was a few bombs dropped on Tbilisi by the Germans, possibly by mistake. But Georgia had had its fair proportion of casualties in the Soviet/German war, and many Georgian officers and generals had earned some of the highest distinctions. Were they, however, "Soviet patriots" in the same sense as the Russians? Here all kinds of tricky questions arose, and we had some long and candid discussions with Comrade Toidze, an official of the ephemeral Georgian Ministry of Foreign Affairs, whom we met a few days after our arrival and who volunteered to take us on a trip to Maharadze and the tea and citrus-fruit country, and then to Batum, the great Black Sea port of Georgia.

One question which, of course, bothered the Georgians was to what extent they were now being exploited by the Russians as a "colonial territory" which should make a very special effort to help the parts of the Soviet Union which had suffered from the war far more than they. We were received one day by Comrade Mikeladze—a very European-looking high official, who was head of the industrial section of the Georgian state-planning commission and who candidly remarked that before the war Georgia "gave as much to the rest of the Soviet Union as it received from it". But now things had changed: she had to give more than she received. Both industrially and agriculturally, Georgia was practically self-sufficient, and this created something of a problem, since she had to share in "the general austerity" of the Soviet Union, and, much to the disgust of the Georgian housewives, rationing in the cities had to be enforced, just as in Moscow and other Russian cities. Georgia had a monopoly of tea and almost a monopoly of citrus fruit in the Soviet Union; also she was producing great quantities of wine and silk, and all this now went, as it were, into a common pool. But the rest of the Soviet Union, which had suffered from the war, was unable to provide Georgia with the consumer goods she needed. It was a one-way traffic, and the Georgians were not too pleased about it. Of course, things would sort themselves out by the end of the present five-year plan, which provided among other things for a high degree of industrialization in Georgia, which would soon begin to produce her own agricultural machinery needed for the tea and citrus-fruit plantations, and also machinery for her silk industry.

Our most interesting contact was Comrade Toidze of the Ministry of Foreign Affairs. Not that he took his Ministry seriously. It had been set up at the time when Stalin had hoped to get all the sixteen Soviet Republics into the UN; and the Georgian Foreign Ministry now seemed to consist of four rooms in which nothing much was happening. Toidze was a highly cultured official who spoke perfect Russian, but was, for all that, a very ardent Georgian nationalist. He was a man about forty, who had been transferred to the Foreign Ministry from the Ministry of Education. He said that there was some idea of having Georgian

Legations (independently of Soviet Embassies) in a few countries like Persia and Turkey, but seemed a little sceptical about the whole idea. "As you know," he said, "we can't get a separate seat at the UN, and although the Ukraine and Belorussia got them, there's no hope for us any longer." I remarked that there had been a good deal of unpleasantness between the Soviet Union and the Western powers lately about Persia and Turkey.

"Yes," said Toidze, "it's the same old question of Anglo/Russian rivalry in Iran, and the same old question of the control of the Straits. We Georgians are particularly sensitive on both counts, and, as a Black Sea country, we feel very strongly about the Straits. After all, we *were* occupied by the British in 1919. So in these disputes we are 100 per cent with Moscow. But I realize that today we aren't in a strong bargaining position. We're in a bad economic mess, and it's going to be not better, but worse, next year; and especially with the Americans having their atom bomb, we can't afford a major showdown, though we have a perfectly good case in both Iran and Turkey. . . ."

Whether tipped off by Moscow or not—I rather think the Georgian Foreign Ministry wanted to show some independent enterprise—Toidze offered to take us to Maharadze and Batum and to visit some of the tea plantations in the area. We went by train, and had some interesting talks with him. He made no secret of his dislike of the present "colonial exploitation" of Georgia by the Russians, though he thought it was "understandable", in view of the devastations caused by the war in Russia, the Ukraine, etc.

"And what's the feeling about Stalin in Georgia?"

"Well," he said, a little hesitatingly, "to a lot of Georgians Stalin is a very great man, and they are very proud that a Georgian should stand at the head of the Soviet Union. But—and I trust you won't repeat what I say—it makes me, and not only me, pretty sick to see the biggest square and the finest garden in Tbilisi called 'Beria Square' and 'Beria Gardens', and all the slush in our papers about our dear Lavrenti Pavlovich. You remember 1936-7. They didn't know much about Beria in Moscow then, but *we* saw plenty of Beria here and, I can tell you, it wasn't funny. *We* had more than our share of the purges, and those in Georgia—and there are plenty of them—who had some experience of the purges have no love for Beria, and—not per-

haps even as much love as they should have for Iosif Vissarionovich. . . ." This was really a mouthful—in *those* days. Toidze
must have felt very strongly about it, or he would scarcely have
said this to people who were, after all, strangers to him. And he
added:

"We Georgians are Southerners, nice, easy-going people, fond
of eating and drinking and running after women, and Stalin,
Beria—all this is something much too harsh for us. Not that we
dislike the Soviet system as such; it's done no end of good in
health, education, housing, and so on. But the hand of Moscow
is sometimes pretty heavy, and today there's a good deal of
escapism among the young people into a sort of Georgian
nationalism—and you even find it in our approved school books."

Later, on our return to Tbilisi, he even presented me with a
copy of the standard *History of Georgia*—a pretty remarkable
piece of nationalist self-glorification. "If Stalin were a Georgian
nationalist," he remarked, "we'd love him. But he's a *Russian*
nationalist—to him the Russians are the salt of the earth. So if he
wants to rave about Tolstoy and Suvorov, we feel we have a
right to rave about Queen Tamara, and Georgi Saakadze, and,
of course, our great national poet, Shota Rustaveli. . . ."

However, one day he took us up on the funicular up the hill,
where we visited a small cemetery and saw the grave of Stalin's
mother, a simple Georgian woman who had died only a few
years before. "It's a funny thing," said Toidze, "but when I see
the old woman's grave, I still can't help feeling proud of Georgia;
for if it hadn't been for Stalin, God knows what would have
happened during the war. . . ."

We stayed the night in the large town of Maharadze in
Western Georgia, and then Toidze took us to an enormous tea-
growing state farm which had a population of 1,100 people,
including 600 workers, many of them women. Of its 900 hectares,
600 were under tea. Attached to the farm was the "tea factory",
where the leaves were dried, sorted, cut and packed. The workers
on this state farm were much better paid than on state farms in
Russia, and although most of them were Georgians, there had
latterly been an influx of Russian and Ukrainian workers, chiefly
from Rostov and Odessa, who were finding life here much easier,
and food more plentiful. Here again was a symptom of that 1946
migration to the south—a flight from the drought-stricken areas.

Most of the workers on this *sovkhoz* lived in blocks of flats built on the crest of a hill, for in the valleys there was still some malaria. Hundreds of eucalyptus trees had been planted, partly to drain the soil, partly to discourage the mosquitoes, and eventually to become valuable timber. Enormous trees grew in eight or nine years. As in the *kolkhozes*, so in the *sovkhozes*, each worker had his individual plot. Here most of them grew vegetables, oranges and tangerines, which they then either ate or sold in the market. The work on the *sovkhozes* was paid "by results", and the earnings ranged from 500 to 1,200 roubles a month. As distinct from the *kolkhozes*, they were paid in cash, not in produce, and there were also cheap canteen meals. The centre of the *sovkhoz* was a large pool with jumping Garbusia fishes, specially imported from Italy, which snapped up mosquitoes.

The enormous tea plantation was an impressive affair, and the Georgians never tired of repeating that one-third of all the tea consumed in the Soviet Union came from Georgia. The rest was imported from India and Ceylon, but the proportion of Georgian tea would rapidly rise. The tea industry had been started in a small way before the Revolution with plants imported from Ceylon and India.

The *sovkhoz* also contained a "cooperative store", and some consumer goods—including some rather shoddy textiles—could be bought at "ration" prices. But the shortage of consumer goods was very marked, and so was the shortage of modern agricultural machinery. Even so, this was a part of the Soviet Union which, apart from some severe military casualties, had not suffered in the war. The director of the state farm naturally invited us all to a jovial supper party of some twenty people, he himself presiding over the proceedings as the *tamada*, or toast-master. It went on for hours, and although the food was not very plentiful the wine was horrifyingly so, the "ration" per head being five litres! The women did the serving, and did not sit down to supper. The toasts ranged from that to Comrade Stalin to the much more fanciful ones later on in the proceedings—for instance: "To the little birds who, sitting on the telegraph wires, welcomed our dear guests on their way to our *sovkhoz*." The trouble was that it was not done to drink less than a full glass with each toast. After nearly three bottles, Ziemowit and I gave up, and an embarrassed Toidze, mumbling excuses, had to pack us into

the car and drive us back to Maharadze. Having driven out of our
hosts' sight, we begged for the car to stop, rolled out of it and
brought up our three litres of wine. Oriental hospitality, we
thought (if we could think of anything), sometimes went too
far. The next morning Toidze said our behaviour was regrettable,
but since we weren't Georgians our hosts had taken it very well.
If we had been Georgians, they would have been mortally
offended.

We took the train to Batum, and during the latter part of the
journey the line followed the Black Sea coast. A damp heat was
rising from the tropical tangle of vegetation, and the air was
filled with the scent of flowers and eucalyptus. All the alarmist
talk in the Western press about a "Russian invasion of Turkey"
seemed quite nonsensical—the hills we could see fifteen miles to
the south *were* Turkey, and no place seemed sleepier, lazier and
less martial than Batum. In the west end there was a magnificent
park and a promenade along the sea front, and some modern
hotels built shortly before the war. The east end had the usual
"oriental" appearance. Here was the same kind of market, and
also a theatre where they were playing *Oedipus Rex* in Georgian.
The harbour was not busy, but in the crowded sea-front cafés
they were still talking about the ship that, the day before, had
brought 3,000 more Armenians repatriates from Syria. The
repatriation of thousands of Armenian from all over the world
to Soviet Armenia, and especially from the Middle East, was in
full swing.

The attitude of the Georgians to the Armenians was a rather
mixed one. In the course of our supper that night at the Dukhan
Simpatia, our charming Intourist girl told us the sad story of how
she was engaged to a very handsome young man and how, when
her parents learned that he was an Armenian and not a Georgian,
she had to break off the engagement.

While at Batum, Toidze received an urgent phone call from
Tbilisi and looked distinctly flustered. It seems that, at least in
Moscow's view, he had exceeded his powers, and should not have
taken us to Batum. So he packed us on to the night train—where
we suffered mercilessly from the bedbugs—and took us back to
Tbilisi. But I still do not believe there were any Russian troop
movements along the Turkish border. I was sorry to think we
might unwittingly have got our Georgian friend into trouble.

He was a very civilized human being and seemed to have forgotten for a few days that Moscow "harshness" to which he himself had referred.

At Tbilisi we were back in the clutches of Intourist. We had one more jovial party at the Dukhan Simpatia—with its beautifully primitive Douanier-Rousseau-like portraits of celebrities, including Queen Tamara, Pushkin, Lermontov, President McKinley and Thomas Edison, all painted by one Gregoriants in 1904—and then took the plane back to Moscow. Except that the pilot was a war pilot and a peculiar kind of practical joker who liked to frighten passengers by suddenly diving a thousand feet, the journey was uneventful and positively a bore compared with our slow journeys through Kabardia and Ossetia and down the Georgian Military Highway.

What conclusions could one draw from these travels in the summer of 1946? First, that life was slowly, but only very slowly, returning to normal in the areas that had been hit by the war; that the drought in an enormous part of the country was causing new anxieties and the promise of even greater privations; and that this was causing quite a considerable migration from the hunger-threatened areas to the more favoured ones like the northern Caucasus and Transcaucasia; then that in the northern Caucasus the deportation of whole nationalities to the East had left a deep and painful impression and that, in a relatively highly favoured country like Georgia, they were talking of Russian "colonial exploitation", and were conscious of the "heavy hand of Moscow" pressing on them; finally, that there was much disappointment at the way things were going internationally, and that the American atom bomb was having a depressing effect, but that on the whole this disappointment had not yet reached the anxiety and anger of six months or a year later. Nobody was much concerned about Iran and Turkey, except some people in Transcaucasia who felt that Russia had a good case there but that she was in no position to force a showdown.

NINE

The Satellites in 1946

Although the history of the East European countries more or less under Soviet domination is outside the immediate scope of this book, much of what went on in these countries is relevant to the question of East/West relations and of their rapid deterioration. Broadly speaking, Rumania and Bulgaria were toeing the Soviet line in 1946, though, significantly, young King Michael, who had been awarded the highest Soviet decoration for the role he had played in the anti-German revolt of August 1944, was still on the throne. True, he had been mercilessly bullied by Vyshinsky about the time of Yalta into replacing the "pro-Western" Radescu government by the "pro-Soviet" Groza government, but on the surface relations continued to be correct, and in 1946 the King organized a great reception in honour of Marshal Tolbukhin, one of the victors of the Germans in Rumania.

In Czechoslovakia, with Benes still as president, parliamentary democracy continued, and in 1946 Maurice Hindus wrote a rapturous book on Czechoslovakia showing it to be the ideal example of peaceful East/West coexistence. The communists—with their 40 per cent vote—held many important government posts, but they were on the friendliest terms with the other members of the government coalition. Finland, continuing to make her punctual reparations deliveries, presented no problem. Yugoslavia was more enthusiastically communist than any of the other East European countries, and the Soviet press was particularly enthusiastic about it, though Stalin had, on the quiet, some mental reservations about Tito, and the Yugoslavs' extreme aggressiveness towards the United States at the Paris Peace Conference was sometimes even excessive. The Russians had to restrain them and even made them apologize and pay compensation for the American planes shot down over Yugoslavia.

Apart from that, however, relations between the Soviet Union and Yugoslavia seemed wonderfully good. In April 1946 a Soviet film on Yugoslavia, directed by Leonid Varlamov and with a script by Ehrenburg, was released in Moscow which not only celebrated the indissoluble bonds between the Soviet Union and Yugoslavia, but even went out of its way to exalt Tito as a great hero, showing him, for instance, addressing frantic crowds from a balcony in Belgrade. In April 1945, a friendship, mutual-aid and post-war cooperation agreement had been signed between the two countries, and this was now followed up, in June 1946, by an even more extensive economic agreement, which provided for Soviet arms supplied to the Yugoslav army and for close cultural and political cooperation. Tito had come specially to Moscow to sign this agreement, which was to contribute within two years, to the great crisis in Soviet/Yugoslav relations. But now all *seemed* well, and it almost appeared that not the Soviet Union but Yugoslavia was the greatest beneficiary under the agreement. *Pravda* of 12th June 1946 printed on its front page a large picture of Tito and, with it, his farewell words:

We are deeply moved and happy that the Soviet government and, in particular, the great Stalin should have fully appreciated our difficulties in the restoration of our country, and should have come to our aid in all matters.

The agreement we have reached is of the greatest importance to the restoration of war-devastated Yugoslavia. It shows that Yugoslavia has, in the Soviet Union, the most sincere friend and defender.

Generalissimo Stalin is a great friend of Yugoslavia. Long live the great Stalin!

So there was little for the Russians to worry about in the case of Yugoslavia, which was if anything being even more communist than Russia. Bulgaria, where the communists were on the whole in full control too, Rumania, which was doing as she was told, with the Western powers having more or less washed their hands of her, albeit reluctantly, and Finland and Czechoslovakia, each in her own way, also presented no immediate political problem.

East Germany had not yet reached satellite "status" and was, for the present, being chiefly used as a source of reparations, its future still wrapt in mystery pending further East/West negotiations on the future of Germany as a whole. Not that there were not already very strong grounds for the suspicion that the final split of Germany was making rapid progress.

There remained the peculiar cases of Hungary and Poland. In the case of Hungary the Russians were playing a relatively "liberal" game. Stalin had stressed to Byrnes in December 1945 that the general election in Hungary during the previous October had not been favourable to the communists, and he sounded quite reconciled to that. Since the end of the war, Hungary had adopted a new republican constitution, had built up afresh the administrative machinery of the state, had carried out a radical land reform, and had restored the railways and 80 to 90 per cent of its pre-war industrial capacity. It had lived through the biggest and fastest inflation on record, and had successfully established a new and stable currency.

Not that all was well. There were great difficulties in getting coal and other fuel. In 1946 Hungary had been hit by a drought, and the harvest was 40 per cent below normal; but despite the land reform 97 per cent of the pre-war acreage had been sown. One observer wrote:

> Budapest is in much better shape than Vienna. The war damage had been restored. Restaurants and shops are flourishing. There are two new bridges over the Danube. . . . In Vienna the black market is the main topic, but there is no black market in Budapest. . . . The oppressive occupation atmosphere of Vienna and Germany is absent in Budapest, and the Red Army here is inconspicuous.*

All the papers, the same writer reported, were run by the various political parties. Not that the Red Army was popular with the local population—the excesses had not been forgotten. But the behaviour of the Red Army had radically improved in the last six months, and requisitionings and industrial removals had ceased. The laws passed by the Hungarian parliament had to be submitted to the Allied Control Commission's approval, but this had caused no major difficulties. Russian influence, Kaldor

* Nicholas Kaldor, *Manchester Guardian*, 29th October 1946.

commented, had manifested itself in only two things: the land reform carried out in 1945, and the complexion of the coalition government appointed after the election.

The land reform was instituted by the provincial government of Debrecen (that is, before the end of the war) largely on Russian insistence. Without this, it would have come about more slowly, and less thoroughly. There was, however, no disagreement among the political parties, except the Right, on the necessity of the reform. One quarter of the larger estates being owned by the Church, it was doubtful whether any government on its own would have carried the reform into effect.

This was clearly a point in the Russians' favour.

As regards Russian influence on the make-up of the cabinet, this was a more arguable matter.

In the general election the Communists had polled 17 per cent of the votes; the Socialists 17 per cent, the National Peasant Party 8 per cent; the Smallholders 57 per cent. In the government the Communists did not get an excessive number of seats, but they had exceptional influence, since the Ministry of the Interior controlling the police went to them.

The anti-Fascist and anti-Horthyite purge went further than the smallholders would have liked; it amounted in fact almost to the wholesale dismissal of the class of "gentry" that traditionally dominated the public offices of Hungary.

This elimination of the class of feudal landowners and of the traditional bureaucracy represents a social revolution of . . . permanent significance to Hungary. For both these reforms the Russians rather than the internal forces of the revolution must be held responsible.

Now, it is quite clear that neither in 1945 nor in 1946 did the Russians want to set up a communist dictatorship in Hungary. This emerges very clearly and explicitly from Kaldor's well-informed report. Hungary was in the peculiar position of having remained the last of Hitler's satellites. But by the end of the war the pro-Hitlerite Hungarians had largely vanished from their country. This created an odd situation.

The Germans were followed by members of [Salasi's] Arrow-Cross Government and an indefinite number of officials of the earlier Horthy administration. So when the Russians came, the Hungarian government machinery was almost non-existent. . . . The population of the villages, politically enfeebled by long years of dictatorship or feudal semi-dictatorship, was not in a mood to revolt or organize. . . . It simply expected a communist dictatorship.

But, says Kaldor, *a communist dictatorship is not what the Russians wanted.* Instead, they wanted a new government, both on the national and local level, built on the coalition principle and composed of the representatives of all the anti-Fascist parties: the communists, the social democrats, the smallholders, the national peasants and various small liberal groups.

The Hungarian communists from Moscow not only organized the new Hungarian Communist Party, but also saw to it that the national committees in each village had a fair proportion of each party. The organization of the parties preceded, in fact, the building of the administrative machinery of the state, and the parties became powerful groups, owning cinemas, papers and a variety of commercial enterprises.

In the general election, the first to be held in Hungary with universal suffrage and under secret ballot, six parties took part— the communists and social democrats, with a working-class clientele; the national peasant party, representing the landless peasants; the smallholders, representing the small farmers; the liberals and radicals, representing the town bourgeoisie. In the absence of a proper right-wing party, all the reactionaries, clericals, conservatives and fascists, voted for the smallholders, which got 57 per cent of the votes; but of these only 15 per cent represented the real smallholder vote.

The absence of a Right and Catholic Party in the 1945 election was a serious mistake. The result was that the real opposition was not inside, but outside parliament, centring round the young Primate, Cardinal Mindszenty. And Kaldor concludes:

> The Coalition now is not a working combination of social groups with largely parallel aims, but an uneasy partnership of mutually antagonistic forces. . . . If the Catholic Right had been represented in Parliament, the four Coalition parties would still have polled 60 per cent—enough for a working majority, and a large right-wing opposition would have given added cohesion to the coalition. Instead, the Smallholders' Party, supported by reactionaries, is being pushed steadily to the Right. The more enlightened leaders of the

party like Ferencz Nagy are anxious to combat this tendency. . . .
(But it is not easy) and while the Right cannot take over, or even
participate in the government . . . they have a large but undefined
influence on the strongest party in the government, and this leaves
them far more room for manoeuvring than they would have in
open parliamentary opposition. The socialists and communists
would not be opposed now to the creation of a Catholic Party;
they'd be glad to have it. But the real opposition to this comes
from the group round Mindszenty.*

Here was a very curious situation for the Russians, without any
exact parallel in any of the other Eastern European countries.
They had given a fair chance to "free elections", but had limited
them to "anti-fascist" parties; as a result, the "fascists" came in
by the back door.†

With the Cold War developing, and not only the "Mindszenty
group" but also many of the smallholder leaders seeking salvation from the West, the Russians' "liberal" and "parliamentary"
experiment in Hungary came to an end. But it seems highly
significant that they should have started their Hungarian policy
in this way, just as until February 1948 they fully tolerated a
regular Western form of democracy in Czechoslovakia.

A few words should be said here of Hungarian/Soviet economic
relations, as they developed just after the war, for this also is
typical of the period under review. Since the armistice, Russia
had a share in Hungary's output, because, for the following six
years—later extended to eight years—she was due for reparations.
Russia had also acquired an interest in Hungarian industries
through the Potsdam agreement and the Soviet/Hungarian agreement on the creation of joint Soviet/Hungarian firms. Moreover,
the Soviet/Hungarian trade agreement showed that large-scale
trade between the two countries was contemplated. Under the
armistice, Hungary had agreed to pay $300 million (1938 pur-
chasing power) in reparations—$200 million to the Soviet
Union and $100 million to Yugoslavia and Czechoslovakia.
Under the reparations agreement Russia was to take about 25 per

---

* *Manchester Guardian*, 30th October 1946.

† Perhaps the closest parallel is to be found in post-war France, where most of
the "reactionaries" voted for the MRP, the most right-wing of the "Resistance"
parties, who, indeed, did not fail to turn the MRP into a remarkable reactionary
party.

cent of all the factory production, or 15 per cent of all industrial production, and in the first year about 5 per cent of Hungary's industrial equipment was taken as "war booty". But in 1946 this was stopped. Under Potsdam, Russia was entitled to all pre-war German property in Hungary, that is, thirty or forty large or medium firms. The Soviet/Hungarian companies were concerned with civil aviation, Danube shipping, oil and bauxite, the Russians providing the planes, ships, etc. Under the commercial agreement, Hungary received from Russia $20 million of raw cotton. The agreements made showed that Hungary was to be part of Russia's economic sphere of influence, the Soviet Union holding in relation to Hungary much the same kind of place as Germany held before the war. The important difference lay in this: Germany was interested in Hungary as a source of food and raw materials and as a market for manufactured goods. With Russia the opposite was true: Russia was interested in Hungary primarily as an industrial country, with an emphasis on light industry. Whereas Germany hampered Hungarian industrial development, Russia was now, on the contrary, encouraging it. At the time, at any rate, the Russians saw no objection to the Hungarians selling cereals and other food surpluses to the West.

If, in allowing free elections in Hungary—even though limited only to "anti-fascist" parties—the Russians were prepared to take a chance there, they were not going to take any such chances in Poland.

In the West, the "rape" and "betrayal" of Poland have been described in great—and lurid—detail. There is no doubt that the Russians were highly conscious from the outset that they were dealing with a country whose population was in the main hostile to them. Several factors contributed to this hostility: the "partition" of Poland between Nazi Germany and the Soviet Union in 1939; the deportation of many hundreds of thousands of Poles to the Soviet Union in 1939; the almost general conviction that the Russians, and not the Germans, were responsible for the massacre of over 10,000 Polish officers at Katyn; the strong suspicion, if not the conviction, on the part of many Poles that the Russians had consciously "betrayed" the Warsaw rising of August 1944, as a result of which some 300,000 Poles lost their lives and the Nazis turned the city into a heap of rubble. To probably the great majority of the Poles, influenced by the Catholic

Church, the Polish London government was the "real" government of Poland, while the Lublin Committee, set up in July 1944 and recognized by the Soviet government in January 1945 as *the* Polish government, was nothing but a bunch of usurpers and Russian stooges. The anti-German Polish underground army (the *Armija Krajowa*) was under the orders of the Polish government in London and was essentially anti-Russian. When I went to Poland in August 1944, in the district of Lublin alone some 2,000 AK men had already been arrested by the Russians, and by the time Poland came to be discussed at Yalta in February 1945 many more thousands—according to Mikolajczyk as many as 40,000—had been arrested or deported.

Mikolajczyk, the leader of the Polish Peasant Party, had resigned from the premiership of the Polish government in London at the end of 1944 and was replaced by Mr. Arcyszewski. This government had been totally uncompromising in its attitude to Russia and in particular would have nothing to do with the "surrender" to Russia of the whole of what they still regarded as "Eastern Poland"—and what was, to the Russians, "Western Belorussia" and the "Western Ukraine". More realistic than his former London colleagues, Mikolajczyk was prepared to accept the Curzon Line, marking in effect the ethnographic border between Polish-inhabited and predominantly non-Polish parts of the country, in return for large parts of Eastern Germany, up to the Oder/Neisse Line. Mikolajczyk and a few of his colleagues thus became Churchill's last hope of introducing into the Russian-formed Polish government certain "Western" elements who would at least create the semblance of what might be called an "East/West" coalition government. Churchill was highly conscious of the fact that Polish soldiers had fought in France in 1940, and then in Libya, in Italy, in Normandy; and that in 1939 England had "gone to war" for Poland. Most of the unpleasantness with the Russians between Britain and Russia had been precisely over Poland; but if Churchill knew that, of all the East European countries, Poland was the one with the deepest grievances against Russia. Stalin, while also fully aware of this, was determined that it was precisely Poland that it was most important for the Russians to tame. He had no great illusions about winning over the Poles in the immediate future, but though more in terms of a long-term accommodation, as a result of which the Poles would "get used" to their alliance with Russia and their dependence on Russia.

The nucleus of a pro-Russian Poland was created by the constitution on Russian soil of several Polish divisions in 1943 and 1944, by the setting-up of a pro-Soviet Polish government and the creation of a powerful Polish—even if largely Russian-controlled—police apparatus.

It would be untrue to say that there were no genuine pro-Russians in Poland. Only too many remembered that in 1939 Chamberlain's "guarantee" to Poland had done nothing to save her from seven years of the most ruthless Nazi occupation. In spite of everything, Enemy No. 1 was still Germany, and the Russians could be depended upon, more than the West, to protect Poland against the Germans. And the very fact that enormous areas of Eastern Germany, including Danzig, Silesia and even Stettin, right up to the Oder/Neisse Line, were now, thanks to the Russians, being incorporated in the new Poland was a strong point in their favour. These areas, with their good agricultural land and their enormous industrial wealth, were more valuable than the bogs and forests of "Eastern Poland". Moreover, with Poles colonizing all these areas, from which the Germans were being driven out, Poland would be an almost entirely homogeneously Polish country for the first time. True, there were in the East Lwow and Vilno, which the Poles regarded as essentially "Polish" cities, but on these two points the Russians would not yield.

Very much under pressure from Churchill, and after numerous abortive negotiations during the previous year between the "London" and "Lublin" Poles, Mikolajczyk finally agreed, after long discussions in Moscow, to enter the Warsaw government, and on 28th June 1945 its formation was officially announced. In Mikolajczyk's words, fourteen out of its twenty-one members were, as agreed, "Lublin" Poles; the rest were "London" or "pro-Western" Poles who had been in Poland all the time. But the very next day two more government posts were created, and these went to communists; this was the first, albeit minor, violation of what had been agreed. The principal members of the Polish provisional government were the Premier, a "socialist" called Osobka-Morawski; the two Vice-Premiers, Gomulka and Mikolajczyk himself; Rola Zymienski, Minister of Defence;

Radkiewicz, Minister of Public Security; Hilary Minc, Minister of Industry; Jan Stanczyk (a London Pole), Minister of Labour; etc. To Mikolajczyk, Gomulka, a genuine Polish communist, was nothing but a "maniac" and a "raving lunatic".

Great hostility developed almost from the outset between the "Russian stooges" and Mikolajczyk, who came to symbolize, as it were, "the Western ideal of freedom and democracy" and who, as leader of the Peasant Party, claimed to have the great majority of Polish opinion behind him. What complicated his task, however, was that, as he himself says, Britain and the USA, having achieved the semblance of a "compromise" with the Russians over the Polish government, had then in effect washed their hands of it. For all that, he had a great following in the country, and was particularly popular among the peasant masses and in strongly clerical and anti-Russian cities like Cracow.

At first Mikolajczyk was not without influence. He got the government to approve, as early as August 1945, an amnesty for the rank-and-file of the AK, the Home Army, though the "Lublin" Poles refused to have this amnesty extended to the AK leaders. Even so, 200,000 members of the AK became "normal citizens". He also used his influence, partly for humanitarian reasons, but partly no doubt also for political reasons, to secure from the West substantial UNRRA help—significantly amounting, in the case of Poland, to over $400 million (the Ukraine, a much larger country, received only $180 million).

But soon Mikolajczyk began to be sabotaged in a variety of ways: the communists and socialists, fully conscious of the fact that, though a member of the government, he was in fact *the* Opposition leader, created a Peasant Party of their own, bearing the same name of SL (Stronnitzwo Ludowo); Mikolajczyk's attempt to "merge" the two seemingly identical peasant parties into one met with violent opposition from the communists, particularly Jakob Berman, "Stalin's principal Russian agent" as Mikolajczyk invariably describes him. In the circumstances, Mikolajczyk renamed the SL the PSL (Polish Peasant Party); and already in September 1945 the terrorism against this party was begun. Without saying anything about the numerous murders of communists by remnants of the AK and other right-wing organizations (for there was, in fact, a minor civil war which continued to rage in Poland at least up to 1948), Mikolajczyk describes in lurid detail the murder by the Security Police of a certain Kojder, a leading member of the PSL, in September, and of one Scibiorek a few months later. The PSL press met with continuous obstruction from the censorship, but more important still, according to Mikolajczyk, were the mass arrests among members and supporters of the PSL by the Polish security police working hand-in-hand with Russian NKVD "counsellors". He tells of numerous cases of murders and tortures which occurred even as early as the end of 1945.

In the provisional parliament the PSL were given many fewer seats than originally agreed to, but Mikolajczyk still used this parliament as a place where he could publicly denounce the police terror, even though his speeches were never published, except in an expurgated form, in any Polish paper. The communists meantime never ceased denouncing Mikolajczyk's party as being part of "the criminal underground".

On 30th June 1946 came the referendum. There were three questions: one concerned the abolition of the Senate under the 1921 Constitution; the second, the economic structure of Poland (land reform, nationalization of key industries, maintenance of private enterprise); the third, the Oder/Neisse Line. Mikolajczyk did not quarrel with points 2 and 3, but advocated a negative vote on the first question—by way of a protest against "the police state". According to Mikolajczyk the voting on the first question was No, 84 per cent; Yes, 16 per cent; the official figures published by the government were No, 32 per cent; Yes, 68 per cent. The "free and unfettered" elections, as provided by the Yalta and Potsdam agreements, took place a few months later, in January 1947. During the preceding weeks, an abortive attempt was made to get the PSL to join the "government bloc" in the coming elections. When this attempt failed, as many as 100,000 PSL members (again according to Mikolajczyk) were arrested and 130 murdered. Much also was made of Mikolajczyk's friendship with the USA, whose Secretary of State Mr. James Byrnes, had shortly before, in his speech at Stuttgart, declared himself against the Oder/Neisse Line. Thus, in Polish government propaganda, the PSL became the "pro-German party", even though its leader had protested against the Stuttgart speech.

The "free and unfettered" elections were, of course, a swindle, rather like the French-controlled elections in Algeria. Judging from a small number of constituencies where Mikolajczyk succeeded in keeping a close watch on the count, over 70 per cent voted for the PSL and less than 30 per cent for the government bloc. But, as Stalin had told a Polish socialist and communist delegation who had gone to see him in Moscow shortly before the election:

> Don't worry about the Americans and the British. There will be no war because of the Polish election results; no doubt they will protest, but it will be one more protest. You just get on with the job, and declare that Mikolajczyk has been beaten, because he is associated with the criminal underground. He is, like the Americans, against the Western frontier of Poland; he is a reactionary who wants the capitalists and landlords to take over Poland. He is also a foreign agent. If you repeat this often enough, you will even find a good many people in England and America believing you. . . . Now you can go; but you must send me [secretly] the real results of the election; I want to see how much influence you are really gaining in Poland.*

In the new parliament which met after the election, 327 seats went to the government bloc, 24 seats to the PSL of Mikolajczyk and 21 seats to some minor parties. Although he was against breaking diplomatic relations with Poland, Mr. Arthur Bliss Lane, the US Ambassador, resigned by way of protest against the "election swindle".

After the election Mikolajczyk and two others resigned from the government, and the new parliament hastened to replace the 1921 Constitution by a provisional "Little Constitution". This set up a "State Council" (modelled, in Mikolajczyk's words, on the Supreme Soviet). On 7th February 1947 a "coalition government" was formed. Out of the twenty-four ministerial posts only five went to communists; the others went to the other members of the bloc, and even a few to the small parties outside the electoral coalition. A number of economic laws were passed. Under one of them private trade was handicapped in favour of state enterprises; another limited the number of private businesses and industries; another heavily taxed *kulaks*; further, the old type of independent cooperatives was abolished, as well as the independent trade unions; strikes were made a criminal offence. All heavy industry was nationalized. A rent law was calculated to

* S. Mikolajczyk, *Le viol de la Pologne*, pp. 208–9.

pauperize and finally ruin the owners of houses, who were to let flats at the pre-war rate in now-devalued zlotys. Twenty-eight per cent of the budget was to be spent on the army and police; the security police totalled 230,000 men, besides the auxiliary ORMO police of 120,000. In central Poland large estates were split up into smallholdings, but in the formerly German territories a number of state farms were also set up. According to Mikolajczyk's figures, the economic relations between Poland and the Soviet Union were highly beneficial to the latter.

Mikolajczyk, of course, makes all the Polish leaders out to be simple Russian stooges—whether Gomulka, the overlord of the Western territories, or the other members of the Politburo, Berman, Zambrowski, Minc (the economic "dictator"), Radkiewicz, head of the police, Spychalski, political chief of the army, or Modzelewski, the foreign minister. Oddly enough, to Mikolajczyk, Gomulka was the worst "maniac" of all, and "scarcely sane". Written after his escape from Poland in October 1947, Mikolajczyk's book is little more than preventive-war propaganda, as the following passage suggests:

> The Western democracies must always remember: if Russia today had the atom bomb and other weapons of mass destruction—provided they had them in sufficient numbers—they would immediately destroy the United States and the British Isles, and any other moral and material force standing in the way of their ideology.

One must, therefore, accept with some reservations the horrors upon horrors he piles up in describing conditions in Poland in 1947, with his stories of countless murders committed against the PSL and other enemies of the regime, and his complete silence on the "counter-murders" committed by the right-wing underground. In reality, conditions in Poland calmed down after the 1947 election and the various amnesties. Not that the campaign against Mikolajczyk himself abated for a moment, and when in October 1947 he learned that his parliamentary immunity was about to be lifted (which meant certain arrest) he hastened to escape from Poland.

The elimination of Mikolajczyk from Polish affairs in 1947 was typical of the evolution of the Cold War in Eastern Europe. He unquestionably represented the "West" in Polish politics, and was, to say the least, a major nuisance to the new regime. In view of the unquestionably wide support the "West" was enjoying in Poland, the Russians could not afford (as they could, at least for a time, in Czechoslovakia and even Hungary) the luxury of those "free and unfettered" elections which had been agreed upon by the Big Three at Yalta and Potsdam. What Mikolajczyk did not, however, foresee was the temporary, if reluctant, acceptance of the "minority regime" by the Polish people, and their gradual emancipation from Sovietization and Stalinization— a process which, oddly enough, was conducted by the very man whom Mikolajczyk considered the most "maniacal" of all the Russian stooges—namely Gomulka. In 1950 Gomulka was imprisoned as a sort of Polish "Titoite" and did not re-emerge as the genuine leader of Poland—but of a socialist Poland—until 1956. By then the Soviet bloc was loosening. But in 1947 a hard and Russian-controlled regime was set up. In the years that followed it became harder still, though it never went to the extremes of the Stalinist regime in Rumania, Hungary or Czechoslovakia. Oddly enough, President Bierut, "NKVD Bierut", as he was commonly known, was credited even by his political opponents with having done much to save Poland from the worst rigours of Stalinism. Gomulka, it is true, was arrested in 1950; but Poland never had anything like the Rajk, Kostov or Slansky trials. . . . The rebellious Polish national character, which even Bierut had to take into account, had something to do with it.

What even at the worst of times favoured the Russians in Poland was the threat of Germany to both Poland and Russia. Freed of Stalinist coercion, the Poles readily accepted the alliance of Russia—the country which, unlike the United States, had always insisted on the permanence of the Oder/Neisse frontier. Moreover, socialism—without collectivization—was also acceptable to Poland. An anti-Russian and pro-Western Mikolajczyk Poland was wholly unrealistic. Stalin knew that even Harry Truman would not go to war because the 1947 Polish election had been a swindle according to the more purist Western standards.

Some of the more wicked absurdities of Stalinism during the late 1940s, such as Lysenkoism in science and Zhdanovism in literature and the arts, had no parallel in Poland, and when at the international Cultural Congress, held at Wroclaw, in August

1948, the Soviet delegation headed by Alexander Fadeyev advocated—with Ehrenburg alone assuming a somewhat ambiguous position—a Zhdanovist cultural line, the Poles, without openly objecting, looked distinctly embarrassed.

And even at the height of Russian military and police control in Poland—and this went on in fact until 1956, with Marshal K. K. Rokossovski as "Polish" Minister of Defence,★ and with the skyline of a newly reconstructed Warsaw becoming more and more dominated by its Stalin-Gothic skyscrapers, the "Palace of Culture", which was as much a symbol of Russian domination as the giant Orthodox Cathedral built under Alexander III and demolished in 1924 had been—even then one of Warsaw's most flourishing industries was that of anti-Russian jokes and wisecracks, and these were circulated with almost complete impunity.

★ He was of Polish parentage, and temporarily re-acquired Polish citizenship.

TEN

Russia Weakened by Hunger

It was not only hunger that the disastrous 1946 drought had produced, but in some parts of the country actual famine. When, in 1964, shortly before his fall, Khrushchev had to explain why the Soviet Union had had to buy large quantities of wheat in the United States and Canada, he said that he cared more than Stalin did for the lives and well-being of the Soviet people. In 1947, he said, there were places in Russia, notably in his own native province of Kursk, where people were *dying of starvation*. Despite this, for strictly political reasons Stalin had thought fit to send hundreds of thousands of tons of grain abroad—an allusion to the shipments of grain to France, Finland, Czechoslovakia and Rumania.

The Foreign Ministers' Conference which was to meet in Moscow in March 1947 was taking place in a hungry, if not a starving, country; and there was a defiant and shocking propaganda purpose in making the huge Moskva Hotel, where most of the delegates and foreign press stayed, a scene of luxurious living, with torrents of wine and vodka and cognac, unlimited supplies of caviare and smoked salmon, and interminable menus of opulent dishes. The most indecent item, somehow, was the milk-and-vermicelli soup that figured on the menu. Not an attractive item at the best of times, it was now a particularly revolting one when one considered that the children of Moscow were short of milk, as of nearly everything else.

If there was no actual starvation in Moscow, people in Moscow —and even more so in other parts of the country—were having a worse time than during the later stages of the war and in 1945.

There were many long-term reasons why agriculture was showing a very low yield; and on top of it had come the drought of 1946. Speaking before the Supreme Soviet on 20th February 1947, A. G. Zverev, the Minister of Finance of the USSR, said:

The very severe drought has had a deplorable effect on our agriculture in 1946; this drought has affected a very considerable part of the European territory of the Soviet Union. There has been no such drought in the last fifty years, and the area affected was greater than was the case in 1921.*

However, thanks to the advantages of the socialist organization of agricultural production, both the overall harvest and the quantity of marketable grain in 1946 were incomparably higher than in 1921, and in areas not affected by the drought, the total production of grain, sunflower seed and sugar beet showed an improvement over 1945. However, as a whole, the output of all these three crops was lower than in 1945.†

No doubt the "socialist organization" to which Mr. Zverev referred had, here and there, limited the damage, but it was cold comfort to the population as a whole. The long-term causes of the food shortage went back to the war years:

(1) There was a lower yield per hectare all over the country owing to the decline in the mechanization of agriculture. This had already made itself increasingly felt during the war, when tanks had to be produced instead of tractors; and since then the reconversion of industry to peace-conditions had been disappointingly slow. Tractors and agricultural machinery had fulfilled in 1946 only 77 per cent of the Gosplan target for the year.

The Kharkov tractor plant, after two years of rebuilding, was now turning out only two or three tractors a day, as against twelve or fifteen before the war; at Stalingrad the tractor plant was still in the process of rebuilding, and at Rostov, Rostselmash, the agricultural machinery plant, was working at only one-sixth pre-war capacity, and the restoration scheduled for 1946 had

---

* 1921 was the year of the great famine when, much to Lenin's disgust (for he suspected the "charitable" Americans of the most villainous designs and altogether this appeal for foreign aid as a deplorable confession of failure), the ARA, headed by Herbert Hoover, saved millions of people from starvation in the famine-stricken areas of Russia, particularly in the Volga country.

† *Zasedaniya Verkhovnogo Sovieta SSSR, 3-ya sessiya, 20–25 Fev. 1947,* Moscow, 1947, p. 15.

14

been fulfilled only to the extent of 46 per cent. The Rostov plant evacuated to the East was slow in its reconversion. Altogether, 1946 proved a difficult and unproductive transition year.

The agricultural machinery and tractor situation in the Ukraine was very bad. Mr. Paul White, one of the UNRRA officials there, went at the end of 1946 to the USA in the hope of getting a few hundred tractors which had been promised, but had not then been delivered. If in Poland—no doubt for political reasons— UNRRA's help (largely as a result of Mikolajczyk's appeals to the USA) was considerable—above 400 million dollars—the Ukraine was not a privileged customer of UNRRA's.

The great question was whether in 1947 the tractor and agricultural machinery industries would show any marked improvement.

(2) Very largely owing to the drought, civilian consumption of food in the Soviet cities had been drastically cut down from 4th September 1946. It was done in this way: the price of rationed foods in the Soviet Union was admittedly low, and had not been increased since rationing was first introduced in July 1941. The value of the rouble, as a result of wartime inflation, was very low, *except* in the case of rationed goods. And it was precisely here that the rouble lost the greater part of its value. The price of rationed food was suddenly increased $2\frac{1}{2}$ times ($3\frac{1}{2}$ times in the case of bread). The effect of this on Russian living standards was little short of disastrous. Thus, a family of four earning, say, 1,500 roubles (the husband earning 1,000 roubles, the wife 500 roubles and two children nothing) used to spend 200 roubles on their regular rations; now they had to spend 600 or 700 roubles. Where, as in countless other cases, the family income was much lower, there was very little left over for buying anything in the "free market". Now many people, as a result of the rise in the price of bread, were even refraining from buying all the bread to which they were entitled; hence a reduction in the overall consumption of bread, which was obviously one of the government's aims in enforcing higher bread prices.

The capacity to buy anything "over and above the ration" was greatly reduced not only because rations were much more expensive and there was little left for anything else, but in addition as a result of the drought the free market (or *kolkhoz* market) prices had risen enormously since the autumn of 1946. If in early 1946 bread and potatoes were plentiful in the *kolkhoz* markets, they were no longer so now. Potatoes had risen from 3 or 4 roubles a kilo to 13 or 15 roubles; bread from 8 roubles to 40 roubles in Moscow, and to 50 or 60 roubles in some provincial towns. Vegetables and dairy produce were three to five times dearer in early 1947 than they had been in early 1946. A very high proportion of families could not in fact afford to buy *anything* over and above the rations.

The relatively good harvest in Siberia and a few other areas had helped to avert widespread starvation; nevertheless, conditions (except for a few lucky areas) were lamentable in central and south-east Russia, as well as in the Ukraine. It was obvious that the termination of UNRRA in Belorussia and the Ukraine was adding to the harships of the urban (and part of the rural) population of Belorussia and the Ukraine. During the winter of 1946–7 plans had been made for giving superior rations to heavy workers, such as the Donbas miners. Even so, the all-round increase in hardships and undernourishment was inevitable, and only a good harvest in 1947 could save the situation.

And the rations on which the population could, more or less, depend (though not everywhere) were still very meagre. Workers' rations in urban areas were:

Bread, 550 grams a day (a little over 1 lb.)
Fats, 800 grams a month (just over 1½ lb.)
Sugar, 500 grams a month (1 lb.)
Cereals, 1½ kg. a month (3 lb.)
Meat or fish, 2·2 kg. a month (4 lb.)
Tea, 50 grams a month (1¾ oz.)
Matches, 3 boxes a month

True, there were the factory canteen facilities, and produce was in many cases additionally supplied from the factory's farms, besides certain food bonuses for extra-good work, etc. Nevertheless, many workers depended, in the main, on their meagre rations.

But even these were superior to Class II and Class III rations, the former for clerks and "employees" generally, the latter for "dependents", that is non-employed housewives, old people and—with some variations—children. Class II rations were 20 per cent below Class I, and Class III 40 per cent below—in other words, approaching starvation level. If in 1945–6 a fair proportion of the bread was white, in 1946–7 it was 400 grams black and 150 grams white on Class I rations, and all-black in the other categories. On the fats coupons only children, as a rule, received butter (and miserably little at that), and Class II and III ration-cards were often not honoured until a month or even two months later. Also, inferior merchandise was frequently given instead of that marked on the ration card. Thus, instead of sugar, people were given sweets made of saccharine, of low nutritive value. In Moscow, where undernourishment virtually disappeared towards the end of the war and in 1945 and early 1946, many people were beginning to show signs of malnutrition. There had been nothing quite like it since 1942.

All government departments were greatly concerned about the food situation and the harvest of 1947. To the government it was also politically of the utmost importance to have a good harvest, so that it could counteract what was already being referred to as "American food blackmail". Some countries like Finland were already receiving certain quantities of food from the USA that they had originally expected to receive from the Soviet Union and the delivery of which had, at any rate, been "delayed". This Soviet/American rivalry in food deliveries was, as we shall see, going to prove of major historical importance in the case of Czechoslovakia. It seemed doubtful whether, in early 1947, Russia had anything in the nature of a large "political food fund" hidden away.

In a small way Russia was buying food abroad, for instance fish and whale-oil from Norway and Iceland, but this was small stuff and, for international prestige considerations and with an eye on the top priorities of the Five-Year Plan, the government was hoping that the country would somehow pull through till the next harvest.

The drought had some far-reaching effects on the general economy of the country. It was expected that the livestock in the Ukraine would be back to pre-war by 1947; but owing to the drought many cattle had to be slaughtered in the autumn, so that an abnormal amount of meat suddenly appeared in the market, but the livestock rehabilitation programme was set back perhaps for years. Oddly enough, even the "moneyed" people in the

Soviet Union were feeling the pinch. In early 1946 the "commercial restaurants" were crowded with writers, theatre and cinema people, factory executives, army officers and others with money to spend—and these even included some fairly small industrial fry. Many of these people had now little money available for even occasional luxuries, while others no doubt had some qualms about such "binges" in a hungry Moscow. Except on Saturdays and Sundays the commercial restaurants were now half or three-quarters empty.

If the food situation was very serious, the housing situation was no better. In 1946, the transition year, a good deal of patching-up had been done in the devastated areas, and a high proportion of villages had (often very primitively, it is true) been rebuilt. But in Moscow the number of new houses under construction compared with the number needed was still wholly negligible.

In that year of 1947, which was to see the birth of the Marshall Plan in June, the whole of Europe—with a few lucky exceptions like Sweden and Switzerland—was, in varying degrees, feeling hungry. In April and May 1947 there were food riots in France. The winter of 1946-7 was the hardest and hungriest Britain had ever experienced (I remember how, in the down-at-heel restaurants of London, one had to choose between bread and soup —one couldn't have both!) But these hardships were still mild compared with those of most parts of Russia and many other countries in Eastern Europe.

Probably the most tragic plight of all was that of Rumania. On 25th February 1947 there appeared in the *Manchester Guardian* a letter from Mr. Ion Murgu, press counsellor of the Rumanian Government Mission in London, saying that he had just returned from Rumania and could only report that the situation was highly tragic:

> Hundreds of thousands are on the verge of starvation. By the end of March the scanty stocks of grain will have been completely exhausted, and if nothing is done, tens of thousands will die; children's lives being particularly endangered. Help from abroad is the only hope. . . .
> The Soviet Government has given the lead in renouncing this year its entire quota of grain to be delivered under the Armistice terms, and last year the Soviet Union sent us 300,000 tons of cereals which saved thousands of lives. Rumania is rich and will be able to

repay.... But today, after two years of drought, Rumania is the only war-ravaged country that received no help from UNRRA....

Another letter in the *Guardian* from a Rumanian said that 500,000 people were dying of hunger in Moldavia.

The truth is that in 1946–7 *both* Eastern and Western Europe were in dire need of food—and everything else. This should be borne in mind when one comes to consider the enormous economic and political implications of the Marshall Aid which Western Europe gladly accepted (much to the embarrassment, one might add, of the local communist parties) and which Eastern Europe more or less reluctantly rejected owing to the strong political pressure of Moscow.

ELEVEN

Zhdanovism: The First Phase

It is scarcely a coincidence that Zhdanovism, or what one might call the cultural counter-revolution, with its all-out regimentation of thought, should have begun in August 1946, just as the Cold War was becoming increasingly acute and the Soviet Union was moreover faced, as a result of the threatening famine, with even more difficult economic problems than had been anticipated only a few months earlier, at the time of the first post-war meeting of the Supreme Soviet. No doubt ever since 1944 there had been some rumblings about an ideological tightening-up after the war, and official warnings in the Party press that there must be a return to "Leninist purity" in all fields. Already hints were dropped by papers like *Bolshevik* that there must be no "toadying to the West" and that, valuable though the British and Americans were as allies in the war against Nazi Germany, this did not mean that there could be anything like artistic and ideological coexistence, still less "fusion", with their bourgeois and more or less degenerate cultures. Not that there seemed any serious danger, at any time during the war, of Soviet culture going "soft", in a pro-Western sense, or escapist, even if there were a few new works of art which caused some uneasiness to the Party—for instance, Shostakovich's eighth and ninth Symphonies. The composer was let off reasonably lightly, rather with the suggestion that a great and prolific Soviet artist could not be expected to be at his very best all the time.

Art and literature, music, the cinema and the theatre were scarcely a problem during the war. Everybody was doing his or her best for the war effort. It was known, of course, that there were some poets who were not quite as conformist at heart as most, but even they—Boris Pasternak and Anna Akhmatova for instance—were writing patriotic poems like everybody else— even though it was in their *own* way, rather than the *usual* way. The Stalin Prizes that were awarded in January 1946 went to works that were, on the whole, no more and no less orthodox than the rest of the works produced during the 1943-4 period. These prizes had been established in 1939 and were now being awarded for the fourth time. Apart from a very long list of scientists, technicians and industrialists who were given them in 1946 (and these people, it is worth noting in view of what happened in 1948-9, included a large number of Jews), they were awarded to typical wartime works of art, whose quality was usually taken into account when the awards were granted.

In music, first prizes went to a Shaporin oratorio, to a Miaskovsky quartet (No. 9) and to Khachaturian's 2nd Symphony. Second prizes went to A. N. Balanchivadze and G. N. Popov for symphonic works, to Feinberg for a piano concerto and N. Rakov for a violin concerto; to Shostakovich for his Piano Trio, to Chemberdji for a string quartet and V. Zakharov for his *Ode to Stalin* (*Velichalnaya Stalinu*) and other songs. In the theatre, first prizes went to I. Moskvin and other outstanding actors of the Moscow Art Theatre, and to Yuri Zavadsky for his production of Leonid Leonov's remarkable play, *The Invasion*, at the Mossoviet Theatre; a second prize was awarded to S. Obraztsov, head of the superb Moscow Puppet Theatre. In the cinema, first prizes went to Petrov's historic film, *Kutuzov*, and to S. E. Eisenstein for the first part of *Ivan the Terrible*, as well as to its main actors—N. Cherkasov, S. Birman, etc.—to cameraman E. Tissé, and to Prokofiev, who composed the music. Other first prizes went to L. O. Arnstam for his film *Zoya* (about the heroic Komsomol girl, Zoya Kosmodemianskaya, who was hanged by the Germans in a village outside Moscow in November 1941), to M. Chiaureli for the patriotic Georgian film *Georgi Saakadze* and to M. Donskoy for *The Rainbow*, based on Wanda Wasilewska's novel on the German occupation in Russia; second prizes went to A. Room's film on Leonov's *Invasion*; to I. Pyriev's *Six Hours after the War*, and M. I. Romm's *Man No. 217*, a grim film on German captivity. Among documentary films given

Stalin Prizes were *The Rebirth of Stalingrad*, and *The People's Avengers*, on partisan warfare. In fiction the two first prizes went to major historical novels, the veteran V. Shishkov's *Pugachev* and to A. N. Stepanov for his anti-Japanese novel, *Port Arthur*. Second prizes went to Boris Gorbatov's novel on the German occupation of the Donbas, *The Unconquered*, to novels by V. Kaverin and W. Wasilewska, and to K. Simonov for his *Days and Nights*. In poetry first prizes went to Kuleshov, Tvardovsky (*Vasili Terkin*) and Surkov for various wartime poems, and to Lozinsky for his masterly translation of Dante; second prizes were awarded to Antokolsky, Pervomaisky and Alexander Prokofiev. The only play to receive a first prize was Alexie Tolstoy's *Ivan the Terrible*—an obvious glorification of Stalin as a state-builder and a terror to the invaders of Holy Russia.

Since the Stalin Prize Committee was dealing solely with works written during the war, most of these awards seemed fair enough by almost any standard. Even if "oversophisticated" and "neuropathic" works like Shostakovich's Eighth Symphony were given no prize, his far from "socialist-realist" Trio was still given a second prize. That literary quality still mattered could be seen from the fact that only a second prize was given to Simonov's ideologically no doubt perfect, but still in many ways remarkably silly, novel *Days and Nights*, with its sickly love story in a Battle of Stalingrad setting.

The paintings given Stalin Prizes were, on the whole, routine wartime paintings, though some account was still taken of craftsmanship.

After the war the artistic and literary life of the Soviet Union seemed for a time to go on unruffled. More and more novels about the war were being produced and at first it seemed that the Central Committee had no cause for alarm. The theatre was very much on the conservative side, with a preponderance of pre-Revolution classics. Thus, in February 1946, the following were played in Moscow: at the Bolshoi, Tchaikovsky's *Nutcracker* ballet and Glinka's opera *Ivan Susanin*; at the Filiale of the Bolshoi, Rimsky-Korsakov's *Tsar's Bride* and Verdi's *Rigoletto*; at the Malyi, an Ostrovsky play and *Twelfth Night*; at the Moscow Art Theatre, a stage version of Gogol's *Dead Souls* and another Ostrovsky play; at the Kamernyi, a stage adaptation of *Madame Bovary*; at the Vakhtangov, *Mlle Nitouche* and *Much Ado about*

Nothing; at the Red Army Theatre, Gorki's *Petty-Bourgeois*. Only three Soviet plays were shown in the whole of Moscow—two on the war and one on the post-war period, Simonov's *Under the Chestnut Trees of Prague*.

In Soviet cinema something of a landmark was created when, at the end of July, Chiaureli's film *The Oath* (script by P. Pavlenko) was announced and shown soon afterwards in dozens of cinemas in Moscow and in thousands throughout the Soviet Union. Its central character was Stalin himself, and the central episode was the oath he swore on the day of Lenin's funeral to follow in the master's footsteps. Stalin, played by the Georgian actor M. Chekovani (Caucasian accent and all), was represented as a faithful disciple of Lenin, and also as a man with a deep human feeling for the Russian people, symbolized in the film by an elderly heroic Russian woman, Varvara Mikhailovna. Here is a typical *Pravda* commentary on the film:

> Here we see Stalin at Gorki in January 1924, the day Lenin died. We see him winding his way along the snowbound path to the bench where he and Lenin used to sit together so often. Deep is Stalin's sorrow, and he weeps, as do the pilgrims who have come to see Lenin and who have just been told the bitter news. . . . Here is Stalin in Lenin's study, wrapped in thought about Lenin, his life's task, and the future of the young Soviet Republic. His hand is seen scribbling Lenin's profile. . . . And here is Stalin uttering his oath, and the Soviet people are seen repeating every word of that great oath.

And the producer, Chiaureli, is quoted as saying:

> To me the most moving, most beloved episode is the final one, showing the meeting between Josef Vissarionovich Stalin and Varvara Mikhailovna, that noble symbol of the Russian people. . . .

This double process of the "humanization" and "Leninization" of Stalin is fairly significant of the immediate post-war period. The emphasis was no longer, as it was in 1943–5, on Stalin's "military genius", but on Stalin as the head of the "Leninist" state, as the guardian of Leninist purity, and, at least by implication, as the one man in the whole world who was standing up against the imperialist forces of evil now beginning once more to beset the Soviet Union. And he was also to be regarded, more than ever, as the father of his people. *The Oath* clearly marked the beginning of that ideological austerity (to be combined, a little later, with Russian super-chauvinism) which was to find its fullest expression in Zhdanovism in the next few years.

Zhdanovism blossomed out suddenly in August 1946, on the face of it almost by accident. What gave it its first push, as it were, was a "Poets' Evening" held in the famous Pillared Hall in Moscow one day in June. The Party leaders were extremely perturbed by it. The young people of Moscow—above all, its students—as good as ignored the numerous "approved" poets who recited their verses there—for instance the Leningrad poet Alexander Prokofiev—and gave a tremendous ovation to two of the least "approved" ones, Boris Pasternak and Anna Akhmatova. I remember that evening only too well. When Pasternak got stuck in the middle of reciting a poem, a large part of the audience, who knew practically all of Pasternak by heart, acted for him as a sort of multi-vocal prompter; I also remember the anger of the hacks, and Akhmatova's remark when it was all over: "This will lead to no good," of which I was told the next day.

This may seem, at first sight, a trivial episode, but it started in effect (though any similar episode would probably had done just as well) the long process of that totalitarian regimentation of thought which was one of the main characteristics of the last years of Stalin. It extended to almost every realm of human thought, science and art—starting with literature, but going on to the cinema, the theatre, philosophy, history, genetics, economics, the plastic arts, and even music. In genetics, Lysenko (of whom more later) was raised to the pinnacle of an infallible dictator who was able to terrorize scientists clinging to "Mendelianism"; while in most other fields the Party's No. 1 hatchet man was Andrei Zhdanov, who posed as the infallible expert on literature, art, philosophy, music and much else.

The question that inevitably arises is *why* this ugly process should have begun in 1946, and a highly plausible answer is given to this question by Julian Huxley in a book published in 1949:*

Central to the present state of affairs is the historical fact that Soviet policy has undergone a radical change since the war, apparently with the view to preparing the people of the USSR for a long struggle, possibly involving war, with the capitalist world in general and the USA in particular.

* *Soviet Genetics and World Science*, London, 1949, pp. 153 ff.

> The wartime glorification of "Holy Russia" . . . has been coupled
> with a glorification of communism . . . Nationalism and patriotism,
> Marxist theory and Stalinist practice, have been combined . . . with
> the intent of making Soviet society as monolithic, and the Soviet
> States as massively powerful, as possible.

Huxley attributes this "radical change" to the hostility shown by
the West to the Soviet Union's policy of "expansion and consolidation of its power" in Central and Eastern Europe, coupled
with its expectation of obtaining large loans or credits from the
USA. When these hopes failed to materialize "angry disillusion-
ment set in" and "the Kremlin began, at first stealthily, to
transfer the symbols of hostility and aggression from Nazi
Germany to 'imperialist' America".

To Huxley, these fears of capitalist countries are "eminently
understandable", as is also Russia's desire for security.

> In view of those fears and that desire it was natural, and perhaps
> inevitable, that the Soviet authorities should have wished to develop
> a strong and unified national sentiment based on national pride
> [but also] directed towards the triumph of the system.

It was therefore necessary to mobilize and regiment not only
public opinion in the ordinary sense, but also all the higher
activities of the mind, both intellectual and aesthetic. "Thought
and creative expression had to become a weapon of foreign
policy and an instrument of domestic policy in the struggle of
the Soviet State to survive and to achieve its aims in the difficult
post-war world" (Huxley, op. cit., p. 155).

As we have seen in an earlier chapter, the discipline of the
Party itself had been strengthened since 1944, and much had
been done to intensify the political and ideological indoctrination
of its members. This indoctrination was also extended in various
ways to the population at large. The imminent decay of capitalism
was "scientifically" prophesied—despite a few dissenting voices,
such as Professor E. Varga's—and the vast superiority of the
Soviet system exalted. "Apolitical" attitudes began to be sharply
condemned, and it is precisely in this context that one has to
observe the first great outburst of Zhdanovism in the literary
field.

Zhdanov was a top *apparatchik,* and one of the toughest in
Stalin's entourage. Born in 1896 the son of a Tsarist Inspector of

Schools, he received a good middle-class education, and is said to have learned both French and German. But according to his official biography he became a revolutionary at the age of sixteen, and joined the Party in 1915.

During the 1914–18 war he spread Bolshevik propaganda among the troops; during the civil war he conducted party work at Shadrinsk in the Urals, and later at Tver. He was chairman of the Tver provincial executive committee, and from 1924 to 1934 held a leading party position in the Gorki province. He rose in the party hierarchy during the following years, becoming a member of the Central Committee, and in 1934 candidate member of the Politburo. That same year he succeeded Kirov (who had been assassinated on 1st December) as head of the Leningrad party organization. He was also a member of the executive committee at the Seventh Congress of the Comintern.

In the course of the Second World War he was the Party chief of Leningrad during the blockade. The question has often been asked to what extent he was to blame for the city's total unpreparedness for the siege and whether, without his ruthlessness in handling food-rationing, fewer lives could have been lost in the famine. Nevertheless, by 1946 he had acquired the reputation of the man who had "saved" Leningrad.

There is, of course, no doubt that he played a ruthless part in the Leningrad purges that followed the mysterious murder of Kirov in 1934. His unpleasant character was perhaps most clearly revealed at the Twenty-Second Congress in October 1961 in a speech delivered by D. A. Lazurkina, an old woman Bolshevik who had spent seventeen years in a concentration camp. After speaking of the Stalin terror in the 1930s, "when some of our best people perished, and people were shot without trial", she said:

I shall quote just one example typical of the atmosphere of those days. In May 1937 Zhdanov was secretary of the Leningrad provincial Party committee. He called us leading members of the committee together and declared that there were, within our ranks, two enemies of the people, Chudov and Kadatsky. They had been arrested in Moscow, he said. We could say nothing; we felt as if our tongues had been frozen. But when the meeting was over and Zhdanov was about to leave, I said to him: "Comrade Zhdanov, I do not know Chudov. He has not been long in our Leningrad organization. But I can vouch for Kadatsky. He has been a member of the Party since 1913, and I have known him for many years. He is an honest Party member, who conscientiously fought against all the oppositions. So what you say is just incredible and ought to be properly checked." Zhdanov looked at me with cruel eyes and said: "Lazurkina, will you stop this talk?—otherwise things will turn out very badly for you."

Such was the atmosphere in 1937. People were dominated by fear—a fear unworthy of Leninists. People denounced each other, and even denounced themselves. Lists of innocents who were to be arrested were drawn up. We were beaten, so that we should slander others. We were given these lists to sign; if we refused to sign, we were told, we would be tortured to death. . . .*

Whether Zhdanov was directly responsible for Lazurkina's arrest and her seventeen years in a camp is not made quite clear, but what is obvious from her story is that he was steeped up to the neck in all the beastliness of *yezhovshchina*. And it was this glorified Chekist whom Stalin chose to appoint cultural dictator. He had already meddled in literary affairs in the early 1930s, when the Soviet Writers' Union was first constituted, but now he became a byword of intolerance, cultural persecution and dictatorial stupidity.

Oddly enough, it all started with a story about a monkey. In 1945 the most popular Russian humorist, Mikhail Zoshchenko, had written a very funny story called *The Adventures of a Monkey* which became instantly popular throughout the country and was a great favourite with all Russian children. Zoshchenko, now aged fifty, had been popular since the 1920s when, in his very individual colloquial style, he wrote a large number of highly amusing stories on Russian everyday life, in which, it is true, he made no secret of the general poverty, the shortage of housing and consumer goods, and the drunkenness which often led to ugly brawls in the communal flats. In these stories he took a somewhat detached political line—or, rather, no political line at all. Thus, in one of his best, "The Joys of Culture", describing a couple of workers' (and one of the men's girl friend's) visit to a theatre after the introduction of the NEP, he contrasts the theatre in the days of War Communism, when you could go in wearing

* *XXII syezd Kommunisticheskoi Partii Sovetskogo Soyuza*, Moscow, 1962, vol. III, pp. 119–20.

an overcoat, and the post-NEP period, when coats had to be left downstairs. Since the man telling the story had nothing but a nightshirt below his overcoat, he preferred the pre-NEP system. Altogether, his stories were written, as it were, from the unfortunate "consumer's" point of view, and in the Soviet Union the consumer was seldom very happy about life. Zhdanov did not fail to read into them some highly dangerous and seditious thoughts.

His other victim was Anna Akhmatova, one of the greatest Russian poets, who had already been famous before the Revolution. To Zhdanov she represented pre-Revolutionary decadence, and her enormous popularity among young lovers of poetry in 1946 annoyed him particularly. The fact that she had written some of the most moving patriotic poetry during the war—though always with an emphasis on eternal Russia rather than on the Soviet Union—made no difference.

It so happened that Zoshchenko and Akhmatova were both closely associated with two Leningrad monthlies, *Zvezda* and *Leningrad*, and these two journals were singled out for Zhdanov's pillorying operation as an alleged refuge for escapist, unorthodox and plainly "un-Soviet" thought. Nor was it a pure coincidence that both these papers were published in Leningrad, a city which had gone through a worse hell than any other during the war, but which—in spite of this or perhaps because of it—still remained aloof towards Moscow—and Stalin.

In August 1946 a decree had been published by the Central Committee sharply condemning the two magazines and particularly Zoshchenko and Akhmatova. A few days later Zhdanov summoned a meeting of the Leningrad writers and started by attacking *The Adventures of a Monkey*. In this story, which takes place in a town near the Front, a zoo is bombed. The snakes and various other animals are killed, but the monkey escapes from its wrecked cage. There follow numerous adventures in which the monkey tries to fend for itself to get food in the town. Not having any ration-cards, it simply helps itself to some carrots by jumping the queue in the greengrocer's shop. It is then pursued by a big dog which it hits over the nose with a carrot. It has some typically "Zoshchenko" adventures in a bath-house, and is finally given a happy home by a boy called Alyosha, where the monkey learns to behave itself and to eat its semolina pudding with a tea-spoon. Harmless enough? Not in Zhdanov's opinion:

> The real significance of this "work" of Zoshchenko's lies in the fact that he represents Soviet people as so many idlers and moral monsters and as generally stupid and primitive. Zoshchenko is not interested in the labour of Soviet people, in their heroism and their high social and moral qualities. . . . These themes have always been absent from Zoshchenko's "works"; this vulgar and trivial petty-bourgeois has always liked to mess about with the lowest and meanest sides of everyday life. . . . Already in 1934 Gorki ridiculed those so-called "littérateurs" who could never see beyond the soot in the bathhouse and the kitchen. . . . As in his other "works", so in *The Adventures of a Monkey*, Zoshchenko mocks at Soviet everyday life, the Soviet order, and Soviet people, all this mockery being seasoned with empty wit and rubbishy humour.
>
> But look at the story more closely! . . . In depicting Soviet reality in a vulgar, trivial and caricatural form, Zoshchenko endows the monkey with a sort of superior reason; and it is the monkey who is made to utter this vile little aphorism, oozing anti-Soviet poison, about "life being much nicer in the zoo", and about its being easier to breathe in the cage than when living amongst Soviet people.

And he asked how it was possible that the people of Leningrad could put up with such "vile obscenity". And yet, with his "nauseating morality and his poisonous hostility to the Soviet regime", Zoshchenko had made himself at home both in the *Zvezda* and the *Leningrad* monthlies, and, moreover, his foul story of the monkey was being recited in theatres and concert halls. Only the scum of literature could produce such "works", and only politically blind people would tolerate that sort of thing. After recalling that Zoshchenko had been evacuated to Alma Ata during the war, and had done nothing for the war effort apart from writing some "obscene" reminiscences, for which he had been duly attacked in *Bolshevik* in 1944, Zhdanov went back to the 1920s, when Zoshchenko formed part of the "Serapion Brethren" group, who prided themselves on being "wholly unpolitical". And, for twenty-five years, Zhdanov said, Zoshchenko had persisted in this "political hooliganism".

In conclusion, he said that if Zoshchenko did not want to change his ways, then there was no room for him in Soviet literature. It did not need his empty, vulgar and trivial rubbish.

The official report of Zhdanov's speech says that this was followed by "stormy applause".

He then started on Akhmatova, whose "works", he said, were now being extensively published in the Leningrad journals. This seemed to him about as unnatural as publishing decadent pre-Revolution poets like Merezhkovsky, Zinaida Hippius, M. Kuzmin, Andrei Belyi, Sologub and those other writers who, to progressive Soviet humanity, were renegades and bywords of reactionary obscurantism, both in the political and in the literary sense. These people, including Akhmatova, belonged to the years 1907–17, that shameful decade of Russian literature which Gorki had so angrily denounced. Akhmatova, he said, was a typical representative of that counter-revolutionary bog; she belonged to the so-called Acmeist school which, with its extreme individualism and aristocratic drawing-room poetry, was absolutely alien to all that Soviet literature stood for.

> Akhmatova's subject-matter is throughout individualist. The range of her poetry—the poetry of a crazy gentlewoman dashing backwards and forwards between her *boudoir* and her chapel—is wretchedly narrow. What interests her above all are amorously erotic themes mingled with sorrow, sadness, nostalgia, death, mysticism and hopelessness. All these feelings of hopeless resignation, all this mysticism mixed up with erotic dreams—such is the world of Akhmatova, the world of the old nobility, of "the good old days of Catherine the Great". A mixture of nun and harlot, that's what she is. . . .

And there followed a quotation from *Anno Domini* taken out of its context. This nostalgia for the pre-Revolutionary past, for old St. Petersburg, for Tsarskoie Selo, for Pavlovsk, had no room in the Soviet Union; and what was the need to popularize Akhmatova now, in 1946? What was the good of getting such museum pieces from a world of phantoms to teach the young Soviet generation how to live? In the midst of "a lot of other rubbish", there was an Akhmatova poem published in *Leningrad*—a poem written while she was evacuated to Tashkent during the war, and here she talks about her loneliness, with only her black cat to share it with her.

> Akhmatova has already written about this black cat in 1909. All these feelings of hopelessness and loneliness are totally alien to Soviet

15

literature, yet they are the quintessence of Akhmatova's poetry. There is absolutely nothing in common between this kind of poetry and the interests of the Soviet people and the Soviet state. What can Akhmatova teach our young people? Nothing, except a lot of harmful things like defeatism, pessimism, and an anti-social outlook on life. . . . If we had educated our young people in the spirit of Akhmatova, we would have lost the war.

Soviet literature, Zhdanov then proclaimed, was not a private enterprise striving to cater to all kinds of tastes. "We are not bound to make room for tastes and morals which have absolutely nothing in common with the moral standards and qualities of Soviet people." By publishing Akhmatova and Zoshchenko, *Leningrad* and *Zvezda* were playing straight into the hands of the enemies of the Soviet Union; nor was it fortuitous that the same journals should have shown so much interest in the inferior products of Western bourgeois literature. It was unworthy of Soviet patriots to kowtow to the West; for Soviet people represented a regime which was a hundred times better than any bourgeois regime.

After talking at great length on Lenin's and Stalin's views on literature, education, etc., Zhdanov went on to denounce once more the cult of old St. Petersburg. To Akhmatova and Zoshchenko the Bronze Horseman symbolized the city—old St. Petersburg. "To us, Soviet patriots, Leningrad is dearer, Soviet Leningrad, that great centre of Soviet culture, the cradle of the Revolution." In conclusion, he denounced Zoshchenko and Akhmatova as "un-Soviet writers", and ended with a harangue on the decadent art and literature of the West.

After this meeting, Akhmatova and Zoshchenko were "unanimously" expelled from the Writers' Union. My friend Yuri German, the Leningrad novelist, who was at that meeting, later described it to me as "the most painful experience in his life".

"Zoshchenko stood near the doorway, looking like a man condemned to death. Everybody walked past him in a wide circle, as though he were a leper. I went up to him and put my arm round him. He gave me one look, and broke down and wept. 'Thank you, Yuri,' he said."

"But you voted for his expulsion, all the same," I said.

"Yes, I voted for his expulsion. But you shouldn't have asked this stupid question. Just shows you don't know what Zhdanovism was like. . . ."

Zoshchenko and Akhmatova were both condemned to long years of inactivity and poverty. Zoshchenko was a broken man. A few years later a paper published a few miserable little stories of his—allegedly—funny stories about the Germans during the war; they had none of Zoshchenko's sparkle and were a failure.

Akhmatova showed greater contempt and greater resilience. For several years afterwards, she lived in Leningrad in silence and great poverty; and it was not until 1950 that Surkov, then editor of *Ogonyok*, published some of her (admittedly rather conventional) poems on the rebirth of Leningrad.

She did not resume writing to any great extent until 1956-8, and it was during this "second birth" that she wrote some of her most remarkable poetry. Ostensibly, she had made her peace with the Soviet world in the more tolerant atmosphere of the Khrushchev period. Magazine editors were eager to publish her new works, and selections of her earlier poems were reprinted in many thousands of copies. Thousands went to her funeral, among them famous poets like Andrei Voznesensky, but also many of the unknown young poets with whom she thought the future of Russian poetry lay.

The Central Committee's decree of 21st August laying down a rigid literary line and condemning the two Leningrad monthlies, *Zvezda* and *Leningrad* (the first was "reorganized", the second liquidated), and, more specifically, Zoshchenko and Akhmatova was only a beginning. A few days later, on 4th September 1945, the Central Committee issued a further decree "against *bezideinye* and false films" (*bezideinye* meaning films "without ideas" or, more precisely perhaps, "without ideological content"). A violent attack was launched in this decree against a film called *The Great Life*, dealing with the life of miners in the Donbas. This was, the decree said, not a serious film; it told practically nothing about the decisive role played in the restored and reconstructed Donbas mines and factories by the Party; it did not show nearly enough of the modern machinery that was being used; instead, there was far too much drinking and vulgar singing, and too much *tziganshchina*—"gypsy-song stuff".

Worse still, the same decree violently attacked two of the greatest masters of the Soviet film—Pudovkin, for his *Admiral*

Nakhimov, and Eisenstein, for the second part of *Ivan the Terrible*. It attacked Eisenstein for having misrepresented the *Oprichniki*, Ivan the Terrible's "progressive army" (in reality a sort of private NKVD of the Tsar) "as a gang of degenerates, something like the American Ku Klux Klan"; and for having made Ivan himself, a man of strong will-power, to look like a characterless weakling, a sort of Hamlet, who could not make up his mind about anything. This was almost an act of lèse-majesté, since, in the historic mythology of the Stalin era, Ivan the Terrible (like Peter the Great) was a forerunner of Stalin.

It may look ridiculous from a distance, but in reality such pillorying was a personal tragedy to those directly concerned. Eisenstein, who had worked frantically on this second part of Ivan, was so discouraged and frustrated that he developed serious heart trouble and died less than two years later, aged forty-eight. Akhmatova silenced for years, Zoshchenko broken, Eisenstein killed off—here were some of the first casualties of the cultural purge.

It was about this time that the Propaganda and Agitation Department of the Central Committee began to publish a weekly paper called *Kultura i Zhizn* (*Culture and Life*). Its first number opened with a sort of manifesto stating that "all the forms and means of ideological and cultural activity of the Party and the State—whether the press, propaganda and agitation, science, literature and art, the cinema, radio, museums or any cultural and educational establishment—must be placed in the service of the communist education of the masses." The country was war-weary and wanted to "relax", but this could not be tolerated. Now, more than ever, communist morality and a communist consciousness should be cultivated; as for writers and artists, the proper study for them was Soviet Man. And Soviet Man should be educated in the proper spirit and carefully protected against the contamination of degenerate Western culture.

Culture and Life found fault with many things. The press, it wrote, tended to be platitudinous and preferred to "pass over in silence many acute everyday problems"—though the timidity and caution shown by the press had no doubt been determined by the editors' understandable reluctance to stick their necks out; for what was the good of writing of "acute everyday problems" when, as in 1946, they largely concerned the food and housing shortage or the level of wages, which had gone down sharply since September, not to mention the equally "acute" question of Beria's concentration-camp empire. Writers, too, were charged with escapism and an attempt to "dodge Soviet reality":

> Both they and film and theatre producers are hopelessly wrong if they imagine that after the war all that the Soviet people want is rest and recreation and that they can be satisfied with low-quality "entertaining" little plays by contemporary bourgeois playwrights, or with works depicting the luxurious life of aristocrats in the past.

This escape into history was particularly bad in the Soviet cinema. To avoid "acute present-day subjects", film producers were finding it less troublesome to "escape into the distant past".

> Of the nineteen big films produced in 1945, eight are adaptations from old plays, or else historic films. History is, of course, important, but this shouldn't be overdone. . . . We find this post-war tendency of escaping from present-day reality into the distant past and this interest in old-time legends and fairy-tales abnormal. Is it not a kind of indifference to present-day life and to the spiritual wealth of Soviet man which has created this strange enthusiasm for old-time history?

And there followed another particularly vicious attack on Eisenstein's *Ivan the Terrible* (Part II) for having distorted the true historic image of that "progressive statesman". In view of this and other distortions, the film, the paper firmly said, could not be released.

Bolshakov, the Minister of the Cinema Industry, declared in a long article that in the films to be produced in 1946–7 Soviet Man in war and peace would be the central character. He would be seen in different roles and contexts—as a musician in *The Ballad of Siberia*; as a geologist in *The Great Diamond*; as a teacher in Donskoy's *The Education of Feeling*; as a Belorussian *kolkhoznik* in *The New House*; as a soldier in *The Brandenburg Gate*; as a member of the Soviet underground in Gerasimov's *Young Guard*, based on the Fadeyev novel; as a Lithuanian partisan in *Maria Melnikaite*; as a worker in the polar regions during the war in *The Arctic Ocean*; as a Latvian partisan in a film called *Victory*; and so on. There were to be documentaries on Yugoslavia and

Czechoslovakia, biographical films on Pavlov (Romm), Michurin (Dovzhenko), and Glinka (Arnstam), besides various Georgian and Uzbek heroes, etc.

In another article the paper complained that the new theatre repertory was very thin. Apart from a few successful plays written during the war (Simonov's *Russian People* and Leonov's *Invasion*, for instance) most of the new plays were doubtful. Vodopyanov's *Forced Landing* was "a silly love vaudeville about a *sovkhoz* girl dressed up as a tractor-driver who falls in love with a pilot, a Hero of the Soviet Union.... In such plays Soviet people are shown to be a bit half-witted and uncultured, using vulgar speech and trivial colloquialisms and provincialisms."

The Government's Art Committee was blamed for having encouraged the production of Western plays, such as Somerset Maugham's *The Circle*, or plays by Pinero. All these "drawing-room dramas, with their variations on love themes, might be attractive to the bloated and corrupt Western spectator, but why bother showing this stuff to Soviet audiences? Shakespeare, Sheridan, Calderon, Bernard Shaw and Lilian Hellman are appreciated by Soviet audiences; but why show plays in which bourgeois society appears as a natural and eternal form of society? All this mild and good-natured satire of this or that aspect of bourgeois society had no connection with a "properly critical attitude to bourgeois civilization". On the other hand, however, Soviet playwrights were not producing much of any interest, which would explain why the Moscow Art Theatre had, in the last three years, produced only two modern Soviet plays. And the Mossoviet Theatre's record was just as bad.

Funnily enough, the paper also attacked *Krokodil* for not aiming higher in its satire than the *upravdom* (manager of a block of flats), the *kolkhoz* chairman, or the director of a bath-house. Why not deal, instead, with embezzlers, black-marketeers, stupid and brutal bureaucrats, bribery and corruption, careerism and sycophancy? Why not follow in the footsteps of Gogol, Chekhov or Saltykov-Shchedrin—the great satirists of the Tsarist era?

This sort of question—"why don't you write like Gogol or Saltykov-Shchedrin?"—is, of course, one of those questions which crops up in the Soviet Union from time to time—it did under Stalin and has done so since. The trouble, of course, is that these self-appointed Gogols and Saltykovs are apt to end up in jail, as Siniavsky and Daniel did even in the more clement post-Stalin era; but to have tried in 1946 to paint, say, a portrait of Zhdanov in the manner of Saltykov's Tsarist satraps was, of course, more than a man's life was worth.

The paper also frequently dealt with the necessity of intensifying Marxist/Leninist education among the masses and noted with satisfaction that millions of copies of the Stalinist *Short History of the Communist Party* had been published since the war, besides vast printings of the selected works of Lenin and Stalin. In 1946 a six-volume edition of Lenin's works had had a printing of 500,000, as had Engels's *Anti-Dühring*. In 1945 already 20 million copies of the Marxist classics had been published. Altogether, during those years *Culture and Life* became the most vigilant watch-dog of Soviet ideological purity in all fields. Its tone was largely set by the indefatigable Zhdanov.

There is no reason to suppose that Zhdanov was any more an expert in philosophy than he was in literature or music. Nevertheless, as Stalin's cultural dictator, he had to go through all kinds of surprising motions. If his "lecture" on literature in August 1946 and his "lecture" on music two years later were, to all appearances, his "own work", with their combination of crudeness, amateurishness and plain (though aggressively camouflaged) ignorance, he must have received some preliminary coaching before he embarked on the demolition of the *History of West European Philosophy* by G. F. Alexandrov, who was, during the war, one of the leading ideologists of the Central Committee. A conference of philosophers was called to discuss this offending work, and at the end of the discussion on 24th June 1947, he delivered his indictment. Very much in passing, he admitted in his introductory remark that he was a novice "on this tempest-tossed philosophic ship". Nevertheless, he talked for at least 1½ hours.

Alexandrov's book had been written towards the end of the war, when a relatively "tolerant" and "objective" attitude to the West was still possible. By 1947 the Cold War was in full swing, and Alexandrov's almost sympathetic treatment of Western philosophy had now become intolerable. "The very fact," Zhdanov said, "that the book had not aroused any significant protests, and that *the intervention of the Central Committee and of Comrade Stalin himself were needed to reveal all its flaws*, shows that, on the philosophic front, there is a lamentable absence of Bolshevik criticism and self-criticism."

Now, what was wrong with Alexandrov's book? First, it had not clearly defined the limits of the history of philosophy *as a science*. Second, it could not be regarded as a scientific work, since it was not built on the solid foundations of the contemporary achievements of dialectical and historical materialism; thirdly, Alexandrov had, in his scholastic way, failed to link his history of philosophy with present-day problems.

The author [Zhdanov said] represents the history of philosophy and the progression of philosophic ideas and systems as a smooth evolutionary movement marked by an accumulation of quantitative changes. The impression he gives is that Marxism is simply the successor of earlier progressive teachings, such as that of the French materialists, the English political economists and Hegel's idealist school of thought.

What Alexandrov, in short, had failed to make clear was that Marx and Engels had created a new philosophy, qualitatively different from all earlier philosophies, even the progressive ones. Everybody knew that Marxism had revolutionized philosophy *by turning it into a science*. The trouble with Alexandrov was that, instead of pointing to the revolutionary nature of Marxism, he dwelt too much on the links between Marxism and pre-Marxist philosophy. For had not Marx and Engels themselves said that their discovery meant the end of the old philosophy? (There followed a long quotation from *Anti-Dühring*.) Alexandrov had failed to make it clear that Marxism was not a philosophic school like any other; on the contrary,

Marxism is a repudiation of the old philosophy which was the domain of the happy few; Marxism marked a new period in the history of philosophy when this became a scientific instrument in the hands of the proletarian masses struggling for their liberation from capitalism.

By stopping his history in 1848 Alexandrov had made his book worthless as a textbook. By omitting all mention of Russian philosophy, he not only implied its insignificance, but subscribed as it were to the Western idea that Marxism somehow belonged to the regional Western current of thought.

Unlike Lenin, Alexandrov did not bite his opponents (the

idealist philosophers). His attitude to them was that of "a tooth-less vegetarian", with his professorial quasi-objectivism. Marxism was pugnacious and merciless to its idealist enemies. Instead, Alexandrov always found something good to say about Kant and Fourier and Hegel, to the point of becoming himself a prisoner of the bourgeois historians of philosophy. In the case of Hegel, he went out of his way to show that, if there were reactionary elements in Hegel, there were also progressive elements. This was a kind of objectivist eclecticism which resulted in presenting Hegel as an at least 50 per cent progressive thinker. In short, Zhdanov said, it was no good drawing favourable attention to philosophic systems which had long ago been killed and buried. Alexandrov's placid and objective treatment of the Germany of Kant, Fichte and Hegel compared most unfavourably with Marx's and Engels's savage indictment of that country.

Alexandrov, Zhdanov said, was not alone among Soviet philosophers to neglect present-day problems in their philosophic work and to adopt a slavish attitude towards the Western philo-sophy. It was important that Soviet philosophers remembered that Marxism/Leninism was a live, creative science, growing richer every day from its experience of socialism and from the latest successes in the natural sciences. Also, the question of Bol-shevik criticism and self-criticism was, for Soviet philosophers, not only a practical one, but also a profoundly theoretical one.

Marx used to say that the old philosophers only explained the world; but our task now is to change it. We have, indeed, changed the old world and have built a new one; but our philosophers, un-fortunately, neither explain this new world, nor do they take a sufficiently large part in changing it.

Then came a conclusion on the international significance of the discussion. A great struggle, Zhdanov said, was continuing, but the centre of the struggle against Marxism had now shifted from Germany to Britain and America. Here obscurantism and reaction were waging their unholy war against Marxism. Bourgeois philosophy had become the handmaiden of atomic and dollar democracy, allied to all the other obscurantist forces—the Vatican and American racism, the yellow press and decadent art. Other forces were being mobilized for the struggle—gangsters and pimps and spies and common criminals.

Let me give you an example. The other day I read that *Temps Modernes*, a paper edited by the existentialist Sartre, was praising to the skies a criminal writer called Jean Gênet for his book *A Thief's Diary*; this opens with the words: "Treachery, theft and homosexuality—these are going to be my principal subjects. . . ."

Referring to Germany, where idealist philosophy had finished by corrupting a whole nation, Zhdanov said that the same kind of thing could now be observed from the example of Jean Gênet, whose popularity was also great in America. Pimps and criminals as philosophers—that was what the West had come to!

TWELVE

Breakdown over Germany

Nineteen forty-seven, the year of the abortive Foreign Ministers' Conference in Moscow, of the Truman Doctrine and the Marshall Plan, and of the constitution of the Cominform, marked a further stage in the inexorable process towards the splitting of Europe into two hostile camps. Officially, the Russians were not yet reconciled to the thought at the beginning of 1947, but if they still had any mild illusions left of "friendly coexistence" with the West these soon vanished in the spring and early summer of 1947.

During the winter of 1946-7 Russia was hungrier than she had been since the tragic winter of 1941-2. The Soviet press scarcely made a secret of it. *Pravda*'s 1947 New Year editorial admitted that living conditions in Russia were very hard indeed, but tried to show that they were worse still in the West:

> The black shadow of an approaching economic crisis is hanging over the capitalists' plants and factories, and the unemployed run into millions.

There were some, the paper suggested, who thought that only by unleashing another war could these difficulties be overcome. Yet Comrade Stalin had clearly said that there would be no war.

> The Soviet Union is on the other hand marching in the vanguard of the peace-loving nations of the world, and the Soviet people are engaged in constructive and creative work, and are healing the country's wounds by rebuilding cities, industries and villages destroyed by the war.

And yet, *Pravda* went on, 1946 was a very hard year.

> We are suffering from the hard consequences of the war and, moreover, we had a serious shortage in grain production in 1946 as a result of the drought.

Even so, the new five-year plan had become a reality, and Moscow and Leningrad had overfulfilled the plan for the first year. More and more iron and steel were being produced; the Donbas was rising from the ruins, and the rebuilding of towns and villages was continuing. In the previous ten months of 1946 in the RSFSR alone 190,000 rural houses had been built or rebuilt, out of the 712,000 built in the last three years.

Three weeks later, in a speech made in Kiev, N. S. Khrushchev, the Ukrainian Premier and Secretary of the Central Committee of the Ukrainian CP, gave further details of industrial reconstruction:

> Of the 279 basic coal mines wrecked during the war, 142 had already been restored and were in production; the iron and steel industry was being successfully reconstructed, as was also the Krivoi Rog iron ore area. The engineering industry was making good progress: of the 104 plants that were being restored, 102 had already gone into production. The hydro-electric Dnieper Dam had been restored to the extent of 48 per cent. More than $1\frac{1}{2}$ million rural houses had been rebuilt. Unfortunately, the grain harvest had been "very much lower" than could have been expected after the enormous reconstruction work done by millions of *kolkhozniks*.[*]

The Gosplan's report on the Reconstruction and Development of the National Economy published about the same time dwelt more fully on the disastrous harvest of 1946:

> Having begun at the end of March in Moldavia, the drought rapidly spread to south-western Ukraine, and then to the entire central-*chernozem* areas, including the northern Ukraine. By the middle of May the drought spread to the Lower Volga areas . . . thus embracing a very considerable part of the whole of the European part of the USSR. Our country had not known such a drought in the last fifty years; the area affected was larger than in 1921, and approximately the same as in 1891. Although the harvest

[*] *Pravda*, 23rd January 1947.

was good in Kazakhstan and western Siberia, the total output of grain, sunflower seed and sugar-beet was considerably lower than in 1945. . . . Measures have been taken to help the stricken areas, and to economize in food.

One of the effects of the drought was, as we have seen, the sharp reduction in food consumption throughout the country, and although the Soviet press did not dwell on this at the time the food shortage had, in 1946 and 1947, a very marked effect on labour productivity. Coming on top of the food shortage and the nervous strain of the war years, these new privations were having a deeply depressing effect on the working-class generally. It was, to them, something of a vicious circle; though physically weak and exhausted, men and women still had to do overtime in order to make ends meet as far as possible.

Even in relatively privileged Moscow, people were showing growing signs of malnutrition. I remember, in the winter of 1947, once going to see my "courier", Klavdia Ivanovna, in her little cottage just off the Leningrad Chaussée, where she was living with her husband and fourteen-year-old son. Even during the war she had always tried to be gay and cheerful, and whenever I had visited her she had always produced something out of her meagre reserves. Now she fussed, as usual, in her little kitchen, and then came in with two glasses of very weak tea and a tiny crust of black bread. "I am sorry," she said, "but that's all I can treat you to." And there were tears in her eyes, And she talked of Misha, her son (who wasn't there), and said she dreaded that, with those wretched snacks he was getting at school, he might develop TB. He was losing weight all the time. "I suppose the Americans are rejoicing at our difficulties," she remarked. However, pulling herself together, she added: "Oh, never mind, we Russian people are pretty tough. We'll pull through somehow till the next harvest. We've seen even worse times than this. . . . But I'm sorry I haven't any sugar for the tea today. . . ." and then: "No, I didn't think the post-war years would be quite so hard. No doubt Truman *chortu molilsya* (prayed to the Devil) to bring this drought upon us!"

On the face of it, however, life went on as usual during that winter of 1946–7, and there were even occasional signs of relations continuing to be friendly with the Allies. Much publicity was given in the press in January to Field-Marshal Montgomery's visit to Moscow, and to the warm tribute he paid "to the Russian people, who suffered in brave silence more than any other people". On 11th January, the press carried large pictures of Stalin and Montgomery after the Kremlin banquet given in Monty's honour (no sign of any food shortage there, one can be sure!). Montgomery made another statement on the very warm reception given him by the Soviet military authorities, his "wartime comrades", among them Marshal Vasilevsky and General Golikov, both present at the Stalin banquet.

But this pleasantness was already something unusual. The papers were full of explosive and controversial stuff: the "arbitrary actions of the American troops in China"; Mao Tse-Tung's New Year Message saying that the Kuomintang was "preparing for civil war . . . the guns would soon go off . . . the Kuomintang was under the thumb of the American government . . .", etc. TASS, for its part, denied a Kuomintang story that the Soviet Union was sending a lot of arms, including some received during the war from the USA, to the Chinese communists in Manchuria and in China proper. This information, it said, was "provocative and untrue".

There was, of course, also a lot of trouble over the Polish election. The press reported on 16th January that Ambassador Bedell Smith had presented a note to Molotov complaining of the terror that had accompanied it. Molotov replied that "all these stories" came from Mikolajczyk, who kept talking about the "repression" against members of his Party. What the US government was ignoring were "the well-known facts concerning the participation of many of Mikolajczyk's men in the underground, which resorted to threats, violence and murder". After many more complaints in the Soviet press about the PSL's "terrorist activities" —which, of course, could not be tolerated by the organs of Poland's State Security—the Soviet press joyfully announced on 22nd January, "the brilliant election victory of Polish democracy", adding that even in a stronghold of reaction like Cracow 66,000 had voted for the Democratic bloc, and only 31,000 for Mikolajczyk's PSL. There were, of course, all kinds of protests from the West, and Mikolajczyk himself held several press conferences a day denouncing the election as a swindle. UNRRA help to Poland was stopped. Even before the election, as reported by the *Evening Standard*, which was quoted by the Russian press,

Poland and Yugoslavia had been warned that UNRRA help to them would soon stop, and Western help would be shifted to more "reliable" countries like Greece and Austria. It was already an early straw in the wind which the Russians did not fail to notice.

On 10th February 1947 the satellite peace treaties were at last signed in Paris. The Russian comments were rather on the acid side. Although there is no doubt that the Russians had overcome the Yugoslavs' reluctance to sign the Italian peace treaty, the Soviet press still reported that Simic, the Yugoslav Foreign Minister, had warned Bidault that

> Yugoslavia's signing of the Italian peace treaty did not mean that she was renouncing her claims to ethnically Yugoslav territories, such as Venetian Slovenia, Gorizia, Monfalcone, Trieste and parts of north-western Istria.

The Russians, as we know, considered that the Yugoslavs had no serious claims on any of these places, and were later to accuse Tito of having tried to drag Russia into a war with the West because of his unreasonable territorial ambitions. But in 1947 appearances of Soviet/Yugoslav unity still had to be kept up.

The Soviet press commented, on the whole, rather unfavourably on the peace treaties. However, it congratulated the Soviet negotiators on having succeeded at least in cutting down "Monarchist Greece's" exorbitant demands on Bulgaria to a much more reasonable amount ($45 million instead of $985 million). Further, the West had not succeeded in establishing its exclusive domination over the Free Territory of Trieste, and a few other minor concessions had been secured; and "though unsatisfactory", *Pravda* said, "these treaties are the best we could get."[*]

On the whole, however, the Soviet government seems to have been glad that these peace treaties were out of the way and that they could now tackle the much more important question of the peace treaties with Germany and Austria.

This was made clear by various speakers at the Third Session of the Supreme Soviet which met in the Kremlin between 20th and 25th February. Thus, N. P. Bazhan, one of the Ukrainian representatives, referred to a memorandum which, in view of the peace treaty with Germany which was shortly to be drafted, the

[*] *Pravda*, 16th February 1947.

Ukrainian government had just sent to the deputies of the four Foreign Ministers. This memorandum recalled that, quite regardless of the appalling human losses, the Ukraine's material losses in the war had amounted to 285 billion roubles, clearly implying that, like the rest of the USSR, the Ukraine was vitally interested in reparations.

The Supreme Soviet's session of February 1947, the main purpose of which was to approve the Budget for 1947 presented to it by Finance Minister A. G. Zverev, was about as dull as usual. A few interesting facts and figures nevertheless emerged. Zverev (like the press before him) dwelt at some length on the almost unprecedented drought of 1946. Nevertheless, despite the "serious difficulties" this had created, he declared himself reasonably satisfied with the progress made in the reconstruction of industry, housing, etc., suggesting, however, that the "real turning point" in reconstruction would be reached in 1947 rather than in 1946. Significant were the 1947 figures he quoted for education:

> In 1947, the number of pupils in elementary and secondary schools would, with 31·3 millions, very nearly attain the 1940 level of 32·9 millions; by the end of the year there would be, in the universities and other higher-education schools, 696,000 students, which was 91,000 more than in 1946 and 155,000 more than in 1940; there was an even greater increase among the students of technical schools—some 700,000, which was 42 per cent more than in 1940.

It is significant of those post-war years that despite widespread shortages, hardships and housing difficulties a very special effort was being made to train every kind of *cadres* in universities, technical schools, etc.

One of the more incongruous facts that emerged from the February session of the Supreme Soviet was that although not much was being done to remedy the housing shortage in Moscow (priority was given to the war-devastated cities) the Council of Ministers had decided, "on Comrade Stalin's initiative", to build a large number of "skyscrapers" (officially called many-storey buildings) in Moscow, ranging from sixteen to thirty-two floors.

> These high buildings will be constructed according to the latest building techniques. . . . They will broaden the experience of our builders. . . . These monumental multi-storey buildings will add

great beauty to the city and will constitute a valuable contribution to the reconstruction of Moscow. We have no doubt that the ministries concerned and the building organizations of Moscow will successfully carry out the task that Comrade Stalin has set them.*

The result was to be the numerous "Stalin-Gothic" skyscrapers (later to be supplemented by the university on Lenin Hills), which were clearly intended as a monument to Stalin himself. It is odd to think that these extravagant building projects should have been adopted by the Supreme Soviet at a time when Russia had reached about its lowest economic ebb. The decision suggests, however, that Stalin—and not only he—were considering the great economic difficulties of 1946–7 as something transient.

Did the Russians have any serious illusions that the crucial Foreign Ministers' Conference, which was to meet in Moscow on 12th March, would really produce a satisfactory draft peace treaty with Germany, and perhaps one with Austria too? During the weeks preceding the meeting, the Russian press refrained from directly criticizing the British or American governments, though it gave some prominence to criticisms to which they were subjected in their own countries, frequently quoting such speakers as Harold Ickes and Henry Wallace in the USA and Mr. Zilliacus in England. That Mr. Zilliacus was by no means typical of the Labour Party as a whole was, somehow, never suggested; the implication, on the contrary, was that Ernest Bevin had to reckon with a strong left-wing opposition inside the Labour Party.

In Eastern Europe, meanwhile, things were going as well as could be expected from the Russian point of view. The temperamental Yugoslavs had been forced by the Russians to accept the Italian peace treaty. In Hungary, Czechoslovakia and especially Rumania the food situation was extremely serious, but otherwise there were no major political problems yet. The results of the election in Poland—however badly "cooked"—had given the Russians particular satisfaction; at the end of February, the new Polish premier, Mr. Cyrankiewicz, and other members of the Polish government were received in Moscow with a great show of cordiality, and the Soviet Union granted Poland a gold loan of 30 million dollars.

In the West, the picture was less rosy. The position of the

* *Zasedaniya Verkhovnogo Sovieta SSSR, 3-ya Sessiya*, Moscow, 1947, p. 65.
16

communists in the French government for instance—partly as a result of American pressures, partly because of the outbreak of the war in Indo-China, partly also because of the wage-freeze imposed on the French working class by the Léon Blum government in December 1946—had become extremely precarious. The discussions at the UN, particularly on the Baruch Plan, were leading nowhere, and suggestions of "the absolute prohibition of atomic weapons" made at great length by the Soviet spokesman on the Security Council on 5th March were falling on deaf ears.

Still, at the beginning of March the Russians seemed to have some serious illusions that, even if the Moscow Conference of Foreign Ministers did not produce complete drafts of the German and Austrian peace treaties, it would make enormous progress towards this cherished goal. The announcement of the Truman Doctrine, only a few days after the opening of the Conference, should have finally shattered these illusions, but they still persisted in trying to thrash out a peace treaty with Germany, and the Conference went on for over six weeks.

On 8th March, Ernest Bevin was the first to arrive, to be followed soon afterwards by Marshall and Bidault. Bevin came by train, together with Lord Hood, Hall-Patch, Pierson Dixon and the inevitable Mr. Ridsdale, the Foreign Office press officer who headed a large group of diplomatic correspondents from London—"the trained seals of the sealed train", as we Moscow correspondents used to call them. "Rids"—or "Ribs", as Bevin liked to call the skinny little man—had no use for the undisciplined Moscow correspondents and expected us, in our reports, to stick strictly to his "briefings", giving what he called "the British point of view", and not to bother about what the Americans, the French and—God forbid!—the Russians were saying at *their* press conferences after each of the plenary meetings of the Foreign Ministers or their deputies. On the whole, the "trained seals" closely followed Rids's briefings, with only a few rare exceptions, such as Iverach MacDonald of *The Times*, who showed a commendable curiosity in what "the others" also had to say. Rather typically, Rids had Frank Lesser, the *Daily Worker* correspondent, excluded from his briefings.

Despite frequent displays of joviality and good humour—often he would even break into song—Bevin was, of all the three heads of the Western delegations, by far the most pugnacious and truculent in his dealings with the Russians. Secretary of State George Marshall, on the other hand, always behaved with great calm and dignity, though the same could not be said of some of the persons accompanying him. The most violent among them was General Mark Clark. I remember visiting him in his room at the Moskva Hotel. Here, sitting in front of a radiator, which he said was chock-full of microphones, he took a particular joy in shouting obscenities about Stalin. "Here," he would exclaim, "you sons of bitches, play this record to that big shit! Let him know what we Americans think about him!" In his dealings with "fat boy" Ambassador F. Gusev, who like himself was working on the Austrian peace treaty, he was scarcely less abusive, and very nearly reduced the unfortunate Gusev to a nervous breakdown. On one occasion Gusev all but broke into tears.

Georges Bidault—Ernest Bevin's "dear little man"—tried at first to act as a sort of moderating influence between the Anglo/Americans on the one hand, and the Russians on the other; but soon after the announcement of the Truman Doctrine he told me, I remember: "After this I'm afraid it's all going to be rather a waste of time. If the Russians don't help us with the Saar, we shall inevitably drift into the Anglo/American camp." He obviously meant that, with the announcement of the Truman Doctrine, the Cold War was going from bad to worse, and that, in her economic plight, France had only the United States to look to. It is also clear that Bidault's opposition to a central German government and his support of German "federalism" already clearly foreshadowed the splitting of Germany in two, even though at that stage he was still unwilling to see the French zone incorporated in the Anglo/American bi-zone, which was already giving Molotov such bad dreams.

The Foreign Ministers' meetings took place at the large Airmen's Club, about two miles north of the Kremlin, on the Leningrad Chaussée. Most of the delegates and the visiting journalists were living in great comfort and even luxury at the Moskva Hotel, which a few days before the Conference opened had been requisitioned for the purpose, all the Russians living there—among them some very important people—having been simply turned out. The huge dining-room, with a big band playing every evening, was, as we have already seen, a picture of high living, with luxurious menus to choose from, and with unlimited quantities of vodka, wine and champagne to consume. Once or twice it came to drunken brawls, some pugnacious young Americans shouting abuse at the Russian staff, and even hitting them. In the hungry Moscow of March 1947 there was something obscene about those menus, but the Russian authorities obviously felt that a show of frugality and austerity might suggest to the foreign delegations that Russia was in a very poor economic way —which, of course, she was, as they must have known from the Russian press and from the recent speeches at the Supreme Soviet, not to mention the undernourished look of so many people in the streets of Moscow. It seemed an unnecessary display of opulence, all the more so as France and especially Britain were also having a particularly thin time during that winter of 1946–7.

It seemed at first that the Western delegations had come to Moscow to do really serious business about the German peace treaty, and the Russians treated the meeting with the utmost seriousness, the Soviet newspapers giving very full summaries not only of Molotov's and Vyshinsky's speeches, but also of Marshall's, Bevin's and Bidault's. On 12th March, the papers printed on their front pages large photographs of the first plenary meeting of the Conference. Here, among the Russians, were Molotov, Vyshinsky, Gusev and Marshal Sokolovsky; among the British, Bevin, Lord Hood, Hall-Patch, Sir William Strang and Pierson Dixon; among the Americans, Marshall, Cohen, Murphy, "Chip" Bohlen, General Mark Clark and John Foster Dulles—yes, he too; among the French, Bidault, Ambassador Catroux, Couve de Murville, etc.

There can, of course, be no question of describing here in great detail all that happened during the Big Four discussions, which went on for nearly six weeks, but some of the main arguments used should be mentioned, for it was this conference, or rather its failure, which laid, as it were, the foundations for that divided Europe, in which, for better or for worse, we are living to this day. Not that the seeds of this division had not already been sown. We only have to remember Stalin's determination, ever since 1943—and even before—to include Poland in his sphere, or the Churchill/Stalin spheres-of-influence deal of October 1944, or the very strange and far-reaching territorial reparations "settlement" finally agreed at Potsdam between Byrnes and a reluctant Molotov.

It may be said at once that in March 1947 the Russians had already become highly suspicious of what was going on in Western Germany. At the very first meeting of the Conference Molotov complained about the Western allies being "very slow in dismantling the West German war industries"; he also alleged that there were still a lot of "Nazi" troops in the West, as well as a variety of other military and paramilitary "fascist" formations, such as a "Royal Yugoslav Army", and units composed of Chetniks, Ustashi, Hungarian Salasi fascists, Anders Poles, Ukrainian Bandera terrorists, etc. He saw no objection to Germans being used for demining the towns and the sea, but why keep German military formations? Everywhere except in the British zone the demining had been completed; but what did the British need 80,000 German soldiers for?

The discussion continued the next day. Bevin argued that they could not forcibly send these people—Poles, Yugoslavs, Hungarians, Ukrainians, etc.—to their own countries; and the Germans were not really troops, but a sort of labour corps wearing special uniforms and trained to do demining work. As for dismantling—a question on which Bevin felt very strongly— he simply said that it was particularly difficult to decide what constituted, and what did not constitute, "military potential". And it was no use going on with indiscriminate dismantling until it was a little clearer what exactly had been removed from the Soviet Zone.

Molotov noted that Bevin had, in fact, admitted that there *was* a German army in the British Zone, besides various fascist formations, and rejected the "absurd" rumours Bevin had mentioned about German soldiers and officers entering the service of the Soviet armed forces. The American press, Molotov said, had talked of 3 million German war prisoners in Russia, many of whom were being drafted into "the Seydlitz Army"—that is a Russian-controlled army under the command of General Seydlitz (taken prisoner at Stalingrad). All this he dismissed as nonsense, but promised to provide figures on the number of German war prisoners in Russia.

Another important point of principle which arose early on in the discussion was whether (as the Western powers were proposing) there was to be a peace treaty *for* Germany, or (as the Russians were proposing) a peace treaty *with* Germany. The point was important, because the Russian formula implied the existence of a regular German government, or as Vyshinsky put it, "there must be a peace treaty *between* the Allies on the one hand, and Germany on the other". To which Sir William Strang replied that "no one can tell yet *when* there will be a central German government". The matter, as we shall see, was to prove one of the main stumbling-blocks of the conference. As Yuri Zhukov wrote in *Pravda* on 14th March, "the difference between *for* and *with* is the difference between a peace treaty with Germany and a *Diktat*".

There were also some heated discussions over denazification. After Marshall's statement on 13th March intending to show that denazification had been proceeding satisfactorily in the West, Molotov argued that the Potsdam decisions on denazification were very far from being fully applied. In the West, he said, many high economic and administrative posts were held by people who had been active Nazis in the past. Thus Dinkelbach, who was head of Vereinigte Stahlwerke under Hitler, was now head of the iron and steel industry in the Ruhr. Some of the top judges in the British Zone were Nazis; and a delegation of the WFTU which had recently visited Western Germany had, he said, found the state of denazification "very unsatisfactory" in all the three zones. In the Soviet Zone, on the other hand, 390,000 Nazi officials had been sacked—a much higher figure than anywhere else. The Soviet government therefore insisted that the Allied Control Council take the following measures: (1) remove from responsible official and semi-official positions all former active Nazis; (2) speed up the work of the courts and tribunals dealing with Nazi war criminals; (3) make a serious effort to bring all active Nazis before the courts, without, however, bothering about the small fry. Bevin promptly hit back by giving a long list of top Nazis in big jobs in the Soviet Zone, and by saying that in the British Zone alone 34,000 Nazis were interned.

These exchanges were proceeding when suddenly the news came from Washington of the announcement of the Truman Doctrine.

The Russians did not take long to gauge its full significance. On 15th March *Pravda*'s editorial on Truman's message to Congress said:

It all goes far beyond the aid of one country to another. It is a most unusual act. . . . Under British tutelage, the fascist-monarchist regime in Greece has reduced the country to a state of complete chaos. But Truman is not aiming at helping the Greek people; all he wants is to support the reactionary Greek government, since Britain has proved unable to carry out her obligations to Greece. . . . Under the guise of "charity", the USA has shown her expansionist ambitions.

The paper then commented acidly on the "choice personnel" the USA was proposing to send to Greece. As for Turkey,

She also is to be helped, though Turkey did not suffer from the war. Why then this urgent and even "indispensable" aid to Turkey? Turkey wanted, of course, financial aid from Britain, but Britain is broke, so the Americans have got to take her place in order, as Truman says, to secure Turkey's "national sovereignty".

But no one, *Pravda* said, was threatening Turkey. It was not the "modernization" of Turkey but her domination by the United States that Truman was aiming at. And if, as Truman said, he had to struggle against "totalitarian communism", then why should he not deal through the UN? In all this business, Truman had shown the greatest contempt for the UN, and had violated America's obligations to it. And, after ridiculing Truman's description of the Tsaldaris government as a "democratic' government, supported by the Greek people except for a few thousand armed communists, it concluded on this ominous note:

All this business of protecting "free peoples" against totali-tarianism goes far beyond Greece and Turkey. Hitler also protected other nations from "Bolshevism". . . . *This is a turning point in American foreign policy.*

And it added that, significantly, the "Truman Doctrine" was being most loudly approved by Churchill, General Franco and all the most reactionary papers in the world.

In the next few days the Soviet press gave much space to ad-verse criticisms of Truman, such as Henry Wallace's statement:

Coming two days after the opening of the Moscow Conference, Truman's message is undermining the position of Marshall, whose aim is to establish lengthy cooperation with France, Britain and the Soviet Union. . . . Why not hand Greece over to the UN?

or Zilliacus's:

Truman is the Father Christmas of all reactionaries, monarchists, fascists, quislings and collaborators. . . . American imperialism is threatening the world with another world war.★

With the Truman message almost coinciding with the opening of the conference on the German peace treaty, the Russians had every reason to suspect that, to the US government, this Moscow Conference was already an anachronism; and although Western delegates pretended that nothing had changed, the correspondents in Moscow—particularly the French—spoke as early as 15th March of Truman having knocked the conference on the head. Nevertheless, the negotiations continued, though often in a somewhat unsystematic way.

From the discussion on German war prisoners and on displaced persons (DPs) it emerged that there were still 631,000 of them in French hands; over 500,000 were being used "in the French national economy"; 19,000 were in French North Africa, 18,000 in the French Zone of Germany; and in the British Zone there were 435,000 war prisoners. The Soviet Union now held, according to Molotov, 890,000 German war prisoners, but since the German capitulation 1,004,000 had been sent home. The Americans held only 31,000, of whom one half were in the US Zone and the other outside Germany.

Bevin expressed some doubts about the accuracy of the figures Molotov had supplied, but more unpleasant still was the discussion on DPs. Vyshinsky claimed that there were still 827,000 DPs in the Western Zones of Germany, among them 221,000 Soviet citizens, 236,000 Poles, 24,000 Yugoslavs, 7,000 Czechs, etc. The Soviet Repatriation Commissions had repatriated, up to 1st January 1947, over a million people, among them 315,000 French, 24,000 British and 22,000 Americans. There were no Allied DPs left in the Soviet Union, but there were numerous Soviet citizens in DP camps in the West who were being subjected to intimidation and anti-Soviet propaganda. In this "work" Ukrainian, Lithuanian and Latvian Nazis and fascists were being given the greatest freedom of action. Bevin replied that all this business about "anti-Soviet propaganda" was greatly exaggerated; the truth was that these DPs were too frightened to return to Russia, and Britain was not going to force them to go against their will.

★ *Pravda*, 17th and 18th March 1946.

Many of the Foreign Ministers' meetings were to be devoted to the questions of German economic and political unification, reparations, the possibility of a German central government, and so on. Despite the ominous undertones of the Truman Doctrine, the Russians still seemed to take all these discussions extremely seriously. Did Marshall, Bevin and Bidault? And, if not, why did they have to go on with them for another month? On one occasion Bevin said that this conference was "the last chance". Did he mean to get results in Moscow, or did he already know that the division of Europe was now inevitable?

Whatever Bevin thought at heart, it is interesting, if only for the historical record, to see what the Russians in particular were striving to do about Germany.

On 19th March the Foreign Ministers began to discuss economic principles and reparations. Bevin recalled that at Potsdam the "economic unity of Germany" had been agreed upon. The Russians were now complaining about zonal barriers, though they themselves, he said, had pretty well sealed off the Soviet Zone. He agreed that zonal barriers must go, but the bi-zone would stay as it was, whatever the Russians said about it, so long as there was no agreement on all-German economic unity. Bevin said that the whole reparations problem would remain indefinite so long as it was not clear whether Germany was to be treated as a single economic unit or not. Nor, he said, had anything been definitely settled about the future frontiers of Germany.

None of this pleased Molotov, who promptly remarked that in the Russian view there could be no question of going back on the Oder/Neisse frontier.

At Potsdam, he said, Stalin had proposed the creation of central German administrations, which would provide the economic and political unity of Germany; but the others had disagreed. Nevertheless, it was decided at Potsdam to set up central German economic departments, each headed by a German secretary of state working under the Allied Control Council. These departments would deal with industry, finance, transport, communications and foreign trade. But although the Soviet Union was favourable to all this, nothing was actually done to bring these central administrations into being.

As regards the Ruhr, which contained three-quarters of Germany's coal and engineering industry, the British took over the coal industry there as early as December 1945, thus confront-ing the Control Council with a *fait accompli*. In August 1946 the same happened to the Ruhr engineering industry. Yet at Potsdam, the Soviet Union had advocated a four-power control over the Ruhr.

> Shortly before that, in July 1946, I raised the question at the Foreign Ministers' Conference. But no, the British went on with their unilateral treatment of the Ruhr. The Soviet Union now in-sists that the Ruhr be placed under four-power control. It is wrong to leave the Ruhr under the control of one power in Germany. Four-power control alone can safeguard against the Ruhr becom-ing once again the economic base for a new German aggression.

Molotov went on to say that the French, for their part, had unilaterally separated the Saar from Germany—another *fait accompli* with which the Control Council was faced.

This charge against the French in the name of "German unity" was particularly significant. By not condoning France's "unilateral action" in the Saar (as Bidault had confidently hoped), Molotov hastened the process whereby France, abandoning her between-East-and-West position, finally threw in her lot with Britain and America.

Molotov had other complaints to make. In December 1946, he said, the USA and Britain had agreed on the administrative and economic unification of their two zones, with a joint three-year economic plan. These two zones were thus virtually sepa-rated from the rest of Germany. Trade with other zones was calculated in dollars, instead of marks—which was another *fait accompli* for the Control Council. All this, Molotov said, went contrary to the whole idea of the economic unity of Germany.

As for reparations, Molotov described the situation as "in-tolerable". It had been agreed at Potsdam that by 2nd February 1946 the programme for the removal of equipment would be completed; and that equipment would be delivered by way of advance reparations payments. The British and Americans had, under one pretext or another, delayed all these payments and deliveries. No doubt the Soviet Union was taking reparations from the Soviet Zone, but all this was quite insufficient. Here Molotov became positively plaintive:

> For three years the Soviet Union had to wage war single-handedly

against Nazi Germany and her satellites. The damage done to the Soviet Union amounts to 128 billion dollars. 1,700 towns were destroyed and 70,000 villages; 25 million people were left homeless; 31,000 industrial enterprises were destroyed, employing 4 million workers; 65,000 kilometres of railway track were destroyed and 4,000 railway stations; 98,000 collective farms and 1,800 state farms were destroyed or looted; 7 million horses, 17 million head of cattle, 20 million pigs, 27 million sheep and goats had vanished; 40,000 hospitals and dispensaries, 84,000 schools, 42,000 public libraries had been destroyed.

And, in addition to all this, there were many millions of people who had lost their lives. So, out of $128 billion, the Soviet Union was asking for only $10 billion in reparations from Germany.

Molotov now proposed that, in addition to what came from the Soviet Zone and from German assets in Eastern Europe, the Soviet Union should receive 15 per cent of the available equipment from the rest of Germany—that is, equipment not essential to Germany's own peace economy. But that was not all. At Yalta, Molotov recalled, it was agreed that reparations would come from three sources: (1) equipment and machine tools; (2) current production; (3) German labour. There also the USSR and the USA had agreed on the figure of $20 billion, half of it going to the Soviet Union; Britain had refused to name a figure.* As regards current production, the Soviet Union now agreed to increase the level of German industry. The Soviet Union stood for the economic unification of Germany and for knocking down all economic barriers. Molotov therefore proposed the following measures:

Set up *immediately* central German administrations as provided by Potsdam, adding to them an agricultural administration; thus the foundations would be created for a German government.

Increase the German level of production, cancelling the Control Council's ruling of 26th March 1946; the steel production to be increased to 10 or 12 million tons a year.

All-German measures should be taken to strengthen the country's financial and monetary position.

The Ruhr should be placed under four-power control.

German industries should be helped to import raw materials.

* In reality, this figure had been accepted by the USA at Yalta merely as a "basis of discussion".

The Control Council should be instructed to hand over to the German State the German *Konzerne*, *Kartelle* and trusts; the demo-cratic parties and free trade unions should be associated with this measure.

The economic unification of the British and American Zones, being contrary to the principle of the economic unity of Germany, should be cancelled.

As regards reparations, Molotov proposed that the Soviet Union receive $10 billion, out of which she would pay Poland's share. Reparations would consist of equipment, current produc-tion, various services, and German assets abroad, the removal of equipment to be terminated in the Soviet Zone on 1st July 1947 and in the Western zones a year later. All German reparations were to be terminated within twenty years of the Potsdam Conference (that is in August 1965). He also proposed that the Allied Reparations Commission, comprising the Big Four, be revived.

The Soviet government's interest in reparations was, of course, understandable, even though, as Molotov insisted, the $10 billion the Soviet Union was asking for represented only a small fraction of the damage caused by the German invasion. More significant in the context of 1947 was the persistence with which the Russians were pressing for German economic unity and for the establish-ment of a central German government. The explanation for this is simple. When I asked Vyshinsky about it, he said with a charac-teristic snarl: "If there isn't a central German government, there will be before long a militarist and West German govern-ment. Don't quote me, but just remember what I said." Openly the Russians refrained from making this allegation, but it was certainly at the back of their minds, especially since the announce-ment of the Truman Doctrine and in the light of numerous Western press comments on "the West going its own way". There was something else, too: from the *German* point of view, the Russians were doing the popular thing in advocating a central government.

Bevin, needless to say, took Molotov's proposals very badly. On 19th March he said that he was in favour of all-German administrations but wholly against a four-power control of the Ruhr. He rejected Molotov's reparations plan, his proposal for setting up the Reparations Commission, and his demand that bi-zonal arrangements should be cancelled. On the following day he ominously remarked that this was the most important Foreign Ministers' Conference ever to be held, but if no agreement were reached now, *he doubted whether any agreement would ever be reached.*

On 22nd March Bevin used some peculiar arguments for rejecting Molotov's plea for establishing a central government in Germany.

> We British have had to fight two world wars against Germany, and we don't much like the idea of a strong German central government; and even if there is to be a central government, it must have strictly limited powers.

Marshall, on the same day, seemed to take a kind of intermediate position. The German people, he said, should be allowed to set up a provisional government dealing with all state affairs; but no such government was possible as long as no agreement had been reached on the bases of economic unity, and *if there were no fundamental freedoms guaranteed to all parts of Germany.* Without this, there could be no provisional or permanent central German government. He therefore proposed the constitution of a provisional government composed of the heads of the present Länder and States, as well as Berlin; there must be a new Constitution and the Länder governments must be freely elected; the Constitution must be German in origin, and be based on democratic principles and decentralization. Thus, the central government must have only limited powers, the Länder governments remaining powerful on a local level.

Ignoring Marshall's insinuations that the Russians were unlikely to allow free elections to be held in the Soviet Zone, Molotov strongly attacked federalization, which, he said, was at the root of both the British and the American policy statements. Without recalling that at Teheran Stalin had wholeheartedly supported the partition of Germany, and had done so (though much more half-heartedly) at Yalta, he stressed that on Victory Day, 9th May 1945, Stalin had declared: "The Soviet Union is today celebrating victory; but she has no intention of either dismembering or destroying Germany."

Taking up Bevin's argument about Britain's dislike of a strong central government in Germany, Molotov said:

Federalization will, of course, weaken Germany. But, in the long run, it is dangerous. For it will play into the hands of the militarists playing on the German people's longing for "German unity".

He therefore proposed the following plan:

Germany is to be restored as a single, peaceful, democratic republic with an all-German parliament, consisting of two Houses, and with an all-German government, the Länder, with constitutional rights of their own, forming part of the German State.

The President is to be elected by parliament.

The all-German constitution is to be valid for every part of Germany—this constitution having been approved by parliament, and the Länder constitutions having been approved by the respective Landtäge.

Both the German and Länder constitutions are to be democratic, and are to guarantee free education, free activities to all the democratic parties and trade unions, etc.

All German citizens, regardless of race, sex, language or religion, will, under the German and Länder constitutions, be guaranteed the democratic freedoms of speech, press, religion, public meetings and association.

The central parliament and the Landtäge are to be elected by direct, secret and universal suffrage under proportional representation; the lower local government bodies are to be elected by the same democratic method as the Landtäge.

For a few days a slight *rapprochement* between the Russians and Western viewpoints could be detected. Thus on 26th March the calling of the Peace Conference and of its composition was discussed, and Bevin even agreed there ought to be "a German government" to sign the peace treaty. He did not clearly specify what he meant by such a government, but certainly it was one with "limited powers".

Despite this momentary *détente*, the Russian press was getting gloomier as time went on. Yuri Zhukov quoted Molotov as saying that all that the Soviet Union had got from Western Germany since Potsdam was $5 millions' worth of free reparations deliveries, plus $7\frac{1}{2}$ million dollars' worth for which she had to pay with "other commodities", that is food from Eastern Germany. Both the Soviet Union and the other claimants were being done out of West German reparations deliveries. On the other hand, the UK and the USA were generously helping themselves to Germany's foreign assets (*Pravda*, 31st March 1947).

The other vital question, the "future political regime of post-war Germany", was also discussed in the same issue of *Pravda*. Leontiev now openly charged that "influential circles in Britain and America" were now "already talking about the *inevitability* of the world splitting in two"; but "what they really mean is that such a split is *desirable*", which clearly implied that the West was about to include Western Germany in *its* sphere, and was—for the time being—abandoning Eastern Germany to the Russians. There was therefore no question of the Russians sharing in the control of the Ruhr, or of a central German government being set up.

Marshall, alluding to these charges in the Soviet press, tried to pour oil on the troubled waters at the meeting on 1st April. He even began by saying that the conference was "making progress". He was sorry, however, that the Russians were making their demands for reparations out of current production a condition for their accepting the economic unity of Germany. He appreciated France's need for coal, Russia's need for consumer goods, and Britain's unwillingness to increase her burden in keeping Germany afloat. Even now, he said, German rations amounted to no more than 1,500 calories. If the Russian reparations demands were accepted, this figure would drop to 1,100 calories—not enough to keep anyone alive for long. The USA did not want Germany to become an over-populated slum in the middle of Europe. The USA, Marshall said, *did* want an economically united Germany, because the partition of Germany would mean the partition of Europe.

Bidault was chiefly concerned about the Saar, and obviously disliked the idea that this talk of "German economic unity" might interfere with France's special interests in the Saar coal. He said he could not agree to any proposals concerning economic unity, the level of production or reparations unless an agreement was reached on German coal deliveries and the status of Saar.

> We must know how much German coal is available for export and how much for German home needs. Also, we cannot agree to economic unity unless there is a firm agreement that the Saar is economically and monetarily joined to France. We have no objection to reparations from current production, and this, as Mr. Molotov

has explained, has already been organized in the Soviet Zone. . . . As for the German level of production, we have no objection to its being raised provided this does not constitute another threat to peace.

Now, this French demand for a special status for the Saar was precisely what clashed with Molotov's thesis of a "united Germany" and, as we have seen, it was the Russians' failure to agree to the French demands—which Britain and the USA were, for obvious reasons, beginning to treat more sympathetically— which finally pushed Bidault into the Western camp.

During the fourth week of the conference the discussion became increasingly involved and ill-tempered, Bevin, in particular, attacking the Russians with even more than usual truculence. He was, he said, in favour of building up a democratic Germany, but it could not be done in a day, as the Russians seemed to imagine. The German people, he said, were still poisoned by Nazi propaganda. With overpopulation, shortages and no prospects, there was a vacuum in Germany and the situation looked dangerous. In short, he was against the establishment of a central government on the lines Molotov had proposed. There was also the question of frontiers, which Molotov had not mentioned; yet one could not ignore this question in dealing with the German problem.

Bevin said that the Russians loved to talk about the "economic unity" of Germany. Britain demanded in this connection freedom of movement for persons and trade and the spread of ideas; neither the Russians nor the French were in agreement on this. German exports should, in the first place, pay for German imports; here the Russians disagreed. The financial burdens of the controlling powers should be fairly distributed; the French and Russians disagreed with this. The German central departments should be endowed with executive powers; but no, here the French objected.

Worse still,

The Russians make German economic units subordinate to German reparations from current production; they also want four-power control of the Ruhr, though this is in the British Zone; they want the economic merger of the British and American zones cancelled. No, we cannot accept these terms.

Germany is today unfit to pay reparations out of current production; this would also mean a further burden to the British taxpayer. And so long as the zonal system exists, we can't accept four-power control of the Ruhr.

Not that Bevin seriously meant the Russians to have a finger in the Ruhr pie—ever:

Once economic unity has been achieved, I agree that the production of the Ruhr industries and the distribution of Ruhr steel should be managed by the Control Council acting through the relevant German administrative bodies, as in the case of all other German industries. But I can't go further.

Again he rejected the cancellation of the bi-zone merger; the artificial barrier in the past had made the situation intolerable. He said he sympathized with French demands, but was opposed to coal deliveries being included in the peace treaty. He approved of raising the level of production, and "we should like reparations to be paid as soon as possible; but the present standard of living in Germany is exceedingly low; nor is it possible to go on with dismantling for years to come!" And then, turning on the Russians, he added:

We are in favour of the Germans going up to 10 million tons of steel a year, but we must have full details on what has already been removed from Germany (that is from the Soviet Zone). The Germans are in a helpless position so long as they don't know what reparations are expected from them, and when; and what's to be dismantled and not to be dismantled.

Here, indeed, was a mouthful: The Russians were not saying what they were removing from the Soviet Zone, and even if production in Western Germany were to be greatly increased, this still did not mean that the Russians need depend on reparations payments. That, at any rate, was how the Russians—probably rightly—interpreted Bevin's harangue. And he concluded on a highly ambiguous note:

We all agree that Germany must be regarded as an economic whole; but agreement on all the aspects of this problem will not necessarily be reached at this conference; maybe at the next one.

But *was* there to be a next one? As we have seen only a few

17

days earlier Bevin had as good as stated that this was the last
chance of coming to an agreement on Germany.

Molotov, in answering Marshall and Bevin, said he was glad
that Marshall had remarked that the Foreign Ministers should
"build solidly, rather than quickly". But remarks had also been
made among the Western delegates to the effect that Potsdam
was "a paper plan". The Soviet Union, on the contrary, strongly
felt that the Allies should closely stick to the Potsdam decisions.
He was glad, too, that Bevin and everybody else were agreed
on the need for Germany's economic unity. But the Soviet
Union did not agree that there could be a settlement of the
German problem without a reparations settlement being reached
at the same time. This was the opinion not only of the Soviet
delegation, but of the entire Soviet people. The Soviet Union was
still suffering great hardships as a result of the German occupation.
Of course, she sympathized with France's need of coal. France,
too, had suffered from the five years of German occupation. The
Americans did not seem to appreciate either France's or Russia's
point of view. Molotov reiterated that the Soviet Union's
right to reparations had been recognized at both Yalta and
Potsdam, and he argued that Germany *could* pay. During the
war she had spent 620 billion marks on war needs, and this was
not counting all that she had spent on preparing for war. It was
not necessary, as Bevin had said, to reduce German rations from
1,500 to 1,100 calories. A land reform had been carried out only in
the Soviet Zone; in the other zones the Junkers were still in possession of the land, and were sabotaging the Allies. Bevin had also
raised the question of the land given to Poland, but this was
totally irrelevant to the question of "German economic unity".

In the main, Molotov agreed with Bevin about raising the
German level of production, but the French seemed opposed to
this and the American position was far from clear. If the industrial
level were raised, there would be no need for Mr. Bevin to go on
talking about the burdens of the British taxpayer. In the Soviet
Zone, as distinct from the Western zones, all measures were
being taken to develop industry.

What we want [Molotov said] is the economic unity of Germany
under the joint control of the Allied powers. Already at Potsdam
we proposed the creation of a central German administration, but
this was then rejected. . . . Now we are again told about the un-

desirability of dividing Germany in two, and we couldn't agree more.

And Molotov again charged Britain and America with inconsistency, if not downright hypocrisy:

> If you are really in favour of German economic unity, then don't undermine it with your bi-zone; cancel the bi-zone arrangements, because what you have done *can only lead to a separation of Western Germany from the rest of the country*.

On 6th April the Coordination Committee's report came up for discussion. It emerged from this that while the Russians, British and Americans favoured setting up central German administrative departments, the French did not. (The Russians, needless to say, suspected that Bidault was being difficult with Marshall's and Bevin's tacit approval.)

The deadlock on German economic, as well as political, unity now seemed complete. It was then that, on 8th April, Molotov produced a new proposal for an all-German plebiscite: the question to be put to the German people was whether they wanted Germany to be a single country or a federation. In a single country, Molotov said, there must be a central government, though without "excessive centralization"; if the Germans wanted a federation, then the responsibility would rest chiefly on the governments of the Länder. The plebiscite, Molotov proposed, should be carried out under the control of the four Allied powers.

Bevin would not hear of it. He could not, he said, place the fate of Britain once again in the hands of the German people who had approved Hitler. To Britain it was a question of her own security. She distrusted the Germans, and if there was to be a central government it would have to be one with very limited rights.

Bidault agreed with Bevin, and Marshall also said that he distrusted the Germans, and suggested a return to an earlier American proposal which provided that a provisional German government should elaborate a new German Constitution, which would then be submitted for approval to the Allied Control Council. Within a year of the formation of the provisional government, the Constitution would be submitted to the approval of the German people. Molotov replied:

The Soviet Union is just as much concerned about security as the others are, and even more so. But we don't agree that the German people and Hitler are the same thing. . . . Moreover, German aggression can be prevented if we are all equally resolved to carry out the demilitarization and the democratization of Germany. This is something in which the German people themselves can help. Secondly, German aggression can be prevented by the four occupying powers' strict control.

After repeating his earlier objections to federalization, Molotov said he thought German unity was best for both Germany and the Allies. That was why he had proposed a plebiscite. He rejected the suggestion made by some Western delegates that the Russians were trying, in this way, to "play a tricky game of seducing the German people". What the Americans had previously proposed was not very different from the Russian plebiscite plan, but now they seemed to be hedging. So who was playing tricks—the Russians or the Americans?

As for the British, they were paying lip-service to German unity—political, juridical, financial, economic, etc.—but at the same time they were opposed to the plebiscite. Why? Bevin had said that Hitler had used the plebiscite machinery. But that was no reason why the Germans should not be asked a question about their own future. The plebiscite would in any case be carried out under four-power control, so there could be no abuses, as there were under Hitler.

Bidault, Molotov said, had also objected to the plebiscite, arguing that the plebiscite machinery might be applied to other questions, too. This was nonsense. The German people were obviously not going to be consulted on their obligations to the Allies.

But on the internal regime of Germany we must have the opinion of the German people. It is important that we should settle this question of a United Germany or a Federation once and for all. Obviously, the Germans will want a United Germany. And if, instead, we forced on them a situation of 100 years ago, when there was no German state, then we would never find a common language with the German people.

In answer to Bevin's proposal that the Control Council should veto any decisions of the German provincial government with which it disagreed, Molotov said that such a veto could apply only if all the Four agreed, but if not, then the Germans could play on disagreements between the Four.

These frantic Russian attempts in 1947 to create a United Germany are of the greatest interest, especially when one considers that only a few years later, with the establishment of the DDR—following the constitution of the Federal German Republic in the West—the Russians became the staunchest supporters of the two Germanies. Why, in 1947, this advocacy of a United Germany? There seem to be several obvious reasons. Since the setting up of the bi-zone, the Russians saw that the danger of Western Germany splitting away was a very real one. They tried to prevent this. Secondly, they still hoped against hope that, in a united Germany, the good old resolutions about democratization and denazification would be more or less adhered to by all the four powers, whereas, if Western Germany split off, an anti-democratic and militarist country might well, before long, emerge there with the blessing of the three Western allies, and especially the United States (the Russians were by then only too keenly aware of Truman's disposition). Also, a united Germany was the only kind of Germany in which the Russians could hope to obtain reparations on an all-German basis, and have a finger in the Ruhr pie. And, finally, was there not also a long-term political manœuvre in the "seduction" of the German people? If, as was only too likely, Germany was to be split in two, then the Russians could claim that this was entirely the fault of the West.

In the second week in April the Foreign Ministers resumed their discussion on reparations. There was much futile haggling on whether or not to revive the Interallied Reparations Commission. Everybody except the Russians was against it. Molotov complained that the old Commission, set up as a result of Yalta and Potsdam, had in effect been liquidated by the British and the Americans.

BEVIN: Nobody liquidated it. It liquidated itself. It just lay down and died.

MOLOTOV: This is no joking matter, Mr. Bevin. The three of us took certain decisions at Yalta and Potsdam, and we insist that they should be carried out.

BEVIN: The Potsdam decisions have never been carried out, anyway.

MOLOTOV: The Soviet Union carried them out. The incapacity of the Reparations Commission in Berlin was due to the absence of the British and American representatives. My impression is that Britain and the USA simply refused to carry out the Potsdam and Yalta decisions about the Interallied Reparations Commission. . . .

MARSHALL: I'm against re-establishing this Reparations Commission. It waited for the Soviet representatives in Berlin for a fortnight, and they never turned up. However, I may be wrong there.

BEVIN: No, you are right. They went to Paris instead.

MOLOTOV: Both Mr. Marshall and Mr. Bevin are wrong. The Soviet Union always carried out its obligations. . . .

This is a fair sample of the utter futility of most of the discussions during the later stages of the Conference.

The discussions on German frontiers that started a few days later were just as futile. Marshall challenged the Oder/Neisse frontier, saying that it badly handicapped Germany's economy. Bidault, for his part, harped on France's desire to see the Rhineland become a separate country (or a number of countries), with an autonomous status and under Allied occupation. He wanted the Ruhr to be internationalized, given a special statute and placed under control by the Big Four, to whom he proposed to add the Benelux countries. Either, he said, an international commission should govern the Ruhr, or there should be a local German government under the supervision of a High Commissioner who would act as a link between the local German government and the international organization. The High Commissioner would have great powers, including the power of veto.

Bevin rejected all this. As long as there was no peace treaty in sight, it was no use talking about any special statute for the Ruhr. Nor would he hear of any separation of the Rhineland. Bidault then returned, *faute de mieux*, to the Saar. On 11th April, Molotov sharply rejected Bidault's proposals, saying that, with his ideas on the Rhineland, Ruhr and Saar, the French Foreign Minister was simply proposing the dismemberment of Germany, and with this the Soviet Union could not agree.

He admitted, in criticizing Bevin's "historic retrospect", that the dismemberment of Germany had been discussed at both Teheran and Yalta, but no discussion had been taken, and on 9th May Stalin had firmly declared himself against any dismemberment. Then, turning on Bevin, he said that it was "quite abnormal" that the Ruhr should be solely under British or Anglo/American control. As for frontiers, he had made his views on the French proposals clear, while the Oder/Neisse frontier had been "settled at Potsdam".

In the last few days of the conference the discussions reached further heights of futility. When the Russians proposed that, at the time the draft peace treaty was approaching completion, a central German government should be set up, the three Western powers objected to the phrase "central government". Again, when one of the Western delegates proposed that "responsible representatives of Germany be given the opportunity of expressing their views at the peace conference", Vyshinsky said: "No, it must be the German Government." There was also much disagreement on what powers were to be represented at the peace conference.

The Conference was getting nowhere. On 12th April Vyshinsky held a press conference at which he declared that reparations deliveries from the Soviet Zone were proceeding in a satisfactory manner, but that in the Western Zones reparations to the smaller powers and to the Soviet Union were being sabotaged. Like Molotov before him, he treated German "economic unity", the level of production, and reparations, including those from current production, as inseparable.

By 14th April the end of the conference was clearly in sight. Among Western delegates, its "collapse" was already being openly talked about. This was reflected in a large part of the Western press. On that day *Pravda* sharply attacked the Western correspondents in Moscow for "misinforming" their papers. And it angrily quoted several papers—the *New York Herald-Tribune* for saying that a collapse of the Moscow Conference "would be no tragedy", since the Truman Doctrine had already shown which way the world was moving; the *News Chronicle* for saying that there was "a chasm" between Russia and the others on the question of the Polish frontier; and the *Washington Post* for going in "for pure blackmail": "This paper now tells us that the USA should 'take the lead in helping the Western Allies to restore Western Europe'. This is becoming a familiar tune: these gentlemen would prefer the Moscow Conference to collapse."

One of the few small positive achievements was the decision, taken on 24th April, concerning the repatriation of all German war prisoners by the end of 1948, in accordance with a plan to be elaborated in the next two months by the Control Council.

During one of the last meetings, Marshall complained that Molotov had rejected the American twenty-five-year plan for the demilitarization of Germany. Molotov said this was not true. The Russians had proposed to extend it to a forty-year period, and the USA had agreed to this. But the text of the treaty needed improving, for the American text spoke only of demilitarization, not of democratization. Also, the treaty should embody Germany's obligations to pay reparations; it should also provide for the four-power control of the Ruhr, the de-cartellization of industry, the de-junkerization of agriculture, etc., all of which formed part of the demilitarization and democratization process. The American take-it-or-leave-it attitude was wrong, and unacceptable to a self-respecting power like the Soviet Union.

On 25th April Molotov proposed that the next Foreign Ministers' meeting take place in London in November. Bevin, Marshall and Bidault all thanked the Russians for their hospitality, and Molotov concluded by saying:

> We have spent much time and energy on the agenda of the present session. Our task is not finished, but we have done some substantial preparatory work. And I hope this will help us at our future meetings.

We need not say anything about the parallel discussions on Austria. Before long, they also reached a complete deadlock. At a late stage of the Conference, Mr. Kardelj arrived in Moscow to talk to the Foreign Ministers and to give a press conference at which he presented Yugoslavia's claim to "Slovene Karinthia", where, he said, there were 200,000 Yugoslavs. No one, least of all the Russians, took him very seriously. Kardelj was visibly annoyed by the casual way in which the Russians treated him. In reality, he might have known that they had quite enough trouble on their hands without having to bother about Southern Karinthia.

I remember Ernest Bevin's last minutes in Moscow. On the platform of the Belorussian Station he was in one of his most exuberant and back-slapping moods. Vyshinsky had come to see him off. No sooner did he see him than he burst into song:

The more we are together, together, together,
The more we are together,
The merrier we shall be. . . .

"What a jolly man!" Vyshinsky venomously remarked. He was in a foul mood, but tried to restrain himself. He may have wondered if there was any political significance in the song—would the Allies continue as before, or would the Western world all merrily gang together against the Soviet Union?

Officially, the Soviet line was that the conference had *not* been a failure. On 29th April a *Pravda* editorial said that for $1\frac{1}{2}$ months the whole attention of the world had been focused on the conference.

> Germany is, of course, an immense subject, which requires a lot of time and patience. The much simpler satellite treaties took fifteen months to complete. The conference was marked by some tense and even violent struggles. . . . The Soviet Union strictly adhered to the Yalta and Potsdam decisions; the others tried to sidetrack them. . . . Nevertheless, some appreciable results have been achieved.

But the list was a rather thin one: the "liquidation" of Prussia; "a number of decisions on the demilitarization and denazification of Germany", and on DPs and war prisoners; "considerable progress" concerning the procedure in preparing the German peace treaty. The conference had also shown that in the Soviet Zone denazification and democratization were proceeding satisfactorily, but not in the Western Zones; here also the liquidation of Germany's military potential was quite inadequate. Many important posts in the West were held by Nazis. Nevertheless, said *Pravda*, "we can say without hesitation that the Conference marked the beginning of the solution of the German problem" even though the examination of many important questions remained uncompleted, such as the economic issue and reparations, both of which, in the Soviet view, were insolubly linked. The non-settlement of the reparations problem had also delayed the Austrian treaty; here disagreements had arisen over German assets. But while trying to sound reasonably optimistic, the leader concluded that there were still many difficulties ahead. If, it is said, a large part of the Western press was saying that the conference had "failed", it was because the Western delegations had "failed to wreck the Potsdam decisions".

Were the Russians seriously hoping that this conference on the German peace treaty would prove a "useful beginning", and that much better results would be achieved at the next meeting? After all, even while the conference was still in progress, the Soviet press published some sharp comments on Truman. On 3rd April, Henry Wallace's Madison Square Gardens speech, in which he said that the Truman Doctrine was "a threat to peace", was reported. On the same day Harold Laski was reported as having written in *Avanti* that the Truman Doctrine was a policy of "economic imperialism" and one striving to create a new *cordon sanitaire* round Russia. It was hypocrisy, Laski wrote, to speak of "helping democracy" and of making the Greek tyranny the first objective of this help: "It is all obviously contrary to what UN stands for. . . . The Truman Doctrine is the biggest menace to peace since Hitler's advent to power."

Taken together, the Wallace speech and the Laski article took up five columns of *Pravda*. In the Soviet Union such things do not happen accidentally.

No one could have any serious illusions that this Foreign Ministers' Conference of March–April 1947, coinciding with the announcement of the Truman Doctrine, was anything other than a major step towards future East/West conflicts.

Already on 28th April it was announced that a coal deal had been made between France and the two other Western powers. Clearly, the bi-zone was soon to become the tri-zone, the last step before the final division of Germany in two. Ultimately, this division of Germany—and for that matter Europe—was to suit both sides. But by the middle of 1947 the two blocs had not yet congealed, as it were; and their temporary fluidity was to create a dangerous situation which was to continue for a number of years, with policies of "containment" and "roll-back" on one side and "consolidation" on the other. The Russians wrote off Western Germany before very long, but the satellites needed "consolidating"—Hungary, Poland, Czechoslovakia. Then there was the anomaly of Berlin, originally a symbol of that four-power control of Germany which, on the face of it, no longer meant anything after the failure of the conference. Having accepted the *fait accompli* of a separate Western Germany, the Russians tried to put an end to the Berlin "anomaly" with their 1948 blockade of the former Reich capital.

THIRTEEN

The Stormy Summer of 1947

One of the first things to happen after the breakdown of the Moscow Conference was the government crisis in France, as a result of which the communists—who had been in the French government ever since the Liberation—were turned out of the cabinet under the veteran socialist premier Paul Ramadier. The official reasons for the communists' departure were the support they had given the Renault strikers and their unwillingness to support the government in its wage-freeze, but the international reasons for their dropping out of the government were much more important. For several months they had grown increasingly uneasy over the war in Indo-China, but, more important still, the United States had made it amply plain to France that she need expect no great economic help as long as there were communists in the French government. And in the spring and summer of 1947 France was in the greatest economic difficulty, and food was extremely scarce. There were similar developments, at about the same time, in Belgium, Italy and other countries, where the communists were eliminated from their governments in one way or another.

This was part of the division of Europe to which the failure of the Foreign Ministers' Conference had already so powerfully contributed. The Russians were conscious of the hostility to them that was being worked up everywhere in the West, and they did not try to make any secret of it, even though officially it continued to be denied that the Moscow Conference had been a failure or a waste of time. But almost every day the Soviet press quoted bloodcurdling speeches by American congressmen, which were bound to have an effect. Some were saying that the USA, without necessarily attacking Russia just then, should work hard on perfecting "more and more fearful weapons of mass-destruction". Congressman Rankin was advocating the breaking-off of diplomatic relations with the USSR. Mr. Crawford, of Michigan, argued that if the Soviet Union refused to disarm at once, atom bombs should be dropped on her.

The military parade and civilian demonstration on May Day passed off in the usual festive atmosphere. Later, there was a Kremlin reception which Stalin attended, but Molotov acted as toastmaster and Stalin made no speech. Among the mass of the people of Moscow, food continued to be short, though an effort was made to provide a few extras for May Day. But a few days later the second post-war 20-billion rouble loan was launched, with the slogan "subscribe three or four weeks' wages for the good of your country", and although Finance Minister Zverev declared that the subscriptions to the loan "must be absolutely voluntary", in practice this was by no means the case, a very poor view being taken of any worker refusing to subscribe. True, the subscription could be paid for in ten monthly instalments, and the "premium bond" character of the loan (with the prospect of winning 50,000 roubles on a 100-rouble bond) offered a certain attraction. But the loan itself added to the people's daily hardships.

On 8th May, the Soviet press published a (slighly expurgated) version of Stalin's talk with Harold Stassen on 9th April. Stalin was both conciliatory and rather gloomy about the future, and continually asked Stassen whether an economic slump could be expected in the USA.

In answer to Stassen's question whether he—Stalin—thought that Soviet economy and the free enterprise economy of the USA could coexist, Stalin replied: "Not only can they coexist, but they can also cooperate; if they did so during the war, why not now? Lenin first said that the cooperation of the two systems was possible, and Lenin is our teacher."

And he added:

The Soviet system is being treated as dictatorial and totalitarian in the USA, while the Soviet people talk of America's "monopoly capitalism". But when Roosevelt and I met, we did not call each other such names. I am neither a sectarian nor a propagandist. I am a *delovoi chelovek*, a "man of business". I hold that the possibility of cooperation is always present, but the same is not true of the *desire* for cooperation; and when there is no such desire, there can be war. That was what happened to us with Hitler's Germany; we wanted to cooperate even with her, but she refused.

STASSEN: Are you in favour of an exchange of ideas, students, teachers, artists, tourists, etc., if cooperation is established between the USA and the USSR?

STALIN: It is inevitable if cooperation *is* established. The exchange of goods leads to the exchange of people.

In answer to a question by Stassen, Stalin then criticized Western correspondents in the Soviet Union.

One of them went to Teheran, and said that I had hit Timoshenko —who wasn't even there. Two years ago, we abolished the censorship for a short time, but had to put it on again. One of your correspondents wrote that Molotov had exiled Stalin, but that Stalin would soon return and then sack Molotov. Our government was shown as a kind of zoo.

Having finished with this question, Stalin said that he hoped the international control and inspection of atomic energy would be initiated, and the use of atomic energy for war needs totally prohibited. He remarked that things were "very bad" in Europe just now, particularly in Western Europe.

STASSEN: Some countries which didn't suffer too much from the war are not too bad; Switzerland, for instance, and Czechoslovakia.

STALIN: Those are small countries.

STASSEN: Yes, in the bigger countries things are very bad—their finances are in a mess, and there is a shortage of food and raw materials.

STALIN: Yes, it's a tragedy. But isn't it strange that there should be not only a very low output of coal in the Ruhr, but also in Britain?

STASSEN: Fortunately, there is plenty of coal in the USA, and we are sending a lot to Europe.

STALIN: The USA is lucky, protected, as it is, by two oceans, and with only weak neighbours—Canada in the north and Mexico in the south.

STASSEN: We've done very well, and we've successfully reconverted our industries since the war. Our problem now is to avoid a depression and an economic crisis.

STALIN: Are you expecting one?

Stassen assured him that with the existing controls a repetition of the 1929 slump could be avoided. Stalin said that the USA was lucky—having eliminated Japan and Germany as rivals, she had European, Chinese and Japanese markets thrown open to her.

> STASSEN: Yes, but they've got no money.
> STALIN: There are ways of overcoming that difficulty. . . . All the same, the American press is talking of a coming American slump. Is that true?

Again Stassen assured him that a slump could be avoided.

> STALIN: But aren't business people protesting against controls and regulations?
> STASSEN: Yes, but they remember 1929.

It was curious that Stalin persisted in asking about the possibility of a slump in the USA and that he should have suggested that there were ways of overcoming the "lack of money" in Europe and elsewhere. Obviously he already had in mind the financing of West European post-war reconstruction by the United States. Twice he remarked that the United States was "lucky"—both geographically and economically. But the publication of the Stassen interview *after* the breakdown of the Moscow Conference is hard to explain. Perhaps it was a demonstration that there were still a few sensible people like Stassen in America, that the Soviet Union was in favour of cooperation, and that perhaps, threatened with a slump, the USA would *still* agree to it. If Stalin (as he actually seems to have done) hinted that the Soviet Union would be glad to receive a reconstruction loan from the USA, this phrase was omitted from the interview as now published. After the breakdown of the Moscow Conference, such a loan was more than unlikely. What the Soviet press, commenting on the Stalin/Stassen talks, stressed instead was the importance of Stalin's statement in favour of cooperation, at a time when "some American papers are favouring trade discrimination against all powers not adhering to the American way of thinking" (*Pravda*, 13th May 1947). In other words, without specifically asking for an American loan, Stalin was proposing to develop large-scale and unhampered trade with the USA which, in the state of Russia's economy in 1947, necessarily implied certain important credit arrangements (there was the precedent of the huge Swedish credit of 1946), which in turn would be in America's interests as an anti-slump measure. Stalin persistently assumed that the USA *was* threatened with a slump.

Although this interview was published on 8th May, it was by then becoming clear to the Soviet public that despite Stalin's avowed will to "cooperate" and trade with the United States this will was lacking on the other side. On 11th May the Soviet press reported that Truman's Bill for aid to Greece and Turkey had been approved by both Houses of Congress and added Vito Marcantonio's comment: "This is aid to Fascists." The same day the press dismally commented on the five communist ministers in the French government having been replaced by socialists and MRP men, and quoted an article by Henry Wallace saying that "France may well become the next 'beneficiary' of the Truman Doctrine". Meantime, in Italy, the right-wing press was urging de Gasperi to "follow France's example, and turn out the communist ministers". Indeed, as was to be expected, de Gasperi had followed "France's example" by the end of May. B. Leontiev, in *Pravda* on 1st June, attributed the split in the Italian Socialist Party, as well as the formation of the new Gasperi government without the communists and without "those socialists who refused to break with the communists", to the pressure and machinations of the US monopolies and the reactionary forces inside Italy. Linked with all this was de Gasperi's problem of raising a loan of 500 billion lire and an American credit of $600 million. He spoke of the "shooting down of the May Day demonstration in Palermo" as part of the American-inspired reactionary offensive in Italy.

In 1947, after the breakdown of the Moscow Conference, there appeared the very striking phenomenon of the "parallel advance" of East and West. It was as if every American move to eliminate communists from West European governments and make these countries benefit under the Truman Doctrine was accompanied or closely followed by a parallel Russian move to strengthen the Soviet hold on the countries of Eastern Europe. At the end of May, coinciding with the far-reaching changes in France and Italy, a "plot" headed by the general secretary of the Smallholders' Party, Bela Kovacs, was discovered in Hungary. Premier Ferencz Nagy "went on a visit" to Switzerland, but, on being summoned by phone to return to Budapest, refused to do so. Soon afterwards he called on the Hungarian Legation at Berne to say he was throwing up his job as Premier. The communist leader, Mathias Rakosi, vice-premier and acting premier in the absence of Ferencz Nagy, was becoming increasingly influential as the guardian of "Hungarian democracy". He did not become premier himself, but expressed his confidence in the new premier, Lajos Göngös. Speaking before the *aktiv* of the CP of Budapest, Rakosi said that the democratic Three-Year Plan would be carried out and that all the foreign stories about a *coup d'état* or a *putsch* in Hungary which had allegedly eliminated Ferencz Nagy were untrue; but he warned Nagy's and Kovacs's followers in Parliament that if there was more trouble from them there would have to be new elections—obviously on more "Soviet" lines than before, though Rakosi did not of course say so. According to *Pravda* a few days later, "Truman spoke very sharply about events in Hungary" and said that the State Department was "making a thorough inquiry". The Russians, for their part, claimed that President Zoltan Tildy had appointed the new premier without any "outside pressure" (the Western press claimed that the Russians had threatened to deport Göngös if he did not play their game), but at the suggestion of the Smallholders' Political Bureau itself.

There was another striking Soviet/American parallel which should be briefly mentioned before coming to the Marshall Plan, for which so many of the events just enumerated had psychologically prepared the ground. Both in the United States and in the Soviet Union spy-mania was rapidly developing— though, for the time being, in a rather more virulent form in Russia than in the USA. Early in May, asking Congress for $25 million for the purpose, Truman set in motion the machinery of loyalty tests of government officials. In Russia there was a parallel development. True, on 27th May, there was at first the seemingly reassuring Ukase of the Presidium of the Supreme Soviet abolishing the death penalty, which said:

> Our victory in the last war showed not only the might of the Soviet State, but also the remarkable devotion to their Soviet country and its government of the entire population.
> The international situation is such that the cause of peace is safe for a long time, even despite the attempts made by aggressive elements to provoke a war.

In view of this, (1) The death penalty is abolished in times of peace. (2) It is replaced by twenty-five years' confinement in a corrective-labour camp.

This was, of course, little more than a "gesture", but it was one which was no doubt meant to demonstrate the government's benevolence and its conviction that there would be no war— which was what people, rattled by the news in the press, were anxious to hear.

But much more important was another Ukase, three weeks later, on 10th June, by the Supreme Soviet on "the responsibility for disclosing state secrets and the loss of documents containing such state secrets". There followed an enumeration of "secrets" of an economic and military order, but most remarkable was the general principle enunciated in the decree: that in effect no information on the Soviet Union could be published which had not already been officially published; thus, "any information on negotiations and agreements with foreign countries, as well as any measures in the field of foreign policy and foreign trade not already disclosed in officially published documents" were to be considered state secrets.

This, needless to say, put the foreign press in Russia in an extremely awkward position—it was like a warning to them not to attempt to write anything factual—whether military, economic or diplomatic—which had not already been published in the Soviet press. Even to write about the negotiations between the Soviet Union and another country on the strength of what could be learned from representatives of that other country could be interpreted by the Russians as a "revelation of state secrets" and therefore a criminal offence. The Russian censorship, never very easy even at the best of times, became exceedingly difficult in the summer of 1947. There were even frequent cases when they suppressed the reproduction of certain news items in the Soviet press, if their publication abroad was, for any reason, considered undesirable. The censorship itself had been moved shortly before from the Ministry of Foreign Affairs—where correspondents at least had the opportunity of arguing reasonably with the censors— to the Central Telegraph, where officials of the Glavlit—the Russian censorship, working under an official and the Central Committee, and with no experience of the foreign press— handled copy with great ruthlessness and with a kind of inhuman

18

anonymity. The telegram was handed in at a window and a copy returned to the correspondent with the deletions after an indefinite number of hours. Meantime the cut top copy had been telegraphed abroad.

There was, in effect, no longer any distinction between "friendly" or "hostile" correspondents; all were *ipso facto* suspect. I remember a very curious experience at the end of May or beginning of June. I wanted to make another "unaccompanied" trip, like my 1946 one only this time to Siberia. I put the idea to Konstantin Zinchenko, then head of the Foreign Ministry's press department—a very charming man, with whom I had been on the best of terms for a long time (I had first met him in London, where in 1940–41 he was Maisky's right-hand man). He listened to me, and then shook his head.

"No," he said, "I don't think anything can come of it."

"But last year," I said, "you let me go to the Caucasus. . . ."

"Oh, last year and this year aren't the same. I know you did no harm in going to the Caucasus, but now, you know it as well as I do, the international situation stinks—yes, *stinks*. No matter where you go, you'll be treated with distrust and suspicion. If, let's suppose, you were ill and needed to go to a sanatorium, it could no doubt be arranged. But Siberia—it's economically important, and you know how stringent present-day views are on economic espionage."

"Mr. Zinchenko, you've known me long enough—have I ever been a spy?"

"Look," he said impatiently, "it's no use arguing. *I* may not think you're a spy, in fact I don't, but how are these people in Siberia to know that you're not? Do please understand that there's nothing personal in this; but the international situation today is such that my answer must simply be no."

I realized that it was no use arguing. Zinchenko was a good friend, but I knew that he was simply carrying out instructions he had received from above.

"Oh, I suppose you're perfectly right about the international situation. But it's no use being nasty to me—I didn't cause it."

"I know you didn't, and I am sorry, but that's just how it is." We shook hands and he gave me a sad smile.

Back at the Metropole Hotel the same day, I ran into Jack Margoulis. He was a little East End London Jew who had come

to Russia before the war and had now for years been an obvious
NKVD stooge at the Metropole. Officially he was the "Assistant
Administrator". For all that, he always had a furtive and slightly
frightened look. (I heard that he had had some rough experiences
around 1937–8.)

"Where are you going for your summer holidays, Mr. Werth?"
he asked.

"Well, Jack, I wanted to go to Siberia, but it doesn't look as
if they'd let me go."

"Oh, Siberia," he said breezily, "I can fix up a trip for you there
—one way of course—ha! ha! ha!"

We both laughed heartily, both pretending we thought it all a
great joke. Margoulis probably thought the joke even grimmer
than I did.

The story of the Marshall Plan is too familiar to need re-telling
here in detail. The essence of the story is simple enough: Europe,
particularly Western Europe, was financially and economically
in a bad way, and rapid reconstruction was scarcely conceivable
without important financial help from the one country that could
provide it—the USA. Already since the war, America had been
spoon-feeding various countries of Western Europe and, mostly
through UNRRA, even several countries of Eastern Europe,
including (in a very small way, it is true) the Ukraine and Belorussia. But UNRRA help had been "humanitarian" and more
or less politically unconditional. The political purpose of Marshall
Aid—and no one even pretended that it was pure charity—was
that Western Europe should put its house in order along pro-
American and more or less free-enterprise lines, and eliminate
the communists from public affairs, or at any rate greatly reduce
their influence. It was very largely in anticipation of large-scale
American aid that both the French and Italian governments,
soon after the proclamation of the Truman Doctrine, eliminated
their communist ministers on one pretext or another. That this
was one of the conditions on which aid would be given had
already been made perfectly obvious. When Léon Blum went to
Washington in 1946 to borrow some money, it was made quite
clear to him that France could expect far more, and on better
terms, if there were no more communists in her government.

The problem of large-scale American aid had been in the air
for a long time. The Truman Doctrine, though confined for the

time being to Greece and Turkey, foreshadowed the extension of help to many other countries. In his talks with Stassen, Stalin clearly anticipated that to avoid a slump at home the USA would have to find ways of increasing her exports, even though Western Europe "had no money". George Marshall's famous Harvard Address of 5th June 1947 outlining what soon came to be known as "Marshall Aid" did not come as a great surprise to the Russians. But it took ten days before there were any official comments on it in the Soviet press. The reason is clear. The Harvard Address was not sufficiently precise, and the Russians waited for further details: what, in particular, did the whole project mean with reference to Eastern Europe, including the Soviet Union?

At last, on 16th June, eleven days after the Harvard Address, *Pravda* spoke up: This, it said, was a new version of the "Truman Doctrine". For the last ten days the European press had been discussing the Harvard speech. What did it mean? Speaking of the serious economic condition of Europe, Marshall had referred to "the consequences this might have on the American economy". Thus, economic help to Europe meant that it had in the first place to save the USA! This was the primary purpose of the contemplated dollar expansion. American loans to separate European countries had not justified themselves. Therefore, Marshall cautiously advised America's European debtors to join together and to set up a sort of system of joint responsibility. Europe was thus advised to elaborate a "common" programme, and the USA would help "so far as this seemed expedient". In other words, the programme had to be okayed by the USA.

Pravda went on to say that, despite the rather condescending and unceremonious way in which the offer was being made, there was no lack of servile and fawning reactions from Britain, France and other countries. The *Observer* was saying it was "like Lend-Lease" and *The Economist* was talking of a "customs union of Western Europe".

But, though outwardly "new", the Marshall Plan was in reality the same thing as the Truman Doctrine, with its dollar pressure, its interference in the internal affairs of other countries, etc. In Hungary, which had been disobedient, the dollars had been cut off! But if, as distinct from the Truman message, the Marshall speech was "misty" in its wording, it was because the Truman Doctrine, outwardly more aggressive, had made a bad impression in the USA. *Pravda* then got to the real crux of the matter—would Marshall Aid extend to Eastern Europe or not?

In a press conference on 12th June, Marshall said that, in proposing that the European countries work out a programme of economic reconstruction, he "included among them the whole of Europe, i.e. everything west of Asia, that is, Eastern Europe and the Soviet Union. . . ."

Sounding for once a little bewildered, *Pravda* remarked that this was, surely, in flat contradiction with American policy in Eastern Europe (as implied by the Truman Doctrine).

So it now looks as though there were a desire to show the American people that Marshall would like *the whole of Europe* to take part in its economic reconstruction; and the idea these people now want to put across is that the Soviet Union and the other East European countries *are excluding themselves from Europe, since the terms of American "aid" are unacceptable to them.*

Some very puzzling things now began to happen. Had the Russians firmly decided, despite this trenchant *Pravda* editorial of 16th June, to have nothing to do with Marshall Aid? The French communists first took their cue from *Pravda*, Maurice Thorez saying publicly that the whole thing was nothing but "a Western trap", and Pierre Courtade saying in *L'Humanité* that the Truman Doctrine and the Marshall Plan were inseparable: "To subscribe to the Marshall Plan without any guarantee is to accept that American 'world leadership' that Truman talked about."

But then, a few days later, Foreign Minister Georges Bidault said that neither France nor Britain wished to see Europe "shrink", and he declared that he and Ernest Bevin had invited Molotov to come to Paris for preliminary three-power talks. Molotov, much to most people's surprise, accepted the invitation, and the French communists began to pull their punches, Thorez now denying that he had ever spoken of "a Western trap"—even though he had publicly used the phrase only a few days before. Had he spoken too soon? Had Stalin and Molotov had second thoughts about the whole thing?

What raised hopes among those who genuinely did not want to see Europe "shrink" was that Molotov arrived in Paris with a whole army of officials and experts.

But it was no good. Five long meetings took place between Molotov, Bevin and Bidault, Molotov constantly stressing the need for close economic cooperation among all the countries of Europe, with each country's "sovereignty and independence" being respected, and saying relatively little about American aid—this, in his view, was still rather vague and "hypothetical"— and Bevin and Bidault, on the contrary, making this American aid the real cornerstone of the whole programme of European reconstruction. The truth is that Bidault, and certainly Bevin, were terrified of the Russians genuinely entering into the game, since it was highly improbable that Congress would allocate any vast sums for the reconstruction of Europe if a large—or even small—proportion of these sums were to go to the Soviet Union. At the same time, Molotov was fully aware of the fact that one of the clear implications of Marshall's offer was to throw the door open for "dollar diplomacy" in Eastern Europe. Later, in his *Memoirs*, Harry Truman was to write that the purpose of Marshall Aid had been "to help save Europe from economic disaster and lift it from the shadow of enslavement by Russian communism" (vol. 2, p. 139). It is remarkable that in these *Memoirs* Truman should not once specifically mention the Soviet Union as one of the prospective beneficiaries under Marshall Aid, despite Marshall's own statement on 12th June to the effect that the offer was addressed to the Soviet Union, as to all other European countries "West of Asia".

That there was no intention on the part of the Truman administration to include Russia in the future aid programme is quite clear from the President's *Memoirs*, which not only talk of America saving Europe from "Russian communism", but also of the interest shown in the Marshall Plan by Russia's satellites. Thus, Truman quotes a "French diplomatic observer" as saying at the time of the Molotov visit to Paris:

> The Soviets want to put the United States in a position where it must either shell out dollars before there is a real plan or refuse outright to advance any credits,

while Bidault is quoted as remarking:

> Molotov clearly does not wish this business to succeed, but, on the other hand, his hungry satellites are smacking their lips in

expectation of getting some of your money. He is obviously
embarrassed.

Of course Molotov *was* "embarrassed"; even after the Big Three
meeting in Paris was over, Czechoslovakia still accepted the
Bidault/Bevin invitation to the "European" conference of 13th
July, and Poland was tempted to do so, too. Both were prevented
by the Russians from going, as we shall see. What had Molotov
and his experts hoped to achieve by going to Paris?

On 1st July, after long and fruitless discussions, Bidault
produced a Three-Power draft proposal. This stressed the
importance the Three Powers attached to the problem of speeding up the reconstruction and economic development of the
countries of Europe that had been affected by the consequences
of the war, and that they agreed that their task would be greatly
facilitated by economic aid, as offered by Mr. Marshall on 5th
June.

> In the first place, Europe must help herself in developing her
> principal branches of industry; but US aid would be of decisive im-
> portance in achieving this aim. . . . All this would help the countries
> of Europe to secure their economic reconstruction and their in-
> dependence.

Bidault then proposed that a special organization should be set
up which would collect the necessary information for preparing a
programme based on Europe's present resources and her needs;
all countries (except Spain) would take part in this organization
if they wished to do so.

> This organization will not interfere in the internal affairs of the
> states concerned, and will undertake nothing that might be regarded
> as a violation of their sovereignty. No damage would be caused
> to the necessary European exchange. . . .

There then followed the proposal for the establishment of a
special committee which would draw up a report not later than
1st September 1947 enumerating Europe's resources and needs
during a number of years. Moreover, it would also indicate what
each country would need from extra-European sources by way
of industrial equipment, food, etc. The Committee would consist of the representatives of France, the UK, the USSR "and
some other European countries".

The Report would define the development of production arising from the effort made by each country, and from the intra-European exchange of available resources. There would be consultations amongst all countries, with the temporary exception of Spain. The allied commanders-in-chief would provide the information on the resources and needs of Germany. The development of German production would be subject to the decisions of the Foreign Ministers and of the Control Council.

In accordance with Mr. Marshall's proposal, the Committee would request the United States to give its friendly help in drawing up the Report.

Bidault further proposed that six sub-committees dealing with various economic branches be set up.

What were Molotov's objections to this? Here, in part, is what he said at the final meeting of the Big Three on 2nd July:

> Like the earlier British proposal, the French proposal advocates an elaboration of an economic programme for the whole of Europe. But, as we know, most countries haven't got any economic state programmes of their own. Now, with a view to elaborating such an all-European programme, it is being proposed that a special organization be set up which would not only draw up an inventory of each country's resources and needs, but would also define the future development of the principal economic branches in all these countries and only after that seek to discover what economic help can be expected from the United States.

Most significant perhaps, Molotov was not yet taking the promise of American economic aid very seriously. Indeed, as far as the Soviet Union was concerned, he had every reason to be sceptical. But, for the present, he started by charging not the United States but Britain and France with trying to secure a "dominating position" in Europe, with the prospect of American aid as a good pretext.

> Nothing very definite is known about this American aid [he said] but the very idea has given Britain and France a good excuse for trying to set up an organization which would stand above the European countries and interfere in their affairs, including the laying-down of the programme which the main industrial branches of these countries are to follow. France and Britain and certain other countries standing close to them are aiming at securing a dominating position in this organization. . . .

He then made a broad hint that Britain and France were acting as America's agents in these "preliminary" talks. He dismissed as so much verbiage the assurances that there would be no interference with the independence and sovereignty of smaller countries. On the contrary, everything showed that "certain strong powers" intended to place the other powers of Europe under their control.

And, in any case, the possibility of obtaining credits from the United States is closely connected with the obedient behaviour of this or that country in respect of the said organization and its "guiding committee".

Under this scheme, there was no guarantee that pressure would not be brought to bear, say, on Poland that she should produce more coal, even if this meant curtailing her other industries; or Czechoslovakia might be called upon to increase her agricultural production and import her machinery from elsewhere.

The Soviet government, Molotov said, could not accept these proposals, nor could it share the French government's enthusiasm for American aid.

It was wholly in favour of the closest cooperation among the countries of Europe and of European self-aid generally; but it was not in the interests of the European states not to depend on themselves, but to depend primarily, as the French were suggesting, on the United States. . . .

And then came this proud claim:

Even in the most difficult conditions, the Soviet Union always depends, in the very first place, on her own strength, and, as you know, she is going ahead along the path of continuous economic reconstruction.

There were, Molotov said, two forms of international cooperation. One was based on the development of political and economic relations between sovereign states, free of foreign interference; the other was based on the dominating position held by one or more powerful states. The Anglo/French plan, with its interference in the internal affairs of other states, particularly of those in the greatest need of help, was wholly unacceptable to the Soviet Union. As regards Germany, Molotov remarked that the Anglo/French proposals were totally ignoring the vital

problem of reparations. Moreover, nothing was being done to set up a central German government. On the contrary, the rapid federalization process going on in Western Germany showed that this part of the country was being rapidly torn away from the rest. . . . The hope of seeing the establishment of a single democratic German state was vanishing into thin air.

He concluded by saying that the Anglo/French proposals could lead to no good. Europe would be split in two, and American credits would not help to restore Europe economically, but would merely utilize one set of European countries against the other set—all in the interests of certain strong powers seeking to acquire a dominating position (*Pravda*, 3rd July 1947).

In his *Memoirs* Truman expressed some surprise that Molotov should have accepted the invitation to come to Paris, and even says that "for a short while it appeared that the Marshall proposal might not only result in economic reconstruction, *but also in a lifting of the iron curtain*" (p. 140). As we have seen, Truman was more than vague about the possibility of giving economic aid to the Soviet Union, despite Marshall's statement of 12th June, but he was quite definitely interested in using Marshall Aid as a key to opening the door into the satellite states, in the first place Poland and Czechoslovakia. In the latter, there was still (practically alone among the East European countries) a Western-type democratic government, and although it included numerous communists it was the only one openly to accept the Anglo/French invitation to the European Conference that was to meet in Paris on 12th July—ten days after Molotov had slammed the door.

But Molotov, needless to say, applied something of a double standard where "sovereignty and the non-interference in the internal affairs of other countries" were concerned. Pressure was brought to bear by the Soviet Union on both Poland and Czechoslovakia so that they did not attend the Paris Conference of 12th July.

The Polish government, though practically communist-controlled, showed great interest in the Marshall Plan at first, while the Czechoslovak government, which was a coalition of communists and Western-type democrats, simply accepted, without much hesitation, the invitation to attend the Paris "Marshall Plan" conference that Bevin and Bidault had called for 12th July. For a few days they were even undeterred by the news that Molotov had walked out of the Three-Power Conference on 2nd July. Hubert Ripka, the Czech Minister of Foreign Trade and one of the leaders of the pro-Western National-Socialist Party, was particularly enthusiastic about the prospect of American aid. Economically, it was immensely important for Czechoslovakia to get dollars, but American aid, to him, also meant that politically the democratic parties in Czechoslovakia would be propped up and protected against a communist stranglehold on the country. According to Ripka, the news of the Marshall Plan was received in Czechoslovakia "with immense joy", and although the communists, with a nearly 40 per cent vote in the 1946 election, were powerful both in the country and in the government, they were careful not to reject American help. To do so, Ripka says, would be to make themselves very unpopular with the Czech people, who had already attributed to communist protests about "dollar imperialism" Mr. Byrnes's refusal in September 1946 to grant new credits to their country.

Equally significant were the first Polish reactions. Hilary Minc, the communist Polish Minister of Industry and Commerce, happened to be in Prague at the time of Molotov's exit from the Paris Conference. He saw at once that Molotov's refusal to discuss Marshall Aid might complicate matters for both Czechoslovakia and Poland, but he was not unduly perturbed. "Our countries," he said to Ripka, "are not in the same position as a great power like the USSR. We need American help, and I am convinced that the Soviet government will take that into account." On the following day Prime Minister Cyrankiewicz and Foreign Minister Modzelewski, the latter a communist, also arrived in Prague, took the same view as Minc, and proposed to accept the Bevin/Bidault invitation to Paris. On 4th July, the Czechoslovak government met and Foreign Minister Jan Masaryk's proposal that the Czech Ambassador in Paris attend the Marshall Aid conference was adopted unanimously. In reply to Premier Gottwald's question what the Soviet Union thought about it, Masaryk answered that he had mentioned the matter to Bodrov, the Soviet *chargé d'affaires*, and that the latter had raised no objections. The ambassador was instructed not to make any hasty commitments, but to find out first what strings were to be attached to the American aid. But for all that, according to Ripka, the Czech government was unanimous about the country's dire need of dollars, since its industries were largely dependent on raw materials from the West.

It so happened that three Czech ministers were due to fly to Moscow to discuss not only a new Soviet/Czech trade agreement, but also the Franco/Czech alliance that had been on the stocks for some time. Gottwald, Masaryk and Ripka were to go to Moscow, but Ripka, having fallen ill, was replaced by Drtina, the Minister of Justice. It did not take long before Ripka learned that Stalin had presented the Czechs with an "ultimatum": if Czechoslovakia had anything to do with the Marshall Plan, the Soviet Union would consider her alliance with Czechoslovakia as null and void. This produced, on Ripka's part, the following reflections:

> Could we risk a complete break with Moscow? The Soviets might well incite the communists, in that case, to effect a *coup d'état*. [In that case] we were unfortunately unable to expect effective help from the Western powers. . . .
>
> But there was another reason, still more serious. I know that we could not win over the majority of the people for such a policy. . . . [They] might well be revolted by the brutal interference of Moscow, but they would never have agreed . . . to a complete break with our Russian allies. Moreover, we had . . . no detailed information on the help which America was offering, nor on the conditions she would attach to it. And Soviet propaganda was already spreading the idea that the American capitalists . . . were seeking to reconstruct Germany first of all. This sort of argument was very dangerous, and did not fail to have an effect on a large part of our public opinion. . . . Offered the choice between American credits and our alliance with Russia, our democrats themselves began to hesitate. All Czechs have constantly in mind the German danger. . . . Ever since Munich [our people's reliance on Russia] had greatly increased.*

The Czech democrats, as well as President Benes himself, did not take long to see that there was no alternative to accepting Stalin's ultimatum.

Now what exactly happened in Moscow? It is quite clear that in Stalin's view the Marshall Plan was designed not only to place Western Europe under American tutelage, but also to break up

* H. Ripka, *Czechoslovakia Enslaved*, London, 1950, p. 59.

the Eastern bloc, by extending American influence to the Soviet satellites, in the first place to Poland and Czechoslovakia. He did not at first receive the three Czech ministers, but had a heart-to-heart talk with the communist Prime Minister, Gottwald. Gottwald had kept the meeting dark from his two colleagues until after it was over. He then informed them that he had found Stalin in a state of great anger, and Gottwald now reproached the "bourgeois" ministers for having rushed the Czech government into accepting the Anglo/French invitation. He said that Stalin wanted all three of them to go to see him at 11 o'clock that night. With them also went a Czech foreign office official and Jiri Horak, the Czech Ambassador in Moscow.

When the question arose of the Czech acceptance of the invitation to the "Marshall Plan" conference, Gottwald, according to the account given to Ripka by Masaryk,

> defended himself with skill. The invitation had been accepted with serious reservations. . . . The Czechoslovak government, he said, had decided from the beginning to recall its representatives in case of need. "Now," he went on, "we find ourselves confronted with a new situation, since we are the only Slavic state and the only state in Eastern Europe to have accepted the invitation. Is it not natural, therefore, that the Czechoslovak government should wish to know the point of view of the USSR?"

Stalin then spoke and said that after Molotov's return from Paris the Soviet government was informed of the Yugoslav point of view; the question had also been raised by Tatarescu, the Rumanian Foreign Minister. At first the Soviet government thought it would be better to go to the conference, with the possibility of leaving if necessary. But after receiving the more detailed reports of Molotov on what had gone on in Paris, "another point of view prevailed". The Marshall Plan credits, Stalin said, were very uncertain, and it was clear that "through the bondage of these credits, the Great Powers were seeking to form a Western bloc and to isolate the Soviet Union". France and Britain were both in a financial and economic mess—

> Yet, in spite of this, these two great powers are seeking to draw up the programme for the economic recovery of Europe. Now the principal creditor is the United States, for neither France nor England has a cent. [Therefore] the Soviet government does not

consider the Paris plan as genuine and ... has come to the conclusion that in reality it is solely a device for isolating the USSR. [It] has consequently sent telegrams to Tatarescu, the Yugoslavs and the Poles. The Poles at first hesitated, but decided later not to accept the invitation. [We are] surprised to note that you are acting differently.

Then came Stalin's "ultimatum":

For us this question puts our alliance at stake. Besides, you will gain no immediate advantages by going to the Conference. You certainly do not want credits which will threaten your economic and political sovereignty. The conditions attached to the loans will certainly be onerous. ... It is a matter of principle on which our friendship with Czechoslovakia depends. By going to Paris ... you will participate in an action designed to isolate the Soviet Union. All the Slav states have refused. Even Albania was not afraid to reject the invitation. That is why, in our opinion, you ought to reverse your decision.

The rest of the meeting with Stalin, as described by Ripka, was not based on the verbatim report which Masaryk had shown him, but on what Masaryk told him on his return to Prague.

Masaryk remarked that he had been surprised (after Gottwald's earlier story about Stalin's rage and fury) "by the benevolence and apparent calm of the Generalissimo", but that his tone was no less categorical. For the rest, he did not think it necessary to explain to us "how the Soviet government had reached the conclusion that the Marshall Plan had for its aim the isolation of Russia".

According to Masaryk, Gottwald said nothing for a long time, but he (Masaryk) and Drtina pointed to Czechoslovakia's urgent need for credits, since she depended on the West for 60 to 80 per cent of her raw materials. To detach herself from the Western countries economically would mean her own impoverishment.

In the end, Masaryk said, "even Gottwald reminded Stalin that we had to pay in foreign exchange, and that we had not enough of it."

But Stalin retorted, laughing: "We know that you have enough." And, turning to Molotov, he said, still laughing: "They thought they could lay their hands on some dollars, and they didn't want to miss the chance."

Masaryk concluded that, since it was necessary to renounce American help, he tried at least to obtain some compensation from Russia.

However, the industrial products he was proposing to buy from us . . . were those we could advantageously sell to the Western countries, and the only effective aid Stalin promised us was 200,000 tons of wheat as well as some barley and oats. We had urgent need of it, because our 1947 harvest was proving a very bad one. This was extremely valuable to us, but it could not make up for the losses that would result from our boycotting the Marshall Plan.

Both the quotation of Stalin's argument from the official transcript and Masaryk's account of the rest of the meeting ring completely true. So also does his summing-up:

Stalin was, as always, very friendly, almost jovial: but he did not give way an inch. The game was clear: he had come to an understanding with Gottwald; the interview with us [i.e. Masaryk and Drtina] was nothing but a formality.

But the subsequent exchanges between Ripka and Masaryk, as written down by Ripka, sound much more doubtful. These, it seems, were written subsequently by an embittered man, who had had to flee from his country, who mourned Masaryk's tragic death, and who was now writing a "Cold War" book.

I asked Masaryk for what reasons, in his opinion, the Soviets had refused American help. Their country having been particularly devastated, they had every reason to accept it and to hasten reconstruction.

"They claim that America wants to isolate them," I remarked. "By rejecting the Marshall Plan, they are isolating themselves."

"I see only one explanation. . . ." Masaryk answered. "They do not want Europe to recover economically; they are afraid of the success of the reconstruction of Western Europe. . . . As I listened to Stalin, I had more and more clearly the feeling that he is counting on war. Everything they do is done with one aim in view: war."

What gives me added reason for believing that Masaryk did not say anything of the kind to Ripka is that I had an opportunity of having a brief talk with Masaryk at the Czechoslovak Embassy during his visit to Moscow. He did not go into any details on what had happened, but merely said that Czechoslovakia "had made her choice" and was not going to send anybody to Paris.

"And the real reason for this, if you must know, is that the Americans will be very happy to bribe both us and the Poles into loosening our bonds with the Russians."

"But the Marshall offer to give credits to Russia, too?" I said.

"That," said Masaryk, "is the real crux of the matter. The offer of credits to us and to the Poles is quite genuine; I am less sure about the Rumanians and the Yugoslavs. But as for credits for Russia, that is the biggest piece of eyewash in the whole scheme. Do you see Truman and Congress forking out billions of dollars to Enemy No. 1, communist Russia, from whom we all have to be saved?"

Masaryk looked very calm and self-possessed and my impression was that he was not greatly disturbed by what had happened.

Was there not, after all, a certain harsh logic in what Stalin had said about the Marshall Plan being designed to "isolate the Soviet Union"? I later wondered whether it had occurred to Masaryk before, or whether he had seen it clearly only after the talk with Stalin, that the American credits to Russia were "the biggest piece of eyewash in the whole scheme". There is no mention of these credits in the record of the meeting, as given by Ripka, but they *must* have been mentioned.

The record of the talks between Stalin and the three Czech ministers seems to me of the greatest interest. In his jovially ruthless way Stalin had dealt very skilfully with an extremely tricky situation. Far from being half-insane or suffering from senile decay, Stalin had acted like a genuine *Realpolitiker* who realized only too clearly the full implications and challenge of Marshall Aid. He was prepared to see Western Europe go her own way—as she had, indeed, been doing for some time, and nothing was more obvious than that during the abortive Foreign Ministers' Conference in Moscow only three months before—but Eastern Europe had to be "saved" at any price.

Ripka's claim that Masaryk believed that Stalin and the Soviet Union were "counting on war" and that their "one aim in view was war" is totally unsubstantiated, and more than improbable. That the Russians in 1947 *feared* war is true enough; that they *wanted* it is plain nonsense.

At the end of July 1947 I went to Poland, and spent over a month there. I had not been there since 1945, and was much impressed by the enormous amount of reconstruction that had been achieved since then. In the course of this visit I had long talks with Hilary Minc, the Minister of Industry, Modzelewski, the Foreign Minister (both of these were communists), and the socialist Premier, Josef Cyrankiewicz. It was a valuable experience, coming so soon after the Polish government's refusal to attend the Marshall Plan conference in Paris.

The progress of reconstruction in the last two years had, indeed, been remarkable, all the more so since Poland had been more devastated by the war than anywhere else except the occupied areas of the Soviet Union. Moreover, unlike any other country, Poland had been "shifted" several hundred miles to the west, and had to assimilate the large new territories taken over from Germany, now practically cleared of its German population.

The loss of the territories in the east, which Russia had taken over, was being taken with resignation, though there were still many who regretted the loss of "truly Polish" cities like Lwow and Vilno. The country was now more homogeneous than before the war, when Poland had to cope with huge Belorussian and Ukrainian minorities. Moreover, the Jews had been eliminated by the Germans, which, to only too many Poles, caused no excessive regrets; if the Jews were exterminated in that horrible way, that, after all, was the Germans' responsibility. Even then, in 1947, there were still plenty of traces of Polish anti-semitism. In the government and in the Communist Party, many people were saying, there were still too many important jobs held by Jews. There was Minc, the "industrial dictator", for instance, and Jakob Berman, the "chief Russian stooge" in the Party, and many, many others. For all that, there was a widespread feeling that, Jews or no Jews, the government was pretty efficient, and was getting things done. Warsaw was rapidly rising from the ruins. Gomulka, who was in charge of the Western Territories, was rapidly turning them into an integral part of Poland; and most of the top people—Gomulka, and President Bierut (though a "Russian stooge" in his own way) and Premier Cyrankiewicz and Foreign Minister Modzelewski—were, after all, perfectly genuine Poles. And there was much progress to be observed everywhere. There was a larger goods traffic on the railways than before the war. Although there was still a bad shortage of passenger carriages, there were more goods wagons than in 1939. Many of them were German, but many also had been built in the last two years at the great rolling stock plant at Wroclaw, which was now also producing locomotives. This restoration of the Wroclaw plant in 1946 was now proclaimed, in somewhat Soviet style, as the "proudest achievement of Polish industry" during that year. The 500 million dollars of UNRRA aid had, of course, been of great help, but help and credits had also come from Sweden and other countries. Now the recent State Department's decision to stop all post-UNRRA help had come as a great blow.

Life in Poland was not easy, but patriotic, rather than socialist, enthusiasm was making people work hard. Miners, builders, railwaymen, textile workers were working with great devotion. The land reform had gone through fairly smoothly. But there were still serious food shortages and, worse still, there were still the after-effects of the six years of German occupation; 7 per cent of Warsaw's population was tubercular; most people, especially in Warsaw, were living poorly, and were miserably housed. Even so, in 1947, Poland could not rank as one of the very hungry countries of Europe.

A very important difference between Poland in 1945 and Poland in 1947 was that there was now almost complete internal peace in the country. During my stay in Poland I travelled in a car all over the Polish part of former East Prussia and large parts of Byalystok province. A year before, these areas were considered highly dangerous, but now seldom anything unpleasant happened. The February amnesty had virtually ended the activities of the anti-government underground. Over 60,000 men had laid down their arms and had returned to civilian life. Most of them, in the government's view, had given up the struggle for a Western-type (or fascist) Poland for good, though on some no doubt the police continued to keep an eye. The disintegration of the underground bands had been foreshadowed, even before the amnesty, by the diminishing support they had been getting from the peasantry. For although the peasants were, in the main, anti-government, they, like the rest of the population, wanted peace and quiet above all.

During my travels through Poland I acquired the clear impression that, although the government was not popular with the peasantry, the shopkeepers and the "disinherited" classes, it still commanded considerable respect, simply because it was "getting things done"; and, even at the lower level, the government bureaucracy was not inefficient.

One had, I felt, to see the Poland of 1947 in a certain perspective: after all, three years before, the Germans were still occupying the greater part of the country. In 1945 there was a sort of civil-war atmosphere in Poland. Now all looked remarkably quiet and normal—for the first time since 1939.

A member of the American Embassy I met in Warsaw put, of course, a different slant on it. The Poles, he said, were wonderful people, with a great desire to put their country in order, and the country was reviving, not so much thanks to the government as in spite of the government. But the fact remained that it *was* reviving. Among the industrial workers there was, of course, a different attitude: they said they wanted some, but not all, the features of the Soviet system, and if they (and a good many intellectuals, for that matter) were attracted by the PPR (the Polish CP), it was because it had some of the best organizing brains in the country, and, under their organization, Poland was beginning to show excellent results in many branches of the economy. The sort of arguments one would hear from Warsaw intellectuals fairly, though not unreservedly, sympathetic to the government can be summarized thus:

"Of course, the Polish government is not strictly democratic in the Western sense, but then we in Poland never had any 'strictly democratic' government, and according to Western standards the last election was nothing but a swindle. Only, the problem with which we were faced was this: Was Poland to rise from the ruins or not? If the government had left the decision, 'in the name of pure democracy', to a few million ignorant, priest-ridden peasants, we might well have had a Mikolajczyk government, to be followed before long by a plainly reactionary one, which would inevitably have bred internal strife. We had had enough of that in 1945–6. There would have been no proper planning, only chaos, like there is today in Greece. The Russians, for their own protection, might have brought intolerable pressures to bear on us—or even occupied the country."

Relatively speaking, Poland was still a great deal freer than Russia in 1947. There was a censorship of the Polish press, but it did not apply to Western correspondents. Though Mikolajczyk was "on his last legs", as they were saying, there was still a

Mikolajczyk press of sorts, and "an enormous clerical press". This, without being personally offensive to members of the government, still used much of its space to denouncing socialism and communism.

I was interested to meet Hilary Minc, Poland's "economic dictator", a brilliant talker, a man of the liveliest intelligence, who looked exactly like Harold Laski.

He spoke with satisfaction of the genuine progress made by Poland since the Liberation. She was now producing 57 million tons of coal. The present five-year plan was harmonious, coherent, and—within the limits of Poland's possibilities—neither doctrinaire nor pedantic. He talked of Poland's mixed economy, with its three sectors—state, cooperative, and private. The wholesale trade was in the hands of the cooperative, the retail trade in private hands; the transition to socialism would be gradual.

The 1945-6 requisitioning of food amongst the peasants had been abandoned. Peasants were now paid the free-market price for their produce by the state. Of course, the economic conditions among the peasantry were very uneven still. Some peasants (among them some wartime profiteers) were very prosperous. Also, the land greatly varied in quality: the per-hectare yield of grain north of Warsaw was only 4 quintals: in the Lodz province it was 16 or 17 quintals.

Ration cards had been reduced from 11 to 8 million. Those without ration cards were paid higher wages. Altogether, however, the food situation was far from perfect. The number of livestock were still half of pre-war; under the three-year plan, by 1949 there would still be only 58 per cent of the pre-war cattle, and 75 per cent of the pigs; owing to bad weather, there was also a serious grain shortage in 1947, and, as regards grain, Poland was unlikely to be self-supporting before 1949. But on the whole Poland was going to concentrate less on grain-growing than on stock-breeding and dairy-farming—which would also be important from the point of view of her export trade.

Minc was particularly pleased with industrial development since the Liberation and said she was producing 1,000 railway wagons a month, and twenty locomotives. But steel production was still under 1 million tons a year (the iron ore had to be imported from Sweden and the Soviet Union). Her main asset was still her coal; but her home needs of coal were growing. There was, he said jokingly, something caballistic in these figures—before the war 35 million people used 24 million tons of coal; now 24 million people used 35 million tons of coal; 6½ million tons of coal were exported to the Soviet Union, besides considerable quantities of textiles, etc. Of Poland's foreign trade of $300 million, one-third was with the Soviet Union. So even after the deliveries of coal to the Soviet Union, Poland still had a coal surplus of nearly 20 million tons.

And we had the following conversation on the Marshall Plan:

A.W.: I understand, Mr. Minc, that your government, and you in particular, was anxious to go to Paris for the Marshall Plan Conference. That is what the Western press was saying, and what I also gathered from the Czechs.

MINC: Yes, quite true. We wanted to see what it was all about. We had no intention of committing ourselves to anything in advance.

A.W.: Then why didn't you go—at least on this exploratory mission? Who stopped you—the Russians?

MINC (smiling): That's a very crude way of putting it. No, the Russians didn't really stop us. If you must know, what stopped us was *your press*—the British, American and French press. At the very idea that we would go to Paris, these papers started screaming that we were "hopping over to the West", that the "Soviet bloc was disintegrating thanks to Marshall Aid", that the Poles were "turning their backs on Russia" and "kicking Stalin in the teeth".

A.W.: Still, since the Russians themselves refused to, they weren't very keen on your going, were they? They pretty well told the Czechs where they got off. And the Czechs say that you, Mr. Minc, were very keen on the Paris meeting.

MINC: I wasn't *quite* as keen as some of the Czechs, but I was interested at first to find out what the Americans were proposing —via the French and the British. But I told you why we decided against going. The Soviet Union is our best protection against Germany; and, as you know, the Americans—whether Byrnes or Marshall doesn't matter—have a soft spot for Germany, and keep on questioning the wisdom of the Oder/Neisse frontier. But that doesn't mean that we are going into some kind of economic isolation, or that we intend to sever our trade relations with the West. We believe neither in any sort of autarky, or in a self-contained Eastern bloc. I am going to Paris very shortly to negotiate a new trade agreement with France. And we do not deny that we want credits—American credits, any kind of credits.

We can even contribute handsomely to the recovery of Germany, but not on the principle of "Germany first". If we get credits to develop our agriculture and our coal industry, we could help Europe.

A.W.: But won't the bulk of your trade gradually turn eastward?

MINC: No, not necessarily, unless the Americans put us in some kind of quarantine. But, of course, our trade with the East will develop in any case. Czechoslovakia is of special importance to us. Under the newly signed trade agreement with Czechoslovakia 10 per cent of all our exports will go to that country, and 5 per cent of Czech exports will go to Poland. The 600 documents constituting this trade agreement provide not only for the exchange of goods, but also for various other forms of cooperation—industrial, agricultural and so on. There's also going to be a joint council of economic cooperation with several countries which will deal with common problems, and such questions as waterways; thus the Czechs will have an outlet to the sea along the Oder all the way to Stettin—I mean Szczecin— where you will see Czechoslovak ships sailing under the Polish flag. . . .

A.W.: Wouldn't Russia benefit most under the development of trade among the Eastern countries? And some of your people grumble to this day about the unfavourable conditions under which you have to deliver coal to the Soviet Union, and about the so-called German assets they collected and dismantled in what is now Polish Silesia, for instance.

MINC: Well, there were some things towards the end of the war which the Russians did which we didn't like, but that's becoming ancient history. Some of the things they took away from Silesia we would have preferred to remain in Poland, but after all they had a claim on certain German assets, as they called them. But we've now gone well past that stage. . . .

A. W.: So you're fairly optimistic about the future, Mr. Minc?

MINC: Yes and no. A lot of the Americans are in a nasty mood, and we've got to sit tight and not lose our nerve. I think you know what I mean.

The refusal of the Polish government to go to the Paris conference was treated in Poland with a mixture of resignation and a touch of cynical amusement. As a taxi-driver remarked: "If Daddy doesn't want to go somewhere, sonny mustn't go either." But, at the same time, the Polish press was making a big song and dance about the USA, in its "reconstruction of Europe", wanting to give top priority to Germany, and this was having a visible effect on the Poles.

Within the next few days I was to see Mr. Modzelewski, the Foreign Minister, whom I had known in Moscow when he was Polish Ambassador there, and also Prime Minister Cyrankiewicz. Modzelewski made the most of the "priority for Germany" angle, and also of the fact that the whole basis of the conference Bidault and Bevin had called in Paris was rather "indefinite". Of course, he said, Poland could do with American credits. Unfortunately, after the last Polish election, an American credit of $90 million had been cancelled, and this had delayed many improvements in the Polish coal industry. He hoped that a "more acceptable" offer would be made by the West—one that would be "acceptable" to all the East European countries; but he was rather doubtful about it. I was left in no doubt that the Polish ministers—even the communists—were interested at first in going to Paris, but that the Russians were not at all keen on their going.

Handsome, spruce, bald-headed Premier Cyrankiewicz— unlike Minc and Modzelewski, who had both spoken in Russian— spoke to me in German (he knew no other language outside Polish). He made no bones about it: "Western Europe," he said, "must appreciate the fact that in the long run it is essential for Poland to keep in with the Soviet Union, because of the danger of a German military revival. There is really no such thing as a Slav bloc—except as a safeguard against German aggression. We are also keen on an alliance with France, and of course our alliance with the Soviet Union and Czechoslovakia is absolutely essential to our security." And breaking, a little surprisingly, into German political jargon, he added: "There are both historical and geopolitical factors which we must consider in shaping a long-term policy which would safeguard the future of the Polish nation. The trouble with the Americans is that there is far too much talk in their country of a 'preventive war'. This is dangerous stuff. As for the Soviet Union, I do not believe that she is in any way threatening Polish independence." And then came this almost Titoite, polycentrist argument: "What is penetrating into Poland is not Russia, but socialism—*socialism of our own making*. And, in Polish political thinking," Cyrankiewicz added, "the German problem has top priority."

He then talked about other things. The present Polish policy was to "bring all the Poles back" from abroad, thus reversing the emigration policy between the two wars; 80,000 Poles had already returned from Britain and the British Zone of Germany. Inducements were also offered to Polish emigrants of long standing to return to Poland—Polish miners in Germany and France, and others who had settled long ago in Yugoslavia and Rumania. "The Poles from Britain are rapidly becoming absorbed in the general population. And though many are still hostile to us, they are impressed by conditions in Poland, and recall with some annoyance all the horror stories they had been told by the Polish émigré press."

Cyrankiewicz admitted that a few Catholic priests had latterly been arrested for "subversive activities", and he had no illusions about the feelings of the Church hierarchy towards the present government. But these arrests had been the first of their kind. The lower ranks of the clergy were rather divided in their attitude to the government, and by and large the Church was pretty careful not to antagonize the government unduly. After all, there were still 300,000 hectares of Church lands which had not been affected by the land reform. "Of course," said Cyrankiewicz, "the Church was having a strong influence with the peasants still, and was interfering with secular education; and the Vatican had not replied to the Polish government's offer to re-establish diplomatic relations. It was all a bit of a problem. . . ."

Turning to the question of the Polish people's attitude to the Russians, Cyrankiewicz said: "The repatriates are pleased to see that there is no sign of any Russians in Poland, except on their communication lines to Germany. There are, of course, many Russian officers in the Polish Army—but that is because of the shortage of trained Polish personnel; after the First World War we had quite a large number of French officers in the Polish army."

Cyrankiewicz then remarked that there still continued a certain traditional dislike between Poles and Russians, and especially after the German capitulation in 1945 the discipline among some Russian troops in Poland "had not been too good". But the fact was being recognized, he said, that it was, after all, the Russians who drove the Germans out of Poland, and the fact that they "didn't stay on in Poland" is chalked up in their favour.

The much tougher Stalinite regime was not to come to Poland until some time later, especially after the spread of Titoism in Eastern Europe. It was then that Gomulka was arrested and jailed, and—this is the general belief in Poland—would have been shot but for President Bierut. Bierut, though nicknamed NKVD Bierut, was at heart a much better Pole than was commonly supposed. The Stalinist terror never assumed in Poland the same proportions as it did in other East European countries. Already in the summer of 1947 Petkov was arrested in Bulgaria and, after a typical "purge" trial, shot as a "Western agent". Many more similar trials were to follow in Bulgaria, Hungary, Rumania, Czechoslovakia and other countries, especially after the break between Moscow and Belgrade in the summer of 1948.

But Poland, in the summer of 1947, still left a rather reasssuring impression. Warsaw, with one-third of the working population engaged on rebuilding the city, was a stimulating sight. The music of Warsaw was the music of sawing and hammering. In 1945 the "fourteen flower stalls of Warsaw" were a pathetic symbol of the city's revival. Now there were several thousand shops in Warsaw, mostly in temporary one-storey houses built in front of the ruins. In cafés they were serving coffee and whipped cream, and there was a wide range of buns and cakes. There were also a number of privately run and expensive restaurants.

Of Warsaw's houses 10 per cent had survived. In the last two years 20 per cent had been rebuilt and many new houses were being built, notably at Zeliborz. But to obtain a new or even a reconstructed flat one had to be very high on the priority list. A large proportion of Warsaw people were still living outside the city proper, while in Warsaw there was still some fearful overcrowding, with four or five people living in a room. The famous Poniatowski Bridge across the Vistula had been rebuilt, and there were now two theatres and four cinemas in the city.

I travelled by car, with a friend from the British Embassy, all over the Polish part of former East Prussia. In Allenstein, now called Olsztyn, with its aggressively Hohenzollern architecture (more than half the town had survived), there were now 45,000 Poles instead of 56,000 Germans, and the Protestant churches had been taken over by the Catholic clergy. There were still about 100,000 Germans in Polish East Prussia, but many of them ranked as "Masurians", who, though Germanized over the centuries, could still claim Slav descent. The great curios in East Prussia were the *kolossal* red-granite Tannenberg monument and the (now empty) tomb of Hindenburg and his wife. The monument had been blown to pieces by the retreating Germans back in 1945. Altogether there were about half-a-million new Polish settlers in the country. Some 50,000 Germans, who mostly worked as farm labourers, but whose children had no German schools to go to, were waiting to be sent to Germany. Many of the newcomers were Polish peasants from Vilno (now in the Soviet Union), from Rzeczów, near the Ukrainian border, where, until recently, a guerrilla war was going on, or from the overpopulated parts of central Poland. Many of the old Junker estates had been provisionally turned into state farms, the land to be distributed later among the peasant families.

Later I went by train to Danzig (Gdansk), where Warsaw-type reconstruction was going on, then stayed with my friends the Fedeckis at Sopot, now becoming again a fashionable seaside resort. I travelled in slow stages by train to Szczecin, and then explored the new Western territories taken over from Germany. The contrast between now and 1945 was indeed striking. At the beginning of 1946 there were still only 2·8 million Polish settlers in the "Returned Territories"; now there were 4·6 million, or about 20 per cent of the entire Polish population, not counting the Silesians in the industrial areas of Silesia who had not followed the German army and had more or less automatically been given Polish citizenship once the war was over. In many parts of Pomerania there was still much war devastation, and here there were very few new settlers. In principle, all these had to be given adequate houses in their "new" country. Szczecin, with its ponderous Wilhelmian public buildings, looked thoroughly German, but only Polish could now be heard. In Szczecin province, which had had a German population of 2 million, there were now nearly 1 million Poles and only 120,000 Germans, and these were being sent to Germany at the rate of 2,000 a day. Before the end of the year, none would be left.

Of the arable land 40 per cent was still run by state farms, but this land would soon be split up into individual farms, of which there were already several tens of thousands in Szczecin province alone. Farm houses were being built in many parts of the "new" lands, and by 1949 there would no longer be any more fallow patches, as there were now. Swincojsie had been badly wrecked in the heavy fighting, and had not yet been restored. It was strange to recall that this had been Swinemünde until the war, a sort of Brighton of Berlin, merely a couple of hours by train from the Reich capital. It now looked deserted, but, being right on the German frontier, there were many Russian soldiers and officers there, together with their families, Russian women pushing German or Polish-made prams along the desolate sea-front.

Wroclaw (Breslau), after the two months' siege in 1945, was about two-thirds wrecked, and its restoration was proceeding more slowly than Warsaw's. But even so it was a live city, with its new practically all-Polish population. One had to travel through these new parts of Poland to realize how much the Oder/Neisse frontier meant to the Polish people as a whole. Russia, and not the United States, whose leaders had so often questioned this new frontier, was its only real guarantor. Hence also the feeling of inevitability with which Poland regarded her government's refusal to attend the "Marshall Plan" Conference.

FOURTEEN

The Cominform

The events of the first half of 1947 brought about in the mind of Stalin an "agonizing reappraisal". If he was in an exuberantly happy mood at Yalta and still reasonably cheerful at Potsdam, it was because he still believed—or liked to believe—that the victory over Germany would result in the Big Three peace. The foundations—as he saw it—had been laid while the war was still on, and not least as a result of his curious "deal" with Churchill in October 1944. Eastern Europe—Rumania, Hungary, Czechoslovakia, Poland, Yugoslavia and Albania, but not Greece— were to constitute, more or less, the Soviet "sphere of influence", though without purely Soviet or communist regimes being established in all these countries. Germany was to remain under Four-Power control for a long time, and at the Foreign Ministers' Conference in Moscow in March/April 1947 Molotov and Vyshinsky had put up a desperate fight to prevent the splitting of Germany. It was clear after the breakdown of this conference that this was not to be, and that a United Germany, or a peace treaty with such a United Germany, had become a myth. Already throughout 1946, and even before, there had been ominous signs that Stalin's cherished "spheres of influence" peace was precisely what the Western allies were now challenging with ever-growing vigour. Unlike Roosevelt, Truman had been hostile to the Russians from the start, and had encouraged Churchill to make his "Iron Curtain" Fulton speech.

Less than ever were the Russians going to take any chances with "doubtful" allies like Poland. Hence the cooked Polish election of January 1947—a Russian counterpart of the equally cooked

pro-monarchist plebiscite in Greece which the Western powers
had engineered there. For a time, Stalin still tolerated a semblance
of Western-type democracy in Hungary and Czechoslovakia,
and throughout 1946 and even the early part of 1947 he made one
conciliatory statement after another, still suggesting that there
was nothing he wanted more than "peaceful coexistence" with
the former Western allies. It was after the breakdown of the
Foreign Ministers' Conference in April 1947 and the introduction
of the Truman Doctrine and the Marshall Plan that Stalin became
wholly disillusioned and embittered. People who were well
acquainted with Stalin and his immediate entourage have told
me in recent years a great deal about the way in which he became
an "angry old man" at some time during 1948 or 1949. During
the greater part of these two years, and right up to his death in
1953, he was seldom seen in Moscow. He lived nearly all the time
at his government *dacha* at Kuntsevo, outside Moscow, and
governed, as it were, mostly by proxy. Up to the time of his
death in August 1948, Zhdanov was his principal factotum. Then
Malenkov took over, and during the 1949–53 period Malenkov's
influence with Stalin was immense. Another man who had
Stalin's ear was the sinister and ever-present Poskrebyshev; and
the only other man who had fairly easy access to Stalin was the
virtual head of the MVD, Lavrenti Beria, who had moreover
been placed in charge of the all-important atomic industry.
Stalin lived a strange sealed-up life during those years at Kuntsevo.
He ate and drank heavily, but was wholly careless about his
clothes, unwilling to discard the old tunics he had worn during
the last years of the war. Contrary to rumours, he had no wife,
either official or unofficial, and he hardly ever admitted his two
children, his son Vasili and his daughter Svetlana, into his presence. He regarded the former as a dissolute drunk, and the
latter, with her succession of husbands and love-affairs, as a
nymphomaniac.

Except for Zhdanov (and after him Malenkov), Beria and
Poskrebyshev, Stalin's distrust of his "colleagues" became increasingly acute as time went on. Without having to take as
gospel truth Khrushchev's "revelations" on Stalin during the
last years of his life, still less the even more axe-grinding accounts
by Yugoslavs like Djilas and Dedijer, it seems obvious that he
suffered from an increasing degree of paranoia and persecution

mania, easily detecting enemies or potential enemies among his close collaborators (with the above exceptions) and amongst certain groups of the population—notably among the Jews.

A curious kink which he developed in the last years of his life —though this can be traced back to the war years—was his extreme Russian nationalism, and, one might even say, his *Muscovite* nationalism. Hence not only his distrust of Ukrainians and other nationalities, whose loyalty during the war had not been impeccable, but also his acute dislike of Leningrad, with its peculiar individuality, which its grim experiences during the war had only tended to heighten. The twenty-nine-months' blockade had not only increased the Leningraders' local patriotism, but had also aroused something of the old antagonism that had always existed between Petersburg-Leningrad and Moscow. The question often arose in the Leningraders' minds whether their city had not suffered more than it would have done had Moscow (that is, Stalin) given it as high a priority as Moscow had had in 1941. Stalin's growing irritation against Leningrad produced in the end, in 1949, that "Leningrad Affair" in which dozens of men who had taken a leading part in the defence of Leningrad were to be shot.

A look at the Soviet press in the middle of 1947 gives one a clear idea of the exasperation that existed in the Stalin entourage against the Western ex-Allies, of the artificially worked-up "Muscovite" nationalism, of the campaign intended to show Russian "superiority" in all things, and of much else that characterized that period.

Typical of Russian anger against the new policy of the United States was the *Pravda* article on 19th June 1947 singling out Under-Secretary Dean Acheson for special abuse—

> The cynicism of dollar and atomic diplomacy and the thirst for expansion, covered up by the fig-leaf of the "Truman Doctrine", have finally liquidated the great former prestige of American foreign policy, which F. D. Roosevelt had shaped.
>
> In his book, Elliott Roosevelt refers to men like Acheson as "people who are destroying that unity among the Great Powers which had come into being during the war". . . . In his speech the other day Acheson spoke of the promises that the Soviet Union had broken—but *what* promises he doesn't say.
>
> Acheson regards Lend-Lease not as a contribution to the common

war effort, but as a sort of financial-political investment permitting
the United States to dictate its will to the Soviet Union. . . . He
is also trying to convince his American provincial audiences that
victory over Germany was brought about with dollars, not with
the precious blood of the Soviet people.

With maniacal persistence Acheson now says that the Soviet
Union has set up in Eastern Europe "communist regimes". In
reality, the Soviet Union scrupulously carried out her promises
not to interfere in the internal affairs of other states. In no country
of Eastern Europe liberated by the Soviet Union is there a
communist regime, and all these states are ready to maintain close
trade relations with both East and West.

In this there was of course much quibbling. Except in Yugoslavia and Albania, which had not, strictly speaking, been
"liberated by the Soviet Union" and whose regimes could be
called "communist", a semblance of "coalition governments" (a
genuine one in Czechoslovakia) had still been maintained by the
middle of 1947. And, anyway, who was Acheson to talk about
self-determination?

Equally dreary are Acheson's assertions that the Soviet Union
"prevented" the political and economic reunification of Korea,
"prevented" the economic unity and was "threatening" the restoration of Greece. . . . It is surely the height of cynicism for Acheson to
claim that US policy in Greece arises from America's determination
"to preserve such places on earth where free man remains free".

In the weeks that followed there were more and more angry
articles in the Soviet press on the "monarcho-fascist" terror in
Greece and on the 1,500 arrests made among the leaders and
rank-and-file of the EAM (*Pravda*, 10th July 1947). Soon afterwards much higher figures were given. On 18th July, the figure
for the arrests made in the previous week alone was 15,000.
These people had been sent to islands where concentration camps
had been set up.

In a report from Belgrade, General Markos, described as "the
supreme commander of the Greek Democratic Army", was
quoted as describing the direct and indirect interference of the
British and American authorities in the Greek fascists' struggle
against the Greek Democratic Army. The British, he said, were
sending masses of equipment to the Greek government forces,
who in northern Greece were "shelling undefended villages with

their artillery" and committing other untold atrocities. British and American officers and soldiers were directly participating in many of these operations and American officers were present at the Greek government's General Staff meetings.

That summer and autumn Greece was to hold a central place in the mud-slinging contests at the UN. On 19th August, *Pravda* commented:

> Greece is where the Truman Doctrine was first applied. Since then the debate on the UN Security Council has shown that there are two approaches to Greece: the Soviet Union wants the Greek people to do as they like; the USA believes in dictating its will to them. The Soviet Union rejected the American resolution attributing the misfortunes of the Greek government to Yugoslavia, Bulgaria and Albania.
>
> Thereupon the US representative at the UN thundered against the "veto", and said that the USA would bypass UN. The USA are now planning to send 12,000 "military specialists to Greece".
>
> The civil war in Greece is developing unfavourably for the hated Greek government. . . . The Greek democratic forces which had been created to fight the German invaders have had, since December 1944, to fight against British and Greek government troops; but now even the Greek government army of 120,000 men is unable to cope with the Resistance forces, and is begging for American reinforcements to finish off the partisans. . . . Today the Greek government can hold out only if it gets help from the USA.

The truth is that if in 1944, in virtue of his spheres of influence policy, Stalin abandoned the Greek resistance to the tender mercies of General Scobie, the Russians now showed an ever-growing concern for Greece, chiefly as a retort to all the Western criticisms of "undemocratic" Russian behaviour in Poland, Rumania, Hungary, etc. There is little evidence to show that the Soviet Union gave any military or financial support to the Greek guerrillas in 1947, though some help came to them from Albania, Bulgaria and especially Yugoslavia, whose territories they could use as "sanctuaries". After the Stalin/Tito quarrel, the Russians seem finally to have washed their hands of the Greek resistance, though Markos—who was something of a Titoite—continued for a short time to be helped by the Yugoslavs, who also allowed Greek refugees to settle in their country. A small pro-Soviet

Greek faction under Zachariades was supported, also for only a short time, by the Albanians.

But during the rest of 1947, the Russians continued to plug the Greek theme at the UN. In September Gromyko and in October Vyshinsky thundered for hours against "foreign intervention in Greece".

The Western powers, for their part, never ceased attacking the "violations of democracy" in Hungary, Rumania and Bulgaria. At the beginning of August, there was a new general election in Hungary, and this time (as distinct from the 1945 election) the communists and their allies scored a great "victory". The social-democrats suffered heavy losses. It is ironical to think that only a month before, in an interview with *Reynolds News*, Anna Kethly, one of the leading Hungarian social-democrats, should still have approved of Russian policy in Hungary. She said that the Russians "were quite right to defend Hungary against fascism" and claimed that Ferencz Nagy and his friends had been guilty of an anti-republican conspiracy, whose aim was to restore the feudal order in the country. What had happened as a result of this abortive conspiracy could not, she said, be regarded as a communist putsch. On the Russian occupation forces, she said that it was only natural for the Russians to think, in the first place, of their own security. They were quite right not to allow a fascist regime to be set up in any neighbouring country; this was explicitly stated in the Hungarian armistice terms and the peace treaty with Hungary. She added that relations between the communists and the social-democrats were good, and that in Hungary the communists had half the working class and a large part of the poorer peasantry behind them:

They fought together with us against the fascist dictatorship. We shall be faithful to our alliance with the communists. Our enemies are on the right, not on the left. If we were to split, the counter-revolution would destroy us one by one.

Here, in a nutshell, was the whole tragedy of social-democracy in Eastern Europe, at least as seen from the more traditional Western point of view. After the August election, Mathias Rakosi, the communist leader, noted with some satisfaction that in this "democratic election contest" the social-democrats had lost a very large number of votes; but fortunately, he said, the social-democrats' "somewhat hysterical nervousness" had given

20

way to the realization that nothing was more important than "the workers' unity"—even if this meant that the social-democrats had been overshadowed, if not entirely swallowed up, by the communists.

On 9th September, the "New Bulgaria" celebrated its third anniversary. In this connection *Pravda* ridiculed the British and American claims that "the dissolution of the anti-people's opposition and the death sentence passed on N. Petkov" were "undemocratic."

In Rumania, too, the "anti-people's" opposition was rapidly dissolved. Very odd things happened. In August, the Rumanian parliament approved by 294 votes to 1 the government's decision to dissolve the National-Agrarian Party, which, *Pravda* said, now "contained all the terrorist and reactionary forces in the country". This was how the case against the Rumanian "reactionaries" was presented:

After their crushing defeat in the parliamentary elections, the Agrarian Party and its leaders, Maniu, Michalake and Penescu, started on their criminal activities, on their anti-democratic conspiracy, and their open betrayal of the national interests of Rumania.

Needless to say, the Rumanian people "cordially welcomed parliament's decision to rid the country of these criminals". This satisfaction was expressed "at numerous mass meetings". And *Pravda* went on:

The Agrarian Party is politically dead. It is an absurd anachronism. Maniu, that arch-conspirator and intriguer, has lost all contact with the people. . . . On the eve of the Second World War Maniu joined the pro-fascist camp. He was a friend of Ribbentrop, an admirer of Mussolini, an ally of Horea Sima; later he joined up with the German puppet Antonescu, and welcomed Rumania's entry into the war against the Soviet Union. . . . Later, when the tide turned, Maniu became a "friend" of the USA and Britain. In the autumn of 1944 he objected to Rumania's joining in the war against Nazi Germany. He defended the war criminals, he was against the land reform, and supported Radescu and his bloody gang.

General Radescu, it will be remembered, was the "pro-Western" Premier who was dismissed early in 1945 as a result of a Russian ultimatum to King Michael.

The agrarians opposed Rumanian democracy—the bloc of the peasant party (the Ploughman's Front), the communists, the social-democrats and the national liberals, who were having such a hard time in restoring the country's economy.

It was a familiar enough pattern—the same arguments had been used, with minor variations, in respect of Bulgaria, Hungary and Poland, and were going to be used before long in respect of Czechoslovakia, too—the East-versus-West pattern, just as in Greece there was a West-versus-East pattern. But now Rumania was at last on the road to recovery, and the triumph of the "democratic" forces could only help in this.

For now, in the autumn of 1947, after two years of drought, Rumania is enjoying a good harvest at last. She is now also taking measures to stabilize the currency, to confiscate the profiteers' hoards, to nationalize the banks, and to place industry under state management (even though most of it will remain in private hands). Maniu and Co. are against all this; the American press is furious, and talks of the dissolution of the agrarians being "the last act in the liquidation of political freedoms in Rumania". The State Department is sending an angry note to Rumania, and Vansittart, that bison of British reaction, is roaring like mad.

At the end of October there began the trial of Maniu and his friends.

It is clear that by 1947 the Russians had decided to eliminate from public affairs all the "pro-Western" elements in Rumania, Hungary, etc. In all these countries, the social-democrats had in effect either to submit to the communists—or get out. Czecho-slovakia still continued to be a "normal" democracy—but not for long.

This *gleichschaltung* of the satellites went together with the new role that was to be assigned to the communist parties in the capitalist countries of Western Europe, in the first place France and Italy. We shall deal with this when we come to describe the first meeting of the Cominform in September 1947.

The Russian leadership was very conscious of the economic superiority of the group of powers now under the tutelage of the United States, and this partly accounts for the outburst of extreme Soviet, or rather Russian, nationalism with which the year of 1947 was marked.

This nationalism took a variety of forms. One very persistent campaign was directed towards giving the Russians a feeling of superiority vis-à-vis the West. Granted that the United States, but not the Russians, had the atom bomb, it was important to impress upon the Russian people that they were every bit as "brainy" as the Americans—the implication being that they would soon have an even bigger and better atom bomb. Russian nationalism, as we have seen, also pervaded the cultural field: the worst sin of any writer, artist or musician was to "kowtow to the West" or "ape the West". Russian art and literature had to be in the great Russian tradition. It was no use trying to imitate decadent art when there were the great ancestors in whose footsteps one only had to follow—Repin in painting, Tchaikovsky and Glinka in music, Tolstoy in literature. And in science the Russians were proclaimed to be as clever as the Westerners, and indeed much cleverer.

In the summer of 1947 there appeared spates of articles showing that many of the great discoveries of modern science and technology had been made by Russians, not by Westerners. Although during the war the Russians were only too pleased to receive penicillin from the West, one article claimed that penicillin had in fact been invented by a Russian surgeon in the 1870s; he had used some kind of green mould for treating wounds, and this was the original penicillin. In Pravda on 21st August Prof. A. Zvorykin sharply criticized a Soviet history book for its servility to the West. Its author had "erroneously" stated that Bessemer, Siemens and Marten had "invented" new ways of making steel, and had omitted to say that just as important an invention had been made by a D. K. Chernov. The author had also committed the unpardonable error of saying that the electric bulb had simultaneously been invented in 1879 by Edison in America and Ladygin in Russia. This was untrue. The earliest electric lamp had been invented by the Russian scientist Yablocktov; but this was replaced by a greatly improved bulb. Only whereas Ladygin had invented this improved version in 1873, an almost identical bulb had been invented by Edison in 1879. Edison had, in fact, plagiarized the Ladygin bulb. No doubt he improved on it, but Ladygin's claim to have invented it was unquestionable, and this was recognized even by American scientific journals.

Then there was radio. The text-book in question declared that a Russian physicist called Popov had invented wireless telegraphy in 1895, but added that "an analogous invention" was made by Marconi; in reality, Marconi had simply stolen Popov's idea. Zvorykin went on to say that even before the Revolution the Russian Society for Physics and Chemistry, angered by the "Marconi myth", clearly established that Popov was the first to have invented wireless telegraphy. He quoted an American scientist who said that "Marconi hadn't invented anything". Nor was it Stephenson but a certain Cherepanov who had invented the first steam engine. Similarly Morse had invented nothing that a Russian scientist before him had not invented, while Watt had been preceded by a Russian scientist called Polzunov. Many other examples were quoted of Russian scientists having been first in the field. Zvorykin admitted, however, that both Marconi and Edison were better businessmen than Popov and Ladygin, and that they had the backing of big financial capital which was not so easily available in the conditions of Tsarist Russia. Moreover, there was too much "toadying to the West" in Russia, and Peter the Great was not free from this vice. When a Russian, Grigori Kapustin, discovered coal in the Donbas, Peter the Great got a number of English experts, at great expense, to examine Kapustin's discovery. In reality, the English added nothing to what the Russian prospector had discovered.

Russian industry before the Revolution was largely in the hands of foreign capitalists, who tended to treat Russian engineers like dirt. Also, a firm like Siemens did all it could to prevent a native Russian electrical engineering industry from developing. In the same way a Königsberg German called Bayer had tried to "humiliate" Russia by inventing his "Normanist" theory of Russian history, according to which the Varangians had brought culture and political consciousness to Russia, until then inhabited by cultural and unorganized Eastern Slavs. "These rotten theories were in vogue in Russia before and even after the Revolution; this is typical of the toadying to the West of which some traces can still be found in the Soviet Union today."

All this may seem absurd enough. But in the atmosphere in Russia in 1947 it makes a certain rough sense. The country was living poorly after the war. There was a certain defence mechanism in running down things foreign, particularly

American. It was like saying "give us a little time to show that
we are just as clever as they are; we've shown it in the past—
even under the Tsars—and we'll show it again". And un-
Russian ways of thinking were crudely condemned. This was to
develop later, in 1948–9, into a new campaign against "cosmo-
politanism", which, in turn, took before long an anti-semitic
twist.

On 7th September 1947 a very curious celebration took place—
that of the 800th anniversary of the foundation of Moscow. It
was recalled that in 1147 a certain Prince Yuri Dolgorukov had
laid the foundation-stone of a city-fortress called Moscow. For
days the Soviet papers were full of "materials for lectures" on
this somewhat obscure episode of Russian medieval history,
and exalted Moscow, "where the great Stalin lives", as the centre
of *everything*.

When the great day came, the press published Stalin's
"Greetings to Moscow", a very strange document indeed.

> Thrice Moscow liberated our country from the foreign yoke—
> from the Mongols, the Poles and Lithuanians, and from the French
> under Napoleon. . . . Moscow is great, because it initiated the
> creation of a centralized Russian state.
> When, by the will of the great Lenin, Moscow was proclaimed
> once more the capital of our country, it became the standard-
> bearer of the Soviet epoch. Today Moscow is the herald of the
> liberation movement of labouring humanity against capitalist
> slavery.
> Moscow is the symbol of Soviet democracy, which rejects all
> inequality among citizens, and which pays equal wages for equal
> labour.
> Moscow is building a new everyday life, and is free of poverty.
> In other cities of the world there are slums. All slums in Moscow
> have been liquidated, and the workers have been able to move
> into the houses of the bourgeoisie and into new dwellings, built
> by the Soviet regime.
> Moscow is the herald of the great struggle for a lasting peace and
> for friendship among nations.

The "liquidation" of all slums in Moscow was, of course,
nonsense. In 1947 the great majority of people lived poorly and
in overcrowded houses. But the glorification of Moscow as the
great hope of humanity was curious in the context of 1947. So

also was its glorification as the symbol of the centralized Russian state, which no one represented more worthily than he, Stalin. Significant, too, was the implication that the 200 years of Russian history when Petersburg was the capital was a sort of anomaly, which the great Lenin ended. The Soviet regime, in short, was a continuation of pre-Petrine Muscovy, an Eastern rather than a Western city. The anti-Leningrad innuendoes in this tribute to Moscow are apparent enough.

The people of Moscow did not take these celebrations of the "800 years of Moscow"—which were followed by an unveiling of an equestrian statue of the obscure Prince Yuri in Gorki Street—very seriously, and there were some caustic *sotto-voce* comments on Stalin's assertion that there were no slums in Moscow. But a sort of "pyramid-mania" marked Stalin's last years. The statue of Yuri Dolgorukov was a fruit of that mental process which also resulted in the building of the "Stalin-Gothic" skyscrapers in Moscow. These were to be the "pyramids" of that "Third Rome" which in Stalin's mind, Moscow was destined to be in the post-war history of the world.

In the past this "Third Rome" had had the Comintern, but it had proved unwieldy and ineffective, and had also made a very large number of grievous mistakes, for example in Germany in 1932-3, when it had discouraged any united action between the German communists and social-democrats, and again in 1939-40, when it had launched its anti-"imperialist war" propaganda among the Western, particularly the French, working class. There can be little doubt that to ingratiate himself with Hitler Stalin had fully approved this line; having realized its folly, he tended to blame it on Georgi Dimitrov and other leaders of the Comintern. In 1946, according to the Yugoslavs, "Stalin spoke of the Comintern during a Moscow meeting with the Bulgarian and Yugoslav leaders in biting terms, and ... rebuked Dimotrov to such an extent that the old man turned first pale and then red, to the acute embarrassment of the other guests."*

The Comintern, it will be remembered, had been dissolved on Stalin's instructions (though, officially, it had "dissolved itself") in May 1943, partly as a gesture of goodwill *vis-à-vis* the Western allies. Typical of Western comments on the dissolution of the Comintern was former US Ambassador Joseph Davies's remark

* V. Dedijer, *Tito Speaks*, London, 1953, p. 301.

that "when he was Ambassador in Moscow, he used to say to Litvinov that the Comintern—the stick with which everybody beat the Soviet Union—had been the real source of all the trouble".*

It is historically interesting to observe that, so long as there was still some hope left of reasonably good relations with the Western powers after the war, Stalin was very chary of reviving the Comintern in any shape or form, and that the idea of the Cominform, a sort of pocket-size version of the Comintern, should have first been raised, not by Stalin, but by Tito. The Yugoslavs, according to what they wrote *after* their breach with Stalin, had merely thought in 1945 in terms of "an international organization, which would be a consultative body" among the communist parties. Such a body "could be of major service in the exchange of views, and in the exchange of the wealth of experience acquired through the developments of the past few years". In 1945, according to Dedijer, Tito himself submitted this idea to Stalin, who "welcomed it with open arms" (Dedijer, op. cit., p. 300). Now, in retrospect, the Yugoslavs argued that *their* conception of the Cominform was entirely different from Stalin's: to him such a "consultative body" was of no interest; what he wanted was "an obedient undemocratic tool in Moscow's hands". This, as it happened, turned out to be true. But the fact remains that, whereas Tito had proposed something on the lines of the Cominform in 1945 and Stalin had allegedly welcomed it, the latter did not follow it up. The question was again raised during Tito's, Rankovic's and Kidrić's visit to Moscow in June 1946; but even Stalin hesitated, no doubt realizing what capital against the Soviet Union would be made in the West of this new organization, and merely said: "It would be best if you Yugoslavs took the initiative," which was, in reality, a polite way of shelving the whole matter for the time being.

By the middle of 1947 the whole international situation had drastically changed for the worse as a result of the Truman Doctrine, the Marshall Plan, and the Russians' failure to prevent the division of Germany. If, in March 1946, Churchill already spoke of the "Iron Curtain" that had descended on Europe between Stettin and Trieste, the Russians were still reluctant to accept this as an accomplished fact. But by the middle of 1947

---

* On the dissolution of the Comintern, see *Russia at War*, pp. 607-9.

they no longer had any illusions that Europe had not in effect been split in two.

So the Cominform (the Information Bureau of the Communist Parties) was not founded until the autumn of 1947. Unlike the old Comintern, which in theory covered the whole globe, the Cominform was limited to a small number of communist parties, those of the Soviet Union and of her East European friends—Poland, Czechoslovakia, Rumania, Yugoslavia, Hungary and Bulgaria (though not Albania), and, moreover, the two most important communist parties of Western Europe—those of France and Italy. Neither the Chinese communists nor those of any other country outside Europe were included. The formation of the Cominform was very closely related to the new international situation *in Europe*, and its purpose was to coordinate the efforts of the member-parties, including those of France and Italy, which a few months before had been eliminated from the coalition governments in which they had been represented ever since the Liberation in 1944–5. What role were they to play, now that they had been driven into opposition? The Yugoslavs later expressed some surprise that the Greek communists had not been invited:

> The Greek Party was, at the time, conducting an armed struggle which was attracting the attention of the whole of international public opinion. But bearing in mind the spheres-of-interest agreements that the Soviet Union had concluded during the war with the other great powers, when it was decided that Greece should not fall within the Russian sphere, it is easy to understand why Stalin did not invite the Greeks (Dedijer, op. cit., p. 302).

The first meeting of the Cominform was held at the small spa of Szklarska Poremba in Poland at the end of September 1947. The Soviet party was represented by Zhdanov and Malenkov; Yugoslavia by Djilas and Kardelj; Rumania by Gheorghiu-Dej and Anna Pauker; Hungary by Farkas and Revai; Bulgaria by Chervenkov and Poptomov; Czechoslovakia by Slansky and Bastovansky; Poland by Gomulka and Minc; France by Duclos and Fajon; Italy by Longo and Reale.

> The meeting lasted seven days, and all . . . stayed in a sanatorium of the Polish Ministry of State Security, in the middle of a park measuring 500 or 600 yards across. The conference hall and the

dining-rooms were in the same building. The building and the park were strongly guarded. (ibid., p. 303.)

Since this book deals primarily with Russia, special attention should be given here to the long opening statement made by Zhdanov, for this can be regarded as nothing less than the Soviet "answer" to the Truman Doctrine and the Marshall Plan. Significantly, it dwelt on the division of the world, and particularly of Europe, into what Zhdanov described as "two camps"—one, the "imperialist and anti-democratic camp", the other, the "democratic and anti-imperialist camp". An ever-recurring theme was the "enslavement" of Western Europe by "American imperialism", and the reasons why Eastern Europe had not fallen for the tempting offers of Marshall Aid. Another frequent theme was that "preventive war" against the socialist world that was being widely preached in the USA.

After briefly dealing with Munich and the ambition of the "imperialists" to weaken, if not destroy, the Soviet Union with the help of Nazi Germany, and after practically omitting any mention of the wartime coalition against Germany and Japan, Zhdanov came to deal with the post-war world. Of the six "so-called great" imperialist powers, three—Germany, Japan and Italy—had "dropped out"; France had been enormously weakened; so had Britain, now wholly dependent on the USA for its survival. Only one imperialist power, the USA, had come out of the war enormously strengthened, both economically and militarily. Since the end of the war, the USA was determined to maintain its profits on a high level and to continue to develop its foreign markets, especially in Europe. There had been a complete departure from the pre-war isolationism. The great military and economic might of the United States now had to be used not only to consolidate the positions won during the war, but also to extend them, and to replace Germany, Italy and Japan in the markets of the world. This expansionism was now aiming at the world domination of American imperialism. Britain in particular was to be reduced to the position of an American vassal, and her overseas possessions would become part of the American sphere of influence.

The main obstacle in America's bid for world domination was the Soviet Union, together with the countries of the "new democracy". The American reactionaries, therefore, had made it their object to act as the "saviours" of capitalism throughout the world. Their ambitions were "remarkably like" those of the Nazi and fascist aggressors of only a few years ago.

"Literally on the very first day after the war had ended", the American imperialists set about to create "a vast front hostile to the USSR and to world democracy". Following in Churchill's footsteps, the most vicious and unbalanced American politicians were now advocating a preventive war against the Soviet Union, now that the USA was enjoying a temporary monopoly in atomic weapons. This blackmail and intimidation was being applied not only to the Soviet Union, but also to countries like China and India, which the USA was trying to keep under their political and economic domination.

So the crystallization of the world into the two "camps" had become more and more apparent since the end of the war. The USA counted among its satellites France and Britain (the fact that these had "socialist" governments did not worry the Americans in the least); Belgium and Holland, with their colonial empires; countries with ultra-reactionary regimes like Turkey and Greece; and countries economically and politically dependent on the USA, such as those of the Middle East, South America and China. The fundamental aim of the "imperialist camp" was war against the Soviet Union and generous support to reactionary, anti-democratic and pro-fascist regimes and movements.

On the other hand, there was the anti-imperialist camp: this included the USSR and the countries of the "new democracy"; it had the support of countries like Finland, Indonesia and Vietnam, and the sympathy of India, Egypt and Syria.*

The real basis of Soviet foreign policy, Zhdanov said, was *the long-term coexistence of the two systems*—that of socialism and that of capitalism. Unfortunately, this was not the attitude of the imperialists. Thus, in the case of Germany, the Soviet Union stood for "the formation of a united, peaceful, demilitarized and democratic Germany"; but, as the Moscow meeting of the Foreign Ministers in March/April 1947 had shown, "the USA, Britain and France are not only ready to turn their backs on the

* These references to Egypt and Syria, even twenty years ago, as the natural allies of the Soviet bloc are significant in the light of the Middle East crisis of 1967.

democratization and demilitarization of Germany, but are prepared to liquidate Germany as a single state and to dismember her by reaching a separate agreement with one part of it."

Zhdanov then dealt with the immense military power of the United States, which, apart from stockpiling atom bombs, was now also busy making weapons of bacteriological warfare. Its "imperialist expansionism" took three different forms: (a) military and strategic measures; (b) economic expansion; and (c) ideological war.

The military activity provided the creation of a large number of army, naval and air bases in places as remote from the USA as Japan, Italy, South Korea, China, Egypt, Iran, Turkey, Greece, Austria and Western Germany; and the Arctic was being utilized for purposes of military aggression. Britain took part in these aggressive measures of so-called "self-defence".

Economically, like a usurer, the USA was taking advantage of Europe's post-war difficulties—the purpose of the "aid" offered to Europe was to enslave her. This economic control went together with the capture of military springboards, and the "aid" was almost automatically followed by a change in the foreign policy of the country concerned. As the case of France and Italy showed, parties and persons obedient to Washington were placed in control. The ideological war consisted in putting across the idea that the socialist bloc was aggressive and that the Anglo-Saxon powers were "protecting" their friends from a new world war. The peoples of the world had not forgotten the glorious part played by the Soviet peoples in the Second World War; to make people fight against the Soviet Union, they had to be subjected to a long period of ideological reconditioning. The Soviet Union was being deliberately misrepresented as an anti-democratic and totalitarian country. The main argument used against the Soviet Union was that it did not have a multi-party system. The ignoramuses of the Labour Party, in particular, seemed incapable of realizing that, in the Soviet Union, there were no capitalists and land-owners, and no conflicting class interests, and therefore no multiplicity of political parties. Yet these "socialist" advocates of "pure democracy" thought it quite normal for countries like Greece and Turkey to be ruled by bloody fascist dictatorships, and closed their eyes to racial oppression in countries like the USA.

The USA had no respect for national sovereignty. The fancy schemes of certain pacifist intellectuals about a "world government" only played into the hands of the American imperialist ideologists. It was also unfortunately true that certain trade union leaders and social democrats, like Bevin, and that darling of the capitalists, Léon Blum, were fully supporting the Americans' imperialist policy.

Zhdanov then came to the Truman Doctrine and the Marshall Plan—both supreme expressions of US expansionism. The Truman Doctrine aimed at establishing American bases in the Eastern Mediterranean; hence the financial support given to the reactionary regimes of Turkey and Greece, which had been turned into bastions against the new democracies in the Balkans; these were being accused of "aggressive designs".

The Truman Doctrine, with its blatant support of reactionary regimes like those of Turkey and Greece, had caused some embarrassment even among the American capitalists. The Marshall Plan was a more "humanitarian"-looking affair, and was meant to give a more respectable character to American expansionism.

After giving the Soviet version of the Marshall Plan negotiations in Paris and saying that the greatest beneficiary under the Plan would be Western Germany (since she was potentially more aggressive *vis-à-vis* the Soviet Union than either France or Britain), Zhdanov said that the Soviet government had never objected to using foreign, and particularly American, credits for speeding up her own economic reconstruction. But she opposed any credits which would mean the economic and political enslavement of the debtor-country by the creditor-country. Nor did the Soviet government hold that foreign credits could ever be the *main* means of restoring a country's economy. Each country should *primarily* depend on its own resources and on the development of its own industries. The Marshall Plan, on the contrary, provided primarily for consumer goods, not capital goods, and was therefore hostile to the European countries' industrialization and their independence. The Soviet Union's recent trade agreements with the countries of Eastern Europe were all based (Zhdanov asserted) on the absolute equality of both partners. She also aimed at similar agreements with capitalist countries, and he (Zhdanov) was sorry that the Labour government should have allowed outside pressure to put an end to the promising Anglo/Soviet trade negotiations. Moreover, said Zhdanov, it was no use looking upon Marshall Aid as charity; it was largely designed to increase Europe's purchasing power, and so to save the USA from an economic slump.

Zhdanov then came to the crucial question why the Cominform had been established. The dissolution of the Comintern in 1943 had been a necessary measure—it had, among other things, put an end to the myth that "Moscow" was interfering in the internal affairs of foreign countries. His explanation of the origin of the Comintern after the First World War was somewhat confusing to any student of Leninism. Zhdanov's "retrospect" can be summarized thus: After the First World War the communist parties in the world were still very weak; there were no links between the working class of the different countries. It was for the Comintern to strengthen the bonds among them, and to elaborate the theoretical problems of the working-class movement, as well as to facilitate the task of the national working-class leaders by setting down common standards for the propaganda of communist ideas. This had helped to train new leaders, and to turn young communist parties into mass working-class parties. But once such mass parties had developed, it became impossible and inexpedient to give them guidance from one centre. Thus, instead of being a factor of acceleration, the Comintern tended to slow down the development of foreign working-class parties. New relationships had to be established among the different communist parties; and hence the dissolution of the Comintern.

Having got over this hurdle, Zhdanov then said that four years had passed since the dissolution of the Comintern. During this period the communist parties had grown in strength in nearly all countries of Europe and Asia. Communist influence was particularly strong in the countries of the new democracy.

But there were some flaws in the present situation: many comrades had the idea that the dissolution of the Comintern meant the liquidation of all contact among the communist parties. But experience had since shown that such lack of contact was wrong, harmful and unnatural.

Then came what was in effect a warning against the concept of "national communism":

The communist movement develops in its national frameworks, but at the same time there are certain problems and interests which are common to all the communist parties. So we now have the paradoxical position in which the socialists—who climbed the walls to show that the Comintern was simply dictating the will of Moscow to all communists—have restored their own International, while we, communists, avoid meeting or consulting one another on problems of mutual interests just in case our enemies start their usual slander about the "hand of Moscow".

This, he said, created an absurd situation. There were contacts between other groups of different nationalities—scientists, trade unionists, students—but not between communists. Not only was this absurd, but it might be positively dangerous, if each communist party went its own way. And Zhdanov now clearly stated why coordination between the communist parties was essential. For if the socialists—especially the French and British—were agents of American imperialism, then the communists, particularly of the Western countries, had a specific role, too, which was to oppose the Americanization of their countries. They had to support those patriotic forces which were opposed to the enslavement of their countries by American capital, and were determined to defend their countries' national sovereignty. The communists must play the leading role in the mobilization of the anti-fascist and freedom-loving elements opposed to the American expansionists' ambition to enslave Europe.

Here, in a few words, was the Russian blueprint for the French and Italian communists' future policy in their respective countries. As we know, these "instructions" were to result, among other things, in the French political strike wave at the end of 1947.

What Zhdanov said next foreshadowed the enormous peace movement, culminating in the Stockholm Appeal for the outlawing of the atom bomb, which was to prove the most successful communist counter-move at the height of the Cold War of 1948-50:

You have to remember that there is an enormous distance between the imperialists' desire to unleash a new war and the possibility of organizing such a war. The peoples of the world do not want war. If the powers standing for peace are sufficiently considerable and determined to defend peace ... then the aggressors' plans are bound to collapse.

Thus the communist parties of France, Italy, Britain and other countries have a special duty. It is for them to hold firmly the banner of their own national independence and sovereignty.

A question that has often arisen is whether the Soviet government seriously believed, in 1947, in the possibility of a preventive war against the Soviet Union on the part of the United States. The answer is not an easy one. There was certainly enough preventive war talk in the United States to suggest that the danger of such a war could not be entirely excluded. It was precisely about the time of the first Cominform meeting that Vyshinsky (USSR) and Manuilsky (Ukraine) made enormously long speeches at the UN pointing to the alarming proportions preventive war propaganda in the USA had assumed, and these speeches were quoted at great length in the Soviet press. Thus, at the Second Session of the UN General Assembly on 23rd September, Manuilsky quoted Mr. Earle, the former US Ambassador to Bulgaria, as having said: "I am delighted and flattered that Mr. Vyshinsky should have called me a warmonger. If by that he means that I want atom bombs to be dropped on Russia, then he is absolutely right."

It is commonly assumed that if atom bombs *had* been dropped on Russia, the Russians would have retorted by occupying Western Europe with their substantial land forces. There was very little in France, Britain or the USA to stop them. But the Russians, who had already been talking of the "large-scale stockpiling of atom bombs by the USA", were not absolutely sure at the time that the USA had not enough atom bombs to deliver something in the nature of a knock-out blow on the Soviet Union. This knock-out blow theory, especially among those dreading a Russian invasion of Western Europe, both there and in the United States, was a fairly widespread one. Whether out of genuine conviction, or, as seems more likely, as a piece of demagogy, de Gaulle, then the leader of the newly constituted Rassemblement du Peuple Français, never ceased talking of an almost imminent Russian invasion of Western Europe. If he personally refrained from advocating preventive war against Russia, many of his followers did not. And this could only be achieved by means of a massive atom-bomb attack on Russia.

There is reason to believe that among the Russian leaders there was a variety of assessments of the real danger of war. But

Zhdanov, at any rate, considered that there was at best only a 50 per cent chance that there would be no war. Hence the virulence of his opening address to the Cominform, and his appeal—or rather instructions—to the French Communist Party to take the strongest possible anti-war stand. Maurice Thorez's frequently repeated remarks to the effect that "the French people would never make war on the Soviet Union" epitomized this campaign, which the communists undertook against heavy odds, but not unsuccessfully, since public opinion in France was profoundly anti-war and was deeply alarmed by the various manifestations of American bellicosity. If one says that the French communists had to conduct their campaign against heavy odds, it is largely because it was extremely difficult for them to convince the French people, including the French working class, that Marshall Aid was a bad thing, for it was thanks to Marshall Aid that everyday life in France returned to "normal" in 1948-9, after years of food shortages and other privations.

What was the exact purpose of the Cominform? The resolution published after its first session of September 1947 noted that "the absence of contacts" among the communist parties, particularly in the present world situation, was "incorrect and harmful", and the need was particularly pressing for "the exchange of experiences and for voluntary coordination of action among the parties". The resolution then said that an information bureau would be set up on which the nine parties would be represented. This bureau would organize the "exchange of experiences and, if necessary, coordinate the activities of the communist parties on the basis of mutual agreement". Among the other points of the resolution were the decisions to publish a fortnightly, later a weekly, paper, and to establish the bureau's headquarters in Belgrade.

The Yugoslavs, after their quarrel with Moscow and their expulsion from the Cominform in June 1948, were to make the most of these two phrases in the initial resolution of the Cominform—*voluntary coordination* and *on a basis of mutual agreement*—and were to regard the treatment they had suffered as wholly contrary to the avowed purpose of the Cominform. It is all the more interesting to observe that in the whole procedure of setting up the Cominform in 1947, they should have been given

21

a place of honour. Among the member-parties listed, the Yugoslavs came first, though there was no alphabetical reason for
this. The headquarters of the Cominform were to be in Belgrade.
What is more, Kardelj and Djilas behaved with particular
truculence at the first Cominform session, particularly in dwelling
on the heroic wartime history of the communist movement in
Yugoslavia (a hint at the more artificial nature of the communist
parties of such countries as Hungary and Rumania). They
suggested that, unlike other countries, Yugoslavia had in the main
been liberated by the Yugoslavs themselves, and fiercely criticized
the French Communist Party's record since the Liberation.

In retrospect, the Yugoslavs—who had thrown their weight
about at the first Cominform meeting—felt that they had
fallen into a trap set them by Stalin—who had already made up
his mind to destroy the Yugoslav leadership. That is why,
according to them, they had been given a place of honour in the
Cominform, and why Belgrade had been chosen, at Stalin's
insistence, as the place where the Cominform headquarters would
be. Also, they claimed that it was only much later that they
realized that the Cominform was not to be, as they had expected,
a mere "consultative body", where all decisions had to be made
"voluntarily" and "by mutual agreement", but, like the Comintern in the past, "an instrument in Stalin's hands", and, indeed,
"something worse than the Comintern".*

It is very hard to believe that Kardelj and Djilas were as
naïve as all that. They certainly entered the Cominform game
with the greatest relish. Threw their weight about mercilessly
in their effort to play first fiddle on the Cominform, and to
stress their own and Yugoslavia's importance in the "anti-
imperialist camp". It is significant that it was they who, more
than anybody else, launched a savage attack on Duclos, the French
representative, after he had spoken, to show that they, the
Yugoslavs, were better communists than the French were. But
this again was not their fault, but Zhdanov's!

The first Cominform meeting was typical in that its aim was
to create a gulf between the Yugoslav Party and the Parties of France
and Italy. ... *Zhdanov cleverly instructed our representatives*, Kardelj
and Djilas, to speak first in the discussion after the reports delivered

* Dedijer, op. cit., p. 304.

by Duclos and Luigi Longo . . . and to criticize the policy of their two parties. *Kardelj and Djilas needed no persuading* because the Yugoslav Party had deeply critical observations to make on the work of these two Parties during the war and immediately after. (ibid, p. 304; italics added.)

Needless to say, the Yugoslavs, while boosting their own military and revolutionary achievements, charged the Italian and even more the French with not having been sufficiently dynamic, especially after the Liberation. They might have seized power in 1944, but had, instead, acted as a respectable bourgeois coalition party, and had helped de Gaulle, the then head of the French government, by putting the brake on strikes and by supporting his "reformist" economic measures. As we know, in 1944 the French communists had taken the "Stalinist" line that the first and most important thing was to defeat Nazi Germany. After the war, they were determined to become a "permanent government party", and increase their influence in the country by parliamentary methods. With the Cold War growing from bad to worse in the spring of 1947—and the war in Indo-China adding a further complication—they were "expelled" from the coalition government of the veteran socialist leader, Paul Ramadier. But, in any case, they had felt increasingly uncomfortable in that government, which had expected them to support the wage-freeze and the war in Indo-China. Moreover, the Americans were determined that the communists should be eliminated from the French government before any substantial aid could be given to France. The Yugoslav criticisms of the French Party's "reformist" and lily-livered behaviour were of the same nature as those of the "Blanquist" heresy of Marty and Tillon which came into the open in 1952–3, after which Marty was expelled from the Party.

Duclos was certainly furious at the Yugoslavs' assault on the French CP, and after the Tito/Stalin quarrel in 1948 no one was to attack "Tito's criminal gang" more viciously and persistently than Duclos. According to Dedijer, Zhdanov gave some support to the Yugoslav criticisms of the French and Italian communists, throwing at Duclos during the latter's speech: "While you were fighting to stay in the government, they threw you out," and saying to Longo: "You Italian comrades are bigger parliamentarians than Gasperi himself. You are the biggest parliamentary party, and yet they throw you out of the government" (Dedijer, op. cit., p. 305).

Duclos and Longo admitted that they had been "opportunist", but Longo, at any rate, stressed that in remaining for a long time in the Italian government they had closely followed the Russians' advice—which was, of course, perfectly true in the case of both the Italian and the French communists.

Whether, in 1947, Zhdanov had been as critical of the French and Italian communists' past record may be doubted, since their policy had obviously been approved by Stalin; but the criticisms attributed to him by the Yugoslavs in retrospect were intended to show that these were part of the diabolical trap the Russians had set to compromise the Yugoslavs.

Now, a fundamental question is whether in reality the Russians had made up their minds long before 1948 to destroy the Yugoslav leadership through the Cominform by giving them enough rope to hang themselves—which they seem to have done with great relish—and in various other ways. Or is there not a different explanation? Was not the Cominform—with its headquarters in Belgrade, its place of special honour for the Yugoslavs, etc.—intended to *flatter* the Yugoslavs into greater loyalty to Moscow and into becoming one of the most wholehearted members of the "anti-imperialist" bloc? It is certain that Stalin had some serious doubts about Tito, and disliked the superior airs the Yugoslavs struck *vis-à-vis* the more Moscow-bred communist parties of Rumania, Hungary, etc.; but it seems highly plausible that in the threatening international atmosphere of 1947 Stalin was more determined than ever to keep Yugoslavia inside the "anti-imperialist camp". Nothing else would explain the amazing and exclusive flattery with which "heroic Yugoslavia", including Tito, was treated throughout 1947 in the Soviet daily and weekly press (in a special illustrated number of *Ogonyck*, for example), in newsreels and films.

The breach with the Yugoslavs in the early months of 1948—with which we shall deal later—arose from various disagreements which had, fundamentally, nothing to do with the Cominform.

The Yugoslav attack on the Italian and especially the French communists at the first Cominform session, is interesting in itself. But more significant still was the position taken up by Longo and Duclos. Duclos, more than Longo, was on the defensive. He began by describing the extremely difficult economic position that France was in—and the strenuous efforts the Americans were making to cash in on these difficulties, with the blessing of the French socialists and the MRP. Duclos admitted that a violent propaganda campaign had been unleashed in France to show that "without American help France could not survive", since France was in desperate need of dollars, food, coal, etc. France's expenditure, particularly her military expenditure (with the war in Indo-China alone costing 100 million francs a day), was enormous. The living standard of the working class was 50 per cent below pre-war. The country was threatened with runaway inflation. And the argument that "America alone could help" was unquestionably having some effect on public opinion.

Duclos went on to show that between 1944 and 1947, when they were inside the government, the communists had done their best to defend the interests of the working class, to encourage large-scale nationalization, etc., despite the open or secret hostility which they had met throughout from their socialist and MRP partners in the government. At the end of 1946, the communists had won a resounding election victory, but even so, the formation of a coalition government under the premiership of Thorez was sabotaged by the socialists. Then came the short-lived all-socialist government under Léon Blum, which marked, as it were, the beginning of the end. Blum departed from France's between-East-and-West foreign policy, laid the foundations of the Anglo/French alliance, included France in a Western bloc, and started the war in Indo-China. At the beginning of 1947 a coalition government, including the communists, was formed by Ramadier, but their position in that government became increasingly difficult in view of the wage-freeze and the war in Indo-China, which they were expected to support. In May 1947 the communists were eliminated from the government. Here Duclos embarked on a piece of self-criticism: instead of dwelling on the pretexts that had been used to drive them out of the government—which is what they had done—they should have dwelt, instead, on the *deeper reasons* for their elimination— namely, on the intervention of American imperialism in the political life of France:

We must admit that we did not express ourselves sufficiently clearly on this point; hence some doubts about the position we took up, after the events of May, in respect of the Ramadier government.

However, at the subsequent meeting of the CP's Central Committee it was decided that the communists must intensify their struggle against the anti-working class and pro-American policies of the Ramadier government. This firmer communist attitude towards the Ramadier government was all the more essential as, since the elimination from it of the communists, France's foreign policy had undergone some further radical changes.

Now Duclos came to Marshall Aid:

> The part that Bidault played in calling the sixteen-power meeting to deal with the "Marshall Plan" helped to turn our country, much to our grief and shame, into a simple weapon of American imperialism.

Duclos was now placed in an extremely difficult position: how were the communists to convince the French people that Marshall Aid was a bad thing? He as good as admitted that, though it was not easy, the communists should try to do much better than they had done so far. His argument lacked vigour and real conviction:

> Although our opponents are trying to show that France cannot do without American help, there are certain moods in France which are deeply hostile to American expansionism. With an eye on this American aid, our opponents are trying to force France, suffering, as she does, from great economic difficulties, to submit to the USA, and to become a bridgehead of reaction in Europe.

And Duclos added, visibly on the defensive:

> We are struggling against this policy; but it is unquestionable that we must intensify this struggle.

Then, adopting somewhat half-heartedly the Stalinist argument that each country must primarily depend on its own resources, he concluded:

> There is no doubt at all that the European countries can, by their own efforts, by mutual agreement and the exchange of goods, assure their own restoration without the help of the USA. The demonstration of this possibility cannot fail to produce a great impression.

A weak and hesitant ending, if ever there was one. In the final section of his report Duclos thought that in their denunciation of the enslavement of France by the USA—a denunciation which the communists would now undertake with far greater vigour than before—they might find some allies among the rank-and-file and the medium cadres of the French socialist party!

The truth is that in May 1947 the French communists had been driven into a "political ghetto" and that, by and large, French public opinion was only too eager to get Marshall Aid, though by 1949 large sections of French opinion, not least the intellectuals, were becoming more vocal in their opposition to the "colonization" of France and to the brinkmanship of American foreign policy, with a rearmament of Western Germany in the offing.

Unlike Duclos, Luigi Longo, speaking for the Italian communists, did not eat humble pie. It was quite true that, as a result of the split caused by Saragat in the Italian socialist party in January 1947 and the pressure of America and the Vatican, de Gasperi had succeeded in eliminating both the communists and the socialists from the Italian government. This was "a real *coup d'état* carried out on the instructions of de Gasperi's American masters". Now de Gasperi had unleashed a police terror against the communists, but neither they nor the socialists were going to be browbeaten. Longo recalled Togliatti's pledge that despite de Gasperi's *coup d'état* the strategic aim of the Italian CP remained "the establishment of a regime of progressive democracy":

> The political aim of our struggle is to overthrow the de Gasperi government as an anti-national government threatening the very existence of Italy as an independent state. We are struggling for the constitution of a government in which all the popular and republican forces of the country would be represented; but we realize that this can only be achieved under the broad democratic pressure of the toiling masses.

In other words, far from feeling isolated in some sort of "political ghetto", the Italian communists were relying on the democratic parliamentary method for returning them and their allies to power, and they were still full of fight. At the Cominform meeting Longo indicated that the communists and their allies would conduct intensive propaganda and agitation among the masses in anticipation of all future election campaigns—which was perhaps what produced Zhdanov's acid comment that the Italian communists were "more parliamentary than de Gasperi himself".

On Marshall Aid Longo was rather less violent than Duclos had tried to sound. He merely said that it was "harmful to Italy's national economy and dangerous to her national independence", since it aimed at creating an anti-Soviet bloc of powers and at splitting Europe in two, and could only result in economic and political interference in the internal affairs of the European countries. The example of Greece was only too eloquent.

> We are telling the Italian people that what we need is not "aid", but economic cooperation. "Aid" suggests charity and economic enslavement. We have sufficient means and resources to negotiate with the USA as equal partners, and not as poor relations.

One of the characteristics of the first Cominform session was the truculence and boastfulness of the Yugoslavs and the almost apologetic tone adopted by many of the other countries in describing their relatively slow transition from capitalism to socialism. Both Kardelj and Djilas boasted of the Yugoslav people's and the Communist Party's war record, of the People's Front, with its 7 million members, and the Yugoslav Communist Party, with its 400,000 members, and declared that this type of Yugoslav democracy "represented in effect a specific form of Soviet democracy adapted in Yugoslav conditions". There were still "capitalist elements" in the Yugoslav economy. Thus half the retail trade was still in private hands. But the whole implication of their statements was that Yugoslavia had moved much more quickly towards complete socialism than any of the other East European countries. Big landowners and kulaks had, in effect, been eliminated, and three-quarters of the Yugoslav farms were run on "one or other form of cooperation". Kardelj, looking back on the war years, remarked that the Yugoslav people never had any illusions about imperialist "democracy", or any faith in imperialism's possibility of "improving"—perhaps a hint at the "illusions" Stalin had entertained during the war about a Big-Three peace with the USSR, the USA and Britain as equal partners. Kardelj followed with an obvious allusion to the French:

There existed, for instance, a view that every government in which the communists took part was inevitably a government of the new, people's democracy. This is a wrong and very dangerous view. Experience has taught us that the reactionary forces were often willing to cooperate in the government with the communists —but only so long as they themselves felt weak; once these forces felt they were strong, they were only too ready to throw the democratic principles and parliamentary conventions overboard, so as to get rid of the workers' control as personified by the communist members of the government.

And was this not also an indirect criticism of Stalin, who in 1944-7 had encouraged the French communists to belong to coalition governments? Significantly, there were practically no allusions to the part played by the Red Army in the liberation of Yugoslavia, and Belgrade in particular.

Gomulka, in characteristically describing what he called "the so-called Polish way to socialism", made no boasts as extravagant as those of the Yugoslavs, and admitted that Poland was still very far from being a socialist country in the real sense—its economy was still a mixed one. Thus, small-scale private enterprise characterized the majority of Polish farmsteads, a large part of artisan undertakings and small trade; the wealthier peasants, employing constant hired labour, a number of industrial and artisan enterprises, and a considerable part of the wholesalers and retailers, could rank as private-capitalist; and the socialist element was predominant only in the state industries, the state trade, banking, transport, etc. The socialization of the capitalist sector could not be carried out without an acute class struggle. He then read out an eleven-point programme for the gradual socialization of the various capitalist sectors; but, while dwelling on the organization of cooperation in agriculture, he refrained from saying anything on any possible collectivization—which appears to have produced some critical remarks from Zhadnov.

While admitting that after all the destruction caused by the war Poland was having considerable economic difficulties (and these had been further increased by the drought of 1947) and that the living standard in Poland had not yet reached the pre-war level, he concluded that progress was nevertheless being constantly made in reconstruction, in both industrial and agricultural productivity, and in the development of Poland's foreign trade.

But the shortage of livestock as a result of the war, when some 70 per cent had vanished, and the consequent shortage of natural manure, quite apart from the latest drought, had placed Polish agricultural production in a very difficult position. And if some remarkable progress was made in heavy industry since 1945, the same could not be said of light industry. For instance the production of leather for soles was only 23 per cent of the pre-war output. The rural areas were not supplying the necessary raw materials for light industry and, moreover (an obvious allusion to the massacre of the Jews), there were not nearly as many small artisan workshops as there had been before the war.

After giving a long historical survey of the different Polish parties before, during and since the war, Gomulka stressed the importance of the fruitful cooperation between the Workers' (communist) Party (PPR) and the Socialist Party (at any rate that part of the Socialist Party which had entered into alliance with the communists and which had "shaken off its old social-democratic, Pilsudskyite and anti-Russian traditions"). The United Working-Class Front of the PPR and PPS (communists and socialists) had given excellent results, and there were no appreciable ideological differences between the two any longer. The Communist Party had 800,000 members and the Socialist Party about 700,000; and the present government coalition also included the peasant party, the Stronnictvo Ludowo, and two other smaller parties.

Gomulka stressed, however, that the class struggle in Poland was very far from over. In their struggle in recent years with the fascist underground, the working-class parties, and particularly the communists, had lost nearly 15,000 people. These reactionary forces, he said, had now been broken, though not yet entirely uprooted. Gomulka naturally claimed that Mikolajczyk's "Polish Peasant Party" had suffered a *bona fide* defeat in the last election, but said that, if this was so, it was because it had been found guilty of connivance at the fascist underground and with Anglo-Saxon reaction. This had, among other things, committed the cardinal error of condemning the Oder/Neisse frontier. In so doing Britain and America had provided the best possible propaganda in favour of the closest alliance with the Soviet Union. Mikolajczyk's PSL now comprised all that was most reactionary in Poland, both among the wealthier peasantry and the town bourgeoisie, and it would be a mistake to imagine, Gomulka said, that the new Poland had no internal enemies left. These were still numerous and economically powerful. Also, a large part of the Polish intelligentsia was still highly reactionary:

> In higher and secondary educational establishments we have, so far, failed to achieve any serious changes in either the teaching staffs or the curricula; we are only now beginning to make some important changes in these respects. . . . In science there is a shortage of skilled personnel and of people we can fully trust, and the old ideology, conservative and hostile to us, is still predominant among certain parts of the population. Our class enemy tries to reach us through the cracks one finds among some of the other parties forming part of the Democratic bloc. Our young people are often confused and divided. . . .

Gomulka concluded that although he was in favour of maintaining friendly relations with Britain and America, the Polish government could not allow these two countries to create for themselves a "political base" in Poland resting on Mikolajczyk's PSL and the fascist underground. Poland had rejected Marshall Aid, since this aimed at the vassalization of Europe. The example of Greece should be remembered. . . .

We must now deal briefly with the statements made by Rudolf Slansky—who was to be hanged as an "imperialist and Zionist agent" in 1952—on behalf of the Czechoslovak CP; Chervenkov, speaking for the Bulgarian CP; Gheorghiu-Dej for the Rumanian CP; and Revai for the Hungarian CP. The four countries were dissimilar in many respects, though similar in others. The main similarity in all cases was that "reaction" was identified with "Anglo-American imperialism".

Czechoslovakia had suffered less from the war than any of the other East European countries, and it was also economically the most advanced, with a powerful working class and the largest Communist Party, which, in September 1947, had a membership of 1,172,000, and, in the last election in May 1946, had 38 per cent of the votes. In 1947 Czechoslovakia was still a normal parliamentary democracy, and the Czech part of the country there was a "National Front" composed of four parties, the CP, the Socialists, the National-Socialists and the Catholic

"People's Party". Slansky, however, significantly stressed the special importance of the "national committees"—that is local government committees, on which the communists were particularly strong, and these committees, he suggested, acted as a kind of corrective to the more traditional parliamentary system. Parliament could legislate, but it was the national committees who were the real executive organs—they had replaced the pre-war and "predominantly reactionary" bureaucracy.

On the parliamentary and government level there was a constant struggle between the "progressive" forces like the CP and the "conservative" forces like the National-Socialists on such issues as nationalization. Despite resistance the CP had pushed through numerous nationalization measures, and the nationalized industries, or those that had previously belonged to the Germans and had since been confiscated, employed 66 per cent of the workers and accounted for 75 per cent of production. There was, however, a still substantial private sector, which included such important industries as building materials. Remarkable was the difference between Czechoslovakia and, for instance, Poland: in Poland real wages were still 20 per cent lower than before the war; in Czechoslovakia they were 34 per cent higher. Major difficulties had however arisen, Slansky said, as a result of the catastrophic drought of 1947. Slansky also spoke of the land reform, which had been greatly facilitated by the eviction from the Sudetenland of some 3 million Germans. Farmers were paid for their produce on a differential scale, small farmers receiving higher prices than big farmers—a system which had been sharply attacked by the "reactionaries". Slansky made no secret of many of these "reactionaries" being inside the government, and negotiations had now begun with the socialists with a view to eliminating them from the "national front"; here were already the first rumblings of the communist *coup d'état* of the following February. Dodging the tricky point that the CP, including Prime Minister Gottwald himself, had at first been favourable to accepting Marshall Aid, Slansky stressed that the "reactionaries" were most enthusiastic about this, but the "progressive elements" realized that very important help could also be received from the Soviet Union—witness the 200,000 tons of wheat and 200,000 tons of fodder that had been sent by her to Czechoslovakia—"whereas what we get from the West now is only promises". Since the breakdown of their hopes based on Marshall Aid, the "reactionaries" were now trying to provoke panic and chaos in Czechoslovakia, and to "isolate the CP". What should be done without delay was to expel them from the "national front".

According to Chervenkov, Anglo/American "imperialism" had encouraged, and was continuing to encourage, all that was most "reactionary" in Bulgaria—first the Agrarian Party of Dr. G. M. Dimitrov-Gemeto (who later escaped to the USA) and then Nikola Petkov (who was finally shot as a traitor, just as the all-out fascists and German collaborators had been in 1944). Chervenkov quoted Dimitrov's six-point declaration defining the nature of the People's Republic of Bulgaria: it would not be a soviet republic but a people's republic, in which there would be no dictatorship of any kind and in which "the leading role would be played by the great majority of the people"; in which private property, acquired by honest labour, would be protected; which excluded any return to fascism, monarchism or Great-Bulgar chauvinism; which would also eliminate all exploitation of man by man; and which would be independent and sovereign, and wholly independent of foreign capitalist trusts and concerns. Bulgaria would be a promoter of Slav unity and an opponent of all anti-sovietism.

Chervenkov then said that Bulgaria, which had been industrially weak, would seek to achieve a substantial degree of industrialization. However, for the present 78 per cent of large and small industrial undertakings were still in private hands. The programme for agriculture was based on the development of cooperation, not collectivization. But there were many difficulties to be overcome: there were serious shortages of raw materials and agricultural machinery; and the Party also had to cope with "the sabotage and the wrecking activities of hostile elements". The producer-cooperative sector was developing reasonably well, and certain industries, like canneries, belonged chiefly to this sector. Of considerable help in the development of agriculture had been the Dimitrov Youth Brigades, numbering some 80,000 young people, who went from the towns to work in the villages.

The United States had still not recognized the Bulgarian government, and the proximity of Turkey and Greece represented a danger to Bulgaria. Bulgaria had firmly rejected Marshall Aid, and was relying on economic support primarily from the

Soviet Union and the socialist camp. The country was ruled by the five parties included in the Fatherland Front; the CP now had 510,000 members; moreover, in the REMS, the Bulgarian Comsomol, there were 500,000 members. With 54 per cent of the votes and 60 per cent of the seats in parliament, as a result of the last election, the CP was the strongest party in the country. (This was the 1945 election, whose validity the USA had contested.) Foreign trade was "state-controlled", but retail trade was still mostly in private hands, but the "Horemags"—people's and municipal shops—were gradually going to replace the privately-owned shops.

As a result of agrarian reform, 100,000 hectares had been distributed among 88,000 peasants families and new land would be reclaimed through the draining of the Danube marshes; but there was no salvation for Bulgarian agriculture, split, as it was, into very small holdings, except in the development of producer-cooperatives and the establishment of machine-tractor stations, of which there were now thirty—a figure to be increased to fifty in 1948, owning 1,300 tractors and other machinery. The cooperatives—the TKZH, "cooperative agricultural holdings"—were "of course not kolkhozes", Chervenkov said, but organizations in which each farmer held the title-deeds to the land he cultivated. Nevertheless, both economically and from the standpoint of educating the peasants in a collectivist spirit, the TKZHs represented a great advance on what had existed before.

Needless to say, Chervenkov greatly inflated the importance of the Bulgarian partisan and resistance movement during the war, when, he said, they were "active" in the mountains, and then played a leading role in establishing the Fatherland Front and in overthrowing the old regime with the arrival of the Red Army. He mentioned only very briefly that "Great-Bulgar chauvinism" which had resulted in the annexation by Bulgaria, with Hitler's approval, of important areas in Yugoslavia and Greece. But now the closest brotherly relations were being developed with Yugoslavia, and at a recent conference at Bled the foundations had been laid for much closer bonds between the two great Slav Balkan countries—an allusion to those "federal" schemes which were to cause not only Tito but also Dimitrov so much trouble with Stalin only a few months later.

Chervenkov laid great stress on the political education of the

masses in the spirit of Marxism/Leninism, and on the training of
party cadres—of which there had obviously been a great shortage
in 1944-5—and spoke of the 5,000 groups in which 50,000 people
studied the history of Bulgarian and Soviet communist parties
and current international affairs, and of evening classes and other
ways of developing the political consciousness and organizational
abilities of the Bulgarian people. The general impression given
by Chervenkov's report was that Bulgaria was following more
closely and more wholeheartedly in the footsteps of the Soviet
Union than any of the other Eastern countries, even though
she was still the most agricultural and least industrial of the
satellite states. As distinct from countries such as Poland, where
the majority of the intellectuals were "reactionary", in Bulgaria
nearly all the intellectuals—admittedly not a very large group—
were supporting the new regime, and a very high proportion
had joined the Communist Party.

Considerably more complicated was, and continued to be, the
situation in both Rumania and Hungary. If Bulgaria was pain-
lessly liberated by the Red Army in the Two Days' War in
September 1944, fighting had been heavy in Rumania and even
heavier in Hungary. And if Bulgaria was traditionally pro-Russian
(and even pro-Soviet), the same could not be said of either
Rumania or Hungary. In neither country was there a strong
communist party by the end of the war, and pro-Western sympathies were strong. In Hungary, in particular, the strong pro-
German elements among the bourgeoisie, the clergy and part of
the peasantry had turned pro-American.

The "democratization" of Rumania had been a long and
laborious process, and had met with considerable resistance.
King Michael was still on the throne in 1947—though his departure was now very near—but, to begin with, he had tried to keep
the governments after the fall of the Antonescu regime in August
1944 as conservative and pro-Western as possible. According to
Gheorghiu-Dej, the first government of the New Rumania under
General Sanatescu had consisted chiefly of reactionary generals
carrying out the instructions of reactionaries like Maniu, Bratianu,
etc. The Communist and Socialist Parties had only one member
each in that Sanatescu government. In the next government the
CP, the "National-Democratic Front", which had been formed
by the CP, the Socialists and Petru Groza's "Farmer's Front",

were rather more adequately represented, but the "reactionary forces", Maniu's National-Agrarian Party and the National Liberals, still called the tune. In the third Rumanian government, under General Radescu, in which Petru Groza was Vice-Premier, the progressive forces were also reasonably well represented, but the head of the government was "an agent of Anglo/American imperialism" and maintained in office numerous fascist officials. The Rumanian chauvinists were even encouraged to terrorize the Hungarian minority in Transylvania. Land reform was being sabotaged by Radescu and his supporters, and the communists and other progressive forces had to resort to direct action by calling on the landless or poor peasants to split up the large estates themselves, despite armed resistance from Radescu's men. Without referring to the fact that Vyshinsky had forced King Michael to dismiss Radescu in February 1945, Gheorghiu-Dej claimed that the General had been eliminated as a result of the "mass demonstrations" organized by the National-Democratic Front outside the Royal Palace. Radescu finally found refuge at the British Legation and was then smuggled out of the country by the Americans. He was replaced at the head of the government on 6th March 1945 by Dr. Petru Groza. In this government the National-Democratic Front was well represented, and the Ministry of the Interior held three key ministries—Interior, Justice and Transport. Nevertheless, resistance to the full application of the land reform and other measures came from the Tatarescu party, represented in this government by Taterescu himself.

Gheorghiu-Dej went on to say that the period between the formation of the Groza government in March 1945 and the general election in November 1946 had been an extremely difficult one in Rumania.

Our economy was in a state of chaos and general decline. We had suffered from two successive droughts. Even so, much was achieved. The land reform was carried through, and 1·4 million hectares were distributed among 726,000 peasants. . . . Towards the end of the war fourteen divisions took part in the war against Germany. . . . After the elimination of Radescu, more cordial relations developed with the Soviet Union, and with Stalin's approval we were able to set up a Rumanian administration in Transylvania once more. On the other hand, we renounced our claims on Southern Dobrudja, which our imperialists had taken from Bulgaria in 1913; and this area was restored to Bulgaria.*

Being in charge of the Ministry of the Interior under the Groza government the communists undertook a major purge in the Rumanian civil service, eliminating the "reactionary" elements as far as possible. The principal war criminals were executed, and "fascist" generals were removed from the army.

As a result of the two droughts in 1945 and 1946, there was a genuine widespread famine in Rumania. In this respect Gheorghiu-Dej's claims were modest: "We succeeded in avoiding a large-scale famine. . . . We achieved some positive results in saving the children in the famine-stricken areas. . . ." Thanks to Soviet food supplies, a major disaster was avoided.

For five months after the war there was an open conflict between the Groza government and the King—who would not recognize this government. He was supported in his opposition by Britain and America, who thought the Groza government "un-representative", and by the "reactionary forces" inside Rumania. However, thanks to the Soviet Union, a compromise was reached between the three Great Powers in January 1946, and the King re-established normal relations with the Groza government after two "reactionaries" had been admitted to it. At the Paris peace conference Britain and America had made some extravagant compensation demands on Rumania on behalf of their capitalists, but these demands were scaled down, thanks to the Soviet Union.

The main opposition to the "democratic regime" in Rumania came from Maniu's National-Agrarian Party, which by the end of 1945 began to resort to terrorist methods. There were also enemies among the government parties—particularly from right-wing social-democrats like Petrescu, who was, however, finally expelled from the Socialist Party in March 1947. Nor were Tatarescu and his party easy partners.

* Thus, in the case of Transylvania, with its substantial Hungarian population, Hitler had favoured Hungary. Stalin, on the contrary, favoured Rumania—partly no doubt because Rumania had broken with Germany as early as August 1944, while Hungary—or rather a large part of the Hungarian army—had fought on the German side to the bitter end. On the other hand, the return of Southern Dobrudja to Bulgaria was intended to "reward" Bulgaria for her marked pro-Soviet policy, and also to eliminate friction between Bulgaria and Rumania.

22

Even so, the Tatarescu Party, together with the communists, socialists, Groza's party and two other small parties, joined in that "bloc of democratic parties" which was to win the parliamentary election of November 1946. This bloc had a common election platform, but had to put up a heavy fight against "the coalition of reactionary parties who were enjoying the open support of certain British and American representatives in Rumania". These parties "still enjoyed considerable support among the wealthier peasants" and "tried to exploit the very severe hardships from which, at that time, the country was suffering".

The "common election platform" of the "democratic parties" provided for a large number of economic measures, including the nationalization of the National Bank, currency stabilization and the restoration of industry. After the election, the number of ministries in the hands of the communists was further increased, the National Bank, until then controlled by the Bratianu group, was nationalized, and a state control was established over the industrial and commercial enterprises still in private hands. In 1947 there was at last a good harvest in Rumania, but how low the economy had fallen may be seen from the communist proposal to raise the level of industrial production in 1948 to 70 per cent of the pre-war level. Restrictions were placed by the post-election government on the sale of land to *kulaks*, and the sales of land by the poorer peasants during the famine were nullified.

Even after the election victory of the "democratic" parties, reactionary influences were still strong in Rumania. Tatarescu and his followers were adopting an increasingly ambiguous attitude. He himself was now saying in moments of indiscretion that although the Soviet Union was "geographically" closest to Rumania, Rumania was linked with the West "by long years of traditional mutual sympathies". This attitude made it difficult for the communists to continue their cooperation with the Tatarescu liberals. Similarly, they were having some difficulties with the right-wing social-democrats. Two of them had recently had to be thrown out of the government. And, just as in Poland, it could not be denied that the greater part of the intellectuals in Rumania were "reactionary", and there were still "a very large number of reactionaries among university professors".

But the greatest danger to "democratic Rumania" came from

Maniu and his National-Agrarian Party. These had set up a terrorist underground, and Maniu himself had openly advocated Anglo/American military intervention in Rumania, while other members of his group had tried to escape abroad to set up an émigré government there. The Maniu party therefore had to be dissolved, its deputies eliminated from parliament, and many of them, including Maniu himself, had had to be arrested and put on trial.

Gheorghiu-Dej was glad to report that the currency reform had recently created more stable conditions in Rumania, and the big problem now was to create a great united workers' party, comprising both communists and socialists (except the right-wing social-democrats). Such a united workers' party had a sound basis: the CP was now the largest single party, with 710,000 members. And it would be useful in speeding up the socialization of Rumania, where the state sector in both industry and commerce was still weak.

In Hungary, the "reactionary forces" were even stronger than in Rumania, and, as distinct from Rumania, the Church still had a powerful influence. I. Revai, in his report to the Cominform, said that "American imperialism" had done its utmost to prevent new elections being held in Hungary in 1947. The Hungarian reactionaries were hoping, with the help of the parliamentary majority largely consisting of the smallholders, to set up a right-wing government, and only then to have new elections "in an anti-communist and anti-Soviet atmosphere". This would have produced a right-wing majority in parliament, which would have worked hand-in-glove with the "American imperialists". The communists, however, succeeded in bringing about new elections. The American imperialists then tried to get the smallholders and even the social-democrats to boycott them. The social-democrats, without actually boycotting the election, would not, however, agree to the communist proposal that the four "democratic" parties should run a single list of candidates; the smallholders also rejected this proposal.

However, an election agreement was reached among the four parties which prohibited reciprocal attacks during the election campaign. But this agreement was not much more than theoretical, and what the election produced in the end was not so much a fighting alliance of the democratic parties as merely a parliamentary coalition.

Without dwelling on the question of how this was achieved, Revai said that the election had proved a substantial success for the communists, who were now "the leading party" in Hungary. Even so, it had by no means swept the country, having received 22·3 per cent (1,118,000 votes) of the poll; in some working-class areas they had had 70 or 80 per cent of the votes, but in Budapest only 27 per cent. The working-class vote was almost equally divided between the communists and the socialists, but in many places the social-democrats were still stronger. The CP had, however, made some headway in the countryside: of the 1½ million peasant votes, the CP had received 500,000, the socialists 200,000, and the National Peasant Party (a "left" party supported by the poorer peasants) 420,000 votes—far more than in 1945. In short this "left" coalition had received 46 per cent of the votes and 50 per cent of the seats; including the smallholders, the election coalition had got 61 per cent of the votes and 65 per cent of the seats.

It is clear from Revai's report that this was a very odd coalition indeed. The social-democrats were largely dominated, during the election campaign, by their right wing who, anxious to win many of the former smallholders' votes, "were deliberately spreading the malicious rumour that, in the event of a communist election victory, the *kolkhoz* system would be introduced in Hungary". But somehow or other both the social-democrats and the smallholders suffered very heavy losses in the election—the former losing 80,000 votes and the latter as many as 2 million. Not that this greatly helped the communists; the chief beneficiaries of the social-democrats' and the smallholders' defeats were the two new reactionary parties—the so-called Democratic People's Party under Darankovic, which was, Revai said, the party of the greater part of the Catholic clergy (this received 800,000 votes), and the Hungarian Independence Party, under a certain Pfeiffer, which Revai described as "semi-fascist" and an outspoken agency of "American imperialism". It was these two parties which had captured a very large part of the former smallholders' vote, the smallholders having been seriously discredited by Ferencz Nagy's desertion and similar incidents.

Revai said that the election had shown that, although the communists had strengthened their position as a government and parliamentary party, the "reactionary forces" in the country were still very strong. Nor could it be assumed that the present government coalition was monolithically united. All kinds of unpleasant surprises were possible, and the CP had to be increasingly vigilant.

The new government now comprised 5 communists, 4 social-democrats, 4 smallholders, and 2 members of the Peasant Party. This coalition seemed fairly solid, though attempts by the "reaction" to split it could not be excluded. The question whether Hungary would, in the end, be a people's democracy or a bourgeois democracy was still far from having been settled once and for all. Worse still, it was not even certain that Hungary had finally rejected any sort of link-up with Anglo/American imperialism.

For the present, Hungary was a strange amalgam of people's democracy and bourgeois democracy, and American imperialism had not yet given up hope of winning her over and of turning her into an anti-Soviet base. But much had been done to turn her into a people's democracy: 650,000 peasant families had been given land that had formerly belonged to big landlords and the Church; heavy industry had been nationalized, and soon so would be the banks, controlling until recently 60 per cent of Hungarian industry; the Supreme Economic Council, run by the democratic forces, was now controlling the economic and financial life of the nation; and under the new three-year plan, the state sector would become much stronger and the capitalist sector much weaker.

Despite some sharp temporary disagreements between the communists and socialists, it was still possible to speak of a united working-class front, and of an alliance between the working class and a large part of the peasantry. There was an ever-growing influence of the CP among both. The CP and the socialists were exercising a close control over the army and the police, both of which were of the greatest importance.

On the other hand, there were still many strongholds of "bourgeois democracy" in Hungary. A large part of industry and most of trade was still in private hands. The *kulaks*, dodging their duties, were supplying the black market. Many of the civil servants were still pre-war, and had served under Horthy. Clerical reaction was still very strong, as were the reactionary and pro-fascist parties in parliament, and there were right-wing and anti-communist elements among the government parties.

Hungary, Revai said, had suffered serious destructions during the war, and it had been for her a steep uphill road since the end of hostilities. Nevertheless, the progressive forces could claim to have achieved a great deal: in 1945, the land reform had been put through; in 1946 the currency had been stabilized after the fantastic runaway inflation; and industry had reached 80 per cent of its pre-war level; transport, thanks to the communist minister Görö, had been restored; coal production had reached 85 per cent of the pre-war level; nevertheless, living conditions were still very hard, and real wages were not above 60 per cent of pre-war. For three years in succession Hungary had suffered from drought, and in 1947 the harvest would be only 30 per cent of what had been expected—a loss of 500,000 tons.

The Hungarian communists were reckoning on establishing stronger bonds with the left-wing (as against the right-wing) social-democrats, and with the left-wing elements of the small-holders, as well as with the National Peasant Party; latterly it had also been decided to dissolve Pfeiffer's pro-fascist party.

The CP had 750,000 members, and Revai claimed that according to public opinion polls Mathias Rakosi, the communist leader, was now "the most popular statesman in Hungary". One of the troubles with the Hungarian CP had been that some of its older members had imagined that the experiment of 1919 would be resumed with the help of the Red Army, and that a Soviet Hungary would now be firmly set up. It took some time to explain to them that there could be no question of restoring the dictatorship of the proletariat, and that a people's democracy, in which the CP cooperated with other progressive forces, was something quite different. More useful were the numerous young members of the Party, who had done wonders in carrying through the land reform and in repairing rolling-stock, thanks to which it had been possible to prevent a deadly famine in the more remote parts of the country.

All the reactionary forces in Hungary—those which had sided with Hitler in the past—were now pro-American. These people were still resenting the Russian decision to return Transylvania to Rumania. Yet the Hungarian people on the whole were not anti-Russian. The workers were grateful to Russia for their liberation, and so were the 650,000 peasants who had benefited from the land reform. There was no animosity against either

Rumania or Yugoslavia, both of which had given civil rights to their Hungarian minorities.

To Hungary, enemy No. 1 was American imperialism, and the Hungarian CP was preaching a healthy hatred for it, together with a love for Hungary's independence. It attached the greatest importance to economic cooperation with the Soviet Union, Yugoslavia and other socialist countries. In conclusion, Revai said that he welcomed the Cominform meeting, since it was particularly important for the communist parties to close their ranks at a time when the whole international situation was growing more and more complex and ominous.

Such is the gist of the principal statements made at the first Cominform meeting, which was held in Poland in September 1947. These were later published in book-form,* but the book does not include some of the more controversial discussions that took place during that session, such as the furious Yugoslav attacks on the French CP, and the strong reservations made by Zhdanov about the slow progress—or absence—of agricultural collectivization in Poland or, for that matter, the other East European countries. Some of the more ferocious speeches, such as Anna Pauker's, are omitted, although the "inside information" the Yugoslavs later added to this record does not add very much to our knowledge of what went on at the meeting. But these speeches by the communist leaders of the various East European countries are extremely interesting in themselves: they describe Eastern Europe as it looked to the communists at a particularly crucial moment, namely after the rejection of Marshall Aid, and nine months before the Soviet/Yugoslav split. The danger of a Third World War was present in everybody's mind, most of all perhaps in Zhdanov's. In all the East European countries economic conditions were still very difficult, with the partial exception of Czechoslovakia. Everywhere the communists were up against the resistance of the pro-American "reactionaries", though in varying degrees. The "reactionary" menace was weakest in Yugoslavia and Bulgaria, and strongest perhaps in Hungary. In Poland Mikolajzcyk was on his way out, and, by being careful not to antagonize the peasantry and the Church, the communists and their allies had brought about a relatively peaceful state of affairs.

* *Informatsionnoye Soveshchanie Predstavitelei Nekotorykh Kompartii*, Moscow, 1948, 306 pp.

In Czechoslovakia there were no "reactionaries" in the usual sense, but the conflict between "people's democracy" and "bourgeois democracy" was still in the future—though, obviously, not in a distant future. Poland and Czechoslovakia, both hostile to Germany, had special territorial reasons for being pro-Russian. Bulgaria was, in the main, voluntarily pro-Soviet. In Rumania and even more in Hungary a severe class struggle was still continuing, and it was the relative precariousness of the communist position in these countries which made them adopt the most virulent police regimes after 1948. After June 1948, there was also a danger of the Titoite infection spreading to all these countries, and this explains the extreme Stalinization that was enforced on Hungary, Rumania and, before long, also on Czechoslovakia and Bulgaria, with Poland getting off rather more lightly.

A characteristic of the first Cominform meeting was the way the Yugoslavs talked down to the others, rather with the implication that they had, as communists, achieved far more, with much less outside help, than had by the others, who were still wrangling with their various "reactionaries". The Yugoslavs, by virtually identifying the Communist Party with the vast "national front", seemed to suggest that for them there was no more class struggle. A careful study of the first Cominform meeting already points to an imminent ideological conflict between the Soviet Union and Yugoslavia. Also, the Yugoslavs were kowtowing to the Russians—and to Stalin—less than the others. Why?

FIFTEEN

Russia After the Marshall Plan

All kinds of dates have been given as marking "the beginning of the Cold War". Some have spoken of 1917; other suggested dates are March 1943—Moscow's breach with the London Polish government; 12th April 1945—Roosevelt's death; 6th August 1945—Hiroshima; March 1946—Churchill's Fulton speech; March/April 1947—the announcement of the Truman Doctrine and the subsequent breakdown of the Foreign Ministers' Conference in Moscow; or July 1947—when Europe was split in two by Western Europe's acceptance of Marshall Aid and Eastern Europe's refusal of it. Each of these dates can in fact legitimately be regarded as marking a new phase in the intensification of the Cold War. Moscow's and Stalin's own attitude to the West may be said to have drastically changed during the spring and summer of 1947. Until then, in the various interviews he gave, he dwelt on the necessity of what had since come to be known as "peaceful coexistence". Now, by September 1947, if not before, this was no longer possible. The main purpose of the Cominform meeting had been to announce that the world was now divided into two camps—the "democratic and anti-imperialist camp" and the "anti-democratic and imperialist camp". Both internationally and internally, there was a marked stiffening of the regime. Stalin's East European empire needed further consolidation and Stalinization, and by the second half of 1947 it was becoming clearer every day that such luxuries as a Western-type parliamentary democracy in a country like Czechoslovakia would, before long, have to be dispensed with.

Increasingly tough police regimes were set up in countries like

Hungary and Rumania, and the Kremlin was glad to hear that in Poland the embarrassing Stanislaw Mikolajczyk—that "Western stooge"—had fled abroad, with apparently nobody trying to stop him. From the Russian as well as the Polish government's point of view, it was a much easier solution than starting any sort of political trial against him—which might have produced an extremely violent reaction inside Poland.

Czechoslovakia continued to be the one and only obvious anomaly inside the "socialist camp", with a coalition government consisting of communists, some *bona fide* social-democrats, and "bourgeois nationalists" such as the "national socialists", among them people such as Hubert Ripka, the Minister of Foreign Trade. Like President Benes, Ripka had not forgotten the betrayal of Czechoslovakia by the West at the time of Munich. Nevertheless, his sympathies, like those of Benes, were with the West rather than with Moscow. Some very strange things had begun to happen in Czecholsovakia by the end of 1947. In view of the eagerness that country (including even some of its communist leaders) had shown for Marshall Aid—which in the end she had to reject under Soviet pressure—American government was not yet prepared to write off Czechoslovakia as a country finally incorporated in the "Stalinist bloc". But it so happened that in 1947 Czechoslovakia was hit by one of the severest droughts in her history and food there was extremely short. A few months later, in December 1947, I received in Moscow a phone call from my old friend Hubert Ripka, who had shortly before arrived there and who now asked me to lunch in one of the *de luxe* suites he was occupying at the National Hotel. Ignoring the microphones which were certainly installed in this suite, he welcomed me with the greatest cordiality, but then immediately began to bubble over with rage.

"These goddam Americans!" he fumed. "It's because of them that I've had to come here to sign on the dotted line. The point is that Czechoslovakia is threatened with a real famine. We told the Americans, and asked for 200,000 or 300,000 tons of wheat. And these idiots started the usual blackmail: 'Okay, you can have 200,000 or 300,000 or even 500,000 tons of wheat, but on one condition only—that you throw the communists out of the Czechoslovak Government.' They added that they had done this in France, and Italy and several other countries, and they were now making the same demand on Czechoslovakia—'so long as you have communists in the government, the United States won't help you'. We explained that the position in France and Italy on the one hand and in Czechoslovakia on the other were not identical—in our country nearly 40 per cent of the people had voted communist. But they said they didn't care. At this point Gottwald got in touch with Stalin, who immediately promised us the required wheat—200,000 tons to begin with, and more if necessary. And now these idiots in Washington have driven us straight into the Stalinist camp. And Gottwald has sent me here to sign the trade agreement which he drew up with Stalin. The fact that not America but Russia has saved us from starvation will have a tremendous effect inside Czechoslovakia—even among the people whose sympathies are with the West rather than with Moscow, all the more so as they know that it *does* represent a sacrifice to Russia, whereas for America to get rid of 200,000 tons of wheat out of her enormous surplus stocks would have been nothing at all."

And Ripka added sadly: "Lots of people in Prague are now expecting a communist take-over and the exclusion from the government of people like me. But even Benes now seems more or less reconciled to the idea that the days of Czechoslovakia as a sort of bridge between East and West are now numbered. And for me," he said, "it's a great personal tragedy. You remember how I had to leave for France after Munich to avoid being captured sooner or later by the Nazis. Now I shall have to get away again, so as not to fall into the clutches of the NKVD or its Czech stooges—and there are plenty of those in Prague."

What Hubert Ripka foresaw happened, indeed, in Prague less than two months later, in February 1948. The take-over by the communists and their allies took place with little or no opposition, and Benes, now a sad, sick and broken man, gave it its blessing, however reluctantly. He resigned soon after, and died a few months later. Foreign Minister Jan Masaryk, son of Tomas Masaryk, though also accepting to serve under Gottwald, began before long to suffer from acute nervous depression, and committed suicide by jumping out of his fourth-floor window at the Czernin Palace. There were totally unsubstantiated stories that he had been murdered by the communists. On the contrary, Jan Masaryk was a great asset to Gottwald, both internally and internationally, and nothing suited him less than the suicide of "the great Masaryk's" son, whose presence in the new government had a reassuring effect both inside Czechoslovakia and abroad. What seems to have played an important, if not decisive, role in Masaryk's decision to kill himself were the cruel letters from many of his friends in the West, who now accused him of being a "traitor" and a "Stalin flunkey". These friends either did not know, or preferred not to know, that Masaryk had remained Foreign Minister in the Gottwald government at President Benes's personal request.

The economic help for which the Czech government had asked Washington might, if granted, have delayed the communist take-over in Prague. But the rejection by Washington of the Czech request made the change of regime in Czechoslovakia virtually inevitable. Throughout 1947, Stalin had been busy imposing a stern communist regime on all the East European countries. Special agencies like the Soviet/Hungarian, Soviet/Rumanian, Soviet/Bulgarian and Soviet/Yugoslav joint stock companies were a means whereby the Russians were gaining control of these countries' economies. Not until the middle of 1948 were the Yugoslavs to be the first to rebel against this economic enslavement. These countries, as well as Poland and East Germany, "delivered to Russia their coal, machines, bauxite, oil and wheat, either as reparations deliveries or at extremely low prices, while their own people suffered want and poverty. As the parties of opposition were suppressed one after the other, popular discontent found no mouthpieces. A reign of terror stifled any cry or murmur of protest. Soviet administrators and engineers were supervising the industries of Eastern Europe, Soviet generals commanded its armies, and Soviet policemen managed its security forces."*

In Isaac Deutscher's view, there was nothing outrageous in the communist take-over in Czechoslovakia in February 1948:

> At the beginning of 1948, Czechoslovakia alone of all these countries was not yet conforming to the new pattern. Ever since 1945 Moscow had insisted (obviously with a view to pleasing Washington) that the Czech communists should refrain from revolutionary action. Yet Czechoslovakia had emerged from the war in a truly revolutionary condition, its working class armed and

---

* I. Deutscher, *Stalin* (Revised edition, 1966, Penguin Books), p. 571.

clamouring for socialism, and its communist party polling, in free elections, nearly 40 per cent of the national vote. The pro-Russian sentiment of the Czechs was genuine, rooted in national tradition, and, since the Munich crisis, enhanced by a revulsion against the West. Nevertheless, for nearly three years, although it was ruled by a government of which Gottwald, the communist, was Prime Minister, the country remained a bourgeois democracy. Benes was still President, Jan Masaryk was Foreign Minister, and the government depended on the parliamentary vote of communists, liberals and social-democrats. . . . Here was clearly a gap in Stalin's defences, and the Czech communists had to close it. . . . In February 1948 they carried out the long-delayed revolution and seized power.

On the contrary, Deutscher speaks with genuine enthusiasm of this "revolution from below":

Unlike other East European upheavals, this [Prague revolution] bore the mark of a revolution from below, even though it was timed to suit Stalin's convenience. The communists accomplished it by their own strength, supported by the great majority of the workers; they had only to parade their armed militias in the streets to block any counter-action. The Soviet occupation troops had long left the country; and the mere fear of their return was enough to paralyze the bourgeois parties. Gottwald could even afford to observe the rules of the parliamentary game: the bourgeois ministers, hoping to forestall or prevent the revolution, had rashly resigned their posts and left the administrative machine in communist hands; then Gottwald and his comrades managed to cajole the hesitant and divided social-democrats, who rejoined them and formed with them a new parliamentary majority. Benes and Masaryk, overwhelmed and depressed by the evidence of popular support for the revolution . . . bowed to the victors.*

It was not till some time after the Prague *coup* of February 1948 that a police regime of the worst sort developed in Czechoslovakia. It was to prove one of the longest and most ferocious in the whole of Eastern Europe; it took the Czechs nearly twenty years to rebel against it through the overthrow of Antonin Novotny, the last of the Stalinist tyrants, and his replacement at the head of the Party by Alexander Dubček and at the head of the state by General Ludvik Svoboda. This sudden transition from

* It might be added that War Minister, General Svoboda, the future President of 1968, maintained the army's strict neutrality, in accordance with the wishes of President Benes, nominally Commander-in-Chief.

Stalinism to liberalization was more than the Kremlin Politburo, under the leadership of Leonid Brezhnev, could bear, and, violating practically all the treaty obligations the Soviet Union had signed since the Second World War, it sent its tanks into Prague on 21st August 1968. Stalin had never done anything so crude and stupid; as we shall see, he was to handle a very similar anti-Moscow rebellion in Yugoslavia in 1948 with far greater caution and cunning. To take the example of the two principal Western communist parties, the French and Italian, these joined the Kremlin in denouncing the Tito heresy; in 1968, these same CPs sharply condemned the invasion of Czechoslovakia.

The last few months of 1947 in the Soviet Union were marked by a number of important phenomena: the enormously important monetary reform, which went together with the abolition of rationing; a revival—the first since the war—of a "vigilance campaign" which soon developed into a new kind of spy-mania; and an acute deterioration of relations with the West.

In 1945 and 1946 the Soviet press had, on the whole, been cautious not to attack the principal Western leaders personally. The most peculiar welcome Harry Truman gave Molotov less than a fortnight after succeeding Roosevelt at the White House remained a dead secret, as far as the Russian newspaper readers were concerned, and the story was known to only a very closed circle inside Russia. Stalin had still hoped to re-establish reasonably courteous, if not friendly, relations with the United States. By the middle of 1947, after the announcement of the Truman Doctrine, the breakdown of the Foreign Ministers' Conference in Moscow, the setting in motion of the Marshall Plan and the Cominform's announcement that the world was now divided into two hostile camps, the prospect of a *rapprochement* with America or Britain seemed very remote indeed. By the autumn of 1947, there began to appear in the Soviet press some angry personal attacks not only on men like Byrnes, Forrestal and Bohlen but also on President Truman himself. In September 1947 there appeared in *Literary Gazette* an article by Boris Gorbatov on Harry Truman which was so violent that Ambassador Bedell Smith sent Molotov a protest against the publication of the article in which the author, he said, had surpassed Goebbels himself for sheer viciousness. Bedell Smith also said he could not believe that "the Gorbatov article reflected the views of the Soviet government, but, if it did, would Mr. Molotov say so". Molotov replied that the Soviet government could not take responsibility for all articles appearing in the Soviet press, adding that the US government, instead of worrying about the Soviet press, would be well advised to study the American papers, with their war and preventive-war propaganda.

A few weeks later, on 5th November 1947, *Pravda* denounced James Byrnes's book, *Frankly Speaking*, as "a dirty piece of faking", especially those passages where he tried to show that in the last few weeks of his life Roosevelt had spoken of the "deterioration" of Soviet/American relations. This faking, *Pravda* said, went together with Byrnes's ideas on "getting the Soviet troops out of Germany" and with his demand for "more and better atom bombs".

The question whether America would use atom bombs against Russia before Russia made her own had been at the back of many Russians' minds ever since Hiroshima. But in 1945 and 1946 such an attack still seemed improbable, even after so "maniacally anti-Soviet" a speech as Churchill's Fulton address. But in the second half of 1947, nothing seemed impossible any more, and it was fairly widely known that the Soviet armed forces, which had been reduced from 11 million men in 1945 to 3 million at the beginning of 1947, were now being gradually increased again to over 5 million. But immense Russian superiority in conventional arms—with which she would be able to overrun Western Europe within a few days—was the only effective antidote she had against an atomic attack on Soviet territory.*
Such a huge army, however, represented a fearful drain on

* An enormous number of people in Western Europe, notably in France, were fully aware of this danger, particularly in 1947–9, when a highly influential paper like *Le Monde*, for instance, adopted a "neutralist", plague-on-both-your-houses, line. The prospect of Western Europe being overrun by the Red Army was just a shade less unattractive than the subsequent victorious American war in which the Russians in Western Europe—and with them practically everybody else—would be eliminated through hundreds (or thousands) of atom bombs being dropped on Western Europe in the name of the Free World. Such "neutralist" currents—which represented not so much a political doctrine as simply a "mood"—were particularly strong in France, Italy, the Netherlands and all the three Scandinavian countries. (The matter is discussed in detail in the author's *France 1940–1955*, London and New York, 1956.)

Russian manpower and on the very limited economic resources the country possessed, barely two years after the end of the war. For it was the announcement of the Truman Doctrine which started the Soviet rearmament drive.

In the circumstances, the Soviet people heard with particular satisfaction and relief Molotov's announcement that there were no "atom bomb secrets" the Russians did not know, which was interpreted as meaning that the Soviet Union already had the bomb or would have it very shortly. Most Russians did not take the view put forward by many foreign papers that Molotov was merely bluffing, though a few no doubt did—on the quiet.

This Molotov speech, delivered after the "Marshallization" of Western Europe and nearly two years after the adoption of the first post-war Five-Year Plan by the Soviet Union, is historically important in more ways than one.

He began by recalling that the Soviet Union had been industrialized in thirteen years—between 1928 and 1941, the year when she was invaded by Germany and her allies. By 1940—the last pre-war year—the country's industrial production was already twelve times greater than in 1913—the last normal year before the First World War. Claiming that collectivization had proved a great success, Molotov (perhaps rather rashly) asserted that but for the war the Soviet Union would be in "a better agricultural position than any other country in Europe". (Quantitatively, this was of course possible, with France as the only major agricultural country in Europe, but qualitatively it was more than improbable; and this is still true, even twenty years after that Molotov speech.)

But if the agricultural problem was still a serious one, it was for two obvious reasons; the Germans and their allies had occupied in the Soviet Union a territory inhabited at the outbreak of war by 88 million people and representing 33 per cent of the country's industrial output, and containing 47 per cent of its arable land. Fortunately, the Soviet people succeeded in evacuating immediately after the Nazi invasion 1,300 industrial enterprises to the East "and so saved Europe's civilization". But after years of Nazi occupation, most of the arable lands had badly deteriorated, and then in 1946, during the year following the end of the war, when food was so essential to the great reconstruction drive the country had now undertaken, it was hit by one of the worst droughts in her history; but even in these extremely difficult conditions the Five-Year Plan had been fulfilled in 1946 to the extent of 96 per cent, and in 1947 to the extent of 103 per cent, with Leningrad holding the top position in industrial output. By October 1947, the Soviet economic output had reached the monthly average of 1940.

Turning to foreign affairs, Molotov fully justified in retrospect the Soviet/German Pact of 1939; it was by agreeing to this that Stalin had outwitted the Munichites, who had been hoping all along for a Nazi attack on the Soviet Union. But even after the invasion of Western Europe by the Nazis, many Western leaders still had not learned their lesson. Without mentioning Senator Harry Truman by name, Molotov recalled that after the Nazi invasion of the Soviet Union there were "certain people" in the West who wanted as many Russians and as many Germans as possible to be killed, for the ultimate benefit of Britain and the United States. Moore Brabazon, one of Churchill's own ministers, had expressed the hopes that Russia and Germany would "exterminate each other". Despite these influences, the great anti-Hitler coalition had still taken shape. In this connection Molotov quoted what Stalin had said in his "election" speech in February 1946, and then in his interview with Stassen in 1947, in favour of continuing that cooperation which had worked so well among the Allies during the war. But now, said Molotov, this policy of cooperation was being actively opposed in the West, particularly by the United States and Britain, what with the aggressive Truman Doctrine and the setting up of air and naval bases all over the world, particularly in countries close to the Soviet Union.

Some of America's associates observe a dignified silence; others openly grumble—notably Denmark, which wants Greenland back and does not want it used as an American base; and Egypt wants the British troops to go. All the countries who have had such bases inflicted on them, more or less against their will, are fully aware of the aggressive nature of these bases.

And in America itself?

In the American expansionist circles there is a new kind of religion. There is no faith in internal strength, but there is a fanatical faith in one thing—the secret of the atom bomb—*even though,*

23

for a long time now, no such secrets have existed. (Long, stormy applause.)
Yet the imperialists *need* this faith in the A-bomb which, as we
all know, is not a weapon of defence, but one of aggression. All the
more ominous is the fact that the USA will not hear of prohibiting
the A-bomb, or of any reduction of armaments generally; and
meantime propaganda in favour of war is going on merrily, despite
all the good resolutions adopted at UN.

If only the United States and Britain had stuck to Yalta, the
Big Four could peacefully cooperate in Germany today. But the
Western powers are not interested in the democratization and
demilitarization of Germany, or in the payment of German
reparations to the countries which have suffered most from German
aggression. Instead, the USA and Britain are pursuing a bi-zone
policy quite independently of the Allied Control Council. In
reality, as a result of this Anglo/American policy, all Soviet activity
in Germany is now strictly confined to the Soviet Zone; and if
they have succeeded in creating a bi-zone, they have done their
best to prevent the creation of a new Germany.

Molotov, though without any faith that his appeal would
lead to anything, proposed that Britain and the United States
now return to the Yalta principles—that they help in forming a
united democratic Germany. This would be better than building
up the bi-zone with the help of the big German capitalists and a
variety of Nazis, all of them deeply involved in the criminal
Hitler adventure against mankind. Molotov warned Soviet
citizens against the perfidious influence the imperialists were
trying to exercise on them:

> Western journalists in the pay of their press magnates foretold,
> towards the end of the war, that once our soldiers had tasted of the
> fruits of Western civilization, they would want to change the order
> of things inside the Soviet Union. But nothing of the sort happened.
> (*Cheers.*) Nevertheless, there is still a good deal of toadying to the
> West in our country and far too much slavish admiration for
> capitalist culture. We have no use for this, and we shall follow the
> road we have chosen. But it will not be easy. Even in the old
> Bolshevik Party the enemy had his spies and agents—Trotskyites,
> Rightists, and so on, and in the present international situation Soviet
> citizens must be particularly vigilant.

Here Molotov already clearly foreshadowed those witch-hunts
against foreigners and against Soviet citizens guilty of "associating
with foreigners" which were beginning just about this time—the

end of 1947—and which were to continue up to the time of Stalin's death (not that this put an end to this and other forms of witch-hunts).

Finally, Molotov referred briefly to the Cominform:

> Experience has shown that the communist movement in the world is now so great that it cannot any longer be directed from one centre [i.e. Moscow]. But it has also shown that the communist parties, and in the first place the leading communist parties of Europe, must have a joint organization which would help them to exchange views and coordinate their activities on the basis of mutual agreement.

Which is precisely what was not done in the case of Yugoslavia. The Cominform did not, in their case, aim at a "mutual agreement"; it tried, instead, to force on Yugoslavia a policy she was determined to reject.

Whether believing or not in what he was saying, Molotov ended with the usual flourish to the effect that nothing could now save capitalism from an imminent death, since all roads in the twentieth century led to communism; and mankind would be guided along the right road by the genius of Marx, Engels, Lenin and Stalin. (Loud, prolonged cheers.)

This significant speech was delivered on 6th November 1947, on the eve of the thirtieth anniversary of the Great October Revolution. Stalin was apparently on holiday on the Black Sea coast in the Caucasus, since he attended neither the Red Square Parade, nor the Kremlin reception the next day.

The anniversary telegrams received that year by Stalin, Shvernik (who had succeeded Kalinin shortly before as President of the Presidium of the Supreme Soviet), and Molotov, the Foreign Minister, were of some interest. *Pravda* gave top priority to a telegram from Harry Truman to Shvernik:

> On the occasion of the national holiday of the USSR, please convey to the peoples of the USSR the greetings of the people of the United States of America.

There followed telegrams from Bierut, President of Poland, and Zoltan Tildy, President of Hungary; a short cable from Prime Minister Attlee; and then a long gushing message from President Tito wishing the Soviet people further happiness and progress "under the leadership of genius of Comrade Stalin". There were, naturally, many other messages—from Cyrankiewicz, Dimitrov, Gottwald, etc. No doubt the Truman telegram was of no particular significance, but people in Russia still found it reassuring that Truman should still be on speaking terms with the Soviet leaders, and even on "greeting" terms with "the peoples of the USSR".

As we have already said, those last two months of 1947 were marked by a new kind of witch-hunt and by one of the most important monetary reforms in the history of the USSR.

A good deal of witch-hunting had already gone on since 1946. It had begun with Zhdanov's various purges among writers, artists, film directors, historians, philosophers, etc. The Zhdanovite tyranny over the writers was now exercised less by Zhdanov himself than by the bureaucrats of Writers' Union, and in the first place by Alexander Fadeyev, at that time President of the Writers' Union.

Typical of the ruthless tyranny of Fadeyev was the tragic case of Andrei Platonov, a story-writer with a genuine and original talent but also a non-conformist streak which terrified the Fadeyevs and the other bureaucrats of the Party and the Writers' Union. In 1946 he had written a short story dealing with a situation "inconceivable among decent and patriotic Soviet citizens"—that of a soldier who, on returning to his native village, finds that his wife has been living with another man. He was promptly blacklisted, and after that, as he told me himself in 1948, Fadeyev had been "sitting on the manuscripts of his stories and novels" without even allowing them to go as far as the censorship, let alone any magazine or publishing house. Platonov was a sick, undernourished man, deeply embittered, and slowly dying of tuberculosis. He died in 1951, and it was not till some fifteen years later that a volume of his selected stories was published. Its 50,000 copies were rapidly snatched up. He was "recognized" as one of the Soviet Union's major writers. Not that even Fadeyev himself was immune against criticism from the Party bonzes. His novel *The Young Guard*—which is a fictionalized version of the tragic story of the young Komsomol underground at Krasnodon, a mining town in the Donbas— had been a great success when it was first published in 1946. Now, in 1947, Stalin, or somebody high up, decided that the young heroes and martyrs of Krasnodon were behaving, in the novel, in too amateurish a manner, and that Fadeyev had not given nearly enough attention to the importance of Moscow, the Party and Stalin himself in the conduct of anti-German underground and guerrilla work behind the enemy lines. He was ordered to rewrite the novel. The young people of Krasnodon were to be shown as being not merely recklessly brave and patriotic, but as young men and women who are carrying out the instructions of the Party and whose guerrilla warfare at Krasnodon is merely part of a much larger and more effective plan directed and even partly controlled from above. Just as in the case of Leningrad not nearly enough credit had been given for the heroic defence of the city to the Party and to Stalin personally, so, on a smaller scale, in the story of the Krasnodon Resistance, much more should have been made of "the guiding hand of the Party", and less of the spontaneous *partizanshchina** spirit of Oleg Koshevoi and the other young heroes and heroines who died for their country. As a good bureaucrat, Fadeyev rewrote his novel accordingly. The Party line was more important than historical accuracy.

The year 1947 also witnessed the beginnings of another odious witch-hunt—that against the biologists and other scientists who were in disagreement with Lysenko. However, this did not reach its climax until the summer of 1948, when the Central Committee simply *decreed* that Lysenko genetics were right, and all other genetics were wrong!

Before discussing the witch-hunt against foreigners and people "associated" with foreigners, which also started in a big way in November/December 1947, it is important to describe here one of the major landmarks in Soviet economic reconstruction after the war—the great monetary reform of December 1947, which went together with the abolition of rationing.

On 15th December 1947 an important announcement was made, on behalf of the government and the Party, by Prime

---

* *Partizanshchina*, with its derogatory ending often denoting some arbitrary terrorist rule (cf. *Yezhovshchina*, *Zhdanovshchina* and, in the past, *Khovanshchina*) had, on many occasions, especially during the Civil War of 1918–20, been sharply condemned by Lenin for the opportunist and unreliable nature of certain guerrilla formations, which easily changed sides, and whose "revolutionary spirit" was often scarcely distinguishable from plain banditry. The main feature of *partizanshchina* was its insubordination to the Red Army command, or any other high authority.

Minister J. V. Stalin and Secretary of the Central Committee of the CPSU A. A. Zhdanov on the monetary reform and the abolition of rationing that had been agreed upon. This announcement said:

The war made a large increase in the note circulation inevitable. Moreover, the Germans, in their occupied territories, printed a large number of false Soviet notes. As a result of all this, there was a sharp depreciation of the Soviet currency and far more notes in circulation and in existence than was needed by the national economy.

Despite difficult war conditions, the Soviet government succeeded in maintaining without change the *state prices* of rationed goods through the introduction of ration cards for both foodstuffs and manufactured goods. But the shortage of goods in the state shops went together with a sharp rise in prices in the *kolkhoz* markets, where prices have latterly risen to ten or fifteen times compared with pre-war. Speculators did not fail to take advantage of these difficulties, and they also hoarded, over the years, vast quantities of notes. Now it is important that they should not be allowed to use these hoarded notes for buying up goods after the abolition of rationing. The new rouble currency will replace the devalued currency on the following basis:

Cash: 1 new rouble will be issued in return for 10 (depreciated or German-forged) old roubles.

Saving banks: deposits will be transformed into new roubles on the basis of 1-to-1 up to 3,000 roubles, and on a diminishing scale thereafter. With the exception of the 1947 Reconstruction loan, which will be treated as having been subscribed in new roubles, all other state loans will be converted on the basis of 3 old roubles to 1 new rouble. The fact cannot be overlooked that, during the war, loans were subscribed to in depreciated currency.

Wages: these will be paid at the same rate as before; instead of receiving their pay in roubles of ever-dwindling value, wage-earners will be paid the same wages in valuable new roubles.

In this way, the largest sacrifice will be made by the state, though some sacrifices of varying magnitude will have to be made by all. The most hard-hit will be the speculators and black-marketeers, who have always preferred to hoard their notes at home rather than pay them into a savings bank.

The sacrifices expected from *bona fide* workers will be small and short-term, since prices will be rapidly lowered, in both the state shops and the *kolkhoz* markets. The present prices in "commercial" shops and "commercial" restaurants will be abolished;

the fixed prices on rationed goods will be replaced by other prices which will inevitably be higher than the artificial price level in the case of rationed goods, but with one important exception: the new prices of bread and cereals will be not higher, but lower.

The sale of foodstuffs and consumer goods will be now carried out without ration cards; and uniform state retail prices will replace both ration-card prices and "commercial" prices. The new price of bread, for instance, will be 10 per cent below the ration-card price and $2\frac{1}{2}$ times below the "commercial shop" prices. In the case of most other foodstuffs, the same number of roubles will be paid as under the ration-card system; as for consumer goods, their new prices will be rather higher than under the ration-card system, but three times below the present "commercial" prices.

Among examples of the new prices in new, "valuable" roubles, the following may be quoted:

Woman's cotton dress 77 roubles
Woman's woollen dress 510 roubles
Man's suit 430 to 1400 roubles
Man's shoes 260 roubles
Woman's shoes 260 roubles
Man's galoshes 45 roubles
Woman's cotton stockings 7 roubles
Man's socks 17 roubles
Box of matches 20 kopeks
Toilet soap (100 grams) 4 roubles
Laundry soap (400 grams) 5·20 roubles

This kind of monetary reform was, of course, long overdue. If it was delayed a year, it was chiefly because of the fearful shortages caused by the 1946 drought. But the truth is that ever since the German invasion in June 1941 the value of the rouble was becoming more and more uncertain, until it had become little more than a means of making token payments for rationed goods. And ration cards existed, in fact, in the cities, not in the countryside, where a primitive kind of barter system largely replaced any monetary transactions. Thus, at all railway stations there was an active barter trade between soldiers and peasant women—often a whole chicken for 2 oz. of tobacco. Similarly, I heard of cases in Central Asia where the peasants were prepared to pay heavily in poultry and other agricultural produce for a few ounces of ordinary salt, since this was totally unobtainable, often for months on end.

Some years later, around 1956-7, I had a long discussion on this monetary reform with Pierre Mendès-France, who as Minister of Economic Affairs in the first post-Liberation de Gaulle government had also advocated the abolition of a huge proportion of French banknotes, most of them printed under the German occupation. What Mendès-France had in mind was almost precisely the kind of monetary reform the Russians carried out after the war. He considered that the cancellation of surplus notes alone could put an end to the black market in France. However, he was overruled by Finance Minister Pleven, who did not like to interfere with the traditional French "woollen stocking". In the end, de Gaulle supported Pleven, and Mendès-France resigned from the government. Around 1948 I talked to some Treasury officials in London, and they spoke with a mixture of envy and admiration of the Soviet monetary reform: "If we could have done anything along these lines, the pound would be in a much healthier condition, but, like Mendès-France, we are up against 'tradition', and against such sacred cows as treating the national currency with respect, the sanctity of government loans, and so on."

Among the people worst hit by the monetary reform, besides the professional Russian black-marketeers, were the foreign embassies, and not least the British Embassy, at which everybody (except possibly the Ambassador himself and other top officials) had wallowed in currency speculation. Depreciated roubles could, for instance, be bought up dirt-cheap from Russian occupation troops in Germany and Austria, and if one bought up vast quantities of these notes one could still buy with them a good many valuables in "commission shops" and live in grand style. Another racket (and the American diplomats were particularly active in this field) was to import into Russia watches, cameras and every other kind of PX goods and sell them at exorbitant prices to the Russian black market. The "import" of PX goods and almost, but not entirely, worthless roubles was simply done by means of the diplomatic bag. If British and American diplomats went in on a large scale for this kind of speculation, all the other embassies, notably the Latin/ American embassies and the Chinese Embassy, did so too. After all, some highly useful commodities could be bought in the "commercial" shops with very big wads of roubles, and these could be obtained for next to nothing in Vienna, Berlin, etc.

It was not till after the monetary reform that the Russians began to reveal, not all, but at least some, of the black-marketing and speculation that had been going on for years in foreign, and especially Western, embassies. Later, in 1948 and 1949, the books published by a "defector" from the US Embassy, Annabelle Bucar, and one from the British Embassy, "Archie" Johnson (at the time of his "defection" editor of the *British Ally* magazine), and then one by Ralph Parker, the former *Times* and now *Daily Worker* correspondent, gave the Soviet public a somewhat unsavoury view of the kind of people who represented Russia's wartime allies in Moscow. Miss Bucar and Ralph Parker, in particular, did not hesitate to make some pretty damaging charges against the top people in their respective embassies.

But a foretaste of these revelations (most of them substantially true) was to be given by a series of "scandals" concerning allied diplomats almost immediately after the monetary reform. The first did not, it is true, relate to black-marketing, but to plain alleged espionage. The Russian authorities picked, for some reason, on Major-General Richard Hilton, the British Military Attaché, whom a group of patriotic Russians claimed to have caught red-handed taking photographs of "military objectives" on the outskirts of Moscow. He was supposed to have been disguised as a *kolkhoznik*, wearing a "tattered old sheepskin coat". On 3rd November 1947, there appeared in *Pravda* this letter to the editor:

The following case has aroused the deepest indignation among the workers of our plant. At 12 noon on 30 October we noticed on a railway bridge an unknown person in a torn sheepskin coat and wearing working boots who, having turned his face towards our plant, was busy taking photographs. We raised the alarm ... but as the stranger saw our factory guard approaching, he hastily left the bridge and began to make off. He was overtaken. . . . This stranger in the tattered sheepskin coat produced his diplomatic identity card, and called himself the British Military Attaché in Moscow, Major-General Hilton. A member of the department of external relations at the Defence Ministry was summoned to the factory, and here established beyond doubt that the man in the tattered sheepskin coat was General Hilton.

He tried to deny the fact that he had been taking photographs of the factory, and tried to explain his presence by saying that he was looking for a place for ski-ing. . . . We did not find this very convincing. Why should a British general dress himself up in a tattered sheepskin coat . . . to look for a place for ski-ing? . . . Our workers have a different explanation. Do not certain foreign diplomats in Moscow engage in the same kind of activity as did their colleagues in Rumania, as was recently revealed?

Though the name of the plant in question was not mentioned, the letter was signed by several of its workers.

The British Embassy indignantly rejected the Soviet protest against General Hilton's alleged activities, and the General himself later wrote a book in which, like the Embassy, he maintained that he had no camera with him at the time of his arrest, and that the whole thing was a particularly crude and clumsy frame-up. Although the Soviet government rejected the British protest, they did nothing more about General Hilton, who remained in Moscow till the following May. But the legend of the British Military Attaché disguised as a *kolkhoznik* had been created. He appeared on skis and wearing the same old sheepskin coat at the Moscow Circus, and *Krokodil* published a cartoon showing him in the same disguise wading through puddles on his skis, and looking at something in the distance through his field-glasses.

Anyway, General Hilton had been successfully turned into an object of ridicule in the eyes of the Russian general public, though on the protocol level he continued to be invited to official receptions as though nothing had happened. More serious were the charges brought against junior members of the British Embassy. One junior official (or rather his pregnant Russian girl-friend, since the official in question was instructed by the Ambassador, Sir Maurice Peterson, not to appear in Court) was charged, together with this girl-friend, with having imported substantial quantities of cloth from England, and to have sold it in the black-market. Mr. S. was, in fact, only a "sample" of that diplomatic colony which used to thrive on black-marketing and currency speculation before the monetary reform. The girl-friend (partly in view of her pregnancy) was given a lenient sentence, while Mr. S. was simply ordered to leave the country. Later, there was the even more unsavoury case of a Mr. B., a junior clerk at the British Embassy who was alleged to have infected a Russian girl with syphilis. Now, who got it from whom was never conclusively established. Although

Komsomolskaya Pravda wrote an indignant article on "this dandy from Piccadilly" bringing his infected blood to Russia to spread foul diseases there, the British Embassy maintained that he had got "it" from her. Anyway, under some article of the criminal code, Mr. B. was to be tried for spreading V.D. in Russia; but again he was not allowed by the British Ambassador to appear in Court. So he stayed for several years interned at the Embassy, where he was cured of his ailment by the Embassy doctor. In the end, under Khrushchev, he was allowed to go home.

All these unpleasant episodes took place during the winter of 1947–8, and proved a sort of little prelude to the "Little Stalin Terror" of 1948–9—as distinct from the "Great Stalin Terror" of 1936–8. This "little" terror affected in the first place foreigners, and almost any Russian who had, in one way or another, associated with foreigners.

Meantime, there was nothing in Moscow's diplomatic exchanges with the West which would help to improve the general atmosphere. In France the last weeks of 1947 were marked by a powerful wave of at least partly *political* strikes, inspired by the French CP, in response no doubt to the advice the Cominform had given Duclos at its September meeting. The Americans, for their part, worked hard through the American trade-union leaders, assisted by the CIA, to split the French trade-union movement, and indeed succeeded in bringing about a split in the CGT, its socialist, "reformist" wing, under the veteran leadership of Léon Jouhaux, forming the Force Ouvrière federation. It nearly came to a diplomatic breach between France and the USSR.

There was a curious parallel between the Western and Russian moves on the international chess-board. If, in the West, the Communists were being thrown out of the governments (as they were in France and Italy in April/May 1947) so "bourgeois elements" were being eliminated throughout 1947 from the governments of Hungary, Rumania and Poland, and, in February 1948, the last remnants of a Western-type democracy were also being suppressed in Czechoslovakia.

Whether, after the breakdown of the Foreign Ministers' Conference in Moscow in April 1947, the Russians still had any illusions left of being able to save a "united Germany" and to avoid the creation of a West German state, they still went on trying. The last Foreign Ministers' Conference of 1947 was held in London in December of that year, and the results were at least as disappointing to the Russians as had been the Moscow Conference of March/April. After the breakdown of the London Conference, Yuri Zhukov and Boris Isakov wrote in *Pravda* on 18th December 1947:

> General Marshall, supported by Bevin and Bidault, wanted the Conference to break up, even though the agenda was still far from having been exhausted. A few hours later the London papers screamed in their headlines: "Breakdown of Foreign Ministers' Conference." In reality it broke down because such was Marshall's wish. With what plans then had Marshall come to London three weeks ago? The truth is that the State Department wanted the Foreign Ministers to okay the USA's colonialist policy *vis-à-vis* Western Germany, as if it were just another Puerto-Rico. ... Scared of West German competition, Wall Street wants fetters put on West Germany before there is a central German government.
>
> Britain and France are being more and more dependent on the USA, and Bevin is reduced to reading his speeches from an American crib. Bidault's behaviour to the USA is more and more servile.
>
> Molotov was immediately aware of this gang-up, and he said that the Soviet Union would accept no ultimatums; the Soviet Union, he said, was *not* a Greek government. ... There must be a united, independent and democratic Germany; instead of which Western Germany was being turned into the breeding-ground for another world war. What the Soviet Union wanted was a peace treaty with a united Germany; in short, there must be an all-German government, and not one of the bi-zone or tri-zone. Molotov also proposed the formation of all-German economic departments, since without the Germans a united Germany could not be restored. Seeing all this was being rejected, Molotov proposed that at least the establishment in Berlin of an all-German Consultative Council; but this, too, was rejected.

In conclusion, they said that it was only too clear that the French Zone was joining the bi-zone, thus turning it into a tri-zone; and in West Germany a meeting was now being called of those German party leaders who were notorious, above all, as British and American puppets. (Again the same parallel: increasingly obedient American "puppets" in Western Europe; increasingly obedient Russian "puppets" in Eastern Europe.)

In short, as the New Year of 1948 approached, Moscow was haunted by the rapidly approaching sight of a West German government.

Before an "American" regime had been set up at Bonn, the Russians encouraged the communists in Czechoslovakia to seize power. It was, as Deutscher said, a "revolution from below", even though its timing happened to suit Stalin, who was determined now to put an end to the last remaining anomaly in his East European "empire". No doubt there were some of the "bourgeois" Czech leaders who left the country, but by and large the change was accepted by the Czech population, who saw nothing diabolical about their own communists; these, anyway, had the support in the last election of nearly 40 per cent of the voters; and the country's betrayal by Britain and France at Munich only ten years before had not been forgotten. Also, the Czech communists were making great capital out of the fact that the West had refused to give badly needed food to Czechoslovakia without laying down impossible political conditions, and that Stalin had "generously" stretched out his helping hand. Those who, like Ripka, felt bitterly that the West had pushed Czechoslovakia into Stalin's embrace were clearly not very numerous. And all of it had been given a nice appearance of constitutional legality. Benes, though not without hesitation, had given his blessing to the "February Revolution" —if only as a lesser evil.

Whereas the "rape of Czechoslovakia" aroused more indignation in the West than perhaps anything else that had happened since the end of the war, in Russia the February events in Prague were taken very calmly—like something which would have happened in any case in the normal course of things. What was important, from all points of view, was also the fact that the "revolution" had been carried out by the Czechoslovak working class itself, without any outside interference, and the rest of the people accepted the change—at least for the time being—with great equanimity.

What was to create unforeseen new tensions, complications and, before long, the unleashing of a police terror in all the satellite countries, now including Czechoslovakia, was the Titoite rebellion against Moscow in June 1948. At the end of 1947 no one in Russia had expected it; on 29th November 1947 the

Soviet press published the most rapturous articles to commemorate the fifth birthday of the New Yugoslavia. According to the Soviet press, the Yugoslavs were, of all the East European countries, the most enthusiastic communists. Unlike Rumania and Hungary (and, to a lesser extent, Bulgaria), which had been Hitler's allies in the Second World War, Yugoslavia had generated her own communist system and had rejected all demands made on her by the Western imperialists.

But it was precisely this "independence" of Yugoslavia, and the Yugoslavs' boasting to the effect that they had, practically without any outside help—not even much Russian help— liberated their own country from its German and Italian invaders which was to lead to the split between Belgrade and Moscow. It was the first *national* (the Russians preferred to call it "nationalist") rebellion against the Soviet type of communism and against the satellization of their country that was to fore- shadow the other great crises inside the Soviet bloc during the next twenty years, the whole process culminating in the liberaliza- tion of Czechoslovakia, and that invasion of the country by the forces of the Warsaw Pact which may yet prove one of the most fatal errors committed by the Kremlin.

SIXTEEN

*Zhdanov Purges Soviet Music**

Although, since the monetary reform of December 1947 and the abolition of rationing (not that this made life much easier overnight), the ordinary Soviet citizen was developing the feeling that things were at last returning to normal, foreigners, and particularly foreign correspondents, in Moscow were finding the atmosphere increasingly oppressive. Travelling about the country had become virtually impossible. Worse still, a decree† was issued in the second part of 1947 making it a punishable offence for any Soviet citizen to give any kind of information to foreigners.‡ All the numerous contacts correspondents like myself had among Russians during the war and up till about May 1947 (the breakdown of the Moscow Foreign Ministers' Conference) were virtually broken off.

* In this chapter some use has been made of material from the author's *Musical Uproar in Moscow* (Turnstile Press, London, 1949).

† This Stalin decree had long been forgotten, and was certainly not observed under the more clement regime of Khrushchev. But, under Brezhnev, the "authorities" (whoever they were) who were determined that no press conference be given at her house by the mother of Alexander Ginzburg, who had the day before been sentenced to a long detention term for having allegedly smuggled out of Russia his book on the Siniavsky/Daniel Trial, produced this 1947 Decree whose application meant that Ginzburg's mother would be committing a punishable offence in telling the foreign press what had happened at her son's "open" trial—to which the foreign press had, of course, not been admitted.

‡ Exceptions were made only in the case of shops, railway and airline booking offices, and the like; also it was permissible (though not always advisable) for Soviet citizens to talk to foreigners at official receptions—provided they did not tell them too much.

In the autumn of 1947 a particularly savage censorship was introduced. I had to use all kinds of subterfuges to get any news of any real interest to the *Manchester Guardian*, for instance, by going for a week-end to Helsinki, and airmailing my copy (which I had carried from Moscow to Helsinki, not in my pocket, but in my head) from there to London.

Zhdanov was reigning supreme in literature and the arts, in history, philosophy, etc. If there were some good novels still published in 1945 and 1946, original writing was to be strongly discouraged after the Central Committee's Decree on literature in 1946.

In painting things were no better. It was about that time that foreigners like myself were pointedly invited to some VOKS party, where one would have the bad luck of being seated beside the Kremlin's painter-laureate Alexander Gerasimov, who would fulminate against Picasso and Matisse, but declare that there were some excellent painters in England still, like Sir Alfred Munnings, President of the Royal Academy, who specialized in painting Royalty and race-horses, and who "came closest to the Soviet ideas on realist art", but that Soviet art would continue "in the tradition of Repin and Velasquez".

The only branch of artistic activity which the Party had somehow still spared was music. The only circle in Moscow where, until the beginning of 1948, one still had a sense of artistic freedom was among the musicians and composers, and the concert hall was the only place left where one could expect to discover something new and original. The Soviet Union had some of the most famous composers in the world—Shostakovich and Prokofiev among them—and a remarkable wealth in first-rate pianists, violinists and cellists.

In their decisions on literature, the theatre and the cinema Zhdanov and the Central Committee did, in fact, little more than harden a government and Party policy which had, in practice, been pursued for many years. But the Reform of Music in January/February 1948 was much more startling and revolutionary. For here was a case of knocking down idols who had been built up and worshipped for years by the Party and government press; and the theory Zhdanov put forward, that the great reputations of Shostakovich, Prokofiev, Khachaturian and Miaskovsky had merely been built up by "a clique of sycophantic critics" and racketeers was simply not true. In September 1944, *Bolshevik*, the organ of the Central Committee of the Communist Party, had proclaimed Shostakovich's 7th Symphony to be the work of a genius of the first magnitude. Later, *Culture and Life*, another organ of the Central Committee, expressed some disappointment over Shostakovich's 9th Symphony; but it still referred to him as "the composer of immense talent, of whom our Soviet country is so justly proud".

It was, somehow, generally accepted by everyone in Russia, whether they liked symphonies or not, that the Soviet Union was miles ahead of any other country in this branch of music. It was commonly said that the West had stopped producing great orchestral music, but that in Russia this form of art was flourishing as it had not flourished in the West for forty years or more. When Shostakovich's 7th Symphony was accepted only with reservations by critics in Britain and America, the Russians were outraged. The Soviet propaganda organizations had boosted it abroad as a work at least as great as anything written by Beethoven. The buxom Madame Kislova of VOKS (Society of Cultural Relations with Foreign Countries) snorted at the very suggestion that there were any living real composers outside the country of Prokofiev, Shostakovich, Khachaturian, and Miaskovsky. Stalin Prizes were showered, year after year, on the Big Four; Prokofiev scarcely knew what to do with all that money. Then, suddenly, in January 1948, Zhdanov was given the extraordinary job of explaining to the country and to the world at large that it had all been a dreadful mistake, a terrible racket, and that the great composers of Soviet symphonic music were little more than a bunch of artistic spivs, un-Soviet and even anti-Soviet in their activities, "anti-people", formalist, divorced from reality, and, in short, unwanted by the peoples of the Soviet Union.

The way it all started was rather odd. On 7th November 1947, the Soviet Union celebrated the thirtieth anniversary of the Revolution. It seems that the leading Soviet composers did not take the thing seriously enough. Shostakovich, in his spare time, wrote a sort of fantasy on some of the most popular army songs and other ditties; but he was more interested in thinking out his 10th Symphony and a violin concerto. Miaskovsky, who had written many works "for the occasion" in the past, did not

24

bother this time. Prokofiev was too busy completing his 6th
Symphony, which he himself thought as good as the 5th; it was
going to be played in Moscow for the first time on 25th
December, and was to be followed, on the same night, by
a symphonic poem by Khachaturian—this one very specially
written in honour of the thirtieth anniversary of the Revolution.
(It turned out an unhappy idea.) Finally, in the last days of
December, there was going to be the *première*—at a "closed"
performance—of a new Soviet opera by a mediocre, youngish
composer, Vano Muradeli, a Russified Georgian.* This also had
been "specially" written to celebrate the thirtieth anniversary of
the Revolution.

Twenty-fifth December was just an ordinary working-day in
Moscow. For the British there it was still Christmas; but the new
Prokofiev symphony, conducted by the great Leningrad con-
ductor, Mravinsky, was something not to be missed, even if
it meant arriving late at Sir Maurice Peterson's Christmas
party. For a fortnight ahead all tickets had been sold out (I had
to resort to a ticket-profiteer and pay three times the marked
price). On the stair, leading up to the hall, I met one of the
VOKS critics, a man called Sneerson, who wrote a lot of articles
boosting Soviet music for publication in the United States. "I
heard it in Leningrad," he said. "It is wonderful; better than the
usual Prokofiev. It is philosophic, has the depth of Shostakovich.
You'll see!" (Poor Sneerson; for a long time after that concert
nothing was heard or seen of him, until finally, many months
later, he emerged in a musical magazine with an article—
denouncing the degeneracy of American jazz!) But in December
1947, Sneerson still ranked as an authority on Soviet music,
and the programme notes of the 6th Symphony were written
by him; he talked about the depth and lyrical pathos of the
first two movements—qualities which, he said, had long been
suspected in Prokofiev, but which had now blossomed forth
as never before. . . .

It is one of the most beautiful, most exalted of his works, imbued
with the creative spirit of Soviet humanism. . . . It is a great landmark not only in the art of Prokofiev, but in the whole history
of Soviet symphonism. . . . This great work shows once again

* He had distinguished himself in 1945 by composing a "sublime" *Song of
Beria!*

how immeasurably superior Soviet music is to the music of the capitalist West, where symphonism has long ceased to be an art of lofty ideas and high emotionalism and is now in a state of profound decadence and degeneration. . . .

In analysing the themes and development of the work, Sneerson said that while it was not programme music, it nevertheless "reflected the deep feelings of Soviet humanity after war and victory".

I would hesitate personally to comment on a symphony after hearing it only once, except to say that, after the slow and, for Prokofiev, unusual first two movements, one of which had a strange intensity at times almost reminiscent of Skriabin, there came the exuberant, joyful, wildly humorous finale in the best gay-Prokofiev tradition, which made you sit back in your chair chuckling and chortling. The symphony was not to be played in Russia until several years later, in 1948; it was condemned out-of-hand by the authorities as "formalist". How many times, one wondered, could they have heard it? And what kind of authorities on music were these "authorities"? On the day after the concert, *Pravda* published a short notice saying that the audience had been "very appreciative" in listening to the Prokofiev and Khachaturian works.

This, in fact, was not quite true; nobody cared much for the Khachaturian *Poem*, which was a noisy, bombastic *tour de force*, with the organ playing full blast nearly all the time and twenty-three "trombone soloists" blaring away, in addition to the usual orchestra. Whether "formalist" or not, it was crude and eccentric. But beyond that brief *Pravda* notice, nothing more was said in the press about the two new Prokofiev and Khachaturian works. It was obvious, during those last weeks of December, that "something was up". Inside the Composers' Union, at the Bolshoi Theatre and elsewhere, some kind of row was going on. The general public knew little or nothing about it; but musicians, when one talked to them, seemed uneasy. Some whispered that things were working up to some sort of crisis, though few knew what the real trouble was; above all, no one suspected that the Party was preparing to strike a blow of such shattering force. Perhaps, as in 1936, when *Pravda* attacked Shostakovich for his opera *Lady Macbeth of Mtsensk*, this or that work would be singled out for abuse and derision; but no one thought that all

Russia's most famous composers would be thrown off their pedestals.

Yet it happened. And it began, in the strangest way imaginable, over Vano Muradeli's new opera called *The Great Fellowship*. It had already been tried out in the provinces; and, since no one thought Muradeli anything but a third-rate composer, no one could get particularly excited at the prospect of seeing his opera —even at the Bolshoi Theatre. The *première* took place some time about the New Year, and it was a "closed" performance. It is said that Stalin attended; certainly Zhdanov was there, with some 500 other people—members of the Central Committee and others. Zhdanov later claimed that it was a "sufficiently cultured" audience to appreciate the faults and virtues of a new opera. How "cultured" the audience really was may be surmised from the remark made later in January at Zhdanov's conference of musicians by Livanova, the distinguished musicologist, who said she was unable to get a ticket for the Muradeli *première*, "even though all kinds of people from the Food and Fish Ministries were there". Anyway, Stalin or Zhdanov, or both, did not care for the new opera; and it seems that, at the end of the performance, there was an ugly row, so ugly that Leontiev, the Director of the Bolshoi Theatre, had a heart attack, and died.

Only a very short notice appeared in the press, simply recording his sudden death. Nothing was said about the closed performance of Muradeli's opera, but soon the news began to seep through that there was, in the musical world, "just one hell of a row". Then, suddenly, works by modern Soviet composers were omitted from concerts. Richter, already then the greatest Soviet pianist, was to play Prokofiev's new (9th) Sonata; when the time came, he played some Schubert instead—without explanation. Worse still, some arrests were made amongst some familiar figures in the musical world.* This was no doubt intended to be a

---

* Among these was a good friend of mine, the well-known musicologist David Rabinovich, a charming lively little man bubbling over with enthusiasm for modern Soviet music, and especially for his idol and close personal friend, Dimitri Shostakovich. It was while having dinner with "Dodik", as he was known to all Moscow, that I first met Shostakovich in the summer of 1942. Charged, apparently, with "treasonable" contacts with foreign correspondents, among them Robert Magidoff (who was soon afterwards expelled from Russia as an American spy) "Dodik" was arrested in early February 1948, taken to the particularly sinister NKVD prison at Lefortovo, and sent to a camp for

salutary warning to the rest. And then, before long, it was learned—this was about the middle of January—that an important conference of composers and musicians was taking place in the building of the Central Committee of the CP under the chairmanship of Zhdanov.

Various more or less apocryphal stories about this meeting—for instance, that Prokofiev sat on a piano stool, with his back rudely turned to Zhdanov—began to circulate in Moscow. Moreover, the Party also used at that time its technique of rumour-launching, which had already so successfully worked at the time of the monetary reform in December. All kinds of people started saying, nobody knew on what basis, that Zhdanov was a most accomplished musician and a graduate of the Leningrad Conservatory. This "fact" had never been recorded in any official biography of Zhdanov, and the suddenness with which this now became common knowledge was peculiar. Later inquiries showed that there was not a word of truth in the story; but the public nevertheless acquired the idea that Zhdanov was a great musical expert. That this was untrue was admitted at the Composers' Congress in April even by the sycophantic Zakharov. "Comrade Zhdanov," he declared, "is no professional musician. But oh, how well he knows folk song! When he recently visited our Piatnitsky Choir, we asked him: 'Is it true, Comrade Zhdanov, that you know 600 folk songs?' 'No,' he said, 'not 600, but I suppose I do know about 300.' How much better our composers would write if they knew folk songs as Andrei Alexandrovich does!"

At last, on 10th February, the papers published the Central Committee's Decree on Music. It was a most extraordinary document, and much grimmer than anybody had anticipated. It started with an attack on Muradeli's opera. The music, it said, was poor and unexpressive, and without a single melody or aria one could remember. "This opera is chaotic and inharmonious, full of continuous discords which hurt one's ears. Some allegedly melodious passages are suddenly broken off by noises unsuitable to normal human hearing. . . . The vocal side of

---

many years. He did not reappear in Moscow until about 1955. He has since been writing numerous articles and books on Soviet music, including a monograph on Shostakovich and another on famous Soviet pianists.

the opera produces a feeble impression." Further, in writing this opera Muradeli had failed to make good use of the songs and the dance tunes of the peoples of the northern Caucasus, or to learn from the experience of the classical Russian opera, "which is rich in content and melody, and is marked by elegant, beautiful, and clear musical forms which have made the Russian opera the finest opera in the world, and a form of music particularly loved by the people".

After criticizing the libretto for having misrepresented the historic facts of the Civil War years in the Caucasus (there was no enmity, the Central Committee asserted, between the Russian and Georgian peoples at that time, as the libretto made out) the Decree went on:

> The Central Committee considers that the failure of Muradeli's opera is the result of his having followed the formalist road—a road that has been so pernicious to the work of Societ composers. As long ago as 1936, in connection with Shostakovich's new opera, *Lady Macbeth of Mtsensk*, the formalism and anti-people perversions in Shostakovich's music were sharply criticized by *Pravda*. . . .
>
> Despite these warnings, and despite the Central Committee's more recent decisions on literature, the cinema, and the theatres, Soviet music has so far failed to pull itself together. The occasional successes of a few composers who have written songs which became popular with the people, and the music written for some films, etc., do not alter the general picture.
>
> The state of affairs is particularly bad in the case of symphonic and operatic music. The Central Committee has here in mind those composers who persistently adhere to the formalist and anti-people school—a school which has found its fullest expression in the works of composers like Comrades Shostakovich, Prokofiev, Khachaturian, Shebalin, Popov, Miaskovsky and others. Their works are marked by formalist perversions, anti-democratic tendencies which are alien to the Soviet people and their artistic tastes.
>
> Typical of this music is the rejection of the basic principles of classical music, and the preaching of atonalism, dissonance and dis-harmony, which are alleged to be signs of "progress" and "innovation"; the rejection of so important a thing as melody; and a striving after chaotic and neuropathic discords and accumulations of sounds. This music savours of the present-day modernist bourgeois music of Europe and America—a music which reflects the *marasme* of bourgeois culture.

The Decree then deplored the excessive interest shown by these composers in instrumental music and their "un-Russian" lack of interest in vocal music.

Ignoring the best traditions of Russian and Western classical music, which they treat as "out-of-date", "old-fashioned" and "conservative", and haughtily looking down on those composers who conscientiously try to adopt and develop the methods of classical music as advocated of "primitive traditionalism", and representatives of "epigonism" ... many Soviet composers are also ignoring the requirements and artistic tastes of the Soviet peoples, and are happy to live in a narrow circle of specialists and gourmets. Disregarding the great social role of music, they are content to cater to the degenerate tastes of a handful of aesthetizing individualists.

Here is really the crux of the matter. Music for the few, or music for the people? But the Central Committee, or rather Zhdanov, who obviously wrote the Decree, over-simplified the whole matter to a monstrous extent, by attributing all kinds of crimes (atonalism, for instance) to composers like Prokofiev and Miaskovsky, who were scarcely ever guilty of them, and by denying the existence of melody in composers who are extremely rich in melody—at least in most of their works— as are Prokofiev, Miaskovsky and Khachaturian. If Shostakovich was not a melodist in the primitive sense—"a tune you pick up and hum right away"—he was, nevertheless, in his later works (for example his 3rd Quartet) a melodist of rare distinction, though his melodies were no more "sing-songy" than are, say, the melodies of the *Waldstein*, or the later Beethoven Sonatas. Equally significant was the patronage given by Zhdanov to those who "conscientiously try" to copy Russian classical music and the protection he gave them against the contempt of the high-brows, who considered it old-fashioned to be imitative. Small wonder that the small fry in the Russian musical world promptly behaved like a pack of hounds released by the master's hand. Years of accumulated envy were to be used by Zhdanov as a most effective weapon for downing the Big Four.

After deploring the fact that composers were insufficiently interested in writing choral music, songs, opera and popular music for small orchestras, the Decree proceeded:

The divorce between some Soviet composers and the people is so serious that these composers have been indulging in the rotten "theory" that the people are not sufficiently "grown-up" to appreciate their music. They think it is no use worrying if people won't listen to their complicated orchestral works, for in a few hundred years they will. This is a thoroughly individualist and anti-people theory, and it has encouraged some of our composers to retire into their own shell.

This calls for comment. Throughout this whole controversy on music, one fact stands out: Zhdanov did not, at any point, give the slightest thought to so fundamental a question as musical perception by the listener. He constantly referred to the great popularity of Tchaikovsky. Why, he kept asking, was the public not so fond of modern composers? The answer is simple. Scarcely any musical work "registers" right away with the listener. In the past, the Soviet authorities had understood this; they did not allow music critics to write about a new work until they had heard it four times. Tchaikovsky's symphonies were popular because they were familiar; to listen to them required no great mental effort. What chance had a new Prokofiev or Miaskovsky symphony of becoming really popular—in the sense that Tchaikovsky or Rachmaninov was popular—if it is played once, or twice at most, by the Moscow radio? Even a simple tune requires to be heard several times to "catch on", as we know only too well from the Hollywood technique of "plugging". Much of the work of the Big Four was not "easy", though—with the exception of some of their earlier, eccentric and experimental works—it was not as a rule, shapeless, atonal, unintelligible or lacking in melody. Far from it; Prokofiev's *Ode to Stalin* (1937) for instance, had one of the fairest and noblest melodies in all music.

Another question to which Zhdanov gave no thought was that of musical culture. His criterion of a work (a very unfair criterion) was: "the people like this", or "the people don't like this". The idea of raising the musical tastes of the people was ignored. Yet a question inevitably arises: would not the people, like more "advanced" listeners, sooner or later reach a point when they would prefer an invigorating mountain climb with Prokofiev to the familiar Turkish bath of Tchaikovsky? That is, provided they had the chance to become sufficiently familiar with modern music.

Possibly this may have occurred to Zhdanov; but since he had clearly no desire himself to cultivate advanced musical tastes, he considered that it would be an unnecessary, harmful luxury to develop such tastes and interests among the people. In this he was, of course, consistent: since literature, plays and films were expected to make a mass appeal and, as far as possible, an immediate appeal to the simplest and least refined reader and spectator, the same criterion should apply to music. Yet there was something extraordinarily arbitrary and irresponsible in the tributes he paid to the "classical heritage". Actually, your untrained *kolkhoznik* on his farm would be as acutely bored by a recital of Bach preludes and fugues as by a Shostakovich symphony. But, for Zhdanov, Bach was a "classic": the criterion of "popularity" no longer held good.

The most comic example of this inconsistency was provided by the case of Skriabin. If ever there was a composer who suffered from *all* the vices which Zhdanov attributed to Shostakovich, Prokofiev, Khachaturian and Miaskovsky, it was surely Skriabin, who was guilty of atonalism in the most extreme form, disharmony, acute and morbid "neuropathic" egocentricity, total un-Russianism in his themes; and who was, in fact, more "anti-people" than anything in the whole of Russian music. But no! Skriabin was sacrosanct—a classic, who was lucky enough to die in 1915, two years before the Revolution. Had he been still alive in 1948, one shudders to think what Zhdanov would have said. But when somebody called Steinpress very reasonably pointed out in an article in *Soviet Literature*, at the height of the controversy, that if ever there was a degenerate formalist of the worst sort, it was Skriabin and that Soviet listeners should be saved from the degrading experience of having to listen to him, the "lowbrow" pundits of the Composers' Union rose like one man to the defence of Skriabin, and publicly called the ludicrously consistent and over-zealous Mr. Steinpress an ass.

The decree went on to say that the influence of the formalists, especially Shostakovich and Prokofiev, was having a disastrous effect on the training of new musicians; in particular, the Moscow Conservatory (with Shebalin as its director) was a hotbed of formalism. "The work of many of the pupils of the Conservatories in the Soviet Union is blind imitation of Shostakovich and Prokofiev." The critics, too, were blameworthy for praising these composers' subjectivism, constructivism, extreme individualism and the professional complexity of their musical language—contrary to all the canons of socialist realism. Finally various government and other organizations must be held culpably responsible for the dominant position the "formalists" had acquired.

The Organizational Committee of the Union of Soviet Composers became a weapon in the hands of the group of formalist composers and a source of formalist perversions. On the Committee there was a stale and rotten atmosphere, and an absence of creative discussion. The leaders of the Organizational Committee and their hangers-on, the critics, have been praising all kinds of anti-realist and modernist works to the skies, while realistic works, notable for their endeavour to continue the great classical traditions, were being dubbed second-rate, generally ignored, or treated with contempt. Composers who claim to be arch-revolutionary in their music acted, on the Committee, like ultra-conservatives, full of haughty intolerance towards the slightest criticism.

All this, said the Decree, was intolerable.

In recent years, the standard of our people's musical taste has risen very high. The Soviet people expect from their composers works of high quality and high ideological content—whether they be operas, symphonies, songs, choral works or dance music. In our country composers have unlimited creative possibilities, and all the conditions necessary for a glorious future of musical culture. Soviet composers have an audience the like of which no composer in the past ever had. It would be unforgiveable if they did not avail themselves of these rich opportunities and did not turn their creative efforts along the right road of realism.

The Central Committee therefore decreed:

(1) To condemn the formalist tendency in Soviet Music as being anti-people and leading to the liquidation of music.

(2) To propose to the Propaganda and Agitation Department of the Central Committee of the CPSU and to the Government Art Committee that they take the necessary steps for improving the state of affairs in Soviet music, and liquidate the faults enumerated in the present decree. . . .

(3) To call upon Soviet composers to become more conscious of their duties to the Soviet people . . . and assure a great upsurge of creative activity which would lead to the creation of high-quality works worthy of the Soviet people.

Needless to say, though it caused real consternation among a large part of the Moscow intelligentsia, the decree was said by the press to have delighted "the Soviet people". To prove this, *Pravda*, *Izvestia* and other papers published, for three or four days, a spate of letters from workers and *kolkhozniks* congratulating the Central Committee on what they had done. The theme of these letters was always the same: "Why is it that, when I listen on the radio on the Piatnitsky Choir of Song and Dance, or to bits of Tchaikovsky's *Eugene Onegin*, I really enjoy myself and when I listen to all that modern stuff of Shostakovich and Prokofiev, I don't?" As an example of "bad" music, Shostakovich was more frequently mentioned than the others. Significant again; for against Shostakovich Zhdanov had a particular spite. He was too subtle, too delicate a personality to tolerate in Moscow, 1948. The fact that he was completely Russian, and completely Soviet, having spent all his conscious life under the Soviet system, and having scarcely ever been abroad, made it all the worse. Moreover, Zhdanov had a vague feeling that Shostakovich was also a typical product of Leningrad, which he had always suspected of being too independent-minded and rebellious at heart. That delicate boyish face, with its pale-blue eyes that seemed to know so much, was irritating. It is perhaps no accident that the Central Committee's 1946 Reform of Literature should have started with Zhdanov's savage attack on the Leningrad writers.

The publication of the Decree followed the January conference of musicians, but it was not until after its publication that a verbatim report of the conference was issued. This report is of outstanding interest in that it allows the reader to peep through a window of the Central Committee's headquarters. He can watch one of the highest members of the Politburo preside over a "free discussion" by people, many of whom were, obviously, in hearty disagreement with him, but many of whom were, also, extremely nervous and almost hypnotized by his presence. Some, like Shebalin, the director of the Moscow Conservatory, who felt that he had been unjustly attacked, both as a composer and an administrator, spoke up boldly and counter-attacked. Not, indeed, Zhdanov—nobody dared attack him or question his judgement directly—but he let fly at some of the "popular music" representatives, who had Zhdanov's full support. Speeches of a high standard were made by a few, notably Knipper, a gifted young composer both of popular hits like *Polushke-Polye*, and also of distinguished symphonic works. But, in the discussion, Zakharov, composer of pseudo-folksongs, was triumphant. Not only did he know that the popular song writers were now going to be officially proclaimed the most useful and valuable members of the musical community; he wanted to make sure that the highbrows, who had been receiving so much attention and adulation, should be proclaimed useless parasites. The Central Committee meeting was the hour of his revenge: he announced with venom and glee, and with obvious approval from Zhdanov, that *all* the symphonic music written by the Big Four was worthless.

That Zhdanov fully approved of this line may be seen from the fact that, in his two speeches, there was no reference to a single achievement in that field; the implication was that all that the symphonists had written was, if not bad, at any rate, *unwanted*. Zakharov also felt that he would now hold a high administrative post on the Organizational Committee of the Composers' Union, and would from there actively dictate musical policy to the other musicians. It meant the end of the *laissez-faire* regime, in which the Big Four, more interested in composing music than in musical politics, were at the head of the Composers' Union. That they tended to look down on the small fry is, of course, true; and the whole Central Committee discussion gives one an insight into the hatred, intrigue and envy that existed among the members of the Composers' Union. And how jubilant and bursting with *schadenfreude* the envious lowbrows now were! Typical of this attitude was that of Khrennikov, who had written a couple of fair symphonies but, having failed to be acclaimed as a great composer, took to writing cinema music and "popular" songs—some, like his popular *Song of Moscow*, of striking vulgarity, and triviality. Khrennikov must have known, at the time of the Central Committee discussion, that he was the most likely candidate for the presidency of the Composers' Union "under new management". But the worst exhibition of cringing and self-flagellation was that of Muradeli—the Muradeli who, nominally, was at the root of all the trouble. He ate dirt with relish, and went out of his way to have all the leading composers take part of the blame, indeed most of the blame, for the failure of his opera. Shostakovich and others not unnaturally thought that Muradeli was himself primarily responsible for his failures.

Shostakovich made two statements which cannot be taken at their face value. They were the words of a great artist, utterly bewildered by what was happening, and making all sorts of irrelevant remarks, regardless of the fact that a very large part of the whole discussion was directed against him personally, and against his music. His promise, at the end of his second statement, to be good, and his thanks to the Party for all its fatherly care, were part of a pathetic human document. They were the words of a man—still only just over forty—who felt himself crushed and beaten, but who saw no future for himself except in a world where he would henceforth be bossed by Zhdanovs and Zakharovs, and who still hoped against hope that somehow he, Shostakovich, would find a place in it. Perhaps even plain personal, material considerations, combined with the feeling that (for better or for worse) he *belonged* to Soviet Russia till the end of his days, accounted for that pathetically meek behaviour of Shostakovich in the midst of people so many of whom were his enemies.

Miaskovsky's case was tragic in a different way. He had devoted all his life to the cause of musical culture in Russia; by 1948 he had written twenty-five symphonies, besides numerous other orchestral works and chamber music. All his music was of a high professional standard, and some of it remarkable—for example, his 6th Symphony, his 25th Symphony, some of his quartets and his piano music. His works were often described as being "in the Tchaikovsky tradition", though in reality they are much more in the tradition of Brahms and Rimsky-Korsakov; but, less original, admittedly, than Shostakovich or Prokofiev, he could not fairly be classed as an imitative composer. He began to compose long before the Revolution—in 1907. To adapt himself to new Soviet conditions was a difficult and painful task, and some of his inner conflicts are reflected in his profoundly moving 6th Symphony. But in the end this "old intellectual" adapted himself to new conditions and took a deep joy in the thought that he, Miaskovsky, had succeeded in forming the bridge between the great era of pre-Revolutionary Russian music —especially the Rimsky-Korsakov school—and the young generation of composers.

He never became very popular—perhaps for the simple reasons that he wrote too much and was not performed nearly often enough. He would write a symphony each year; it would be performed, usually only once; polite notices would be published; then perhaps the Moscow radio would play it once or twice; and then—then Miaskovsky would write another symphony. He had, however, his small circle of friends who closely studied and loved his work, and no doubt he thought that in time he would become popular. There was nothing in most of his music that did not make easy acceptance by a large public possible. He was not ambitious, and sincerely admired his more loudly praised younger rivals, Shostakovish, Prokofiev and Khachaturian, and at *premières* of their works one invariably saw Miaskovsky in the audience, visibly happy to hear a fine new work by a Russian composer. He himself composed, as Rimsky-Korsakov used to compose, methodically, day after day—not in fits and starts.

There was something noble in the little man, whose neat grey beard and fine features made him look like one of the more lovable characters of a Chekhov play. With diligence he composed, and composed, and seemed a happy man, untouched by envy. And then, all hell broke loose; wild accusations of "formalism" and "anti-people" tendencies were hurled against him, as against the others. He reacted differently from Shostakovich and Prokofiev; the coarseness and the injustice of it all made him sick and disgusted; he did not go to Zhdanov's meeting, and later, when the decree was published, he was the bitterest man in the whole of Russia. He was sixty-eight; all his lifework was declared to be useless; he felt a broken man, and ignored all attempts to drag him into any further discussions. He ignored the summons addressed to him by the Composers' Congress in April, and the votes of censure passed on him meant nothing to him. He died a sad and embittered man three years later, in 1951. In recent years his music has become increasingly popular in Russia, though not yet in the West.

Whether Prokofiev was at the Zhdanov meeting, I am not sure. Rumour in Moscow had it that he was there, and that he behaved truculently, but in the verbatim report there is no record of his having been present. Prokofiev later wrote to the Composers' Union; I shall quote his letter later.

One receives an insight into many other strange happenings from reading the verbatim report—happenings in newspaper offices where favourable criticisms of a musical work were turned, without the critic's knowledge, into unfavourable ones, and *vice versa*; happenings at the Composers' Union where the authority of a *Pravda* or *Culture and Life* article had the effect of paralysing all independent judgement, and where "open" discussion was often absolutely different from the lobby talk. The report also throws some light on the role of the Art Committee, and its unfortunate chief, Khrapchenko, who apparently did his best to encourage the Big Four, and now brought upon himself the wrath of the Central Committee. That sycophancy and cowardice, bordering on panic, were also common enough in that Moscow world of music was made particularly apparent by the courageous speech of the Director of the Moscow Conservatory, Shebalin—particularly when he told of the panic caused at the Conservatory among some people at the thought that they might displease the Party authorities by playing some modern Soviet music—even at a "closed" concert!

A strange case was that of Professor Goldenweiser, a veteran of the Conservatory, and an old friend of Tolstoy's, Rachmaninov's and Skriabin's. His warning against lowering the professional standard of music was, no doubt, sound enough; but in view of his loud praise of Skriabin, one cannot explain his attack on Prokofiev and Shostakovich except by personal enmity, or a desire to keep in with the authorities. Unlike some others, he did not even have the courage to stand up for Miaskovsky. There were also a few pathetically comic remarks, such as the complaint by Dzerjinsky, the composer of numerous rather indifferent operas, that "nobody wrote about him". But the greater part of the discussion really revolved round the strangely anti-Marxist demand made by Zhdanov himself that modern composers should, in effect, write "like Glinka and Tchaikovsky", and not be afraid of being "epigones"—which really amounted to saying that twentieth-century Soviet music should speak the language of mid-nineteenth-century Tsarist Russia! Another ever-recurring theme—and a very important one—to be found in the speeches of the "opposition" was that, while they admitted certain errors and failures and pleaded guilty to occasional "formalist" lapses, they were insistent that the work of the Big Four should not be

dismissed *en bloc* as bad, and that a distinction should be made
between their successful and their unsuccessful works. But the
general tendency of Zhdanov was to condemn all their music as
bad. And this, indeed, was suggested by the decree, of which he
undoubtedly was the author.

It was said that this conference with the musicians was a "democratic" discussion, since everybody was allowed to express his
views. But the truth is that in the end, it was the Party (that is,
Zhdanov himself) who proclaimed to the country who was
right and who was wrong. Zhdanov's figure dominated the whole
debate. Not only did he open it; in effect, he also closed it,
and some of his brief remarks and questions during the discussion
were highly revealing. So also were the "cheers and laughter"
with which some of his jokes were greeted. Many at the conference behaved like schoolboys laughing at teacher's jokes.

The story of how the verbatim report was published is also
strange. In the middle of March 1948 the papers announced
that it would be published, and would, in a few days, be on sale.
But when it came to the point, only very few copies were
available. Full summaries of Zhdanov's speeches were published
in the press, but little else. Was it because the "opposition",
polite though they were, had still made out a very good case
against the Party line? Was it feared that their arguments, if
widely known, might weaken the effectiveness of the speeches
made by the new pundits of the Composers' Union and by
Zhdanov himself?

Before coming to the aftermath of the decree of 10th February,
it is important to get one point straight. What is "formalism",
as understood by the Soviet authorities in 1948? The answer, as
we now know, is this: "formalism" is, in fact, an insufficiently
wholehearted attitude towards Soviet communism. It is no
longer an aesthetic, but a political concept. Neither Zhdanov,
nor any of the new high officials of the Composers' Union, like
Khrennikov, said this in so many words; but it was explained,
with the authorities' obvious approval, by a woman musicologist,
N. Brusova, at the Composers' Meeting in Moscow soon after
the publication of the decree. She said:

> Formalism is usually considered to denote a lack of ideas, a lack
> of content, a complete concentration on form . . . with no reference
> to reality. In "theory" classes our pupils are sometimes taught to

write such exercises in composition. Such "works" are sometimes also written by composers, when they are not creatively alive. . . .

But when we speak of formalism today, we mean something entirely different. One cannot say that the works of Shostakovich, Prokofiev, Miaskovsky, Khachaturian and others are completely divorced from life and reality, or completely lacking in content. Nevertheless, these works have a strong formalist basis. We feel that there is something in these works that prevents them from penetrating simply and directly into our consciousness, and prevents us from seeing life and the world reflected in the feeling and consciousness of these composers. Undoubtedly the composers, or the more truthful among them, felt this too, even before the Decree, but refused fully to realize it, and believed that things were all right as they were, and that, without this camouflage, their works would not be on "a sufficiently high level".

This, however, is not the kind of camouflage you can simply rub off, the kind of mist that will lift, after which there will shine a pure, clear, sunny reality in all its radiance. These men do not lack vision; their vision is distorted.

Socialist realism, as we know, does not require from the artist any sort of abstract objectivism, but an understanding of the true road of life. . . . Formalism manifests itself whenever the composer shows an insufficient creative will to follow this road of life's fundamentals to the utmost limit of his consciousness. If he is creatively lazy, he will stop at the beginning of the road, and the thread that leads him to the final goal snaps. His musical images, as a result, become vague, incomplete, and distorted.

When this happens, it may be due not only to laziness, but to a lack of boldness and courage. Hence the tendency to imitate Western bourgeois art and contemporary modernism. In such cases the composer has not the strength to look our great future straight in the face. . . . The composer must struggle against this tendency to distort, against this laziness, this lack of courage; and in this struggle he should be greatly helped by the stern, but friendly care shown him by the Party.

We know of examples when formalists have successfully overcome these difficulties. . . . We accept with all our heart Khachaturian's "Song of Stalin" in his *Poem of Stalin*. We cannot fail to hear something that is very near and dear to us in Shostakovich's 7th Symphony. . . . This shows that there are great sources of strength in our Soviet composers.

Any deviations from the true road, any mental laziness and lack of creative courage, are, therefore, all the more inexcusable among men who live in the land of the Soviets, who have been brought up on the teaching of Marx, Lenin and Stalin, and who see before themselves, the great road of the Soviet people towards communism, the highest stage of life.

This is important as a definition of formalism, even though to many Western ears it may sound like gibberish. Brusova's observations were, in fact, tolerant in comparison with the still more "official" line taken, after the CC Decree, by the new chiefs of the Composers' Union—Zakharov, Khrennikov and Chulaki—who had replaced the disgraced Khachaturian, Shostakovich, Kabalevsky and the rest of the "formalists".

At two further conferences—the meeting of Moscow composers and music critics in February, soon after the Decree, and the All-Union Composers' Congress in April—Khrennikov, the new Secretary-General of the Composers' Union, laid down the Party line in two very long speeches, each purporting to be a history of Soviet music since the Revolution.

In these two speeches Khrennikov performed, before the musicians, the same function that Fadeyev had performed at the Writers' Union. There was not one appreciative word about a single one of the "condemned" composers.

Miaskovsky was mentioned only a few times—once, in connection with his 6th Symphony, of which Khrennikov said: "The Revolution [here] appears as something fearful and chaotic, breaking into the artist's life. Reality appears as something fearful and horrible to the depressed artist." Not a word of tribute to the great work done by Miaskovsky in maintaining the high professional traditions of Russian music.

In a casual reference, his 12th (*Kolkhoz*) Symphony was quoted simply as an indication that, at one point of his career, he was beginning to get a glimmering of what was wanted, but did not stick to the "only right road".

Khachaturian, too, was mentioned only briefly, and then only in connection with his less successful works, such as his Cello Concerto and his *Symphonic Poem*, which, like Prokofiev's *Ode on the End of the War* (with its harps, eight pianos, brass, and no strings), is an amusing extravaganza and no more. (It is true that the lack of solemnity shown by both these composers on two such solemn occasions as the end of the war and the thirtieth anniversary of the Revolution was enough to rub many an earnest Party member the wrong way.) Khachaturian's fine and popular violin and piano concertos and ballet music were simply ignored.

When he came to Shostakovich and Prokofiev, Khrennikov's treatment of "history" was really a masterpiece of "Marxist" distortion. In his early Leningrad days, Shostakovich undoubtedly did dabble for a time in Western modernism; there was, especially in Leningrad during the twenties, a vogue for modern German composers like Alban Berg and Hindemith. Shostakovich was a youth of infinite vitality and curiosity; Russia had started on her new revolutionary existence, and, for young composers, it was a period of *Sturm und Drang*. Mayakovsky was the poet of that age. Small wonder if young Shostakovich threw himself into that exciting, extravagant world of novelty and experiment. Yet he had a sense of moderation where his work was concerned; his 1st Symphony, which took Russia by storm, and made him world-famous, was a work of extraordinary freshness, and beauty, and not "modernist" in any sense open to criticism. But did Khrennikov as much as mention it? No. Instead, he concentrated all the guns of his heavy sarcasm on Shostakovich's admittedly "silly period", when he wrote his ultra-modernist, deliberately disharmonious, though tremendously dynamic, 2nd and 3rd Symphonies, and delighted in extravagant and *grotesque* forms, which were to find their fullest expression in his opera *The Nose*, based on Gogol's equally *grotesque* and "surrealist" story.

Shostakovich's *Nose* is an extravaganza, and also a "period piece" just as much as Mayakovsky's *Misteria-Bouffe*, Meyerhold's production of Gogol's *Revisor*, the drawings of Nathan Altman, and the "industrial" ballets and music of Deshevov and Mossolov were period pieces. If anything, they showed that Shostakovich was very much a child of his age; and in those early years of the Revolution—up to the late 1920s, when Stalin became the supreme boss in all things—nobody was seriously expected to be "traditionalist". Did anybody ever ask Mayakovsky to "write like Pushkin"—or ask young Shostakovich, for that matter, to "write like Tchaikovsky"?

Young Shostakovich, perhaps with the success of his 1st Symphony gone to his head, was no doubt exuberant and rather silly at times. However, the taboos of the "Zhdanov Era" had not yet come into force, and Shostakovich was, in those days, a most uninhibited young man. And so, in 1934, he composed his *Lady Macbeth of Mtsensk*, based on that powerful Leskov story of a monstrously wicked and sensuous woman. There was something in the subject that specially attracted him.

But let us face it. Today, in decent communist society, sex is profoundly shocking (and this applies just as much to 1968 as to 1948). I remember, soon after the decree of 10th February, meeting Khrennikov at a Molotov reception. He started talking about Shostakovich's *Lady Macbeth of Mtsensk* and was positively grundyish. "Ugh," he said, "why, he gives you a musical rendering of—ugh!—the Sexual Act!!" I remarked that, after all, Wagner had done much the same in *Tristan* and the *Walküre*. "Ugh, yes, horrible," said Khrennikov, "but Shostakovich is *even more naturalistic, even more horrible!*"*

Khrennikov, in his "history", did not mention Shostakovich's 5th Symphony, which according to all the views expressed since 1938 showed that he had mended his ways and had taken to writing good, serene, intelligible and beautiful music. (The official theory now was that he had been "over-praised", and that the 5th Symphony had not nearly enough socialist realism in it.) Khrennikov could not, however, ignore the famous 7th (*Leningrad*) Symphony altogether:

> Shostakovich's musical thought turned out to be more suitable for depicting the sinister images of Hitlerism and his own world of subjective reflections than for giving substance to the heroic images of our age. The abstract atonalism, the cosmopolitan musical language of Shostakovich who, even during the war, did not try to come any nearer the musical language of our people, have prevented the 7th Symphony from being lastingly popular.

The rest of Shostakovich's later work was dismissed by Khrennikov as "frantically gloomy and neurotic". In this, of course, there was a grain of truth: Shostakovich is a highly sensitive artist, he has his moments of deep gloom and "neuroticism", and is incapable of seeing the whole of life through the eyes of a *Pravda* editorial.

Soon after the decree, a Bulgarian government delegation,

---

* It was not until long after Stalin's death that a somewhat revised version of *Lady Macbeth of Mtsensk* reappeared in Soviet opera houses.

with Georgi Dimitrov at its head, came to Moscow, and gave a reception. The decree had made a deplorable impression abroad, and had, of course, played into the hands of every kind of anti-Soviet propagandist. *Time* and *Life* and *Newsweek* had all become terrific Shostakovich fans, and defenders of all the "persecuted musicians". Khachaturian, obviously sent to the Bulgarian party to do a little counter-propaganda among the foreign correspondents and diplomats, was perfectly willing to talk. His line was that "it shouldn't be taken too seriously": the Central Committee, in its decree, had simply laid down certain principles and given certain indications, and it would now be for the composers themselves to sort out the good from the bad. And he added, a little wistfully:

"There is going to be a reassessment of a lot of things; some of the works that I considered least important—such as some of my ballet music—will now be treated as important, and——"

"And your Violin Concerto," I said, "will be considered less important?"

"Well yes, I suppose so. Personally I prefer it to a lot of my other works—but things are going to be different now."

In fact, they were to become even more different than he had expected. In April *Pravda* reported with great approval that Chulaki, a little-known composer from Leningrad, who had just received a Stalin Prize for a "tuneful" symphony, had declared at the Composers' Congress: "Enough of these attempts to distinguish between the bad works and the good works of the formalist composers! All their works stink, and all these attempts to differentiate between good and bad are merely tricks for leaving a lot of loopholes open for a continuation of formalist influences in Soviet music!"

But as the "non-formalists" had not written any serious music of real worth, the "formalists" could not, in practice, be dispensed with altogether—at least for the present. For two months not a single work by Shostakovich, Prokofiev, Khachaturian, Miaskovsky or Shebalin was played anywhere in Moscow; the concert programmes were all Tchaikovsky, Beethoven, Schubert; Tchaikovsky, Rachmaninov, Brahms; Tchaikovsky, Grieg; Tchaikovsky. But, by the end of April, one or two Prokofiev works were allowed to be played, and the concert programmes for the winter, 1948-9, season included a sprinkling of Prokofiev, Khachaturian and Miaskovsky. Shostakovich did not figure in the list; but by May the Bolshoi Theatre had begun to play Prokofiev's *Romeo and Juliet* and *Cinderella* ballets again.

This did not mean that Prokofiev was in the Central Committee's good books again; indeed, Khrennikov's treatment of Prokofiev was just as vindictive as his treatment of any of the other "formalists". In his "historical" addresses, he went out of his way to make Prokofiev out to be an alien influence in Russian music. Having enumerated at length the foreign modernist, decadent, pathological, erotic, cacophonous, religious or sexually perverted monsters—including Oliver Messiaen, Jolivet, Hindemith, Alban Berg, Menotti, and Benjamin Britten*—Khrennikov proceeded to tell Prokofiev how wicked and Western *he* was. He ignored completely the fact that Prokofiev represented, around 1910, the healthiest possible reaction against the stale, Arensky type of drawing-room music on the one hand and against the true decadence of the Skriabin school on the other, and that Prokofiev was in music very much what Mayakovsky was in poetry. Instead, he went out of his way to identify Prokofiev with Stravinsky and Diaghilev—alleging that all three represented "closer to the West at any price" ideas, and that, in presenting an exotic, Petrushka-like vision of Russia to the West, all three lampooned their own country in front of foreign audiences. And "it all ended in Monte Carlo, where the Diaghilev Ballet found its right mission at last—to cater to an audience of gamblers, profiteers, and prostitutes", Khrennikov concluded.

Khrennikov, with characteristic meanness, than made capital out of the fact that Prokofiev was really an émigré (though, unlike Stravinsky, he had had the sense to return to Russia in 1934), and that vile foreign influences had marred his work through and through. Without saying a single word about Prokofiev's best work either before or after his return to Russia, Khrennikov dismissed all his later compositions as "formalist and unsuccessful". So is musical "history" written.

But one may guess that, for all his "Russianizing" and his genius, Prokofiev was considered fundamentally "too European"

---

* Of these, Hindemith and Benjamin Britten, at any rate, have not only been fully "rehabilitated" in Russia, but Soviet records have been made of many of their works.

and not really properly "Soviet". Whatever he did, he would be, even in his simplest works, essentially sophisticated.★

The first statement made by Prokofiev after the decree (it will be remembered that he did not speak—as far as is known—at the Zhdanov meeting) was a letter he sent to the musicians' meeting in Moscow soon after the decree was published. It was addressed jointly to Mr. Lebedev, who, as head of the Art Committee, had by now succeeded the unfortunate Mr. Khrapchenko, and to Khrennikov, who had succeeded Khachaturian as Secretary-General of the Composers' Union. In this letter Prokofiev paid all the necessary compliments to the Party, and promised to do his best in future, but in effect he rejected the general accusation against him as a "formalist". He made a concession to his addressees by blaming foreign influences for his earlier lapses.

The letter began by saying that, owing to ill-health, he was not able to attend the meeting, but that he wished to express his views about the CC's decree.

> This Decree . . . has separated the healthy tissues from the dead tissues in the work of our composers. However painful this may be to many composers, including myself, I welcome the Decree, which creates conditions for restoring the health of Soviet music. The Decree is valuable in having demonstrated how alien formalism is to the Soviet peoples. . . .
>
> There have been formalist elements in my music for the last fifteen or twenty years. The infection must have been caused through contact with certain Western currents. After *Pravda*'s criticism of Shostakovich's opera in 1936, I gave much thought to the whole question, and came to the conclusion that formalism was wrong. . . .
>
> As a result, I looked for a clearer musical language, and one with more content. In a number of my subsequent works I tried to get rid of formalist elements, and I believe I succeeded in this to some extent. . . . If there is still some formalism in some of my works it is probably due to my insufficient realization that our people do not want such music.

But Prokofiev's letter was not all humble pie. There is an undercurrent of sarcasm in the following passage, and a clear allusion to the Khrennikovs and Zakharovs, with their "popular hits":

★ Today Prokofiev is, of course, considered as "the greatest of all Soviet composers".

I never had the slightest doubt about the importance of melody, and consider it by far the most important element in music. *Nothing is more difficult than to discover a melody which would be immediately understandable even to the uninitiated listener and, at the same time, be original. Here the composer is beset by numerous dangers: he is apt to become trivial and vulgar, or else dish out a repetition of something already heard before.* In this connection I must say that the composition of complicated melodies is much easier than that of simple melodies. Sometimes it also happens that a composer messes about so long with a melody that, in the end, he lengthens and complicates it unduly. Such mistakes I have sometimes made myself. *One must be particularly vigilant to make a melody simple, but without allowing it to become cheap, sickly, or imitative rubbish.* (Italics added.)

Prokofiev then said that his lapses into atonalism were rare, and that he considered that the Schoenberg school of atonal music was getting nowhere. Regarding opera, he admitted that he had given preference to recitative, but that this was partly because he loved the theatre and hated to see actors singing away for an hour, glued to one spot, as they sometimes did in Wagner operas.

However, in the new opera he was now writing he would strike a happy medium. It would have as its subject Polevoi's *Story of a Real Man*—the tale of a heroic fighter-pilot who, after losing both legs, trained himself to become a fighter-pilot again. In this opera, he would make use of some of the folk-song material he had gathered in northern Russia, and would make the harmonies as simple as possible. In short, Prokofiev clearly went out of his way to show that he did not consider himself beaten, and that he was going to make the best of a bad job. What his private feelings were about the whole thing one can easily guess.*

The handling by the press and even by a periodical like *Soviet Music* of the two composers' meetings—one in February, the other in April—was extremely tendentious. Almost unlimited space was given to speeches supporting the Party line, while "opposition" speeches were reported in only a few words, accompanied by sarcastic comments. Thus, while Khrennikov's

---

* This opera was condemned outright at the end of 1948 by Khrennikov and the other "Zhdanovite" pundits of the Composers' Union, and was not produced in numerous Soviet opera houses until several years after Stalin's death.

speech at the February meeting was given nine pages in *Soviet Music*, Shebalin's was given ten lines, which began with the words: "Shebalin made an entirely unsatisfactory statement". In fact, what he really said was not revealed to the readers at all. The Central Committee having laid down the law, the "opposition" were not allowed any more publicity, except when they uttered words of repentance, as notably Shostakovich did. Miaskovsky ignored the meetings.

What was one to conclude from all this? Until the end of 1947, Russian music was the one art in Russia which, in terms of Western European values, still continued to thrive. Painting was artistically negligible. Literature was becoming more and more mechanical—except for a few rare books, which were almost like lucky flukes, such as a short novel by Kazakevich, called *The Star*. Music alone was not yet regimented. What was to be done? The composers, above all the "Big Composers", must be told to change their whole creative processes; they must write, not the sort of thing that they thought best, but what the Party thought best. In short, a high-quality trade must become a utility trade.

Some could adapt themselves to such demands more easily than others—not with joy but in a spirit of "Blast you! Take the damned thing!" That was, clearly, Khachaturian's attitude. Such was also perhaps Prokofiev's attitude—unless he felt sufficiently healthy and cynical to write a magnificent pastiche of a Glinka opera, just as, in the past, he had written his *Classical Symphony*—which is, in effect, a delicious pastiche of Mozart.*

Was all this victimization really necessary? The Party had surely had a good deal of experience in these matters. For years, it prided itself on having achieved wonderful results with an occasional warning, like the *Pravda* article on Shostakovich in 1936, followed by persuasion and encouragement. Granted that some 1947 works were not "satisfactory"—would not another warning have been sufficient? But that was clearly no longer Stalin's and Zhdanov's object. They did not want any more 5th

---

* Prokofiev's 7th Symphony, performed and published in 1949, was apparently composed on the "Blast-you, take-the-damned-thing!" principle. It was like an imitation of second-rate Glazunev or Glière. The Soviet press went into raptures over it as an example of the Party's "salutary influence" on Prokofiev!

Symphonies from Shostakovich; they wanted a clean sweep, so much so that if in 1948 Shostakovich had written something on the lines of the 5th Symphony, he would not have received loud praise, as he did in 1938, but abuse. The February Decree was infinitely more drastic than the mere Party *guidance* contained in the *Pravda* attack on Shostakovich in 1936. Was not the whole thing grossly overdone? For there was a vast difference between *guidance* and *dictation*.

Zhdanov died on 31st August, but his policy did not die with him. He had added, perhaps, to the whole process a kind of ruthlessness which others might have avoided. One feels that Shcherbakov, had he been alive, would have handled the matter rather differently. He did not love Zhdanov. Even so, Zhdanov's policy on music, as on literature, was part of a general policy of anti-*élite* and exclusively "popular" art. This, in turn, was part of the conditioning process through which the Soviet people had to be put before they attained the state of "complete communism", or before a war had started with America. Was this policy going to be modified? Perhaps the first promising sign of a reaction to the Zhdanov art policy was to be found in a 1949 attack on Gerasimov, the painter-laureate of the Stalin regime, in Komsomolskaya *Pravda*, which declared that his official paintings of Stalin, Lenin, etc., were lifeless, dreary, uninspiring and a bore. Perhaps it was a good sign, too, that soon after the death of Zhdanov, the Soviet press should have praised Shostakovich's music for the new film, *The Young Guard*, for being "realistic".

Three months after Zhdanov's death, there took place the Plenary Meetings of the Composers' Union in Moscow between 21st and 29th December 1948. During these meetings no fewer than a hundred new compositions were heard, and although some speakers complained that "it was all too much to take in, and to give a considered judgement on these new works", the officials of the Composers' Union, and especially Khrennikov—working in close contact with the Central Committee—felt themselves in a position to draw a number of conclusions.

The main conclusion was that Soviet music had successfully entered a new state, and that there was some progress to report as a result of the Zhdanov reform.

It seemed, nevertheless, curious that, of the works singled out for praise by Khrennikov, the majority should not have been works by Russian composers, but by non-Russians—the *Father-land Cantata* by Aratunian, an Armenian composer; a symphonic work by Amirov, an Azerbaijan composer; a *Stalin Cantata* by Wirkka, an Estonian; another *Stalin Cantata* by Tallat-Kelpsha, a Lithuanian; a violin concerto by Dvarionas, another Lithuanian; a piano concerto by Gasanov, a native of Daghestan in the Caucasus; and a *Simfonietta* by the Jewish composer, Weinberg. It is reasonable to suppose that a certain folk-lorish parochialism in some of these works must have appealed to the officials of the Composers' Union.

But what of the great highroad of Russian music? Apart from a few polite remarks about a new symphony by a young composer, V. Bunin, and two or three other works, there seemed very little to report. None of the pundits of the Composers' Union—Khrennikov and the rest—appear to have produced anything of the least importance—so busy were they, it seems, re-educating the others.

It was interesting and indeed gratifying to learn that, despite all the fearful knocks they had received, the Big Four and the other "formalists" had not given up. Even old Miaskovsky, bitterly hurt by the treatment he had suffered at the hands of Zhdanov, had, as usual, produced his annual symphony. Khrennikov said:

> The new works of the composers who were denounced by the Central Committee as formalists naturally attracted special attention at the Plenary Meetings. The most successful works by these composers were Shostakovich's music for the film *The Young Guard*, and a number of choral works by Muradeli. Extracts from Khachaturian's music for the new *Lenin* film, Miaskovsky's Symphony on *Russian Folk Themes*, and Shebalin's 7th Quartet showed that these composers were trying to take the road to realism, and were not altogether unsuccessful in their attempts. But the Plenary Meeting nevertheless found that there were still some formalist elements in their work, and that their transformation was proceeding rather slowly. (*Pravda*, 4th January 1949.)

Other leaders of the Composers' Union remarked that while these composers were now refraining from "the cruder manifestations of formalism", they were "not yet sufficiently organically welded to the ideals of communist civilization". To be damned with faint praise must have been almost welcome!

If Shostakovich was, a year ago, the principal target of the anti-formalists, Prokofiev now took the place of Surviving Formalist Number One.

Amongst the numerous speeches at the Plenary Meetings later reported in the press, there are none by the "formalists" or "ex-formalists"; the press reports of these meetings were extremely one-sided, and no unorthodox opinions were quoted at all.

It is curious that in spite of all the speeches made by Zhdanov and the other protagonists of "art for the people" in 1948, in favour of starting a splendid new era of Soviet opera, no opera (apart from Prokofiev's) should have been composed, and that the best works (in Khrennikov's estimation) produced in the last year should have been orchestral works, plus a few *Stalin* and *Fatherland* cantatas. True, Khrennikov and some others promised at the meeting to complete their operas "shortly".

Altogether, however, the first year in which Soviet music was rigidly regimented by the Central Committee had not been outstandingly successful. And during the first year even the popular songs and the military marches, we were told, had not been up to standard.

Yet there was at least one point which Stalin and his advisers should have borne in mind. Their art policy had caused Russia more harm abroad, among the left-wing and predominantly pro-Soviet intelligentsia, than anything else. Czechoslovakia, Poland and other countries had adopted a planned economy, and thought very highly of many features of the Soviet economic system. Politically, too, Russia had a profound influence on the post-war structure of many States. The Soviet Union was considered, among millions of people, to be the one country that had something to offer in the way of political and economic ideas and organization to the colonial and semi-colonial peoples of Asia and Africa. Soviet ideas of economic justice were one of the most potent ideological weapons in the world; and when millions and millions of Chinese coolies were being turned into self-respecting citizens, it seemed perhaps silly to worry about the future of Prokofiev's work. Yet the treatment of the artist by the State was still something very important.

The two most powerful communist parties in the West, those of Italy, and France, had the strongest mental reservations about Soviet art policy. In Poland and Czechoslovakia, the whole communist and left-wing intelligentsia were perturbed and embarrassed by what had happened in Russia in the field of culture. In Warsaw in the autumn of 1948, a Polish communist remarked to me: "Glory to the Soviet Union, and glory to the Red Army that tore the guts out of the German army, as your Mr. Churchill said, but thank God we haven't got a Lysenko, a Fadeyev, or a Khrennikov dictatorship yet."

But it so happened that although the dictatorship of Lysenko in biology, and of Fadeyev and his successors in literature, were to continue right up to Stalin's death in 1953, and often beyond, Khrennikov's dictatorship over music did not last long. If socialist realism could still be enforced on literature even twenty years after Zhdanov's death, the absurdity of proclaiming the genuine and even the bogus folk-song to be the highest form of musical art was so patently absurd that, in music, socialist realism (as proclaimed by Zhdanov) scarcely survived Zhdanov himself.

SEVENTEEN

The Great Tito Schism

In the introduction to this book I have spoken of the highly unpleasant atmosphere which developed in Moscow in the early months of 1948—so unpleasant (to put it mildly) that one was forced to the reluctant conclusion that any newspaper work in Russia had now become as good as useless. The agencies would send extracts from the Soviet press, and all there was left to do was to describe the increasingly dreary new films and plays that were produced in Russia in 1948. Travel was out of the question, and even those Russians one knew who had not—or not yet—been arrested for "consorting with foreigners" began to avoid you like grim death. The censorship, too, had become worse than it had ever been, so the best thing to do was to go home and hope for better times. But on my returning to London in June 1948, there came that explosion I had been expecting for some time in Moscow. But the very manner of the few Yugoslavs I knew in Moscow, and the way the Russians reacted if one mentioned Yugoslavia to them, suggested to me that something serious was brewing.

So at the end of June I flew to Prague, only to find that there were no planes to Belgrade "for the time being". I had to wait several days to get a Hungarian transit visa so that I could go to Belgrade by train. I arrived there just in time for the opening of the Fifth Yugoslav Party Congress, at which Tito was going to explain at great length why the Soviet Union and Yugoslavia had quarrelled.

In so far as there was such a thing as "public opinion" in Russia under Stalin, it had, paradoxically with the help of Soviet

380

propaganda—rapturous press articles and wildly enthusiastic documentary films on Yugoslavia—a greater admiration and respect for the Yugoslavs than for any other nation belonging to Stalin's post-war European empire.

Of all the Soviet Union's post-war allies, Yugoslavia alone had what one might call an ideal resistance record. True, there was something both questionable and confusing about the origins of the great resistance movement that was to become by far the largest and most effective the Germans and their allies had to face anywhere in Europe. Hundreds of thousands of men, women and children had simply escaped into the mountains of Bosnia and other wild mountainous parts of the country simply in order to get away from the mutual massacres between Croats and Serbs. It is, indeed, a scarcely disputed fact that of the 1,700,000 lives (at least one-tenth of the population) lost in Yugoslavia in the course of the Second World War, far more people had perished in these mutual massacres, especially between Serbs and Croats, than in the actual military operations. Ante Pavelić, the fiendish head of "independent" Croatia and the chief inspirer of the whole-sale massacre of the Orthodox and non-Catholic Serbs, had moreover the advantage over any Serbian leader of being encouraged and patronized by both Hitler and Mussolini. General Nedić in Belgrade, who was no more than a miserable little quisling in comparison, was merely trying, in Pétain fashion, to save what little could still be saved. A much more controversial figure was Draža Mihailović, the head of the Serbian Četnik army, and for a long time, the symbol of specifically Serbian, but not Yugoslav, national resistance to the Germans and Italians.

It is only fair to say that Mihailović was first in the field of active resistance, but he accepted the authority of the Yugoslav Government-in-Exile in London, and when some time later Tito, at the head of a much more numerous resistance movement, including members of all the Yugoslav nationalities, appeared on the scene, deadly rivalry between the two became inevitable. The fact that Tito was not only a communist but also a Croat by nationality made him doubly suspect in Mihailović's eyes, even though Serbs, Montenegrins, Slovenes and all the other nationalities of Yugoslavia took a highly active part in Tito's movement: Zujović, Ranković and Arso Jovanović were Serbs;

Djilas and Dedijer were Montenegrins; Moša Pijade a Jew; Edvard Kardelj a Slovene, and so on.

As some of the Yugoslav leaders were to show in the post-mortems they wrote after the breach between Stalin and Tito in 1948, Stalin's attitude to Tito in 1948 had been highly ambiguous from the start. For a long time he regarded and treated Mihailović as the sole representative of Yugoslav resistance, and not until Mihailović had begun, on occasion, to collaborate with the Germans, and the British "discovered" that Tito was a much more effective ally in the struggle against Hitler and Mussolini than Mihailović, did the Russians at last begin to take some notice of him, though even then their support of the Tito movement was, to say the least, lukewarm and reluctant.

In Stalin's view, even while Tito and his hardened and ever-increasing forces were of the greatest value to the allied cause, there was "something" about the Yugoslav leader he did not like. Stalin was highly distrustful of any other nation's "nationalism". Also, the very fact that by the autumn of 1944 Tito's armies had liberated the greater part of Yugoslavia without Russian help, and were pretty well treating the Red Army as an equal and no more when it did finally rush to Yugoslavia to take part in the liberation of Belgrade, was not at all to Stalin's liking. He expected his allies in Eastern Europe to be yes-men, and the Yugoslavs were just not that. They were acutely conscious of the fact that *their* military record, though of course on a much smaller scale, was every bit as good as that of the Red Army, and possibly better, considering all the blunders Stalin himself had been guilty of in 1941 and 1942. And it came as a great shock to Stalin when, soon after the joint liberation of Belgrade by Yugoslav and Soviet forces, the Yugoslavs made a strong complaint against the very large amount of rape and even murder of which, they alleged, the Soviet troops had been guilty while on Yugoslav soil. This was something quite new. No Polish or Czech, let alone Hungarian, Rumanian or Bulgarian, leader had dared to complain to Moscow about the similar crimes committed by the Russians in their countries, though the behaviour of the troops there had obviously been no better (and was often worse) than in Yugoslavia.

Also, Tito was exceedingly annoyed to discover that in October 1944 in Moscow Stalin and Churchill had "partitioned" Yugo-

slavia into two equal spheres of influence, and he told both Stalin
and Churchill, in effect, to go to hell. Nor was it, in his view,
for either of them to decided whether the Royal Yugoslav
government was going to be represented or not in the government that had emerged from the nation's vast liberation
effort.

Altogether, Tito and his immediate associates were behaving
much too independently, and Stalin did not like it.

But then, the Yugoslavs had very little reason, even as late as
1944, to be "grateful" to Stalin or the Soviet Union. For at least
two years, Tito's liberation army had been receiving substantial
supplies from the British and Americans and nothing from the
Russians; and it was not until February 1944 that the Russians
first sent a military mission to Tito's headquarters. It was also
not until the day before that the first seemingly cordial messages
were exchanged between Tito and Stalin, who paid tribute at
last to "the heroic struggle of the brotherly Yugoslav peoples
and their glorious National Liberation Army. . . ."

Two months later, Djilas was sent to Moscow as the first
official representative of Tito's Supreme Headquarters. Stalin
agreed to send planes and other equipment to the Yugoslavs, but
would not promise that the Soviet Union would recognize the
National Committee as the legal government of Yugoslavia.
(Djilas already had the impression that some negotiations concerning Yugoslavia had been going on between Moscow, London
and Washington behind the Yugoslavs' backs.)

Tito did not go to Moscow until 21st September. The time was,
indeed, ripe for joint military operations with the Russians inside
Yugoslavia. After their highly successful August offensive in
Rumania, Russian forces made their first contact with the Yugo-
slavs on 6th September, after asking the National Liberation
Army for permission to enter their territory.

Tito was not particularly pleased with his first visit to Moscow.
As he himself later described his meeting:*

> It was for the first time in my life that I met Stalin. Until then I
> had only seen him from a distance. . . . I had several meetings with
> him. One of the first things we discussed was the question of joint
> operations between our two armies. I asked for a tank division to

* Vladimir Dedijer, *Tito Speaks*, London, 1953, pp. 232–4.
26

help our units during the liberation of Belgrade. In the eastern parts of Yugoslavia we had no tanks or heavy artillery, while the Germans were armed to the teeth with the most modern weapons. Stalin agreed to my request, and said: "Walter (it was what I was called in Moscow before the war), I shall give you not one division, but a whole tank corps!"

It is more than obvious from this answer that, though he had deliberately neglected the National Liberation Army until only a few months ago, Stalin now determined that the Russians should play the largest possible part in the liberation of Belgrade. Tito continued his narrative:

> We also reached an understanding on how much of Yugoslavia was to be freed by our joint forces, what point their troops and ours were to go to, and, finally, how long their troops were to remain in our country. We agreed that they were to give us a tank corps to liberate Belgrade, and that, once Belgrade was freed, their forces were to withdraw from Yugoslavia ... their left flank being strengthened for the attack on Budapest.

After that a cordial-sounding joint communiqué was published, "but otherwise", as Tito says, "the first meeting was very cool."

> The basic cause, I think, was the telegram I had sent during the war, which began with the words: "If you cannot send us assistance, then at least do not hamper us." This was confirmed to me by Dimitrov ... after his first meeting with Stalin. He said: "Walter, Walter, the *Hozyain* [the boss] was terribly angry with you because of that telegram. . . . He stamped with rage." Dimitrov wanted me to know that he had actually defended me before Stalin.

It is clear from what follows that the future of Yugoslavia was to Stalin merely a bargaining-counter in his horse-trading with Churchill. He was interested in a Big-Three peace, and if Yugoslavia was to be the object of an Anglo/Soviet compromise, no matter how shabby from the Yugoslavs' own point of view, so much the better.

> I noticed [Tito goes on] that Stalin could not bear being contradicted. In conversations with the men around him, he is coarse and touchy. Only occasionally he turns to Molotov for an opinion, but never listens to him to the end. . . .

I was not used to such conversations, which led to uncomfortable scenes. For instance, Stalin said to me: "Walter, be careful; the bourgeoisie in Serbia is very strong."

I answered calmly: "Comrade Stalin, I do not agree.... The bourgeoisie in Serbia is very weak."

He was silent and frowned and the others at the table, Molotov, Zhdanov, Malenkov, Beria, gaped.

Then, no doubt to please Churchill, Stalin asked about various bourgeois politicians who might be used in any future government of Yugoslavia. Tito dismissed them as scoundrels, traitors and German collaborators.

Stalin frowned again, while Malenkov, Zhdanov and the others looked at me askance.... The talk proceeded in a very painful atmosphere. Stalin assured me of the need to reinstate King Peter. The blood rushed to my head.... I composed myself and said it was impossible, that the people would rebel, that in Yugoslavia the King personified treason, that he had fled and left the people in the midst of the struggle, that the Karageorgević dynasty was hated by the people for corruption and terror.

Stalin was silent, and then said briefly: "You need not take him back forever. Take him back temporarily, and then you can slip a knife into his back at a suitable moment."

At this moment Molotov rushed in with a news cable saying that British troops had landed in Yugoslavia. Tito firmly declared that this was impossible, and Stalin did not press the point. It was pointed out that the arrival of some British artillery General Alexander had promised to send had been mistaken for a British invasion.

Stalin then asked me the direct question: "Tell me, Walter, what would you do if the British really forced a landing in Yugoslavia?" "We should offer determined resistance." Stalin was silent. Obviously this answer was not to his liking. Was he again thinking of the arrangements he had made for dividing Yugoslavia into spheres of influence?

I remember that first Tito visit to Moscow and the reception given in his honour at the Yugoslav Embassy, if I am not mistaken. What struck me most about Tito was his personal appearance. He was handsome, dapper, with something of the elegance of that old Hapsburg Monarchy in which he had grown up. There was human warmth and humour in his conversation.

He completely lacked the solemn poker face of the Stalinite bureaucrat.

Tito flew back to Yugoslavia a few days later. The fighting for Belgrade had begun. Nine Yugoslav divisions, supported by a Soviet tank corps under General Zhdanov, were engaged in these operations. The Germans' resistance was fierce and lasted for six days, ending with the final liberation of Belgrade. Russians, Yugoslavs and Germans all suffered heavy losses.

Tito's next major clash with the Big Three came as a result of the "recommendations" sent him from the Yalta Conference to the effect that a coalition government, comprising members of the London government, should be formed, and that a Privisional Assembly should be set up comprising members of the pre-war National Assembly.

> The National Liberation Movement was deeply indignant at the idea that there should be included in the new Assembly members of the old Assembly which had been elected under the regime of Milan Stojadinović, an Axis man.

About the same time,

> The armed intervention of British troops in the internal affairs of Greece produced quite a commotion in Belgrade. . . . It was said that Churchill's intervention was equally aimed at the People's Liberation Movement in Yugoslavia. (*Tito Speaks*, p. 238.)

However, it did not come to an armed intervention in Yugoslavia, which, by the end of the war, had 800,000 soldiers, but Tito continued to distrust both Russia and the West. A variety of complications arose with the latter over Trieste, American violations of Yugoslav air space, the shooting down of some of these planes, etc. At the same time, the Yugoslavs were furious with Moscow for often not supporting their territorial claims on Italy and Austria; it was only under heavy Russian pressure that the Yugoslavs finally agreed in 1946 to sign the peace treaty with Italy.

As distinct from the real Soviet satellite countries, at the end of the war Yugoslavia was not merely under Western pressure, but under constant pressure from Moscow as well. More than any other East European country, Yugoslavia, with its large mineral wealth, had been the Western capitalists' hunting ground between the two world wars. Nearly 78 per cent of the capital invested in Yugoslavia was foreign, and in the metallurgical industry and mining as much as 90 per cent. But most of these investments bore no relation to the interests of Yugoslavia itself. Thus—

> although the country is extremely rich in bauxite ore, aluminium was virtually not produced. The cause was the economic policy of the aluminium cartel which controlled 99·7 per cent of our bauxite mining.

In short, Yugoslavia had been treated by foreign capital as a source of raw materials, not as a manufacturing country, and, much to the Yugoslav's growing annoyance since the end of the war, Moscow was taking very much the same view of their country.

As for agriculture, the land reform angered, above all, the Churches and the large landowners, many of them pro-Nazi during the war, and now "pro-Western". This land distribution provided that no one in Yugoslavia could own more than sixty acres.

> This hit the interests of the large landowners, especially the Catholic and the Orthodox Churches. . . . In Croatia and Slovenia alone the Catholic Church had to cede to the peasants 160,000 acres. . . . These tasks were accomplished with relative ease. . . . During the war the majority of the people had declared themselves for their enactment. (Dedijer, op. cit., p. 258.)

Collectivization was not seriously contemplated and, after the breach with Tito, Russian propaganda claimed that Yugoslav agriculture was dominated by a "Titoite class of *kulaks*". However, this was a sore subject, since the peasants' objections to collectivization were equally strong in Poland, Hungary and, in fact, all countries outside the Soviet Union proper.

Relations with the West—which had helped Tito's National Liberation Army during the war infinitely more than the Russians had done—nevertheless gravely deteriorated once the war was moving to its close. The Yugoslavs were particularly shocked to find that war criminals like Ante Pavelić, the fascist boss of Croatia, were allowed to escape, unmolested (so they claimed) by the British or Americans, to South America. The Western powers also gave support to King Peter, although "the overwhelming majority of Yugoslavs were against him"—as indeed the elections held for the Constituent Assembly in the autumn of 1945 were to show:

> The overwhelming majority of the population voted for federation, for the republic against the monarchy, and for the legalization of those reforms which had been initiated during the war. (Dedijer, op. cit., p. 258.)

Tito and his friends also greatly annoyed the West with certain of their territorial ambitions, and Stalin considered these excessive too. Thus the Yugoslavs' attempt to cling on to Trieste, even though the large majority of its population was Italian, found no support from the Russians, who later even claimed that, by behaving recklessly over Trieste, by shooting down American planes flying over Yugoslav territory in 1946, and generally behaving in a provocative way *vis-à-vis* the British and Americans in Italy, Tito had very nearly brought about a war between Russia and the Western powers. However, the question of who was provoking whom may be a matter of dispute. In the summer of 1946 hundreds of British and American planes continued to fly over Yugoslav territory, as part of the "war of nerves", despite numerous Yugoslav protests and warnings, before a few of these planes were actually shot down.

Meanwhile relations between Yugoslavia and the Soviet Union, though superficially cordial (and, as we have seen, the Soviet people admired Yugoslavia more than any of the other of Russia's new allies in Eastern Europe), were not good at all. Almost since the autumn of 1944, when Yugoslav and Soviet troops jointly liberated Belgrade, the Russians' secret services, by a variety of means, began to enlist all kinds of Yugoslavs— "from members of the Central Committee to cipher clerks in the Party and state machine" (Dedijer, p. 268). One of the first to fall into the NKVD trap, or rather to be forced into it, was Andrija Hebrang, a member of the Yugoslav Politburo and Secretary of the Central Committee of Croatia. This is how Dedijer explains the methods whereby Hebrang was blackmailed by the NKVD into serving them:

> Hebrang had been arrested in Zagreb in 1942 by the Ustashi [Croatian fascist] police. He gave way under torture and consented to work for the Ustashi intelligence service and the Gestapo. . . . On German orders, he joined the Partisans in the autumn of 1942.

He behaved well, and we suspected him of nothing. When the war ended, his dossier was found in Berlin by the Russians. We in Yugoslavia learned in 1945 that something was wrong with Hebrang, but the Russians gave us no information about him. . . . Even when in 1946 Kardelj and Djilas told Molotov that Hebrang was under Party investigation. . . . Molotov said nothing. Hebrang was tightly in the NKVD grip, and did what the NKVD ordered him. (Dedijer, pp. 26–89.)

The case of Hebrang was by no means unique. Other methods were used to enlist as many Yugoslavs as possible into the Soviet secret service in Yugoslavia, and introduce Soviet agents in every branch of the economy and the government and Party machine.

The NKVD stopped at nothing. . . . It cajoled young communists in Yugoslavia into working for it with slogans about loyalty to the Soviet Union, the country of the Revolution. . . . These things could not be concealed. There were many who refused to work for the NKVD, and spoke to others about it. (Dedijer, p. 270.)

Tito was not at all pleased about this: apparently, it already then struck him as an attempt to build up inside Yugoslavia a sort of Soviet Fifth Column, which, besides being a source of constant information to Russia, might also prove useful in a major emergency.

Another object of complaint to Moscow, which I have already briefly referred to, was the behaviour of the Russian officers and soldiers while on Yugoslav soil. According to the Yugoslavs, there had been 1,219 cases of rape, 329 cases of attempted rape, 111 cases of rape with murder, 148 rapes with attempts at murder, and 1,204 robberies with violence. The Yugoslav leaders lodged an official complaint with General Korneyev, chief of the Soviet military mission, but he would not hear of it: "In the name of the Red Army Command I protest against these things because they are untrue."

Stalin, for his part, pretended never to have heard of this affair, or perhaps he was really not told. When Tito went to Moscow in April 1945, he was accompanied by Milovan Djilas, who told Stalin about this incident. Surprised by this account, Stalin said to Djilas: "Why did you not write to me about all this? I did not know it. I consider the dispute now settled."*

What also characterized those immediate post-war years was the Soviet "cultural" penetration of Yugoslavia, which went together with plain economic exploitation. The Russian representatives in Yugoslavia proposed that as many Russian songs as possible should be included in the Yugoslav radio programmes. As Tito himself later commented:

> Had we accepted their suggestions, there would have been two or three times as many Russian songs as Yugoslav. They also asked us to increase the number of Russian plays in our theatres. We have always esteemed Gogol, Ostrovsky, Gorki, but we refused to flood our theatres with third-rate modern Soviet plays. In 1946 (they forced upon us) Soviet films for which we had to pay in dollars three, four, five times more than we paid for films from the West. Thus we got Laurence Olivier's *Hamlet* for about $2,000 ... and had to pay for the Soviet *Exploits of a Soviet Intelligence Agent* some $20,000.

The Russians also tried to inflict a large number of articles written by Russians on the Yugoslav press. Had the Yugoslavs agreed to all these demands, practically all Yugoslav journalists would have been out of work. Something similar happened with books: in the first few post-war years, the Yugoslavs published 1,850 Soviet books, and the Russians two books by Yugoslav writers!

From 1944 onwards the Russians had begun to exploit Yugoslavia economically in a big way; but, unlike the new Polish,

---

* Dedijer's sober account of how Stalin reacted to the Yugoslav stories of Russian rapes and murders in Yugoslavia seems completely true and in character. On the other hand, what first made me highly suspicious of the veracity of Djilas's own book, *Conversations with Stalin*, first published in 1962, was this wholly improbable story of how Stalin burst into tears. "He spoke emotionally about the sufferings of the Red Army and about the horrors it had undergone fighting for thousands of kilometres through devastated country. He wept, crying out: 'And such an army was insulted by no one else than Djilas! Djilas ... a man I had received so well! And an army that did not spare its blood for you! Does Djilas, who is himself a writer, not know what human suffering and the human heart are? Can't he understand if a soldier who has crossed thousands of kilometres through blood and fire and death has fun with a woman or takes some trifle?'" (*Conversations with Stalin*, London, 1962, p. 88). Many other scenes of Stalin's buffoonery in Djilas's book strike me as almost equally improbable, but the sobbing-and-weeping scene plainly impossible.

Hungarian and Rumanian rulers, the Yugoslavs often raised objections and resisted Russian demands as best they could. Intensive trade developed between Yugoslavia and the Soviet Union from 1945 onwards on the basis of a number of trade agreements. The Russians insisted on trading on the basis of world-market prices. Many of the Yugoslavs thought this very unfair since, in such trade, an underdeveloped country like Yugoslavia, with a low labour productivity, would be an unequal partner. Russia, as a more highly developed country, would make far bigger profits. More important, however, was the nature of the goods to be exchanged. As Tito himself commented:

> The Soviet government insisted on our giving it essential items which our country could have sold without any difficulty on foreign markets, such as non-ferrous metals, ores, hemp and hops. In 1948, for instance, our exports to the Soviet Union consisted of between 40 to 50 per cent ores and metals, although they constituted only 25 per cent of our overall exports. (Dedijer, pp. 276-7.)

One of the favourite Russian devices for pumping wealth out of Yugoslavia, as out of several other East European countries, was the so-called joint-stock company. The Yugoslavs were not opposed to the principle of the thing, and still hoped that, though profitable to the Russians, the companies would also contribute to the industrialization of Yugoslavia. These companies were discussed between the Yugoslavs and Stalin during their meeting in Moscow in the spring of 1946. This was, in a sense, the most successful of the Yugoslav/Soviet meetings. Stalin, in Tito's words, "behaved diplomatically, slyly, and in a great measure demagogically". Raising the question of joint-stock companies, Stalin remarked that some Yugoslav leaders seemed opposed to the idea. Tito said this was not so; on the contrary, he and his colleagues were in favour of them if they helped to industrialize Yugoslavia. It was agreed that the joint-stock companies should be discussed after the Yugoslav's return to Belgrade. After a long discussion on this and other topics Stalin drove all the Yugoslav guests to his *datcha*. It was a thoroughly drunken party, and after several hours of it,

> Stalin rose from his chair, went to the corner where a gramophone stood and began to play record after record, mostly Russian folk music.

Singing softly, he began to dance to the gramophone music. Molotov and the others shouted out at him: "Tovarish Iosif Vissarionovich, how strong you are!"

But Stalin's mood suddenly changed. "Oh no, no, I won't live long. The physiological laws are having their way." Molotov and the others rose to their feet: "No, no, Iosif Vissarionovich, we need you, you still have a long life ahead of you." Stalin shook his head in denial.... Then he looked at Tito, and continued: "Tito should take care of himself in case anything happens to him. Because I won't live long, and he will remain for Europe."

And then came this extraordinary kind of "complaint" to Tito:

"Churchill told me about Tito, he said that Tito was a good man. He repeated this three times, and at last I answered him: 'I don't know, but if you say so, he must be good. I shall do my best to get to know Tito.' " (Koča Popović's account of the Moscow meeting, as quoted by Dedijer, pp. 278–85.)

Below all this good-natured banter there was something ominous. Churchill had repeated "three times" to Stalin that Tito was a good man. But this Kremlin meeting of 27th May took place a little over two months after Churchill's Fulton speech, which had made him Enemy No. 1 of the Soviet Union. So it was a more than dubious recommendation. Another ominous remark of a different kind was made during that seemingly drunken party, when Stalin suddenly turned to Ranković, the Yugoslav police chief, advising him to be careful of Beria, and then to Beria, asking him: "And you two? Which of you will trap the other?"

It is reasonable to suppose that even in 1946 there was at the back of Stalin's mind the idea that, sooner or later, Tito would have to rank as a protégé of Churchill, and also that a showdown between Beria and Ranković, that is between the Soviet Union and Yugoslavia, was also inevitable—though not immediately.

Fundamentally, Stalin was jealous of Tito. Jealousy and envy were deep-seated emotions in his character. He could not bear anyone who threatened to become more popular than he was himself. Hence the story, supported at least by Khrushchev, that Kirov, the genuinely popular chief of Leningrad, had been murdered on Stalin's instructions. It was also known that Stalin deeply envied Nikolai Voznesensky when his book on the Soviet Union wartime economics, published in 1948, was an enormous success and was praised to the skies in the Soviet press; this may not have been sufficient reason for shooting the head of the Gosplan, yet his execution in mysterious circumstances in 1949 (a year after the great success of his book) can scarcely have been a coincidence. And Stalin had even more reason to be jealous and envious of Tito. Tito was the glamour boy of the communist world. He was the soldier who had fought a heroic battle at the head of his troops and had liberated his country almost single-handed. His appearance in Warsaw, Prague, Bucarest and Buda-pest aroused the wildest enthusiasm among hundreds of thousands of people coming into the streets to welcome the great Yugoslav war hero. The appearance in any of these cities of Stalin himself had never been tried out. Even if such a visit were at all con-ceivable, Stalin might well have been given a worse than mixed reception. Visits like those of Molotov or Mikoyan or any other member of the Politburo, if they took place at all, were never publicized. As for all the Moscow-grown and Moscow-bred leaders now ruling the People's Democracies—Bierut in Poland, or Anna Pauker in Rumania, or Gottwald in Czechoslovakia, or Rakosi in Hungary—what kind of enthusiasm would *they* arouse? They were all servants of Stalin, and that is precisely what Tito was not. Moreover, he had spent the war in the mountains of Bosnia and Serbia fighting the Germans and Italians, and not hibernating in the Hotel Lux in Gorki Street. And, as the next few years were to show, in so far as Eastern Europe did produce some authentic communist leaders sprung from the native soil of their country, they became immediately suspect as "nationalists". Gomulka was one of these, and soon landed in prison; another was Lucreciu Patrascanu in Rumania, who was shot as a "Titoite" in 1950. The anti-Titoite witch-hunt was, indeed, to start immediately after the Moscow/Belgrade breach in 1948.

It became clear to the Yugoslavs during that May/June 1946 visit that Stalin was trying to cause serious trouble between them and the Bulgarians. Three top Bulgarians—Dimitrov, Kolarov and Traicho Kostov—had come to Moscow to attend the funeral of Kalinin, President of the Supreme Soviet, nominally head of the Soviet State. Not only were the Yugoslavs called on to be guard of honour at the catafalque, but in the midst of the funeral in the Red Square Stalin invited Tito (but no Bulgarian leader) to come up to the top of the Lenin Mausoleum and stand there with the Soviet Politburo.

During various Kremlin meetings, attended by both Yugo-slavs and Bulgarians, Stalin went out of his way to be offensive to Dimitrov and the other Bulgarians, and to show his far greater esteem for the Yugoslavs. He had started on his game of creating ill-feeling between Bulgaria and Yugoslavia, a game to be marked, as we shall see, by all kinds of startling moves until the final outlawing of Yugoslavia in June 1948. But even then Tito had the secret support and sympathy of Georgi Dimitrov, now an old and sick man, though only fifteen years before the great hero of the Reichstag Fire Trial,

If Dimitrov had been younger and, above all, in better health, he might well have become the Tito of Bulgaria. But when I last saw him in Sofia in December 1948—six months after the Stalin/Tito quarrel—he looked both old and terribly sick. He was known to suffer from acute diabetes. To reassure his listeners when he spoke at the Bulgarian Party Congress that month he used rouge and lipstick to look younger and healthier. Some months later he died in a Moscow hospital. Maybe Stalin or Beria ordered his death to be hastened, but it was probably unnecessary. He had been a physical wreck for many months before.

The Yugoslavs returned to Belgrade in June to start negotia-tions with the Russians for the proposed joint-stock companies. It was clear from the start that the Russians intended to use these companies for enslaving the Yugoslav economy. Yugoslavia was, above all, to be used as a source of raw materials for the "developed" countries (the Soviet Union, Czechoslovakia, and, to a lesser extent, Poland). Yatrev, the Russian negotiator, said on one occasion: "What do you need heavy industry for? In the Urals we have everything you need." The negotiations led at first to nothing. The terms the Russians proposed for joint-stock companies exploiting Yugoslavia's natural resources— whether oil, steel, iron or non-ferrous metals—were worded in such a manner as to ensure that all this wealth would inevitably fall under an ill-disguised Russian monopoly control. This also aimed at running and controlling the biggest copper mine in Europe, at Bor, the big lead mine at Trepča, and the iron works at Zenica.

In addition, the Russians then produced a proposal for a Soviet/ Yugoslav bank. The machinery proposed was of such a nature that its consequences were only too obvious to the Yugoslavs. It was just another device to enslave her economy and to prevent her from developing an industry of her own, which alone would enable her to become a genuinely socialist country. The Russian proposal meant that the joint-stock companies would embrace almost the whole economy, so that through credit and financing the bank would have complete control over Yugoslavia's economy. Yugoslavia's financial and foreign exchange autonomy would be violated by international clearing transactions conducted by a specially privileged "mixed" company, in which the Russians would have the main say. Thus the whole of Yugoslavia's economy would have become dependent on this bank, in which the Russians would soon achieve complete domination, for Yugoslavia's trade balance with the Soviet Union would for a time be adverse sand very large, and the bank would come into possession of substantial clearing funds, thus increasing its working capital and strengthening the Russian position. There were many other snags and pitfalls; and, needless to say, its Director-General was to be a Soviet citizen.*

As Tito later said:

> Naturally, we immediately rejected this proposal. In Moscow this was taken as a hostile act. Some of their representatives ... began to talk about megalomaniac Yugoslav plans, about the utopian industrialization of our country. These were the first signs of the gathering storm. ... The negotiations dragged on until the beginning of 1947. We still had some illusions about the Soviet Union. Finally, in February 1947 we signed an agreement founding two Soviet/Yugoslav companies: the *Justa* air transport company and the *Juspad* river shipping company. (Dedijer, p. 290.)

Both companies soon turned out to be highly profitable to the Russians, but not at all to the Yugoslavs, which caused great bitterness in Yugoslavia. The Russians seem by now to have realized that they had gone too far. When, in March 1947, Kardelj went to Moscow at the time of the four Foreign Ministers' Conference and began to tell Stalin that the Russian idea of joint-stock companies was unacceptable to Yugoslavia, Stalin stopped

* For fuller details, see Dedijer, op. cit., pp. 289-90.

him and declared that joint-stock companies were unsuitable for Yugoslavia anyway, and should be set up only in former enemy countries. Stalin, satisfied with having obtained through *Justa* and *Juspad* a virtual monopoly in Yugoslavia's air and river transport, knew in any case that the Yugoslavs would not agree, after this experience, to any more of these companies. Instead, sounding magnanimous, Stalin offered Yugoslavia extensive credits for heavy industrial equipment, steel plants, complete with a coking plant, oil refineries, etc. But the agreement turned out a mere ruse. Of the 135 million dollars promised, the Soviet Union sent Yugoslavia equipment worth only $800,000. The technical assistance the Russians promised and the training of Yugoslav technicians in the Soviet Union both presented big financial difficulties for the Yugoslavs. The Russian experts in Yugoslavia had to be very heavily paid, and the Russians charged for the upkeep of Yugoslav students in Russia at an artificial 5·30 roubles-to-the-dollar rate which bore no relation to the real value of the then still hopelessly inflated rouble. (The Russian monetary reform did not come until the end of 1947.)

In the middle of 1947 Stalin should have been very pleased with Yugoslavia. Unlike Poland and Czechoslovakia, the former of which was anxious to consider, and the latter simply to accept, Marshall Aid (even communist leaders in both countries were sorely tempted by it), the Yugoslav government rejected the American offer as being totally unacceptable to a socialist country. Very soon after Marshall Aid had been gratefully accepted by Western Europe and finally rejected by Eastern Europe, the first meeting of a new body, the Cominform, took place in Poland in September 1947. A detailed account of that meeting is given in Chapter 14, but here a few further details might be added. The idea of such an advisory body among various communist parties (no list seems to have accompanied this first offer) was submitted by Tito to Stalin as early as 1945. The idea was not followed up until June 1946, when, during another Tito/ Stalin meeting in Moscow, the question was again raised, this time by Stalin, who appeared favourable to this new International "for information purposes". He then said: "It would be best if you Yugoslavs took the initiative." That same night, Stalin had a big party at his *datcha* for both Yugoslavs and Bulgarians. According to Yugoslav accounts, Stalin went out of his way to be particularly offensive to the Bulgarians, and, above all, to Georgi Dimitrov, whom he taunted with the mess that had been made of the old Comintern, the 3rd International. He was, clearly, playing off the Bulgars against the Yugoslavs. But Dimitrov saw through Stalin's game, and when the latter asked Dimitrov who should initiate the Cominform—he, Tito or the French—Dimitrov said: "Tito." Tito, however, refused and suggested the French. Finally, no decision was taken. It was not until over a year later, in the autumn of 1947, that the Cominform (the Information Bureau of the Communist Parties) was founded.

Perhaps with the benefit of hindsight, the Yugoslavs later claimed that the main purpose of the Cominform, from the Russian point of view, was to make it (as, indeed, the Comintern had been under Stalin) an instrument of Soviet Great-Power policy, whose one and only rule was to achieve what was in the interests of the Soviet Union, and that, from the outset, the main purpose of the new organization was to isolate Yugoslavia. By egging on the Yugoslavs at that first Cominform meeting to attack the French and Italian CPs, Zhdanov had caused bitter resentment amongst these against Yugoslavia. It was first suggested that the headquarters of the Cominform be Prague, but Stalin, who was consulted on the phone, insisted on Belgrade.

Despite all these Yugoslav theories, which they propounded with a display of profound conviction, about the devilish long-term plan that Stalin had of evicting Yugoslavia from the communist bloc of powers, I still believe that, irritating though Stalin found Tito and his colleagues, he was anxious in 1947 to keep them inside the bloc—and the best way of doing so was by flattering them, and by making them feel that even Stalin thought more highly of them than of all the other East European countries, with their Moscow-stooge governments. Nothing else would explain the rapturous propaganda in the Soviet press, right up to the beginning of 1948, praising the glories of Yugoslav socialist construction, with the personal glorification of Tito. Highly characteristic was the inspiring and uplifting Soviet documentary on Yugoslavia made in 1947, the script for the commentary of which had been written by Ilya Ehrenburg, a master of journalistic eloquence and enthusiasm. It should be remembered that, after all, the Cold War between Russia and the

West had become extremely bitter and dangerous. Was this a time for Stalin to throw away the militarily most hardened and experienced ally he had in Europe?

The first issue of the Cominform paper, with the unwieldy title *For a Lasting Peace, for a People's Democracy*,* appeared in Belgrade in December 1947. Stalin had insisted that the paper be printed in Belgrade.

The Yugoslavs, like all other non-Russians for that matter, had, however, very little to do with the production of the paper.

> The whole thing was in the hands of Pavel Yudin, a representative of the Soviet Party, and a philosopher by profession. . . . In the Soviet Union there was a joke about Yudin, that he was "the best philosopher among NKVD men, and the best NKVD man among philosophers". (Dedijer, p. 306.)

Yudin's attitude to members of the Soviet Politburo was one of the most abject servility. He moved to Belgrade in October 1947, and asked for one of the biggest buildings in the centre of the city for the Cominform headquarters. He set up a radio-telephone link with Moscow and a radio-telegraph station. The paper was printed at Borba, which had the largest printing press in the country, and appeared in Russian, English, French and Serbo-Croat—to begin with. Yudin brought his own typesetters from Moscow. The work was done in the strictest secrecy. All the Cominform countries were represented on the board, but in fact the paper was censored in Moscow. Dummies of each issue were sent there for approval before the paper could go to press. On one occasion, Moscow (possibly Stalin himself) objected at the last moment, when the paper had already gone to press, to an article which had at first passed unnoticed—one by Zachariades, Secretary-General of the Greek Communist Party. The whole issue had to be burned under Yudin's supervision.

As we have seen, right up to January 1948 relations between the Soviet Union and Yugoslavia could not on the face of it have been more cordial than they were. On 29th November 1947, Yugoslavia's National Day, *Pravda* published a long and

---

* This title was Stalin's idea. He thought that every time the paper was quoted, the full title would be given, and this would constitute so much free propaganda. However, in the West, at any rate, the paper was simply referred to as "the Cominform paper".

enthusiastic article on that country and on Tito. After describing "the heroic struggle of the Yugoslav people under the leadership of Marshal Josef Broz-Tito", the paper said:

> Events in Yugoslavia in the last four years speak eloquently of the immense, truly gigantic strength of its people. The people, under the guidance of the communists, who have come from the very depths of the people, a Party hardened in battle, and deserving all the glory it gained in its battles for Yugoslavia's freedom, has found the right highway towards the country's complete liberty. And the Yugoslav Communist Party has followed the very road of which Lenin and Stalin had spoken. Today Yugoslavia is a country in whose economy the socialist element is predominant. All state and provincial industry is now state-owned, while, in local industries, the state owns 70 per cent. The peoples of the Soviet Union are watching this amazing process of the political and economic development of Yugoslavia. . . . The transformation of a backward country like Yugoslavia into a progressive state is a truly inspiring sight. . . . No wonder the imperialists hate Yugoslavia, their former colony.

The Poles, Rumanians, Hungarians and the rest could put it in their pipes and smoke it. *Pravda* had never spoken in the same way of these countries, where the private sector in industry was still very strong, and whose war record was quite different from Yugoslavia's; nor had any of these countries shown the same national unanimity as the Yugoslavs had.

On 3rd January 1948, *Pravda* published a very full report of Tito's speech on the results of the first year of Yugoslavia's first five-year plan. This had been fulfilled in eleven months to the extent of 106 per cent of the plan. Four hundred and twenty-one kilometres of new railway lines had been built. One hundred and sixty-five medium and 8 large railway bridges had been restored. The 1947 harvest had been 2 per cent above the last 10-year average. Five thousand new houses, 73,000 new rural dwellings, 1,300 new schools, 443 new industrial enterprises had been built, besides many new medical centres, 966 kilometres of main roads, etc.

Tito also stressed that in the countryside over 10,000 co-operatives of various types had been set up and that the anti-illiteracy campaign was making good progress. He paid a warm tribute to the voluntary and enthusiastic work done in the restoration of the country by many thousands of young people.

27

This work by the Tito Youth (*Omladina Titova*), had, indeed, given of Yugoslavia a picture of greater and more spontaneous enthusiasm than could be observed in any other socialist country, including the Soviet Union. It was reminiscent of the spirit shown by the Russian Komsomols in the 1920s and especially 1930s, of heroic exploits such as the building by thousands of Komsomol volunteers of a new city, Komsomolsk, in the depth of the Eastern Siberian taiga, where in the winter of 1932-3 many hundreds of these reckless young enthusiasts died of hunger and scurvy.

Although it is perfectly true that Stalin had an instinctive dislike of Tito, his independence, his self-glorification, his insufferable way of treating Stalin almost as an equal, I think it is quite obvious that the Yugoslav story that Stalin had made up his mind long before the actual breach of June 1948 to "destroy" Tito, that the Cominform was merely a "trap" into which the Yugoslav leaders were to fall, etc., is contradicted by the facts. Until January 1948, Stalin was extremely anxious to keep Yugoslavia and Tito inside his East European empire, and the Soviet press praised and flattered Yugoslavia far more than any other country, except the Soviet Union itself.

Stalin was suddenly made extremely nervous by something that happened in January 1948—the first serious signs of not only Yugoslavia, but Bulgaria, too, assuming a more independent line *vis-à-vis* Moscow. The Friendship, Cooperation and Mutual Assistance Pact signed between Bulgaria and Yugoslavia in December 1947 was perhaps still nothing to worry about. Of this Tito said:

> We have liquidated the powder-magazine in the Balkans. For a long time it was there, between Bulgaria and Yugoslavia. The present twenty-year agreement provides for the territorial integrity of both countries, for security, independence, mutual military and other aid. . . . The foundations for the agreement were laid at Bled four months ago, and now we have this agreement which puts an end to all the ancient feuds between our two countries.

A similar pact was to be signed between Yugoslavia and Hungary and one between Yugoslavia and Rumania during the same month (December 1947).

The reference to the meeting at Bled, Tito's summer residence, between him and Dimitrov can scarcely have been to the Kremlin's liking. This was the first meeting of the kind between two members of the Socialist bloc in which the Russians had not been asked to take part. But worse was to come.

On the one hand, a good deal of irritation had already been caused in Moscow by the enthusiastic reception given to Tito by hundreds of thousands of people during his various visits to Prague, Warsaw, Budapest, Bucarest and Sofia. The treaty with Bulgaria came on top of this, as well as treaties with Hungary, Bulgaria and Czechoslovakia. According to the Yugoslavs, "the Kremlin decided (in January 1948) to begin liquidating the whole process of *rapprochement* among the nations of Central Europe and the Balkans. It was necessary to strike at the nerve centre, at Yugoslavia" (Dedijer, p. 316).

To begin with, Stalin summoned Djilas to Moscow, ostensibly to discuss Albania; war materials for the Yugoslav army, Soviet machinery for the new Yugoslav industries, etc. Talks between Djilas on the one hand and Stalin and the Soviet military on the other seemed to progress reasonably well, when everything suddenly came to a standstill. It was during this Djilas visit that Kardelj reported to the National Assembly at Belgrade on Tito's visits to the neighbouring capitals. The Assembly had also ratified the new treaties with Bulgaria, Hungary and Rumania. At about the same time, Dimitrov went on a visit to Rumania, and here, in the course of a press conference, he made a statement which brought the latent crisis to a head. The question put to him was:

It is rumoured that a federation of Balkan nations and a federation of the areas of Eastern and South Eastern Europe, including Hungary, Czechoslovakia and Poland, is imminent. If such a federation is created, will other countries from these regions also be able to join it?

And here was Dimitrov's reply:

The question of federation or confederation is premature. . . . It is not on the agenda, and it has therefore not been discussed. When the question matures, as it inevitably must, then our peoples, the nations of the people's democracies, Rumania, Bulgaria, Yugoslavia, Albania, Czechoslovakia, Poland, Hungary, and Greece— and mind you, Greece!—will settle it. It is they who will decide what it shall be—federation or confederation, and when and how it will be formed. What we are already doing greatly facilitates our future work. . . . And when it comes to creating such a federation or confederation, our peoples will not ask the imperialists' permission, but will solve the questions themselves, guided by their own interests, which are bound up with the interests and the international cooperation necessary to them and to other nations.

In the words of the Yugoslavs, "The Kremlin reacted furiously to Dimitrov's statement, although *Pravda* published it. Imagine a Balkan Federation without the Soviet Union!"

In *Pravda* on 29th January, on Stalin's instructions, a fierce attack was launched against Dimitrov:

> Many readers . . . have asked questions which boil down to this: Can it be inferred that, since *Pravda* published Dimitrov's statement, it agrees with his views on the expediency of organizing a federation of Balkan and Danubian states, including Poland, Czechoslovakia and Greece, and on the necessity of a customs union among them?
>
> Here is our answer. . . . First, *Pravda* could not but have published Comrade Dimitrov's statement, which had been published in the press of other countries. . . . But this does not mean that *Pravda* agrees with Comrade Dimitrov. . . . On the contrary, the editors of *Pravda* consider that these countries require no questionable and fabricated federation or confederation or customs union; what they require is the consolidation and defence of their sovereignty and independence by mobilizing and organizing their people's democratic forces, as was correctly stated in the well-known [Cominform] declaration.

Djilas, though in the Soviet Union, was not informed of the telegrams sent from Moscow to Belgrade and Sofia summoning new delegations to the Kremlin. Dimitrov left for Moscow, with Kolarov and Kostov. Belgrade sent Kardelj and Bakarić. Tito himself ignored the Soviet Ambassador's clear hint that he was also expected in Moscow. A further minor complication arose over an Albanian request for two Yugoslav divisions to be sent to southern Albania, threatened, according to the Albanian government, by the Greek government forces. The Yugoslavs agreed; but Molotov promptly cabled opposing this Yugoslav/ Albanian arrangement.

The first, extremely tough, meeting took place on 10th February. Molotov said there were serious differences between the Soviet Union on the one hand and Yugoslavia and Bulgaria on the other, which was "inadmissible from both the government and the Party point of view". He then said that the Soviet Union had advised Yugoslavia and Bulgaria not to conclude such a treaty. Now the Soviet government had "learned about it from the newspapers".

These denied that the Soviet government had been neither informed nor consulted. Nevertheless, Molotov said the text finally signed did not quite correspond to what Moscow had been told. It was a meeting from which all the old banter and backslapping were entirely absent. Stalin shouted at Dimitrov, mocking at him and at his statement about the confederation— to which Dimitrov meekly replied: "Yes, I *was* carried away at the press conference." "Yes," Stalin mocked, "you wanted to shine by saying something new. But your federation is just nonsense." And in reply to another remark by Dimitrov, Stalin pounced on him: "Whatever you do, you bandy words around like a woman in the streets. You wanted to astonish the world, as if you were still secretary of the Comintern. . . . And when all these things go on between Bulgaria and Yugoslavia, we have to learn about it at second-hand." In the end Stalin said he had nothing against a federation between Yugoslavia and Bulgaria, but not between Rumania and Bulgaria.

Tito's interpretation of this sudden "concession" is worth quoting, for it gets to the very heart of the matter:

> Stalin thought he had a large number of his own men in the Bulgarian government who had spent ten or fifteen years in the Soviet Union, and imagined that, through a federation between Bulgaria and Yugoslavia, it would be easier to subjugate the latter, which was the strongest element in that part of Europe. Dimitrov was a sick man, and Stalin now tried finally to undermine and compromise him. (Dedijer, p. 327.)

Now Stalin pressed this idea of a Yugoslav/Bulgaria Federation, and said it should be brought about *at once*, even though Tito and Dimitrov had agreed at Bled in 1947 that it should come about only gradually. He added that the two countries should unite and then annex Albania. This was not new; already before he had told the Yugoslavs they could, for all he cared, "swallow" Albania. Fundamentally, the reason why he wanted to see

Albania disappear was that Albania was more likely than any other country of the socialist bloc to initiate a clash with monarchist Greece. At the same time, Stalin was opposed to any help being given to the Greek guerrillas. He said the Yugoslavs should stop helping them; they had no prospect of winning, and dismissed as absurd Kardelj's assertion that the Greek partisans had an excellent chance of continuing and winning the war, if they received substantial help from the socialist countries and there was no increase in foreign intervention on the other side. But Stalin wanted no trouble with Greece, the first protégé of the Truman Doctrine and threw the Greek guerrillas to the wolves. Moscow's breach with Yugoslavia could only hasten this liquidation.

Although Georgi Dimitrov was, with his concept of a vast federation not including the Soviet Union, the first to defy the Soviet Union openly, Stalin did not take him seriously. He was old and sick, and had apparently during his talks with Tito at Bled and elsewhere fallen under the Yugoslavs' influence. It was sad, in the Kremlin's view, to see the former secretary of the Comintern, who had faithfully carried out even the most unpleasant of the Kremlin's orders and had wallowed for years in internationalist verbiage, now fall under the influence of a Balkan nationalist—for that was what Tito had now become. But consistency was something Stalin never worried about. *Pravda*, in rebuking Dimitrov, had said that instead of messing about with unrealistic federations the socialist countries should consolidate their sovereignty; but when it suited Stalin to ignore the high principle of sovereignty, he did so. Bulgaria and Yugoslavia were sovereign states; yet now he had sent them a kind of ultimatum that they federate into one state. The Yugoslavs saw at once that the Bulgarian part of this "federation" would act as the Trojan Horse inside Yugoslavia. This would be flooded by Bulgarians in the service of Moscow.

Events now moved fast. Almost immediately after the stormy meeting at the Kremlin on 10th February, orders were sent to Bucarest to remove all Tito portraits. By the next day, the faithful Anna Pauker carried out this order. Then economic pressure was put on Yugoslavia. At the end of February the Yugoslavs were informed by Moscow that their trade agreement, which expired at the end of 1948, would not be renewed, which meant, among other things, that Yugoslavia would receive no more Soviet oil and cotton, and no industrial equipment either.

On 1st March Tito called a meeting of the Yugoslav Central Committee. Here several speakers denounced the two Soviet/ Yugoslav joint-stock companies as a Russian swindle. Tito, speaking of the non-renewal of the trade agreement, concluded that *the country's independence was even more important*. On the federation with Bulgaria, the opposition was complete. Of all the members of the Central Committee, Sreten Zujović alone expressed no opinion, but took copious notes.

The rejection by the Central Committee of all Moscow's demands was followed by new kinds of pressures. All Soviet military instructors were to be recalled from Yugoslavia, according to the head of the Soviet Military Mission in Belgrade. This was on 18th March. On the following day, the Soviet government also ordered all its civilian specialists to leave Yugoslavia.

There followed that famous exchange of letters between Tito and Kardelj on the one hand and Stalin and Molotov on the other. The latter brought the wildest charges against the Yugoslavs, saying that the Russian specialists had been withdrawn because they had been constantly insulted and spied upon and that there were British spies inside the Yugoslav government. They singled out Djilas, Vukmanović, Kidrić and Ranković for special abuse. One of the Stalin/Molotov letters concluded: "We think Trotsky's political career is sufficiently instructive." By singling out these four, Moscow was trying to split the Yugoslav Central Committee. But nothing came of it. The four offered to resign from the government, if this made things easier for Tito, but Tito said no. Conveniently forgetting what *Pravda* had said on 29th November 1947, Stalin and Molotov, in another letter, which particularly infuriated the Yugoslavs, proceeded to minimize the Yugoslavs' war effort and to suggest that but for the help of the Red Army the partisan war would have been as good as useless.

The plenum of the Yugoslav Central Committee was called for 12th April to discuss the answer to be sent to the Soviet Union to all its various charges. In several paragraphs they refuted all of them, saying, among other things:

What exactly is the issue then? It appears to us that we differ on how relations should stand between our two countries. We share the view that they should be good and friendly. But how to clear them up—there lies our difference of opinion. In our view, friendship must be based on *the absolute respect for the principle of national and state independence*, as expounded by Lenin and Stalin in their works. . . . Also, Soviet citizens in Yugoslavia should remember that *they are in a brotherly independent country and that they should not interfere in that country's internal life*. (Italics added.)

Having read the text of the draft letter to the Kremlin, Tito concluded:

Comrades, we are not dealing with theoretical discussions, or with errors committed by the Communist Party of Yugoslavia, of ideological deviations on our part. We must not allow ourselves to be forced into such a discussion. The issue here, first and foremost, *is the relationship between one state and another*. It seems to me that *they* [Stalin and Molotov] *are using ideological questions in order to justify their pressure on us, on our state*. (Italics added.)

Tito's letter met with general approval. Kardelj spoke with special pride of Yugoslavia's war record: she had freed practically all her territory without outside help, whereas all the other East European countries had been freed by the Red Army. Now Yugoslavia was accused of Trotskyism, Bukharinism and a revival of capitalism. Kardelj was followed by many other speakers, all of whom approved of the Yugoslav letter to the Russians. The only dissenting voice was that of Sretin Zujović, the Minister of Finance, who was now charged with having taken to the Soviet Ambassador the full report of an earlier Central Committee meeting. Commenting on this, Tito bitterly remarked: "This is treason. *No one has the right to love his own country less than the Soviet Union.*"

The session of the Central Committee was resumed the next day. Some of the wording of the letter to the Russians was toned down, but it also counter-attacked on a number of points. Thus, it spoke of the Soviet military and civilian experts in Yugoslavia; already two years before, the Yugoslav government had asked in vain for a reduction of their exhorbitant salaries, but there had been no response from the Kremlin. Now the letter dotted the "i"s:

The salaries of the Soviet experts were four times the size of our army commanders', and three times those of members of the Yugoslav Federal Government. A Yugoslav commander of an army corps had 9,000 to 11,000 dinars a month, whereas a Soviet military expert, with a much lower rank, had 30,000 or 40,000 dinars. ... We felt that this was not only a financial burden, but also a political mistake, because our people did not understand.

The letter also denied that the *Short History of the Bolshevik Party* was not being studied in Yugoslavia. The Yugoslavs claimed that 250,000 copies of this work had been printed in Serbian and Croatian. (Whether this masterpiece of historical falsification, in which Stalin is represented as Lenin's right-hand man in the 1917 Revolution, was taken very seriously by the Yugoslav leadership may, of course, be doubted.)

In conclusion, the Yugoslav Central Committee said that, if the Russians had complaints to make, the Yugoslavs had some serious complaints, too:

> First, we consider it an impropriety on the part of the organs of the Soviet intelligence service to recruit citizens in our country to work for them. ... We know that some organs of the Soviet intelligence service, when recruiting members of our Party, cast suspicion on our leaders, representing them as incompetent and suspect.... We cannot allow a Soviet intelligence network to be set up in Yugoslavia. We have our own state security to struggle against various foreign capitalist elements and the class enemy inside our country, and we can give all the information necessary to the Soviet intelligence people; but it is not for them to do this work in our country.

The letter, signed by Tito and Kardelj on behalf of the Central Committee, was taken personally to Molotov by Ambassador Vladimir Popović. Neither the letter, nor Popović's forty-five-minutes' speech to the Soviet Foreign Minister, who seemed nervous and was biting his lips, produced any more than this:

POPOVIĆ: Have you any questions?
MOLOTOV: None whatsoever.
POPOVIĆ: I am surprised you have no questions.
MOLOTOV (after some hesitation): I can only say that I thought you, personally, would not share the opinion of the others in Belgrade.

The Ambassador left; he and Molotov did not shake hands.

Having thus lost the first round, Stalin now mobilized against

Yugoslavia all his more obedient "allies"—the members of the
Cominform, who were sent the Stalin/Molotov letter to Tito
and Kardelj of 27th March, but without the Yugoslav answer.
Rakosi, the Moscow-trained Hungarian leader, was the first
to toe the Moscow line. This, according to the Yugoslavs, was
particularly absurd, since Rakosi had often privately complained
to the Yugoslavs that the Russians were plundering Hungary and
were also showing anti-semitic tendencies—which Rakosi, himself a Jew, found particularly disturbing. Slansky, also a Jew,
also hastened to join in the attack on Yugoslavia, on behalf of
the Czechoslovak Party. So did the Rumanians. But nothing
came from Dimitrov (Bulgaria), nor from Gomulka (Poland),
and the French and Italian communists also remained silent for a
while. Dimitrov happened to pass through Belgrade just then,
on his way to Prague, and was visited in his carriage by Djilas,
whom he gripped by the hand and said: "Be firm!" The dirty
work in Bulgaria was done by Chervenkov, who, on behalf of
the Bulgarian Party, wrote a particularly insulting letter on the
Yugoslavs, debunking their war effort and saying the decisive
role in their victory over Germany had been played by the Red
Army.

In a further letter from Moscow, Stalin and Molotov took up
the same theme in particularly violent terms, and concluded:

> No one can deny the merits of the Yugoslav Communist Party,
> but they are no greater than those of the CP's of Poland, Czecho-
> slovakia, Hungary, Rumania, Bulgaria and Albania. . . . Yet the
> leaders of these parties are modest and do not split everybody's
> ears, the way the Yugoslavs do, with their boasting.

Men like Tito, Kardelj and the other leaders of the National
Liberation Movement had, of course, an ill-disguised contempt
for the Rakosis, Paukers, Slanskys, Geminders and all the other
Moscow-bred bureaucrats who had never done any fighting,
had lived at the Hotel Lux throughout the war, and were now
the "communist leaders" of the other People's Democracies.
But Stalin now needed these people's wholehearted support, and
it was they who, through the Cominform, were going to help
Moscow to finish off the Yugoslav leadership. The Cominform
was an organ of consultation, information and *mutual agreements*
among its member-parties; now, quite arbitrarily, it was suddenly

turned into a tribunal. This decision to lay the Yugoslav case before the Cominform was announced by Stalin and Molotov at the end of their twenty-five-page letter of insults of 4th May. The Yugoslavs were summoned to attend the Cominform meeting.

The Plenum of the Yugoslav Central Committee met on 9th May. In their letter of 4th May, Stalin and Molotov had singled out for praise two men of the Yugoslav hierarchy: Zujović and Hebrang. These were the obvious heads of the pro-Moscow Yugoslav quisling government the Russians had in mind. The Yugoslav Central Committee not only expelled, there and then, the two men from the Party, but a few days later they were arrested. Moscow sent a telegram full of threats, protesting against their arrest, then made elaborate attempts to kidnap Zujović; but it was too late. Zujović was in jail, in the good care of Aleksandar Ranković, Tito's Police Chief and Minister of the Interior—not exactly a babe-in-arms, as will be shown later.

After further pressing and threatening demands that the Yugoslavs attend the Cominform meeting, scheduled for the middle of June in Bucarest, their Central Committee met on 20th May and unanimously rejected the invitation to it. For one thing, it was not at all certain Tito would return alive.*

On 25th May, two significant things happened: Dimitrov sent birthday greetings to Tito; he was the only one of the communist leaders to do so. Significantly, he also refrained from attending the Cominform meeting which finally met in Bucarest a month later. Secondly, on 25th May the Yugoslav leaders announced that the Fifth Yugoslav Party Congress would meet on 21st July to inform fully the Yugoslav people of what had happened, and to see how much (or little) support Tito would receive from the Yugoslav Party's rank-and-file.

The Cominform meeting opened in Bucarest on 22nd June and lasted several days. Although most of the delegates were typical Moscow stooges—Chervenkov for Bulgaria; Gheorghiu-Dej, Luca and Anna Pauker for Rumania; Rakosi, Farkas and

---

* Tito recalls, in this connection, the case of the obstreperous Ukrainian Politburo which, in 1937, had opposed Stalin's Russification of the Ukraine. Molotov failed to convince any of them. They were then invited to go from Kiev to Moscow by Stalin himself. As they entered the Kremlin, they were all arrested by the NKVD and they were shot soon afterwards. (Dedijer, p. 366.)

Gerö for Hungary; Berman and Zawadski for Poland; Slansky, Siroky, Geminder and Bares for Czechoslovakia—while the French, Duclos and Fajon, were particularly incensed against Tito for reasons of their own, there is good reason to believe that there was some heated opposition to the condemnation of Yugoslavia, as drawn up by the Russians there—Zhdanov, Malenkov and Suslov. It seems certain that this opposition came from men like Kostov (Bulgaria), later to be shot as a Titoite, and almost certainly from the Italians Togliatti and Secchia. Togliatti, the future father of "polycentrism", could not, at heart, but feel some real sympathy for the Yugoslavs. Significantly, too, Dimitrov and Gomulka were not present at the meeting. Dimitrov was soon to die, and a year later Gomulka was imprisoned as a Polish "Titoite".

However, Zhdanov, becoming impatient with so much opposition, put an end to argument by saying: "We possess information that Tito is an imperialist spy."

The Cominform Resolution of 28th June was intended to kill off the Yugoslav leadership. Here are its main points:

The Cominform approved the action of the Central Committee of the CPSU in showing up the wrong policy of the Yugoslav Party leadership, in the first place Tito, Kardelj, Djilas and Rankovic. These people's unfriendliness to the Soviet Union and its CP is shown by the ill-treatment of the Soviet specialists in Yugoslavia, and the constant spying on them by the Yugoslav police. They are guilty of Trotskyism when they speak of the "regeneration" of the CPSU and the USSR. The Yugoslav leadership is not proletarian and working-class and has departed from the Marxist theory of the class struggle. They have adopted the Bukharinist line that during the transition period to socialism, the class struggle is not stronger, but weaker. In agriculture, they are creating a *kulak* society. The Party in Yugoslavia is diluted in the non-Party mass of the People's Front, which is, in fact, the leading force in Yugoslavia, and not the Party. The People's Front is full of the most heterodox elements. There is no democratic spirit inside the Yugoslav party, but a Trotskyite kind of military discipline, and any criticism of the Party leadership is savagely repressed.

But these somewhat dubious theoretical criticisms suggesting that in the Soviet Union, for instance, any "criticism of the party leadership" was *not* "savagely repressed", were only rather meaningless preliminaries to what was the real purpose of the Cominform Resolution:

> In refusing to attend the Cominform meeting, the Yugoslav leaders are dodging the just criticism of the fraternal parties. The Cominform approves the Soviet criticisms of the Yugoslav leaders, and concludes that these leaders have decided to break away from the united socialist front against imperialism. This is a *betrayal of the workers' international solidarity, and a transition to nationalism.* . . . *They accept the bourgeois nationalist concept that the "capitalist states are a lesser danger to Yugoslav independence than is the Soviet Union".* (Italics added.)

And then this desperate attempt to blow up the Yugoslav leadership from inside Yugoslavia:

> The Cominform does not doubt that inside the Yugoslav Communist Party there are enough healthy elements, true to Marxism-Leninism, and to the internationalist tradition of the Yugoslav CP and to the united social front, which must now force the present leadership honestly and openly to admit their errors and to correct them. But if the present leaders prove incapable of this, then replace them by a new internationalist leadership of the Yugoslav Communist Party.

> The Cominform does not doubt that the Yugoslav CP will carry out this task honorably.

This was, needless to say, a blatant attempt to overthrow the Tito government. The Russians were certain of one thing: that they had terrified Tito and "his gang", and that the Cominform resolution would be kept hidden from the Yugoslav people.

What happened was what the Russians had not foreseen. The Plenum of the Yugoslav CP met on 29th June, immediately upon receipt of the Comintern resolution, decided to answer it and, better still, to publish it in every Yugoslav paper the next day, and broadcast it on the Yugoslav radio. There is an amusing (if perhaps apocryphal) story that the moment *Borba* appeared on 30th June carrying the full text of the Cominform Resolution, Yudin, editor of the Cominform paper, rushed to the Soviet Embassy, and here he and Lavrentiev, the Soviet Ambassador, exchanged these two words:

LAVRENTIEV: Published?
YUDIN: Published.

And it was several minutes before they spoke again.

Dedijer gives an accurate account of Yugoslav reaction (I was to arrive in Belgrade soon after, and can confirm the accuracy of his story):

The great majority, who were not conversant with the letters, could simply not believe their eyes. There were people who cried from despair in the streets that morning. But that was the first reaction. After the first pain came a wave of indignation, and pride. ... Feelings rose high.... The air was charged with feeling as previously, during the greatest events in the modern history of Yugoslavia. From many parts of the country cables reported: "People feel as they did on 27th March [1940], when Yugoslavia broke the Axis yoke and challenged Hitler" ... The reaction of my own mother was very typical: "We are a very strange people. When Hitler was at the peak of his power ... we tore up the pact. ...When the Americans, in 1946, were brandishing atom bombs at the world, we shot down their aircraft which had violated our national territory. And now when Stalin is bursting with strength, we reject his ultimatum. It reminds me of little Serbia rejecting the ultimatum of Austria-Hungary in 1914...."

Things were not, of course, quite so simple. Heroism was all very well, but the economic blockade of the Soviet bloc against Yugoslavia, which had already begun, was no joking matter. And there were undoubtedly a good many doubts in the minds of some Yugoslavs. There was a violent Cold War raging between Russia and the Western powers at the time. Was this the right moment for Yugoslavia to "desert" the socialist camp? Also, the father-image of Stalin had been cultivated in Yugoslavia in a big way during and since the war. Doubts arose in many minds whether the Yugoslav leadership had not perhaps behaved recklessly and thoughtlessly in its dealings with Stalin. Some consoled themselves with the thought that it was not perhaps Stalin's fault; that Stalin knew little or nothing about it, but had been kept in ignorance, or been misguided by Zhdanov, Malenkov and Suslov, the Soviet spokesmen at the Cominform meeting, and the authors of the 28th June resolution. This myth of the "good" Stalin had to be kept up for a time. Even Tito concluded his eight-hour report at the Fifth Yugoslav Party Congress of 21st July with the words: "Long live Stalin!"

I arrived in Belgrade shortly before the opening of that

congress, and stayed on for several months. The impression I had was that many Yugoslavs were deeply troubled in their minds about what had happened. And there is no doubt that police chief Alexander Ranković was on the lookout not only for dangerous people, but even for dangerous thoughts. Ranković's UDB (popularly known as the Udba) was a miniature Balkan version of Beria's NKVD, and its methods much the same. But then, after all, was there not in Yugoslavia a Soviet Fifth Column? As we have seen from earlier Yugoslav complaints to the Russians, these had done their utmost to set up in Yugoslavia a secret service of their own; it was now Ranković's job to track these people down. There were supposed to be Soviet agents in practically every branch of the economy, in the government, in the Party itself. Two top leaders had already been eliminated: the Russians' prospective heads of their quisling government, Zujović and Hebrang. Zujović, who had been Tito's finance minister, was arrested and kept in prison for a couple of years. In the end, he recanted. The Rajk Trial in Budapest in 1949, he said, had opened his eyes to the correctness of the Tito line. Hebrang was never to be heard of again, and appears to have died in one of Ranković's torture chambers or simply to have been murdered. But there were a lot of small fry about who had entered the service of the NKVD, some of them quite young people, who had agreed to serve the Russians out of sheer devotion to Stalin. Ranković, as I discovered in 1948-9, had all of them rounded up. Those who sincerely recognized their error were let off lightly, but those who remained suspect were kept for some years in jail or placed under close police supervision.

What is certain, however, is that, quite regardless of Ranković, the Yugoslavs were about 100 per cent behind Tito on the question of the Cominform resolution.

One last attempt was made—this time by Anna Pauker, the Rumanian representative at the Danube Conference held in August 1948 in Belgrade—to set up a pro-Soviet Yugoslav government. It was then that she nearly succeeded in smuggling General Arso Jovanović into Soviet-controlled Rumania, where he would have set up a Yugoslav government which might well, with the help of the Red Army, have been installed in Belgrade. Jovanović, as Tito's Chief of Staff during the partisan war, was a popular and highly-respected figure, but it was now known that the Russians had "worked" on him for some time. During a long period of military training in Moscow in 1946-7, he had also fallen under the influence of a Soviet general's daughter, who had been planted on him by the NKVD.

Anna Pauker and with her Vyshinsky, who represented the USSR at the Danube Conference, had arranged for Jovanović and two other Yugoslav officers to be smuggled into Rumania. But they had not reckoned sufficiently with Ranković. Jovanović was shot dead near the Rumanian border, one of the officers severely wounded, and the third, who had escaped, caught by Yugoslav frontier guards the next morning.

Would Stalin, had the Jovanović operation succeeded, have driven his tanks into Belgrade, as his heirs were to drive *their* tanks into Prague twenty years later?

Paradoxically, Stalin would have had some better excuses for occupying Belgrade in 1948 than Brezhnev had for occupying Prague in 1968. There was undoubtedly a pro-Stalin group in Yugoslavia, including Zujović, the Minister of Finance, and Jovanović, the Chief of Staff, the unfortunate Hebrang, and probably some more, if it had come to the point. These *could* have "invited" the Red Army to come and "save Socialist Yugoslavia". They were not necessarily all bribed by the Russians. Even Titoite literature admits that Zujović was an honest man, though misguided, and not a vulgar Soviet agent. Regardless of his Russian girl-friend, Jovanović, a famous soldier, may also genuinely have believed that it was in Yugoslavia's military interest to have the might of the Red Army on its side.

In Czechoslovakia, in 1968, there was no Russian Party of any kind, and there was literally nobody in the whole country who wanted to "invite" the Russians to occupy the country.

After the failure of the Jovanović experiment, Stalin did not persist. He knew that even if there was a pro-Soviet faction in Yugoslavia it was only a very small one. He proved, in the circumstances, a politically infinitely wiser man than Brezhnev. Stalin also knew that, in his anti-Titoism, he had not only the servile Kremlin stooges in the people's democracies on his side, but also the French and even Italian communists. In fact, he was in a stronger position *vis-à-vis* Yugoslavia than Brezhnev was *vis-à-vis* Prague; but still he refrained from military action, and was content to declare Titoism a horrible heresy (whereupon a witch-hunt against alleged Titoites went on for years throughout Eastern Europe) and to start an economic blockade against Yugoslavia which forced her, before long, to seek help from the West, in whose eyes Tito's "national communism" suddenly acquired a certain respectability. I remember the American Ambassador in Belgrade telling me in 1949: "Sure, they call themselves communists; but we don't give a damn, so long as we know they are not Stalin's stooges." But Stalin knew what was essential to Russia's security, and Yugoslavia was not.

Brezhnev's invasion of Prague twenty years later was the height of folly compared with Stalin's cautious handling of the Yugoslav problem. He turned overnight a wholehearted ally of Russia into a country deeply embittered against the Moscow bureaucracy. This was very harmful to Russia; the loss of Yugoslavia was not—though it seemed dangerous at the time. In the years that followed, Yugoslavia became one of the "uncommitted" countries in the world, and as such her prestige remained high for twenty years or more. In 1955 Khrushchev suddenly flew to Belgrade and publicly apologized to Tito, saying it had all been "Beria's fault".

Historically, the importance of the Titoite revolt and the "outlawing" of Yugoslavia by the "socialist bloc" cannot be over-rated. But in 1948 she was the *first and only one* in twenty years to have rebelled successfully against the Kremlin bureaucracy. Tito put it in a nutshell: "It was a conflict between the Moscow bureaucracy and the Yugoslav people. . . . Already in the days of the Comintern, what mattered to Moscow was not what was in the interests of Yugoslavia, or of any other people, but one thing only: what was in the interests of Russian Great-Power policy. And it has been the same ever since."

In the past twenty years, nearly all the "satellites" tried, in one way or another, to shake off the stranglehold of Moscow, as Yugoslavia had successfully done in 1948. Poland tried it in 1956, Hungary also in 1956, and, finally, Czechoslovakia in 1968; and they all failed, because it was an unequal struggle, as it turned out (to borrow Tito's phrase), between the Polish people and the Moscow bureaucracy, the Hungarian people and the Moscow bureaucracy, the Czechoslovak people and the same seemingly immortal Moscow bureaucracy.

But there is one very important reason why Yugoslavia
28

succeeded where Poland and Hungary failed. Yugoslavia did not have a pro-Moscow bureaucracy as, fundamentally, Poland and Hungary had—at least a bureaucracy which found it essential, for its own survival, to pay lip-service to the Moscow bureaucrats. Not that, to be quite fair, either Hungary or Poland could have done much against Russian tanks (in the case of Hungary) or against the threat of Russian tanks, which Khrushchev was quite prepared to send into Warsaw in October 1956.

Rumania, less impetuously than Poland or Hungary, had also been slipping, or trying to slip, away from the domination of the political and economic bureaucrats of Moscow.

The hardest blow to the Stalinist East European bloc came, however, from the meek, mild, seemingly timid Czechs. They did not ask for much—merely for personal freedom, for a humanization of the regime. They did not want to get out of the Warsaw Pact (as many Hungarians did in 1956); they did not hate the Russians, as the Poles had done for centuries. But to a Brezhnev, the Czechs' crime was even greater than that of the Yugoslav, Polish and Hungarian rebels, or of the Rumanian semi-rebels. They had to be occupied, so that tanks could permanently control the Czechoslovaks' dangerous thoughts. In the case of Yugoslavia, freedom of speech was not a major issue; it was the feeling of *national independence*. In the other countries, the "main issue" is a mixture of both. In Russia nationalism is a great virtue so long as it is Russian nationalism (though it is never called that, but "patriotism"); when it is Ukrainian or Georgian nationalism, it becomes bad; when it is Czech, or Polish, or Rumanian, or Hungarian nationalism, it becomes wicked, and sometimes so criminal that tanks are the only answer.

Sooner or later this biggest anomaly in the modern world, which has now gone on for over twenty years, must stop—this everlasting conflict between the peoples of Eastern Europe and the Stalinite and post-Stalinite bureaucracy. Yugoslavia, though not an ideal democracy or an ideal state of any kind as a result,* was

* As an angry Yugoslav friend once remarked to me, in criticizing many things in his own liberated and fully independent country: "Of course, lots of things are wrong. We have, as Djilas pointed out, a 'New Class', just as the Russians have; we have a pretty beastly police system (there's really not much to choose between *their* Beria and *our* Ranković—except that the scale of their

still not only the *first* but, for the present, the *only* country of
Eastern Europe to have shaken off the domination of Moscow and
its bureaucrats. As such, Yugoslavia will rank as the pioneer of a
process of emancipation which may be painful and perhaps
still very long, but whose inexorable progress even Stalin's
powerful, but stupid heirs (often infinitely more stupid than
Stalin himself) cannot stop forever.

---

activities is not at all the same) (this was before Ranković was finally denounced
as a sadistic brute and demoted)—and we also have a bureaucracy; but it is
at least *our* bureaucracy, and not a lot of interfering Soviet officials and NKVD
men, who buzz around East Berlin, and Warsaw, and Prague, and Budapest
to this day. At least these are *our* own bureaucrats"; and he concluded with an
expressive, if vulgar, Russian proverb—"*govno, da svoyo*—shit, but at least
my own."

Epilogue

BY HARRISON E. SALISBURY

There is no period of time more essential to our understanding of
the late twentieth-century world than the murky, fear-ridden,
suspicious, power-haunted early post-war years and their reflection in the policies of the United States and the Soviet Union.
Nor is there an era more difficult to assess and enlighten, in part,
because so much of the documentation remains tightly locked up
(particularly in the Kremlin files) and, in part, because so much
of what we know or *think* we know is over-laid by emotions and
propaganda which, on analysis, is found to conceal realities
which we did not know existed.

The background of these years and of the swift and dramatic
shift in relations, particularly between the United States and
Russia (but also vitally involving many other nations and specifically Britain) has been meticulously set out in these pages by
Alexander Werth who occupied a unique position from which to
observe events from within. He spent much of the period as a
correspondent in Moscow, a correspondent with unusual abilities
of assessment, possessing many intimate friends among the Soviet
intelligentsia and even within the middle echelons of the Soviet
power structure. As a true European with deep roots in Russia,
France, Britain and eastern Europe he was particularly sensitive
to the cross-current of opinion and of policy which emerged so
swiftly in the debris of defeated Germany.

That relationships would change with the end of the war was,
of course, inevitable. It would be naive to assume that Soviet
policy did not foresee the possibility of an end to the tri-power
association which had worked—by no means brilliantly but at
least fairly effectively—during the period of the war.

Neither Stalin nor any of his chief advisers and associates ever forgot for one moment the fundamentally anti-Soviet views of Winston Churchill. They accepted his attitude as a factor in the equation while deploring it at the same time. As for Franklin D. Roosevelt it is abundantly clear from the memoirs of Ivan Maisky, Russia's war-time ambassador in England, and a few other more frank Soviet studies, that while quite willing to trade upon Mr. Roosevelt's pixy-like penchant for provoking and frustrating Mr. Churchill's more grandiose imperial dreams Moscow was not entirely reassured as to the durability and reliability of a post-war Soviet-American relationship.

The suspicion engendered by the long years of hostile confrontation stemming from 1917 (after all it was not until 1933 that the USA was even willing to enter into diplomatic relations with "Red Russia") had left their mark. In addition (and on this point I would have put rather more emphasis than has Mr. Werth) Stalin had been, was and would remain not merely suspicious but, in varying degrees, paranoid in all his relationships and particularly in his relationships with other governments.

One should not under-estimate the effects of the wartime controversies on the post-war relationships. The controversies were no small matters. The row over the opening of the Second Front which raged, in reality, from autumn 1941, until the Front actually opened in June 1944 was a very real thing. The position of Britain and the United States was *never* accepted by Stalin. Indeed, there was a consistent tendency in Moscow to see both the United States and Britain as attempting to do a bit of fishing in troubled Russian waters.

For example, in the terrible September of 1941 when Leningrad seemed about to fall, when Kiev was lost, when Moscow was in critical danger Stalin rebuffed Mr. Churchill sharply when the Prime Minister offered partially to replace the Baltic fleet if it was lost to the Germans or scuttled in the battle of Leningrad. Stalin snapped back that he would present his bill to the Germans. He demanded instead, that Britain immediately create a second front to draw off thirty to forty German divisions. He also requested the shipment by 1st October to Russia of 130,000 tons of aluminium, 400 planes and 500 tanks. A few days later he asked Britain to land twenty-five to thirty divisions at Archangel or via Iran.

The demands, of course, could not be fulfilled. Instead, the British began to make contingency plans to halt a German thrust to the frontiers of India should the Russian lines collapse entirely. Moscow did not react well to this. Nor were moods in Moscow improved the following year when during the worst days of Stalingrad both Americans and British blossomed forth with plans to "defend the Baku oilfields". This kind of thing left a very bitter taste in Russian mouths for it reminded them immediately of the British intervention in the civil war when British troops and British support of anti-Soviet elements was so prominent in the Caucasian oilfields and adjacent areas of Russian Turkestan.

Throughout the war there had been policy on two levels—the level of collaboration and a common effort to defeat Nazi Germany and the level of continued confrontation and jockeying for power positions. There is no evidence that this shocked the Russians particularly. It merely confirmed them in their understanding of *real politik*.

If policy on two levels was carried on by Moscow it certainly was paralleled by the action of the United States. This was even reflected in the US Embassy in Moscow where during the tenure of Admiral Standley what might well be described as a "premature cold war" attitude prevailed at the Ambassadorial level while in the military attaché's office, headed by General Faymonville, the attitude was one of warm and intimate collaboration. The dichotomy produced such ambivalence in US policy that it was eventually resolved only at the highest level by the dispatch to Moscow of a new Ambassador, Averell Harriman, and a new chief of Military Aid, General Deane. But even this did not completely resolve the contradictory aspects of US policy. While both Harriman and Deane tried conscientiously to fulfil their mandate from Mr. Roosevelt of full, friendly collaboration the tug in the other direction towards a *quid pro quo* policy continued and was remarkably intensified after the arrival of Mr. George F. Kennan on the scene in July 1944, as Mr. Harriman's second.

I do not wish to over-elaborate the argument but any study of the wartime relationships (for instance, the difficult negotiation over the so-called shuttle-bombing bases near Poltava in the Ukraine and for the hoped-for-but-never-granted US bases in eastern Siberia for use against Japan) indicates that neither side was totally committed to post-war collaboration; each was nervous in the relationship, each sought to elaborate an alternative line in event collaboration proved impossible.

For myself I would trace the first important division point to the disputed question of post-war lend-lease by the USA to the USSR. Russia's desire for major US financial and economic assistance to get its economy going again was broached at least as early as Tehran (November 1943). Roosevelt's attitude was encouraging but a little equivocal. By spring 1944 it was apparent that there was a substantial body of bureaucratic (and probably political) opinion in Washington which was reluctant to give Stalin a blank cheque of $6 billion (which I believe was the amount proposed at that time).

The Soviet invitation to the late Mr. Eric Johnson, then head of the US Chamber of Commerce, to make an extended tour of Russia in June and July of 1944 was an open lobbying measure in behalf of this project. But, as Mr. Johnson told me at that time, opinion in the US government, as well as in US business, was inclined against this project—at least on the scale which the Russians proposed—and needed.

The lend-lease proposal, thus, was in trouble long before Mr. Roosevelt died and even if F.D.R. had lived it might not have been approved on a basis which would have been of real value to the Soviet. In the end it was quite literally "lost" in the bureaucratic shuffle of papers that occurred after President Truman came in.

On the Soviet side it is eminently clear from Mr. Werth's reconstruction that at no point were Moscow and Washington ever near an understanding over Poland. Moscow, viewing Central and Eastern Europe from the standpoint of *real politik*, was determined that the *cordon sanitaire* be reversed. To Moscow's way of thinking the manœuvring of the West (particularly of the USA) over the Polish question was nothing more than the politics of propaganda, partly directed to internal US minorities, partly a pressure device to turn world opinion against Moscow. In the Soviet view Mr. Churchill, the open advocate of imperialism, was far more realistic on such questions. I have no doubt that Moscow was right in this connection. The rather cynical "piece of paper" which Stalin and Churchill exchanged on percentages of interest in Eastern Europe at least had the

virtue of realism. (And was realistically followed by both statesmen.) In contrast Roosevelt's assurance to Stalin that he was
sympathetic to Russia's position in Poland but that he could not
express his views publicly because of the need to corral the
Polish vote in the 1944 elections smacks both of naivety and
hypocrisy.

In my view the "Yalta" case has been overdone by both the
conventional and the revisionist historians. The conventional
historians and statesmen of the Truman-Acheson school hold
that Yalta opened Roosevelt's eyes to Stalin's insatiable demands
and Stalin's duplicity particularly as regards Poland; that Roosevelt was a dying man and unable to cope with the situation and
that it was the "betrayal" of Roosevelt's hopes by Stalin which
crushed F.D.R.'s spirit and led to his quick and sudden death in
April 1945. The revisionist view is that Yalta represented
reasonable political settlements that it laid a foundation for a
reasonable degree of post-war collaboration; that the Polish
problem was as much if not more a Western problem than a
Soviet problem (and specifically that it was deliberately used as
a device by anti-Soviet elements in the British and American
governments to enhance their case against Russia); that the
replacement of the friendly Roosevelt by the long-convinced
anti-Communist and anti-Soviet Truman opened the door to a
complete takeover of American and British policy by those who
had always been opposed to detente and a post-war understanding
between Moscow and Washington.

There is much obvious truth in both views—which makes it
plain that neither is entirely correct. To be sure the anti-Soviet
attitudes were deep-seated in both London and Washington and
the tendency was enhanced by President Truman who had been
poorly briefed by his famous principal on the wartime relationships and who had a long-standing suspicion and fear of Russia.

But there was long-standing fear and suspicion on the part of
Russia as well and this was by no means confined to Stalin.
Russia was not going to take another chance on revival of
Germany and once again being overrun in so catastrophic a
manner. To the extent which it was possible for her to secure her
frontiers by her own force of arms Russia was going to secure
them. Alexander Werth points to a most dramatic example of
this determination. This was Stalin's halting his armies in their

drive on Berlin as of about 1st February 1945. This was a deliberate and calculated political move. Zhukov and Konev and Chuikov were certain they could take Berlin in two or three weeks—a month at most. They submitted plans to accomplish this. Their troops were streaming forward. They were suddenly reined back in a manner which the fighting generals never could understand. But politicians had no difficulty in analysing the move. It enabled the Soviet forces to complete their conquests of Hungary, Czechoslovakia, Silesia so that when the victorious Soviet forces finally did storm Berlin Stalin had garnered in virtually all the territory which he needed to complete his new cordon sanitaire. (The increasing influence of political considerations on the Red Army's offensives in the closing stage of the war had been initially demonstrated in the famous "pause on the Vistula" when the Red Army did not advance on Warsaw until after the Polish underground army had been crushed in Warsaw.)

Another dramatic example of Stalin's employment of the Red Army for what was primarily a political rather than a military purpose occurred at the very ending of the war when he threw 1,500,000 men into action in the Soviet Far East against Japan's Kwantung army a few days before Japan's surrender, at a moment when the surrender was utterly certain. To be sure Stalin's intervention against Japan had been pledged at Yalta. It was a firm undertaking. The Soviet troops had been poised for the jump-off. But Stalin knew through the frantic efforts of Japanese diplomacy that Tokyo was ready to throw in its hand. He unleashed his troops in full knowledge that Japan would be out of the war within a few days. But he was determined to secure the political and territorial advantages which entry would gain him in the Far East; to win back for Russia all it had lost against Japan in the war of 1904-5; to take a full place in the post-war Pacific settlement. It was a political decision of first magnitude and it made certain that Russia would at least have a secure glacis for her Far Eastern positions and, hopefully, something more of a say in the post-war fate of China.

Much has been made by revisionist historians of the deception attempted by Truman and Churchill at Potsdam when Truman informed Stalin of the successful testing of the A-bomb but deliberately (at Churchill's suggestion) did so in a manner which both hoped would not arouse Stalin's suspicions. Stalin gave no sign of significant interest in Truman's private word. However, if Soviet historians are to be believed (and the body of circumstantial evidence is steadily growing) Stalin *did* understand Truman's remark; he deliberately concealed his understanding; he told his associates instantly to speed up Russia's own nuclear developments.

If Truman and Churchill played poker with Stalin over the A-bomb Stalin played them the same game. Nor was this all. Even with the A-bomb Truman and his military men believed that Japan would probably fight on to a bitter end. They saw another year's fighting at a minimum. But Truman did not have all of the cards. He did not know what Stalin knew—that for nearly a year and with increasing urgency in the more recent months and weeks the Japanese had been seeking through the Russians to get in contact with Britain and the United States about peace terms. With the fall of Germany these Japanese attempts became almost hysterical. Stalin kept this knowledge to himself. He passed not a word of it on to Washington and London.

Thus, if the question of deception be placed in the Cold War balance it is difficult, indeed, to emerge from a candid study of the record without the feeling that it was far from a one-way game. Both sides were playing power politics. Neither side was offering many bows to the altar of principle.

Against this background the two great watershed speeches of early 1946—Stalin's February election speech and Churchill's at Fulton, Mo., in March—assume a confirmatory character, Churchill's perhaps a bit more so than Stalin's. Stalin's speech however made perfectly plain that Russia was going forward on her own; to restore the damage of war at enormous sacrifice, anticipating a hostile or arms-length attitude from the wartime partners. Churchill, of course, delivered a call to arms and his text was to provide the philosophical foundation for the evolving Cold War so far as the West was concerned.

The warp and woof of this evolution is eloquently and intimately described in these pages. One set of strands, perhaps, could wish for a bit more emphasis—the brutal deepening of terror at home, within the USSR, which can be seen both as a reflection of Stalin's own deepening paranoia and the steady increase of "internal security" measures as the pressures and tensions of the Cold War intensified.

Here again the pattern was well fixed *before* the Cold War. All that was needed was a stronger line. Throughout the Second World War Russian men and officers unfortunate enough to be captured by the Germans and then make their escape back to their own lines—often at enormous cost and sacrifice—were treated not as heroes but as traitors. They were sent back to the front in penal battalions and used as cannon fodder in the most literal terms—chained to machineguns to cover retreats, sent on forced reconnaissance to open up enemy guns, made to run across minefields to explode the mines and make transit safe for the main units. The removal from front lines of officers and men charged with violation of some one of the many state sedition statutes was frequent. These men, as in the case of the remarkable Soviet novelist, Aleksandr Solzhenitsyn, were often sent back directly from the front to Siberian concentration camps.

Even in blockaded Leningrad the security police continued their terrible depredations, hunting out starving peoples and sending them in usually fatal convoys to the concentration camps.

I mention these amenities of the Stalin system only to put in context the horrors which came with the end of the war or even before the war had been wholly won—the sending to Siberia of total populations of such areas as the Crimea, the north Caucasus, the removal of Baltic peoples by the hundred thousand and with the ending of the war the transfer direct to Siberian camps of *millions* of Russian prisoners of war whose survival in Hitler's concentration camps automatically qualified them for a ticket to Stalin's camps.

It is important to stress the continuity of Stalinist policy lest we leap to the assumption that Stalin was motivated to twist the screws because of the rising tensions with the West. No doubt this confirmed him in his security preoccupations. But the fact is that there is an unbroken chain of this conduct which reaches back into the 1930s, was continued through the war and on into the period of the late 1940s and early 1950s with little change except that of detail. For instance, it is hard to see any real distinction between his deportation to Central Asia in 1949 and 1950 of the "foreign" elements in the Black Sea coastal areas (largely persons originally of Greek origin, or Jews or other minorities) and the similar deportations of the end-of-the-war period. The widescale internal purges and campaigns against "cosmo-politans" in 1949 (actually an anti-semitic drive) had its parallel in the anti-semitic undertones of the 1930s' purges and the over-tones of the anti-semitic outbursts of the early war period and particularly the outbreak of open anti-semitism at the time of the Battle of Moscow.

One might suppose that Stalin's purges of foreign communist parties, specifically the purges in Bulgaria, Hungary, Czecho-slovakia and Poland were related to the Cold War in one form or another. They may have been and Alexander Werth seems to feel there was a rather direct connection. But the fact is Stalin purged the leadership of practically every foreign Communist party he could reach in the late 1930s. He was accustomed to purging foreign communists and not in trusting them. Would the purges have occurred without the Cold War? I believe they would because in my view the control factor was not the Cold War but the independence and intransigence of the Yugoslav Party. Once Stalin perceived Tito as an independent (which is to say in Stalin's vocabulary, a traitor) he was certainly not going to permit any analogous action in the remainder of his cordon sanitaire. Hence, the purges of Rajk, Kostov, Slansky, Gomulka and all the rest. Tito did not survive because of Stalin's good will. Stalin made every possible effort to subvert the Yugoslav regime and certainly toyed with the idea of an attack from out-side. But he never followed through—probably because of fear of war with his erstwhile Western allies.

There is one unwritten chapter which belongs in this book. This is a chapter on Russia and China and the role which Soviet-Chinese relations and American-Chinese relations played in the formative years of the Cold War.

It is entirely clear from remarks which Stalin made both to the Chinese and to others (notably the Yugoslavs) that he did not envisage a Communist China as part of the post-war world. This may have been one reason why he was so eager to secure a far-eastern glacis, essentially the sphere of influence which Czarist Russia had striven to obtain in Manchuria and along the North China coast. It is noteworthy that on 14th August 1945, the very date when Soviet armies crossed the border into Man-churia, Stalin signed a pact with Chiang Kai-shek which was obviously intended as the cornerstone of the post-war settlement.

Its most notable provision was a pledge by Moscow not to aid any other Chinese "faction", i.e., not to aid Mao Tse-tung and his Communists. In return Nationalist China recognized, for practical purposes, the *de facto* status of Mongolia (that is, its role as a Soviet dependency) subject only to a plebiscite, the outcome of which was obvious. The fact that in the end the Soviets did afford some modest aid to Mao by permitting him to capture stocks of arms and munitions in Manchuria should not obscure the fact that Stalin interposed his advice and pressure insofar as he could on the side of a Chinese Communist accommodation with Chiang Kai-shek. (Later, he was to admit to the Yugoslavs that he was "wrong" in his advice.)

What is important to establish is that Stalin did not envisage the rise of a powerful Communist state in China. He clearly foresaw a divided China or more probably a China ruled by Chiang Kai-shek in which the Communists continued to struggle from within for a measure of power and influence. Nor did this disturb him. This predicated a weak China and a weak China traditionally had been the goal of Russian diplomacy from long before the ascent of the Communists. If one views Stalin's war-end policy in perspective, examining each of its elements (including eastern Europe, the Middle East and particularly the Dardanelles and the demands on Turkey for Kars, the excursion into north Persia and the basic elements of Soviet policy in the Far East) one is led straight back to the days of Count Witte and the late nineteenth century. A weak China, a divided China was a guarantee against the rise of a powerful continental competitor to Russia—either an independent continental power or one under the guardianship of the United States. And Russian national and defence interests were protected, or so Stalin must have thought, by the strong positions in Manchuria and North China as well as the occupation of north Korea and the return of the Kuriles and Sakhalin.

On the American side there is no evidence at this stage of concern over a Communist "take over" of China or specifically over the emergence of a Soviet-Chinese Communist alliance. There was much concern that civil war should not break out in China and a strong belief that American influence would be able to direct China in the path of national unity so that she could take her rightful place in the peace councils as one of the Big Four—a charming illusion which neither Churchill nor Stalin had shared with Roosevelt.

Thus, Russia's weight at the end of the war was thrown not either for or against the United States in China, nor, to be sure, in favour of a Communist China. But specifically in the direction of policies which Stalin believed would be protective of Russian security in the Far East regardless of what happened in China. There was no ideological factor involved; simply power politics.

The unwritten chapter of this book would demonstrate how all this changed—both for the United States and for Russia. How the United States came to feel that it had "lost" China to Communism, and specifically, to the Kremlin, thus powerfully fanning the flames of Cold War, touching off a terrible witch-hunt under the leadership of McCarthy at home, laying the groundwork for the Korean and Indochinese wars and a quarter-century of American involvement in the Far East in the guise of a crusade against Communism. And for Russia the unexpected (and unwanted) emergence of a new unified Communist China, led by a Communist of vaunted independence and frequently an opponent both of Soviet foreign policy and Stalinist Marxism, radically deepened and transformed Stalin's inherent xenophobic impulses and remarkably reinforced his view of the outer world as one peopled exclusively by enemies.

No assessment of the Cold War policy of Stalin in Eastern Europe is complete without an attempt to grapple with the manner in which Stalin was shaken by the rise of a new and potentially competitive Communist power. If his attitude towards the Communist world beyond Russia's borders had been disturbed by his perception of Tito's independent tendencies how much more profound was the disturbance when he began to feel that he confronted not only Titoist renegades in Yugoslavia (and their underground and about-to-be-detected allies in Eastern Europe) but a heretic of vastly greater weight in Peking.

The chapter on the role of the Sino-Soviet split in the Cold War cannot yet be written in any authoritative terms. Too many aspects are still concealed despite the curtain-lifting of the polemical exchanges between Mao and Khrushchev and Mao and Khrushchev's heirs. But we can already see enough to be certain that everything about Peking reinforced Stalin's suspicions. One of Mao's initial demands upon Stalin was for the "return" of

Outer Mongolia, that very Outer Mongolia whose transference to the Soviet sphere had been so conveniently legalized by Chiang Kai-shek's agreement of 14th August 1945. Not only had Mao won China but he obviously was not prepared to bow to Stalin's *yarlik*. If Stalin had reacted to Tito's lesser manifestations of independence by coming to the brink of war and by summarily purging all of Eastern Europe and launching a new and savage purge in his own country is it likely that he sat by with folded hands as Mao's heresy was revealed. I do not think so.

Nothing so strongly fired the Cold War as Korea. If the United States and Russia had come almost to the brink during the Berlin crisis of 1948 they now or, so it seemed in America, went across the brink in Korea.

And Korea, or so I have long speculated, was one of Stalin's most calculated and machiavellian moves directed, however, not at the United States (as conventional wisdom would have it) but at Mao Tse-tung. The space is not available here to elaborate the whole argument but let me sketch out a few of the main lines. We now know from both Khrushchev and Mao that there was little or no trust between Mao and Stalin in 1949. Indeed, Khrushchev has said that the break between the two Communist powers would have come in that year had it not been for mutual fear of the United States. Mao came to Moscow in December 1949, and spent an unconscionable time negotiating with Stalin—almost two months. It was the longest negotiation on record. Out of it came the Sino-Soviet pact and, I believe, a determination on Stalin's part to place himself in a position in which he could bring whatever pressure he wished to bear on Mao—even to the point of replacing him as he was at that very time replacing all of the "untrustworthy" heads of his Eastern European satrapies. Stalin held very strong cards. Militarily he had the jumping-off points in Mongolia and eastern Siberia which he had used against the Japanese. He also had his new bases in Manchuria at Dairen and Port Arthur and the Manchurian railroad. He had North Korea. He also had an ace up his sleeve in the form of a private understanding—the exact nature not yet revealed—with Kao Kung, ostensibly one of Mao's close lieutenants and viceroy for Manchuria but in reality a secret ally of Stalin's. (Kao Kung's relationship with Stalin was all but spelled out by the Chinese when he committed suicide after

Stalin's death and Beria's execution. The Chinese communique
charged him with treason in conspiring with other parties to
establish himself as an independent princeling in Manchuria.)
With these strong positions if Stalin became the master of all of
Korea he would hold Mao in a vise which could be closed at any
time Stalin desired. Mao would do Stalin's bidding or Mao
would go—such, I believe, to have been the thinking of the
Russian dictator. Hence, the Korean war. Not as we convention-
ally accept it a part of the Cold War between the US and the
USSR but actually as part of the increasingly warm war between
China and Russia. To be sure the game did not play as Stalin
planned. It almost did. But he had not counted on Truman's
intervention. Stalin was a logical man and when Truman's
Secretary of State Acheson spelled out the American defence
line in the Pacific and deliberately left Korea out—Stalin believed
Korea was free for whoever wanted to take it. He learned to his
amazement (as others have before and since) that it was unwise
to take an American Secretary of State at his word. US intervention changed the whole scenario. But Stalin did salvage one
thing. The aggressiveness with which MacArthur drove to the
Yalu alarmed the Chinese and brought them into the war. As
the Chinese have ruefully admitted in recent years the Russians
launched the Korean war and then turned it in such a way as to
exacerbate US-China relations for years.

Thus, in the end Korea served a Cold War purpose. But it was
not, I submit, launched with that specifically in mind. Nor would
I believe that the decision of Truman and Acheson to stand in
Korea was primarily decided by their on-going conflict with the
Kremlin. Korea and the US posture was much more intimately
related to the "loss" of China which had occurred within the year
and to the political assessment which Truman and Acheson made
of the effect upon the Administration of another "loss" in Asia.

The feed-back effects of Soviet-China and US-China relations
into the Soviet-American Cold War confrontation was constant
and complex, and continues even to the present time as the
triangular nature of the great power relationship becomes more
and more silhouetted by the emergence of China as a major
power in her own right, the more or less permanent deterioration
of Soviet-Chinese Party relations and the gradual movement of
Washington and Peking towards a more normal relationship.

In the specific period with which we are dealing—that is the years roughly from the end of the Second World War until Stalin's death—the China factor tended to represent an X in the algebra of both great powers since neither was able to comprehend precisely the nature of what was happening in China and the relationship of either Russia or America to those events.

What was obvious as the last months of Stalin's life spun out was that the super-powers had established a pattern of hostility and competition both military and political. Stalin lived to see his nation not only quickly catch up with the US technology of nuclear weaponry but to construct a formidable armoury of these dread devices. He did not quite live long enough to see Russia match the United States pace for pace in hydrogen weaponry and move ahead of her in rocketry and missiles. But he laid the foundations of these achievements and the spur to them was the Cold War and the overhanging danger that nuclear diplomacy and nuclear blackmail by the United States would actually be employed by Washington to compel Russia to make really major concessions. The thrust and parry of Soviet diplomacy through the early 1950s was to hold back this US threat while making every sacrifice to bring Soviet arms technique up to the American level. Without the spur of the Cold War it seems quite obvious that Russia would not have advanced so rapidly and that the great achievements of the latter part of the decade of the 1950s and the 1960s—sputnik, space exploration and all—would have come far more slowly or possibly not at all.

But this is the realm of the speculative. The Cold War did emerge. Its roots did lie in the war years and the early post-war period. Its conventions became established with considerable rapidity and with the emergence of parity of destructive power the conventions of confrontation took on a very stylized manner which prevails to this day.

The cost of all this to the Russian people was enormous. They were the ones who paid. If there was famine in 1946 and 1947 (as Khrushchev has only recently confirmed) it may be charged back both to the United States which could easily have afforded the foodstuffs to alleviate it and to Stalin who could have put the resources into the farm lands to prevent it. But the United States was in no mood to comfort and aid a Cold War opponent. And Stalin was in no mood to ease the sacrifices of his people so long as he felt himself confronted by superior American power.

It is probably not too much to estimate that the standard of living in the Soviet Union was held back by a margin of at least ten years due to the Cold War. Possibly twenty. The price paid by the United States was not economic. It was political—the terror and the witch-hunt of McCarthy and the smear of emotional anti-communism which still lies across the surface of American politics. For the world the price has been the arms race and the jingoistic rivalries of the super-powers felt in every part of the globe.

The pace of the late 1940s and early 1950s was too intense for either Russia or America. The dangers were growing too great. It was no accident that the first act of Stalin's successors was to move to relax—both at home and abroad. It took a good bit of time for both the Russian people themselves and the diplomatic assessors in the West to understand that the "thaw" was genuine. On both sides there was a strong feeling that it could be just a trick. But gradually the reality of the change became evident. The Cold War as an intense phase of world diplomacy is actually over although its memories are so vivid that much thinking, not only in Moscow and Washington, but elsewhere in the world is still conditioned by it. But President Nixon's declaration that the United States was moving from the era of confrontation to the era of negotiation was realistic. The movement actually began in the late 1950s. It is still in progress today albeit fluctuating and marked quite often by regression. No one can read the record of the years of which Alexander Werth writes without understanding that attitudes were engraved too deeply in the early post-war era to change rapidly and, more importantly, that the impressions left by the fierce passions of that period will never be entirely eradicated. That is why these years are an essential benchmark from which to measure policy of the present and goals for the future.

Selected Bibliography

RUSSIA
Chuikov, Marshal V. I., *The Beginning of the Road*, McGibbon and Kee, London, 1963
W. P. and Z. K. Coates, *A History of Anglo-Russian Relations*, Pilot Books, London, 1944
Joseph Davies, *Mission to Moscow*, Gollancz, London, 1942
Isaac Deutscher, *Stalin*, 2nd ed. Oxford University Press, 1967
Erich Kuby, *The Russians and Berlin 1945*, Ballantine Books, New York, 1969
Alexander Werth, *Musical Uproar*, Turnstile Press, London, 1949

COLD WAR
J. F. Byrnes, *All in One Lifetime*, New York, 1958
J. F. Byrnes, *Speaking Frankly*, Heinemann, London, 1947
John Foster Dulles, *War or Peace*, Harrap, London, 1950
Jenna F. Fleming, *The Cold War and its Origins*, Doubleday, New York, 1961
André Fontaine, *History of the Cold War*, 2 vols, Pantheon, New York, 1969
George F. Kennan, *Memoirs 1925–1950*, Hutchinson, London, 1968
George F. Kennan, *Russia and the West under Lenin and Stalin*, Atlantic Monthly Press, New York, 1961
Harry Truman, *Memoirs*, 2 vols, Doubleday, New York, 1958
James P. Warburg, *The United States in the Post-War World*, Gollancz, London, 1966
William A. Williams, *The Tragedy of American Diplomacy*, Delta Books, New York, 1959

Louis J. Halle, *The Cold War as History*, Harper and Row, New York, 1967

EASTERN EUROPE
Georges Castellan, *DDR Allemagne de l'Est*, Paris, 1955
V. Dedijer, *Tito Speaks*, Weidenfeld and Nicolson, London, 1953
Milovan Djilas, *Conversations with Stalin*, Harcourt, Brace, Jovanovitch, New York, 1962
F. Feito, *Histoire des Democraties Populaires*, 2 vols, Seuil, Paris, 1952, 1969
S. Mikolajczyk, *Le Viol de la Pologne*, Paris, 1948
Hubert Ripka, *Czechoslovakia Enslaved*, Gollancz, London, 1950
H. Seton-Watson, *The East European Revolution*, Methuen, London, 1950
Pavel Tigrid, *Le Printemps de Prague*, Seuil, Paris, 1968

RUSSIAN LITERARY WORKS
Fedor Abramov, *Two Summers and Three Winters*, published in *Novy Mir*, 1968
Ilya Ehrenburg, *Memoirs*, Universal Library, New York
A. Fadeev, *Molodaya Gvardiya*, Moscow, 1946
Andrei Platonov, *Fierce and Beautiful World*, Dutton, New York, 1970
Alesandr Solzhenitsyn, *A day in the life of Ivan Denisovich*, Gollancz, London, 1963
Vladimir Tendryakov, *Stories*, Moscow, 1959

Index